# Economic Issues Today

# Economic Issues Today

## Alternative Approaches

### Eighth Edition

Robert B. Carson, Wade L. Thomas, Jason Hecht

*M.E.Sharpe*
Armonk, New York
London, England

**Library of Congress Cataloging-in-Publication Data**

Carson, Robert Barry, 1934–
Economic issues today : alternative approaches / Robert B. Carson, Wade L. Thomas,
and Jason Hecht.— 8th ed.
    p. cm.
Includes index.
ISBN 0-7656-1500-2 (hardcover : alk. paper)— ISBN 0-7656-1501-0 (pbk. : alk. paper)
  1. Economics. 2. United States—Economic conditions—2001– 3. United States—
Economic policy—2001– I. Thomas, Wade L.  II. Hecht, Jason, 1958–  III. Title.

HB171.5.C2917 2005
330.973′0931—dc22                                                        2004021683

Printed in the United States of America

The paper used in this publication meets the minimum requirements of
American National Standard for Information Sciences
Permanence of Paper for Printed Library Materials,
ANSI Z 39.48-1984.

∞

BM (c)  10    9    8    7    6    5    4    3    2    1
BM (p)  10    9    8    7    6    5    4    3    2    1

We dedicate this edition of *Economics Issues Today* to
Robert L. Heilbroner
for making the dismal science of economics
readable and understandable.

# Contents

## Part III. Problems of Aggregate Economic Policy

## Part IV. Conclusion

# Figures and Tables

## Figures

## Tables

# Preface

More than a quarter century has passed since the publication of the first edition of *Economic Issues Today* (and its macroeconomic and microeconomic split versions). Needless to say, a lot of economic water has gone over the dam since 1978. Accordingly, the content of *Economic Issues Today* has undergone many changes through this, its eighth edition. Yet the underlying philosophy and pedagogical objectives of the book remain the same: to introduce those uninitiated in the ways of economists to the breadth and richness of economic reasoning.

*Economic Issues Today* maintains a distinctive approach with its first-person debate from Conservative, Liberal, and Radical views. The reader is advised not to approach these "ideological" positions as if they were etched in stone and not subject to change and adaptation. While each position has rather fixed philosophical foundations, the actual practice and the day-to-day politics of each has allowed appropriation of small ideological pieces from an opposing perspective on one issue or another. For example, the subject of automobile safety was a torrid debate between Left and Right twenty-five years ago. Now, it has mainstream acceptability and the debate over consumer protection has moved on to different products and problems. However, the comfortable conclusion of "issue solved" or the convenience of "score carding" which side came out ahead on a particular policy always has been fuel for this book's anticipation of the next turn of the wheel. Consider the wave of industry deregulation and other regulatory reversals that gave the impression that the bulk of regulatory institutions was on the path to oblivion. Now, corporate and accounting debacles of painful proportions have reinvigorated the public's interest in managing the ground rules for business conduct and prompted greater intrusion into lightly regulated areas such as financial reporting responsibilities and the broader accounting profession.

At the beginning of the twenty-first century and after more than

twenty years of nearly uninterrupted economic prosperity, the contemporary scene is one where debates and argumentation over public
policy generally have been muted. The tendency toward believing
that old burning issues are solved or at least a high degree of consensus has been attained seems to have gained more traction over the
past few years. Entire generations are weary of the continuing economic problems of farmers, the unemployed, environmental threats,
the sustainability of the Social Security system, trade and budget deficits, poverty, and the like. These problems are supposed to be "fixed,"
not lingering sources of endless controversies! However, economic
issues cannot be dismissed like overplayed songs and news stories or
a bad season for the favorite sports team. The issues are troubling but
it is more troubling when they are regarded as things too complex,
too abstract, or too trivial with which to be bothered.

As it has since the first edition in 1978, *Economic Issues Today*
(and the split versions) continues to plumb the depths of these debates. The book requires no background in the methods of economic analysis, and as much as possible it avoids the use of economic
jargon in favor of everyday language. This edition of *Economic
Issues Today,* like previous ones, stresses the ideological choices
that exist in economic thought and that often cause ordinary citizens
to be confused about what economists *do* and what economists *believe.* As ever, it is meant to be a provocative book, more concerned
with provoking discussion and thought than in presenting "right"
solutions to problems. It remains committed to the belief that real
economic solutions are possible in a democratic society only when
all alternatives are known and considered.

Although longtime users are familiar with the text's philosophy
and perspectives, new readers might benefit from an explanation of
why the authors undertook this project in the first place and how the
book is organized.

All too frequently, students begin their study of economics with the
impression that economists are bland and monolithic when discuss-
ing important issues confronting the general society. We may as well
admit that the profession sometimes exhibits a tendency to blandness
in its public utterances, but surely any supposed unanimity toward
social policy questions has vanished. With the rise of an influential
Radical caucus within the discipline, beginning in the late 1960s, and
the more recent resurgence of variations of laissez-faire ideology, any

facade of consensus has clearly been broken down. The application of economic theory to issues of public policy more and more reflects a range of choice from Conservative to Liberal to Radical.

For the student struggling with basic theory and analytic tools, as well as for the ordinary citizen overwhelmed by economic data in the newspapers and on the TV evening news, it is hard to avoid confusion over what economists really think about the problems facing the nation. This book begins with the assumption that the answers economists give to policy questions can be usefully compared and analyzed according to the particular biases of their arguments and the probable outcomes of their proposals. In other words, differences in economic logic and interpretation of evidence are not so much a function of skill mastery as they are the expression of strongly held social and political opinions. The text also assumes that economics as a body of knowledge takes on greater meaning and is more readily comprehended when it is viewed in this way.

For each issue, a Conservative, Liberal, and Radical analysis and proposed solution are presented in turn as the valid approach to the problem. On one page, there may be a vigorous and unyielding defense of laissez-faire and the market economy; on another, a program for the elimination or modification of the free market. This is not the way economic analysis and theory are usually taught, but it is what the practice of economics is about. In the real world, the citizen and the economist make public policy choices that protect, attack, or modify the market mechanism. We may defend our positions in terms of economic logic, but behind our proofs lies our political and ideological view of the world. This book attempts to examine the relationship between ideological values and the economic theories and policies that are their outcome.

Since the text presents a wide range of perspectives on a number of currently sensitive issues, it should provoke disagreement, controversy, and discussion. In itself, the book does not urge a particular ideological position or a particular variety of economic analysis. The decision to select or reject this or that point of view is left—as it should be—to the reader.

Each chapter is self-contained and may be assigned in any order the instructor chooses. There are relatively few footnotes or direct references to specific economists, although the ideas of many contemporary economists and schools of economic thought will be apparent. The suggested readings at the end are offered for anyone wishing to dig a little more deeply into an issue or a particular economic perspective or approach.

## What Is New in This Edition

The eighth edition represents a substantial revision over the seventh. Updating of critical changes in economic policy was undertaken for every issue. However, the introduction to the text keeps its time-tested development and explanation of the Conservative, Liberal, and Radical positions.

The microeconomic section contains the same seven problems in the marketplace of the previous edition, but each issue has been overhauled. Issue 1 keeps its informative historical basis while incorporating the new direction American agricultural policy has taken since 2002. Issue 2 is a completely modernized and revised presentation of the consumer welfare issue that extends beyond its original focus on automobile safety. The range of environmental problems in Issue 3 is modified to include more than acid rain and, along with it, greater elaboration about pollution control policies and the growing immediacy of environmental issues on an international scale. The mainstay arguments in Issue 4 on imperfect competition are largely retained in this edition, but assisted by newer and better data in support of the debate over the competitiveness of American industries. Economic regulation in Issue 5 relinquishes some of its focus on transportation deregulation in favor of examples in telecommunications, energy, and professional ethics, and considers the potential drift toward reregulation. Poverty and income distribution are more effectively addressed in Issue 6 of this edition with more complete evidence on welfare reform and the use of the Gini index to track income inequality. Issue 7 on financing government concludes the microeconomic topics with a thorough analysis of the three recent federal tax reductions from all three perspectives.

The most noticeable changes are in the macroeconomic side of the book. A new issue on social policy frames the debate about the Social Security system, becoming Issue 13. International economics is moved to Issue 14 where it takes up the intensifying controversies surrounding free trade agreements, recent episodes of protectionism, capital flight, and the outsourcing of American jobs. A revised Issue 8 launches the section with its familiar query regarding macroeconomic stability: "Are we depression-proof?" Issue 9 follows in a tightly designed sequence with a renewed focus on trends and prospects for economic growth and productivity growth in the U.S. economy. Issue 10 takes a sharp turn back to federal budget deficits from the previous edition's indulgence in budget surpluses with a fully revised discussion of causes and consequences. With unemployment once again ascending the ladder of the economic agenda, Issue 11 emerges as extensively redone to consider the various sources of unemployment, including the recent phenomenon of outsourcing, and examination of public policy options to deal with the problem. Issue 12 approaches the inflation debate more comprehensively than in the past edition by presenting alternative indices of price levels and a discussion of interest rate targeting in monetary policy.

The previous Issue 15, "The Market Versus Planning and Controls," takes on a new identity as a "Reprise" to all the material that has gone before it. Placing it in a stand-alone position at the end of the book acknowledges the issue's summation of comparative economic systems.

## Supplements

The instructors manual for *Economic Issues Today* is available on computer disk. Key terms, multiple-choice, true-false, and essay-discussion questions are provided for each issue. Some instructors like to use *Economic Issues Today* in conjunction with their preferred principles text. The instructor's manual provides a "correlation grid" that cross-references the issues from *Economic Issues Today* with related chapters in leading principles of economics textbooks. Potential adopters can request a copy of the grid from the publisher or view it online at www.mesharpe.com. The correlation grid is reproduced for your convenience at the end of the preface.

To assist with classroom presentations, instructors can download PowerPoint slides of all figures and tables in the text from the publisher's Web site at www.mesharpe.com. The authors also maintain a portal that is a quick and easy way to link to the PowerPoint slides and correlation grid at www.EconomicIssues.com.

# Correlation Grid for Using *Economic Issues Today* with Leading Introductory Economics Textbooks

| *EIT* issues / Relevant textbook chapters | Baumol/Blinder | Case/Fair | Lipsey | McConnell/Brue | Mankiw | Mansfield/Bahrausch | Miller | O'Sullivan/Sheffrin | Parkin | Ruffin/Gregory | Samuelson/Nordhaus | Schiller (one-semester text) | Stiglitz |
|---|---|---|---|---|---|---|---|---|---|---|---|---|---|
| Introduction: Alternative Economic Philosophies | 1, 3, 4 | 1, 2 | 1, 2, 3 | 1, 2, 3, 4 | 1, 2 | 1 | 1 | 1, 2 | 1, 2 | 1, 2, 3 | 1, 2 | 1, 2 | 2 |
| Issue 1: Responding to Market Outcomes: Competition or Protection for American Agriculture | 5, 7, 8, 9 | 3, 4 | 4, 5, 6, 10 | 20, 23, 33 | 4, 5, 6 | 16, 17 | 3, 20 | 4, 5, 6 | 3, 4, 6 | 3, 4, 6 | 3, 4 | 3, 5 | 4, 5 |
| Issue 2: Consumer Welfare: Is It Necessary to Protect the Consumer? | 6, 7 | 5, 14 | 7 | 21 | 7, 21, 22 | 16, 18 | 19 | 7 | 19 | 7, 15 | 5 | 4 | 6, 14 |
| Issue 3: Dealing with Externalities: How Can We Save the Environment? | 8, 22 | 14 | 18, 19 | 30 | 10, 11 | 21 | 31 | 17 | 16, 19 | 5, 8, 20 | 18 | 5 | 21 |
| Issue 4: Imperfect Competition: Is Big Business a Threat or a Boon? | 10, 11, 12, 13, 20 | 11, 12, 13 | 11, 12 | 24, 25, 32 | 15, 16, 17 | 19 | 24, 25, 26, 27 | 10, 11, 12, 13, 14 | 11, 12, 13, 14 | 11, 12, 13, 14 | 9, 10 | 7 | 11, 12, 13, 14, 15 |
| Issue 5: Economic Regulation. Which Path: Has Deregulation Worked? | 14, 20 | | 13, 18, 19 | 32 | 6, 7, 11 | 20 | 27 | 13, 14 | 14 | 14 | 2, 17 | 7, 9 | 13 |
| Issue 6: Income Distribution: Does America Have an Income Inequality Problem? | 17, 18, 19 | 15 | 15, 16 | 28, 29, 34 | 19, 20 | 23, 24 | 6, 30 | 19 | 18 | 17, 19 | 12, 19 | 8 | 19 |

| | | | | | | | | | | | | | |
|---|---|---|---|---|---|---|---|---|---|---|---|---|---|
| Issue 7: Financing Government: What Is a Fair System of Taxation? | 16, 26 | 9 | 16 | 21, 22 | 31 | 16 | 5, 6 | 26 | 8, 12 | 31 | 20 | 16 | 21 |
| Issue 8: Macroeconomic Instability: Are We Depression-Proof? | 24, 25 | 10, 11 | 20, 22, 23, 24 | 23, 25, 27, 34 | 21, 22, 24, 30, 31, 32 | 22, 24, 25 | 7, 10, 11 | 4, 5 | 26, 28 | 8, 9, 10 | 21, 23, 24 | 17, 21, 23 | 23, 24 |
| Issue 9: Economic Growth and Stability: Can We Maintain High and Steady Rates of Economic Growth? | 28, 29 | 10, 11 | 20, 22, 23, 24, 27, 34 | 26, 27, 31, 33 | 21, 23, 24, 25 | 23, 25, 26 | 12, 13, 18 | 6, 11, 14, 25 | 25, 33, 34 | 8, 11, 12, 17 | 25, 26, 31 | 19, 25, 30 | 15, 24, 29, 34 |
| Issue 10: Balancing the Federal Budget: Should We Be Worried About the Rising Federal Deficit? | 36 | 12 | 34 | 31, 33 | 31 | 25 | 13 | 12 | 33, 34, 35 | 18 | 32, 33 | 16, 21 | 33 |
| Issue 11: Unemployment: Is Joblessness an Overrated Problem? | 24, 31 | 10 | 31 | 33 | 22 | 21, 29, 30, 31 | 7 | 4 | 28, 33, 35 | 16, 19 | 31 | 26 | 26, 28 |
| Issue 12: Inflation: Can Price Pressures Be Kept Under Control? | 30, 31 | 14 | 26, 32 | 32 | 27, 28, 31, 32 | 21, 28, 29, 30 | 7 | 7, 10, 13 | 30, 33, 35 | 15, 16 | 28, 29, 30 | 23, 25, 26 | 25, 26, 28, 31 |
| Issue 13: The New Population Problem: Can We Save Our Social Security System? | | | 16 | 19, 21, 22 | 34 | 16, 19 | 6 | 26 | | 36 | | 16 | 21, 33 |
| Issue 14: International Economics: Where Does America Fit into the New World Order? | 3, 18, 33, 34 | 17 | 29, 30 | 35, 36, 37 | 33, 34 | 32, 33 | 17, 18, 32, 33 | 27, 28 | 3, 9, 31, 32 | 37, 38 | 35, 36, 37 | 32, 33, 34 | 35, 36, 37 |
| Reprise. The Market Versus Planning and Controls: Which Strategy Works Better? | 37 | 16 | 33 | 21, 22, 38, 39 | 5, 16 | 22, 31 | 5 | 26 | 11, 36 | 16, 31, 39, 40 | 38 | 11, 31 | 36 |

# Acknowledgments

The senior author would like to thank Michael Weber, a longtime sponsoring editor of *Economic Issues Today* at St. Martin's Press (before St. Martin's dropped its college economics line), for signing the book with its new publisher, M.E. Sharpe, Inc. And, as with each new edition, the senior author feels duty bound to note the kind and thoughtful encouragement of Bertrand Lummus, then the college editor at St. Martin's, who made it possible for *Economic Issues Today* to see the light of day in the first place. Similarly, the senior author wishes to acknowledge the efforts of Paula Franklin and Emily Berleth, whose extraordinary editorial skills in the early editions of the work have survived, both directly and indirectly, right down to the current version.

The authors want to express appreciation to several teaching professors for their suggestions and comments that have led to improvements for this edition of the text: Michael McAvoy, William P. O'Dea, and David Ring (all from SUNY Oneonta), and Amy S. Cramer, Pima Community College. We are grateful to Campbell R. McConnell for his expert advice and encouragement over the past three editions of *Economic Issues Today*. The authors also thank Lynn Taylor, economics editor, for her editorial efforts on the eighth edition.

We sadly acknowledge the passing of our good friend and mentor of *Economic Issues Today*, Robert L. Heilbroner of the New School University. Bob Heilbroner was both a teacher and colleague of coauthor Jason Hecht, and we all drew much inspiration and intellectual strength from his numerous books and writings. In particular, the influence of his most famous book, *The Worldly Philosphers,* is evident within these pages. The eighth edition of *Economic Issues Today* is dedicated in memory of Robert L. Heilbroner.

# Part I

# Introduction

# Alternative Economic Philosophies
## A Survey of Conservative, Liberal, and Radical Critiques

The ideas of economists, both when they are right and when they are wrong, are more powerful than is commonly understood. Indeed, the world is ruled by little else. Practical men, who believe themselves to be quite exempt from any intellectual influences, are usually the slaves of some defunct economist. Madmen in authority, who hear voices in the air, are distilling their frenzy from some academic scribbler of a few years back.

—*John Maynard Keynes, 1936*

As of this writing (2005), the American economy had experienced only two brief recessions (in 1990–91 and 2001) during the past twenty-two years. Add to this the fact that the American economy remains the envy of the rest of the world. By such indicators, we should be—at least with respect to economic matters—a content and happy people. Right?

Alas, economic matters rarely seem to be a solid source of shared contentment. As the outcome of the 2000 and 2004 presidential elections indicates, the country remains equally divided on the question of whether or not the American economy was headed in the right direction. This down-the-middle division leads to an obvious conclusion (and one completely independent of who won and who lost the election): A great many Americans are uncertain about their nation's economic future. In fact, the uncertainty does not end there. Each thoughtful member of either side of the great divide in opinion has to wonder about what is going on in the minds of those who went the other way on the question of the "right direction."

As with all such periods of economic uncertainty and disagreement, the citizenry becomes increasingly interested in economic matters and the observations and advice that might be offered by the keepers of economic wisdom: *economists.* Mostly ignored in good times, economists can count on getting the public's attention when worries about bad times arise. And so, economists once again find a growing popular interest in their "dismal science."

Alas, when they are thrust into the spotlight, economists invariably reveal something about their discipline that ordinary citizens tend to forget during the good times. As those recently watching economists on TV or reading op-ed pieces by economists were soon to discover (or, if old enough, *rediscover*), economists are rarely of one mind with respect to matters of deep and immediate economic impact. Some Americans suffering unease about the economy in general may experience a heightening of this malady as a result of the evident lack of unanimity in the economics profession. However, this has been an abiding characteristic of the keepers of economic wisdom for a very long time.

It is well for the reader to remember that throughout the long history of human efforts to understand and explain economic matters, disagreement rather than consensus has been the rule. In a nation that puts great stock in consensus building as the ultimate tool of governance and the principal device for sustaining social order, this may be a disconcerting fact. In any event, it is one we should understand. Even in times of considerable national economic prosperity, real differences of political and economic opinion still circulate. And, as we should know from the historical record, economic prosperity itself has always been a transitory condition; when it fades, debate over alternative economic policies often becomes heated.

When that debate takes place, squabbling among economists over policy alternatives can scarcely be hidden from the public, and such disagreement can be downright unsettling. It often comes as a rude surprise to the person on the street, who, although paying due professional respect to economists, still sees the economist as a kind of mechanic. When one's car does not start, the car owner expects (at least hopes) that the diagnosis of mechanical trouble given at one garage is exactly the same as what will be heard at any other. If there is one mechanical problem, there should be one mechanical solution. The moral of this comparison is that the study of economics is more than studying a repair manual, and economists are not mechanics.

## Economics and Ideology

How is such disagreement possible? Is not economics a science? Economists' answers to that question vary. A common and reasonable enough response is simply that scientists disagree too. While there is much truth to such an answer, it really begs the question. Plainly, economics is not a science like physics. Whereas economists may sometimes talk about the laws of supply and demand as if they were eternal verities like the law of gravity, there is abundant anthropological and historical evidence that many societies have behaved quite contrary to the laws of supply and demand.

To be sure, economists employ (or at least should employ) the rigor of scientific method and quantitative techniques in collecting data, testing hypotheses, and offering reasonable conclusions and predictions. However, economists deal with different "stuff" than their colleagues in the exact sciences. Their data involve human beings, and their laboratory is a world of behavior and perception that varies with time and place. On top of this, economists, like all social scientists, are called on to answer a question not asked of those in the pure sciences: "What *ought* to be?" Astronomers, for instance, are not asked what *ought* to be the gravitational relationships of our universe. That would be a nonsensical question. Economists, however, cannot evade making some determinations about optimal prices, optimal income distribution, and so forth. Their decisions, while perhaps based on a genuine effort at neutrality, detachment, and honest evaluation of the available evidence, finally must be a matter of interpretation, a value judgment based on their own particular world views. To put the point directly: *Economics, as a study of human behavior, cannot avoid value judgments. Struggle as it may, economics as a discipline is never free from ideology.*

The early economists of the eighteenth and nineteenth centuries—Adam Smith, David Ricardo, John Stuart Mill, and especially the heretic Karl Marx—perceived economics as merely part of a broader political economy context, but this view had been largely abandoned by the end of the nineteenth century. By the middle of the twentieth century, the economics profession generally approached ideology as if it were a dirty word, unprofessional, or, at the very best, too troublesome to deal with. The emphasis was on theoretical tools, considered both universal and neutral. All this changed in the 1960s and 1970s when well-known American economists thrust themselves into the powerful debates then sweeping American society. Their views on the war in Vietnam, poverty, civil rights, the extent of government power, the environmental crisis, the oil embargo, the causes of stagflation, high technology versus smokestack industries, and much more could be heard regularly on television talk shows and miniseries or read in the columns of weekly newsmagazines. Often there was the pretension that this "talking out of church" had little impact on the body of professional theory and judgment, but the pretension was unconvincing. For good or ill, the genie was out of the bottle, and the economics profession had again become involved in politics and in recommending political courses of action to pursue economic objectives.

Initially, through the 1960s and into the early 1970s, prevailing opinion among economic reasoners upheld a Liberal perspective on political economy, advocating an active interventionism by government to correct and improve the workings of the economy. However, during the late 1970s, this consensus began to break down as the national economy slipped into a long period of sagging growth, rising unemployment, and escalating inflation. In its place, a new consensus began to build on behalf of a Conservative, minimum-government approach to political and economic matters. As the Liberals' star fell and the Conservatives' rose,

the intensity and bitterness of economic and political argument sharpened. Although the shrillness of the ideological debate calmed a bit during the Reagan years—no doubt a by-product of the long economic
expansion that began in late 1982—the past four decades of shifting
ideological perspectives have left their mark on the economics profession. To a considerable extent, the ordinary economics textbook illustrates this point. While economics texts continue to do what such books
have always done, namely, to introduce the reader to a generally agreed-
on body of theoretical and analytical techniques and tools that constitute the study of economics, most have also found it necessary to identify
and discuss the alternatives of Liberals, Conservatives, and, sometimes,
even Radicals in the practical extension of economic analysis to actual
policy-making situations.

The significance of all this should not be lost on the beginning student of economics. Though many economists may stress the value-
free nature of their studies, and of economics in general, common sense
and observation suggest that this is at best a vastly exaggerated claim.
The content and application of economic reasoning are determined
ultimately by the force of what economists believe, not by an independent and neutral logic. But to say that economics is a matter of opinion
is not to say that it is just a study of relatively different ideas: Here is
this view and here is that one and each is of equal value. In fact, opinions are not of equal value. There are good opinions and there are bad
ones. Different economic ideas have different consequences when
adopted as policy. They have different effects—now and in the future.
As we confront the various policy solutions proposed to deal with the
many crises now gnawing deep into our economy and society, we must
make choices: this one seems likely to produce desired outcomes, that
one does not. No other situation is consistent with a free and reasoning
society. Granted, it is a painful situation, since choice always raises
doubts and uncertainty and runs the risk of wrong judgment, but it
cannot be evaded.

This book is intended to focus on a limited number of the hard choices
that we must make. Its basic premise is that economic judgment is fundamentally a matter of learning to choose the best policy solution among
all possible solutions. The book further assumes that failure to make
this choice is to underestimate the richness and importance of the economic ideas we learn and to be blind to the fact that ideas and analyses
do indeed apply to the real world of our own lives.

## On Sorting Out Ideologies

Assuming that we have been at least partially convincing in our argument that economic analysis is permeated by ideological judgment, we
now turn to examine the varieties of ideology common to American
economic thought.

In general, we may characterize the ideological position of contemporary economics and economists as Conservative, Liberal, or Radical.
These, the same handy categories that evening newscasters use to describe political positions, presumably have some meaning to people.
The trouble with labels, though, is that they can mean a great deal and,
at the same time, nothing at all. At a distance the various political colors
of Conservative, Liberal, and Radical banners are vividly different. Close
up, however, the distinctiveness blurs, and what seemed obvious differences are not so clear. For instance, there is probably *not* a strictly Liberal position on every economic issue, nor are all the economists who
might be generally termed Liberal consistently in agreement. The same
is true in the case of many Radical or Conservative positions as well.
Unless we maintain a certain open-endedness in our categorizing of
positions, the discussion of ideological differences will be overly simple
and much too rigid. Therefore, the following generalizations and applications of ideological typologies will attempt to isolate and identify only
representative positions. By doing this we can at least focus on the differences at the center rather than on the fuzziness at the fringes of these
schools of thought.

We are still left with a problem. How do you specify an ideological
position? Can you define a Radical or a Liberal or a Conservative position? The answer here is simple. As the British economist Joan Robinson
once observed, an ideology is like an elephant—you cannot define an
elephant but you should know one when you see it. Moreover, you should
know the difference between an elephant and a horse or a cow without
having to resort to definitions.

There is a general framework of thought within each of the three
ideological schools by which we can recognize them. Thus we will not
"define" the schools but merely describe the salient characteristics of
each. In all of the following, the reader is urged to remember that there
are many varieties of elephants. Our specification of a particular ideological view on any issue is a representative model—a kind of average-
looking elephant (or horse or cow). Therefore, the Conservative view

offered on the problem of federal deficits, for instance, will probably not encompass all Conservative thought on this question. However, it should be sufficiently representative so that the basic Conservative paradigm, or worldview, can be distinguished from the Radical or Liberal argument. Where truly important divisions within an ideological paradigm exist, the divisions will be appropriately noted and discussed.

## A Brief Footnote on the Paradigms

The reader should be aware that ideological labels and categories presently are used by Americans in an increasingly flippant fashion. For example, TV journalism's efforts to "dumb down" news reporting and editorial commentary on the news has produced the well-known talking-head format where analyses of events are sifted and sorted into "from the Right" and "from the Left" perspectives. Based upon the authors' experiences, this technique of dividing up Conservative, Liberal, and Radical political-economic ideas—handy as it may be for sound-bite making—creates some awful confusion.

Neat division into "Left" or "Right" is a dangerous oversimplification of the range and variety of ideological points of view. The Left presumably includes all Liberals and Radicals, and the Right catches all Conservatives. To dump Liberals and Radicals into a presumably shared-interest category is a monumental error of the first order. True Liberals and true Radicals have been at each other's throats for a century or more. Indeed, they have been at war with each other more than either one has been at war with Conservatives.

The Left-Right designation of ideologies rests on the false assumption that political-economic belief can be neatly segregated and compartmentalized along a continuum—with Adam Smith on one end and Karl Marx on the other. Accordingly, leaning Left or Right is apparently determined by where along this continuum one is located: nearer or further from Marx and Smith. Alas, ideas are not susceptible to arrangement along a continuum. To arrange political-economic ideas as if they were part of a unified spectrum is about as useful as arranging one's personal library according to book size or one's CD collection according to the color of the disks' cases.

However, the most troublesome and misleading aspect of the Left-Right categorization of American opinion is its habit of not sorting outlooks according to the types of issues that individuals might address.

Tasteless as some may find the following "for instances," where on the Left-Right spectrum should we locate a gay or lesbian couple who regularly vote Republican but are also seeking to obtain a marriage license or the aging Pentecostal Christian who is utterly dependent on Social Security monthly checks and Medicare to support himself and his wife?

The point is that sexual orientation or religious belief are questions of personal and social values (as is the matter of one's preferred major league baseball team) and not necessarily a reflection of one's political ideology at all. To be sure, political conservatives may court those who adhere to "conservative" personal values (sometimes called "family values") and liberal ideologues may cultivate those of a "liberal" bent with respect to their personal beliefs, but that is a separate matter from the examination of competing economic ideologies.

The purpose of this "footnote" is to underscore that the following Conservative, Liberal, and Radical paradigms are generalized representations of three long-recognized schools of ideological outlook. The reader is warned that they are not easily short-handed as Left or Right nor should any of our paradigms be presumed to advocate on behalf of specific "social values."

### The Conservative Paradigm

What is usually labeled the Conservative position in economic thought and policy making was not always conservative. Conservative ideas may be traced to quite radical origins. The forebears of modern Conservative thought—among them England's Adam Smith (1723–1790)—were not interested in conserving the economic order they knew but in destroying it. In 1776, when Smith wrote his classic *Wealth of Nations*, England was organized under a more or less closed economic system of monopoly rights, trade restriction, and constant government interference with the marketplace and individuals' business and private affairs. This system, known as mercantilism, had been dominant in England and, with slight variations, elsewhere on the Continent for more than 250 years.

### Adam Smith's Legacy

Smith's remedy was simple enough: Remove all restrictions on commercial and industrial activity and allow the market to work freely. The philosophical basis of Smith's argument rested on his beliefs that (1) all men had the natural right to obtain and protect their property; (2) all men were by nature materialistic; and (3) all men were rational and would seek, by their own reason, to maximize their material well-being. These individualistic tendencies in men would be tempered by competition in the marketplace. There, men would have to compromise with one another to gain any individual satisfaction whatsoever. The overall effect of these compromises would ultimately lead to national as well as individual satisfaction. Competition and self-interest would keep prices down and production high and rising, as well as stimulate product improvement, invention, and steady economic progress. For this to happen, of course, there would have to be a minimum of interference with the free market—no big government, no powerful unions, and no conspiring in trade. Smith's position and that of his contemporaries and followers was known as "classical liberalism." The Conservative label now applied to these views seems to have been affixed much later, when Smith's heirs found themselves acting in the defense of a status quo rather than opposing an older order.

Thus modern capitalist economic thought must trace its origins to Adam Smith. While this body of thought has been built on and modified over the past two hundred years, the hand of Adam Smith is evident in every conventional economics textbook. Common sense tells us, however, that a lot has changed since Smith's day. Today business is big. There are labor unions and big government to interfere with his balanced free market of equals. His optimistic view of a naturally growing and expanding system is now replaced by growth problems and by a frequent dose of pessimism in some glances toward the future. Nevertheless, modern Conservatives, among contemporary defenders of capitalism, still stand close to the ideals of Adam Smith.

Modern Conservative thought is anchored in two basic philosophic ideas that distinguish it from Liberal and Radical positions. First, the market system and the spirit of competition are central to proper social organization. Second, individual rights and freedoms must be unlimited and uninfringed.

Conservatives oppose any "unnatural" interference in the marketplace. In particular, the Conservative views the growth of big government in capitalist society as the greatest threat to economic progress. Milton Friedman, Nobel laureate and preeminent figure in the Conservative Chicago school, has argued that government has moved from being merely an instrumentality necessary to sustain the economic and social order to becoming an instrument of oppression. Friedman's prescription for what "ought to be" on the matter of government is clear:

> A government which maintained law and order, defined property rights, served as a means whereby we could modify property rights and other rules of the economic game, adjudicated disputes about the interpretation of the rules, enforced contracts, promoted competition, provided a monetary framework, engaged in activities to counter technical monopolies and to overcome neighborhood effects widely regarded as sufficiently important to justify government intervention, and which supplemented private charity and the private family in protecting the irresponsible, whether madman or child—such a government would clearly have important functions to perform. The consistent liberal is not an anarchist.*

The antigovernmental position of Conservatives in fact goes further than merely pointing out the dangers to individual freedom. To Conservatives the growth of big government itself causes or worsens economic problems. For instance, the growth of elaborate government policies to improve the conditions of labor, such as minimum-wage laws and Social Security protection, are seen as actually harming labor in general. A wage higher than that determined by the market will provide greater income for some workers, but, the Conservative argument runs, it will reduce the total demand for labor, and thus dump many workers into unemployment. As this example indicates, the Conservative assault on big government is seen not simply as a moral or ethical question but also in terms of alleged economic effects.

Another unifying feature of the representative Conservative argument is its emphasis on individualism and individual freedom. To be sure, there are those in the Conservative tradition who pay only lip service to this view, but for true Conservatives it is the centerpiece of their logic. As Friedman has expressed it:

> We take freedom of the individual . . . as the ultimate goal in judging social arrangements. . . . In a society freedom has nothing to say about what an individual does with his freedom; it is not an all-embracing ethic.

---

*Milton Friedman, *Capitalism and Freedom* (Chicago: University of Chicago Press, 1962), 34.

> Indeed, a major aim of the liberal [here meaning Conservative as we use the term] is to leave the ethical problem for the individual to wrestle with.*

Modern Conservatives as a group exhibit a wide range of special biases. Not all are as articulate or logically consistent as Friedman's Chicago school. Many are identified more readily by what they oppose than by what they seem to be for. Big government, in both its microeconomic interferences and its macroeconomic policy making, is the most obvious common enemy, but virtually any institutionalized interference with individual choice is at least ceremonially opposed.

Some critics of the Conservative position are quick to point out that most modern-day Conservatives are not quite consistent on the question of individual freedom when they focus on big business. In fact, until comparatively recently, Conservatives usually did demand the end of business concentration. Like all concentrations of power, it was viewed as an infringement on individual rights. The Conservative Austrian economist Joseph Schumpeter argued that "Big Business is a half-way house on the road to Socialism." The American Conservative Henry C. Simons observed in the depressed 1930s that "the great enemy to democracy is monopoly." Accounting for the change to a more accommodating position on big business is not easy. Conservatives offer two basic reasons. First, big business and the so-called monopoly problem have been watched for a long period of time, and the threat of their power subverting freedom is seen as vastly overstated. Second, by far the larger problem is the rise of big government, which is cited as the greatest cause of business inefficiency and monopoly abuse. Another factor that seems implied in Conservative writing is the fear of communism and socialism. To direct an assault on the American business system, even if existing business concentration were a slight impediment to freedom, would lay that system open to direct Radical attack. How serious this supposed contradiction in Conservative logic really is remains a matter of debate among its critics.

## The Recent Resurgence of Conservative Economic Ideas

In the United States, until the drab years of the Great Depression, what we now call "Conservative economics" *was* economics, period. Except

---

*Milton Friedman, *Capitalism and Freedom* (Chicago: University of Chicago Press, 1962), 12.

for an occasional voice challenging the dominant wisdom, usually to little effect, few economists, political leaders, or members of the public at large disagreed greatly with Adam Smith's emphasis on individual freedom and on a free market economic condition.

The Depression years, however, brought a strong reaction to this kind of political and economic thinking. Many—perhaps most—of the millions of Americans who were out of work in the 1930s and the millions more who hung on to their jobs by their teeth came to believe that a "free" economy was simply one in free fall. While most staunch Conservatives complained bitterly about the abandonment of market economics and the "creeping socialism" of Franklin Roosevelt's New Deal, they had few listeners. For thirty-two of the next forty-eight years after Roosevelt's election in 1932, the White House, and usually the Congress, was in Liberal Democratic hands. For Conservatives, however, perhaps the greater losses were in the universities, where the old free market "ideas" of Adam Smith and his disciples quickly fell out of style. In their place, a generation of professors espoused the virtues of the "New Economics" of John Maynard Keynes and the view that a capitalist economy requires government intervention to keep it from destroying itself.

Driven to the margins of academic and political influence by the 1970s, the Conservatives seemed in danger of joining the dinosaur and the dodo bird as an extinct species. However, by the late 1970s, in the aftermath of the Vietnam War and the Watergate scandal and in a period when nothing government did seemed able to control domestic inflation and unemployment problems, there developed a growing popular reaction against government in general. As more and more Americans came to believe that government economic and social interventions were the cause of the nation's maladies, the Conservative ideology took off again under its own power.

In 1980, the Conservative economic and political paradigm succeeded in recapturing the White House. Ronald Reagan became the first president since Herbert Hoover to come to office after a private sector career. There was no doubting Reagan's philosophical commitment to the principles of a free enterprise economy.

As might be expected, Conservatives found themselves facing a difficult situation. Implementing a free market policy was, of course, much easier to accomplish in theory than in the real world—especially in a world vastly more complex than that envisioned by Adam Smith.

Reaganomics, the popular catchword for the new brand of Conservative economics, was quickly and sorely tested as the economy slipped into a deep recession in late 1981. To both friendly and hostile critics, Conservatives responded that quick solutions were not possible since the economic debris of a half century needed to be swept aside before the economy could be reconstructed. Despite the fact that Reaganomics proved to be somewhat less than an unqualified success (indeed, a good many Conservatives would now call it a failure), the Reagan years were a time of moderate but sustained economic boom—the second longest peacetime boom in American history. Despite some dark clouds—the near tripling of the federal debt, a worsening international trade situation, and a precipitous stock market collapse in 1987—the Reagan-Bush 1980s remained, in economic terms, a comparatively bright period in American economic history. Meanwhile, the collapse of communism in Eastern Europe and the Soviet Union and the Soviet bloc's shift toward a more open economic and political system in the last years of the decade could only be counted as frosting on Conservatives' ideological cake. As America approached the end of the century, Conservatives basked in the sunlight of success. Important for our study is the fact that a wide range of Conservative economic ideas and political perspectives that had been shunned in serious academic debates for over forty years have again made their way back into economics textbooks.

Indeed, the rise and refurbishing of market-based economic theory—and not simply in the United States—in the last decade or two of the twentieth century is one of the most important recent developments in economics. For today's young reader, who probably believes that market-based doctrine *is* economics, it may be difficult to believe that Conservative thinking in both economic theory and policy making was, not so many years ago, without much influence in the economics profession. That fact is a good one to keep in mind. It illustrates something that is often overlooked: The prevailing ideological mood, what we might call the conventional wisdom, is ever subject to change and reevaluation.

### The Liberal Paradigm

According to a national poll, Americans tend to associate the term *Liberal* with big government, Franklin Roosevelt, labor unions, and welfare. Time was, not too long ago, when Liberal stood not just as a proud appellation but seemed to characterize the natural drift of the whole country. At the height of his popularity and before the Vietnam War toppled his administration, Lyndon Johnson, speaking of the new Liberal consensus, observed:

> After years of ideological controversy, we have grown used to the new relationship between government, households, business, labor and agriculture. The tired slogans that made constructive discourse difficult have lost their meaning for most Americans. It has become abundantly clear that our society wants neither to turn backward the clock of history nor to discuss the present problems in a doctrinaire or partisan spirit.*

Although what we will identify as the Liberal position in American economic thought probably still is alive and well in the teaching and practice of economic reasoning (as we shall see, even some Conservatives have adopted elements of the Liberal analysis), the Liberal argument is undergoing considerable changes. These changes, however, are more cosmetic than basic, and the central contours of Liberal belief are still visible.

### The Interventionist Faith

Whereas Conservatives and Radicals are comparatively easily identified by a representative position, Liberals are more difficult to identify. In terms of public policy positions, the Liberal spectrum ranges all the way from those favoring a very moderate level of government intervention to those advocating broad government planning of the economy.

Despite the great distance between the defining poles of Liberal thought, several basic points can be stated as unique to the Liberal paradigm. Like their Conservative counterparts, Liberals are defenders of the principle of private property and the business system. These, however, are not categorical rights, as we observed in the Conservative case. Individual claims to property or the ability to act freely in the marketplace are subject to the second Liberal principle—that social welfare and the maintenance of the entire economy supersede individual interest. In a vicious condemnation of what we would presently call the Conservative position, John Maynard Keynes directly

---

*The Economic Report of the President, 1965* (Washington, DC: U.S. Government Printing Office, 1965), 39.

assaulted the philosophy that set the individual over society. Keynes argued:

> It is not true that individuals possess a proscriptive "natural liberty" in their economic activities. There is no "compact" conferring perpetual rights on those who Have or on those who Acquire. The world is not so governed from above that private and social interest always coincide. It is not a correct deduction from the Principles of Economics that enlightened self-interest always operates in the public interest. Nor is it true that self-interest generally is enlightened; more often individuals acting separately to promote their own ends are too ignorant or too weak to attain even these. Experience does not show that individuals, when they make up a social unit, are always less clear-sighted than when they act separately.*

To the Liberal, then, government intervention in, and occasional direct regulation of, aspects of the national economy is neither a violation of principle nor an abridgement of "natural economic law." The benefits to the whole society from intervention simply outweigh any "natural right" claims. The forms of intervention may vary, but their pragmatic purpose is obvious—to tinker and manipulate in order to produce greater social benefits.

Government intervention in the economy dates from the very beginnings of the nation, but the Progressives of the early twentieth century were the first to successfully urge an extensive and systematic elaboration of governmental economic powers. In response to the excesses of giant enterprises in the era of the robber barons, the Progressives followed a number of paths in the period from 1900 to 1920. One was the regulation of monopoly power, to be accomplished either through antitrust prosecutions to restore competition or through the use of independent regulatory commissions in cases where a "break them up" policy was undesirable (for instance, railroads and other firms possessing *public utility* characteristics). A second was *indirect* business regulation, effected by such Progressive developments as legalization of unions, the passage of social legislation at both the federal and state levels, tax reforms, and controls over production (for example, laws against food

---

*John M. Keynes, "The End of Laissez Faire," in *Essays of Persuasion* (New York: Norton, 1963), 68.

adulteration)—all of which circumvented the power of business and subjected it to the public interest.

Although the legislation and leadership of the administrations of Theodore Roosevelt, William Howard Taft, and Woodrow Wilson went a long way in moderating the old laissez-faire ideology of the previous era, actual interference in business affairs remained slight until the Great Depression. By 1933 perhaps as many as one out of every three Americans was out of work (the official figures said 25 percent), business failures were common, and the specter of total financial and industrial collapse hung heavy over the whole country. In the bread lines and shanty towns known as "Hoovervilles" as well as on Main Street, there were serious mutterings that the American business system had failed. Business leaders, who had always enjoyed hero status in the history books and even among ordinary citizens, had become pariahs. Enter at this point Franklin Roosevelt, the New Deal, and the modern formulation of Liberal government-business policies. Despite violent attacks on him from the Conservative media, Roosevelt pragmatically abandoned his own conservative roots and, in a bewildering series of legislative enactments and presidential decrees, laid the foundation of public interest criteria for government regulation of the marketplace. *Whatever might work was tried.* The National Recovery Administration (NRA) encouraged industry cartels and price setting. The Tennessee Valley Authority (TVA) was an attempt at publicly owned enterprise. At the Justice Department, Attorney General Thurman Arnold initiated more antitrust actions than all of his predecessors combined. And a mass of "alphabet agencies" was created to deal with this or that aspect of the Depression.

Intervention to protect labor and extensions of social welfare provisions were not enough to end the Depression. It was the massive spending for World War II that finally restored prosperity. With this prosperity came the steady influence of Keynes, who had argued in the 1930s that only through government fiscal and monetary efforts to keep up the demand for goods and services could prosperity be reached and maintained. Keynes's arguments for government policies to maintain high levels of investment and hence employment and consumer demand became Liberal dogma. To be a Liberal was to be a Keynesian, and vice versa.

Alvin Hansen, Keynes's first and one of his foremost proponents in the United States, could scarcely hide his glee in 1957 as he described the wedding of Liberal Keynesian policies with the older government interventionist position this way:

> Within the last few decades the role of the economist has profoundly changed. And why? The reason is that economics has become operational. It has become operational because we have at long last developed a mixed public-private economy. This society is committed to the welfare state and full employment. This government is firmly in the driver's seat. In such a world, practical policy problems became grist for the mill of economic analysis. Keynes, more than any other economist of our time, has helped to rescue economics from the negative position to which it had fallen to become once again a science of the Wealth of Nations and the art of Political Economy.*

Despite the Liberal propensity for tinkering—either through selected market intervention or through macro policy action—most Liberals, like Conservatives, still rely on traditional supply-and-demand analysis to explain prices and market performance. Their differences with Conservatives on the functioning of the markets, determination of output, pricing, and so forth lie not so much in describing what is happening as in evaluating how to respond to what is happening. For instance, there is little theoretical difference between Conservatives and Liberals on how prices are determined under monopolistic conditions. However, to the Conservative, the market itself is the best regulator and preventive of monopoly abuse. To the Liberal, monopoly demands government intervention.

*Varieties of Liberal Belief*

As noted before, the Liberal dogma covers a wide spectrum of opinion. Moreover, the Liberal position has shifted somewhat in response to the economic disappointments of the 1970s and certain successes of the Reagan years.

On the extreme left wing of the Liberal spectrum, economists such as Robert Heilbroner and John Kenneth Galbraith have long argued that capitalism as the self-regulating system analyzed in conventional economic theory simply does not exist. Heilbroner contends: "The persis-

---

*Alvin H. Hansen, *The American Economy* (New York: McGraw-Hill, 1957), 175.

tent breakdowns of the capitalist economy, whatever their immediate precipitating factors, can all be traced to a single underlying cause. This is the anarchic or planless character of capitalist production."* For a time, this critical defect led Heilbroner to flirt with central planning as the only possible cure. However, he eventually backed away from this position, holding instead that capitalism plus government regulation to provide periodic corrections has proved to be more durable than central planning efforts.

To the left-leaning and always iconoclastic John Kenneth Galbraith, who sees problems of technology rather than profit dominating the giant corporation, a more rational atmosphere for decision making must be created. In brief, the modern firm demands a high order of internal and external planning of output, prices, and capital. The interests of the firm and state become fused in this planning process, and the expanded role of Liberal government in the whole economy and society becomes obvious. While Galbraith has in the past maintained that he was a socialist, the Liberal outcome of his program is obvious in that he (1) never explicitly takes up the expropriation of private property, and (2) still accepts a precarious social balance between public and private interest.

Although Galbraith's Liberalism leads to an economy heavily reliant on planning, most Liberals stop well before this point. Having rejected the logic of self-regulating markets and accepted the realities of giant business enterprise, Liberals unashamedly admit to being pragmatic tinkerers—ever adjusting and interfering with business decision making in an effort to assert the changing public interest. Yet all this must be done while still respecting basic property rights and due process. Under these arrangements, business regulation amounts to a protection of business itself as well as the equal protection of other interest groups in pluralist American society.

In the not-too-distant past, business itself adapted to and embraced this position. Whereas certain government actions might be opposed, the philosophy of government intervention in the economy was not necessarily seen as antibusiness. The frequent Conservative depiction of most Liberals as being opposed to the business system does not withstand the empirical test. For instance, in 1964 Henry Ford II organized a

---

*Robert Heilbroner, *The Limits of American Capitalism* (New York: Harper and Row, 1966), 88.

highly successful committee of business leaders for the Liberal Lyndon Johnson, while Conservative Barry Goldwater, with Friedman as his adviser, gained little or no support from big business. However, the extent of government regulation soon reached a level that was wholly unacceptable to the private sector. In the late 1960s and early 1970s, a blizzard of environmental, job safety, consumer protection, and energy regulations blew out of Washington. Added to what was already on the ground, the new legislative snowfall seemed to many observers at the end of the 1970s about to bring American business to a standstill. Many who a decade before frankly feared the economic freedom of the Conservative vision now embraced that position.

The distress of economic *stagflation* in the 1970s (lower growth, rising unemployment, *and* price inflation), for which the Liberals seemed to have no programmatic cures, along with a growing popular sentiment against big government in general, drove Liberals from positions of political influence. Even within universities, the Liberal consensus began to collapse, with some former Liberal theorists deserting to the Conservative camp and most others adopting a lower profile in their teaching, writing, and research. Yet by the end of the 1980s, most of the analytical and policy positions associated with Liberal economic reasoning still survived—a bit subdued from the high-flying days of Kennedy's New Frontier and Johnson's Great Society but distinguishable nonetheless. Among the more reform-minded Liberal reasoners, the old economic agenda items—income distribution, discrimination, the environment, consumer protection, monopoly abuse, labor unions, structural shifts in the economy and their resulting dislocations—remained vital concerns in any policy-making effort. However, Liberal hopes for a fairly swift and sweeping resolution of these problems had diminished greatly from the expectations of the 1960s and early 1970s. The new realities of a slow-growth economy, massive federal deficits, reduced American competitiveness in world markets, and costly entitlement programs put serious constraints on even a visionary reformer's dedication to interventionism. But this commitment had not been extinguished. When the Eastern European communist states toppled like dominoes and the long-time cold war confrontation with the Soviet Union seemed to move steadily toward a peaceful end, there was brave talk among Liberals of the prospects for a "peace dividend." The ending of the cold war was envisioned as freeing up vast sums for favored social agenda items that had long been shelved.

Meanwhile, in the business community, the old propensity to enlist government on the side of improving the stability of domestic markets was given new life in the face of rising foreign competition, the decline of certain basic industries, and the double frights provided by Black Monday (the sudden collapse of the stock market on October 19, 1987) and the savings-and-loan industry crisis. In particular, the last two events seemed to show that too much market freedom might not be as desirable as it sounded.

The present-day ambivalence of Liberals on the degree and type of intervention will be evident in our survey of economic issues in this book; nevertheless, this tendency should not be misunderstood. Specific Liberal approaches to problem solving may be debatable, but the essence of Liberal economics remains unchanged: *The capitalist economy simply requires pragmatic adjustment from time to time to maintain overall balance and to protect particular elements in the society.*

## The Radical Paradigm

For most readers, specification of a Radical paradigm will seem to be a difficult and unfamiliar exercise. The identifications of Right and Left, or Conservative and Liberal, are used nightly on the television news and talk shows, and presumably these labels have self-evident political meaning to most viewers. The Radical label is not so well known, nor is it used very much by the media. For the most part, Americans are generally uninformed about the content and objectives of a Radical social outlook. Yet in a variation on the old adage about familiarity breeding contempt, we find also that ignorance breeds contempt, at least with regard to ideological matters. Quite simply, most Americans—even if they know little about a Radical ideological outlook—believe it to be essentially wrongheaded and, at bottom, un-American. Nevertheless, there is a Radical tradition in American economic thought, and it needs to be understood.

The principal litmus test for accepting the Radical position requires the rejection of production-for-profit capitalism as an economic system —both the free market capitalism of Conservatives and the regulated capitalism of Liberals. Such a minimum membership standard, needless to say, leads to the lumping of a large number of very different anticapitalist critiques into the Radical category. Nonetheless, there is an important shared outlook among true Radicals. The essence of this perspective is nicely illustrated by a comment made some years ago by Tony Benn, a political and ideological leader of the British Labour Party. Queried by an interviewer in 1992 as to what was going to happen to socialists around the world now that the Marxist-socialist regime in the Soviet Union had collapsed, Benn offered a pregnant response. "The real struggle," Benn observed, "was never between capitalism and socialism. It was and is between capitalism and democracy."

In Benn's remark lies the common core of contemporary Radical thought: Radicals espouse a social and economic order in which institutions are expected to respond to people's needs and people are to be empowered politically and economically so as to ensure democratic outcomes.

At such a general level of articulation, Radical ideology may appear deceptively benign. Who, after all, can be opposed to "empowering people?" However, the economic and political empowerment of people quickly takes on a more serious and, to some, more threatening meaning when the Radical analysis is examined in greater detail. As the Radical tradition understands the economic and social dynamic of societies, power is intricately connected to the ownership of property: Whoever owns or controls the use of a society's things invariably possesses political and economic power commensurate with such ownership or control. In capitalism, ownership of things, particularly the things (capital) that produce other things, is disproportionately held in the hands of a comparative few. These owners of the means of production are seen by Radicals as exercising excessive influence for their own personal (or class) gain in the society's decisions about what will be produced, how that output will be produced, and who will share in this output. In our Radical paradigm, empowerment necessarily leads to limiting private and individual economic power and to increasing the social ownership and control of the things within a society. For most readers, a word should spring to mind: *socialism.*

Socialism as a political, social, even religious outlook probably predates the rise of capitalism. And the term *socialism* is an umbrella that can cover a multitude of ideological tendencies. Utopian communitarians, Christian socialists, anarchists, Marxists, syndicalists, communists, guild socialists, and many other ideological variants can crowd under the socialist umbrella. The common thread to membership in any socialist tradition is acceptance of the advocacy for the social or community ownership of all, or most, of the means of production and for a societally determined standard for the distribution of the output of the society.

While it is pretty clear that all socialists would qualify as Radicals, it is by no means true that all Radicals see themselves as socialists. Partly, this is the case because socialism has long been and certainly remains a dirty word among most Americans—an ideological outlook that directly challenges the nation's historical proclivity to explain social and economic life in largely individualist terms. Partly, it reflects the fact that the term socialism is simply too big an umbrella and therefore includes a lot of ideological outlooks that, once you get past a few basic theoretical similarities, do not agree on important issues of specific programs and goals.

Moreover, many American Radicals are not political activists at all. For them, commitment to a Radical perspective is mostly an intellectual and analytical exercise aimed at attacking and revealing the deficiencies of conventional Conservative and Liberal thought. Their purpose is not to build an alternative political party, such as socialism has tended to become, but to supply an alternative critical analysis that Americans might act upon within the constraints of the existing political order. In any case, in specifying a Radical paradigm, it is wise to remember that membership includes many different marchers not necessarily listening to the same drummer, or at least not hearing the same beat even if there is a single drummer. But then again, the same can be said for Conservative and Liberal paradigms.

However, as a practical matter, an extended explanation of the Radical paradigm must be assigned an ideological starting point. And most, but surely not all, American Radicals would admit their intellectual debt to Karl Marx and his nineteenth-century critique of capitalism.

## The Marxist Heritage

Since the Marxist critique is likely to be less familiar to many readers than the basic arguments of Conservatives or Liberals, it is necessary to be somewhat more detailed in specifying the Radical position. As will be quickly apparent, the Radical worldview rests on greatly different assumptions about the economic and social order than those of the Conservatives and Liberals.

According to Marx's view, the value of a commodity reflects the real labor time necessary to produce it. However, under capitalism workers

lack control of their labor, selling it as they must to capitalists. The workers receive only a fraction of the value they create—according to Marx,
only an amount sufficient in the long run to permit subsistence. The rest
of the value—what Marx calls *surplus value*—is retained by capitalists
as the source of their profits and for the accumulation of capital that will
increase both future production and future profit. As the appropriation
of surplus value proceeds, with the steady transference of living labor
into capital (what Marx called *dead labor*), capitalists face an emerging
crisis. With more and more of their production costs reflecting their
growing dependence on capital (machines) and with surplus labor value
their only source of profit, capitalists are confronted with the reality of
not being able to expand surplus appropriation. Unless they are able to
increase their exploitation of labor—getting more output for the same,
or less, wages paid—they face a falling rate of profit on their growing
capital investment. Worse still, with workers' relatively falling wages
and capitalists' relatively increasing capacity to produce, there is a growing tendency for the entire capitalist system to produce more goods than
it can in fact sell.

These trends set certain systemic tendencies in motion. Out of the
chaos of capitalist competitive struggles for profits in a limited market
there develops a drive toward *concentration and centralization.* In other
words, the size of businesses grows and the number of enterprises shrinks.
However, the problems of the falling rate of profit and chronic overproduction create violent fluctuations in the business cycle. Each depression points ever more clearly toward capitalist economic collapse.
Meanwhile, among the increasingly impoverished workers, there is a
steady growth of a *reserve army of the unemployed*—workers who are
now unemployable as production decreases. Simultaneously, increasing
misery generates class consciousness and revolutionary activity among
the working class. As the economic disintegration of capitalist institutions worsens, the subjective consciousness of workers grows to the point
where they successfully overthrow the capitalist system. In the new society, the workers themselves take control of the production process,
and accumulation for the interest of a narrow capitalist class ceases.

## The Modern Restatement of Marx

Of necessity, the modern Radical's view of the world must lack the
finality of Marx's predictions. Quite simply, the capitalist system has

not self-destructed and, in fact, in a good many respects is stronger and more aggressive than it was in Marx's day. Although the present-day Radical may still agree with Marx's long-run predictions about the ultimate self-destructiveness of the capitalist order, the fact is that Radicals must deal with the world as it is. While the broad categories of Marx's analysis are retained generally, Radical thought must focus on real-world, current conditions of capitalist society and present an analysis that goes beyond merely asserting the Marxist scenario for capitalist collapse. Useful economic analysis must be offered in examining contemporary problems.

The beginning point for modern Radical critiques, as it was also for Marx over a hundred years ago, is the unquenchable capitalist thirst for profits. This central organizing objective of all capitalist systems determines everything else within those systems. The Radical analysis begins with a simple proposition about how capitalists understand market activity:

> Total sales = total cost of materials and machinery used up in production + total wages and salaries paid + (– in the case of losses) total profits

Such a general view of sales, costs, and profits is, thus far, perfectly consistent with traditional accounting concepts acceptable to any Conservative or Liberal. However, the Radical's analytic mission becomes clearer when the proposition is reformulated:

> Total profits = total sales – total cost of materials and machinery used up in production – total wages and salaries paid

It now becomes evident that increasing profits depends on three general conditions: (1) that sales rise, *ceteris paribus* (all things being equal); (2) that production costs (composed of wage costs and material and machinery costs) decline, *ceteris paribus;* or (3) that sales increases at least exceed production cost increases. The capitalist, according to the Radical argument, is not simply interested in total profits but also in the *rate of profit,* or the ratio of profits to the amount of capital the capitalist has invested.

With capitalist eyes focused on raising profits or raising profit rates, it becomes clear to Radicals which individual economic policies and strategies will be advanced by capitalists: *Every effort will be made to keep costs low,* such as reducing wage rates, speeding up the production line, introducing so-called labor-saving machines, seeking cheaper (often foreign) sources of labor and materials, and minimizing outlays for waste treatment and environmental maintenance. At the same time, *efforts will be made to keep prices high,* especially through the development of monopolistic price-making power on both a national and an international scale. In all of these activities, capitalists will make every effort to use government economic intervention to their own advantage—both in domestic markets and in expanding capitalist hegemony into the world.

However, taking the system as a whole, the effort of individual capitalists—either on their own or aided by government—to expand profit produces a crisis in obtaining profits. For instance, the capitalist goals of keeping wages low and prices high must lead to situations where workers as consumers simply cannot clear the market of available goods. Accordingly, the aggregate economy deteriorates into periodic recession or depression, with rising unemployment among workers and falling profits for capitalists. With capitalist support, a variety of government monetary and fiscal efforts may be employed to offset these ups and downs in the capitalist business cycle—in particular to improve the profit and profit rate of capitalist enterprises. However, so-called mixed capitalism (a mixture of private sector and government planning of the economy) cannot overcome the fundamental contradictions of a dominantly private, production-for-profit economy. And, of course, with the expansion of capitalism throughout most of the world, the capitalist crisis takes on international proportions. Quite as Marx predicted, the general economic crises deepen and occur more frequently. The search for profit becomes more frantic and more destructive to the lives of ever greater numbers of people living under capitalist hegemony throughout the world.

From the Radical point of view, periodic crisis in capitalism is not the result of excessive tinkering with the market system, as Conservatives claim; nor will the tendency toward crisis be contained by Liberal interventionism. *Periodic and deepening crisis* is *capitalism.*

Radical analysis is, of course, more penetrating than this short résumé can indicate. One further point that should be examined briefly is Marx's view of the relationship between a society's organization for production and its social relations. To Marx, capitalism was more than an economic system. Private values, religion, the family, the educational system, and political structures were all shaped by capitalist class domination and by the goal of production for private profit. It is important to recognize this tenet in any discussion of how Marxists—or Radicals with a Marxist orientation—approach contemporary social and economic problems. Marxists do not separate economics from politics or private belief. For instance, racism cannot be abstracted to the level of an ethical question. Its roots are seen in the capitalist production process. Nor is the state ever viewed as a neutrality able to act without class bias. Bourgeois democracy as we know it is seen simply as a mask for class domination.

Marx, in his early writings before his great work, *Capital,* had emphasized the "qualitative" exploitation of capitalism. Modern Radicals have revitalized this early Marx in their "quality of life" assaults on the present order. In these they emphasize the problems of worker alienation, commodity fetishism, and the wasteful and useless production of modern capitalism. The human or social problems of modern life are seen as rooted in the way the whole society is geared to produce more and more profits.

In addition to their Marxist heritage, modern Radicals derive much of their impulse from what they see as the apparent failure of Liberalism. Liberal promises to pursue policies of general social improvement are perceived as actions to protect only *some* interest groups. In general, those benefiting under Liberal arrangements are those who have always gained. The corporation is not controlled. It is more powerful than ever. Rule by elites has not ended, nor have the elites changed. Moreover, the national goals of the Liberal ethic—to improve our overall national well-being—stimulated the exploitation of poor nations, continued the cold war, and increased the militarization of the economy.

## The Question of Relevance

Quite obviously, the Marxist prediction of capitalism's final collapse has not yet come to pass. In fact, Radicals—particularly those very closely associated with the Marxist tradition—are increasingly obliged to account for what many non-Radicals see as a historical turning away from all collectivist political economic alternatives with the rise of market economies in previously socialist states. These trends, along with certain internal analytical problems of Marxist analysis, are quite sufficient for most non-Radicals to consign the whole Radical paradigm to the garbage heap of worthless, worn-out ideas.

A thoughtful observer may question whether this is an entirely enlightened conclusion to reach. First, the tendency to lump Marxism and real-world communist systems together as one and the same, while long a habit in the noncommunist as well as the communist world, rests on a grossly inaccurate understanding of Marx's philosophy. Second, Marxism—at least as American Radical scholars have developed and used it—is more a way of looking at how our economy works than a prophecy of things to come. It is the technique of analysis rather than the truth of Marx's specific analysis that counts.

A third point might also be worth considering. Freed of the Soviet millstone, Radical critiques, which were easily evaded during the cold war epoch, might take on more meaning and appeal. Radicals no longer have to explain away the Soviet errors of authoritarian politics, decrepit bureaucracies, and failed planning before putting forth their own critique of contemporary capitalism and their own democratic-socialist programs. Moreover, and of increasing importance to the relevance of Radical arguments, the post-Soviet world economy has yet to show the robustness that the victors of the cold war might have expected. Standing unchallenged in the world, capitalism and variants of capitalism may loom as larger targets for Radical attack than is generally appreciated. Consequently, it may be just a bit early to count out the Radical paradigm, as non-Radicals are presently inclined to do.

As noted before, not all Radicals subscribe to all Marxist doctrine, but Marxism in one form or another remains the central element of the Radical challenge. Marx's fundamental contention that the system of private production must be changed remains the badge of membership in the Radical ranks. This sets Radicals apart from mainstream Conservative and Liberal economists.

Critics of the Radical position usually point out that Radical analyses are hopelessly negativistic. Radicals, they say, describe the problems of capitalism without offering a solution other than the end of the whole system. While there is much truth to this charge, we shall see in the following sections that indeed some solutions are offered. But even if their program is vague, Radicals would argue that their greatest contribution is in revealing the truth of the capitalist system.

Despite lessened political influence, modern Radical economic thought still looms as a logically important alternative to the more broadly supported Conservative and Liberal paradigms. The force of an idea is not dependent on the number of true believers. Were that the case, Conservative economic doctrine would have disappeared thirty years ago.

## Applying the Analysis to the Issues

We have identified the three representative paradigms; now we will put them to use. The following selected issues by no means exhaust the economic and political crises troubling the nation; nevertheless, they provide a good-sized sampling of the social agenda confronting us. The issues presented here were selected because of their immediacy and representativeness in illustrating the diverse ideological approaches of Conservative, Liberal, and Radical economic analyses.

In each of the following issues, the representative paradigms are presented in a *first-person advocacy approach.* The reader might do well to regard the arguments like those in a debate. As in a debate, one should be careful to distinguish between substantive differences and mere logical or debating strategies. Thus some points may be quite convincing, whereas others seem shallow. However, the reader should remember that, shallow or profound, these are representative political economic arguments advanced by various economic schools.

The sequence in presenting the paradigms is consistent throughout the text: first Conservative, then Liberal, then Radical. In terms of the logical and historical development of contemporary economic ideologies, this sequence is most sensible; however, it certainly is not necessary to read the arguments in this order. Each one stands by itself. Nor is any ideological position intentionally set out as a straw man in any debate.

Readers should look at each position critically. They should test their own familiarity with economic concepts and their common sense against what they read in any representative case. Finally, of course, as students of economics and as citizens, they must make their own decisions. They determine who, if anyone, is the winner of the debate.

Because of space limitations, the representative arguments are brief, and some important ideas have been boiled down to a very few sentences. Also, within each of the three major positions there is a wide range of arguments, which may sometimes be at variance with one another. Conservatives, Liberals, and Radicals disagree among themselves on specific analyses and programs. For the sake of simplicity, we have chosen not to emphasize these differences but arbitrarily (although after much thought) to select the most representative arguments. Each paradigm's discussion of an issue presents a critique of present public policy and, usually, a specific program proposal.

In all of the arguments, the factual and empirical evidence offered has been checked for accuracy. It is instructive in itself that, given the nature of economic facts, they can be marshaled to prove a great variety of different ideological positions. Different or even similar evidence supports different truths, depending on the truth we wish to *prove.*

# Problems in the Marketplace

Part II focuses on issues generally accepted by economists as *microeconomic* in their analysis. Microeconomics examines specific economic units—households, firms, industries, labor groups—and the behavior of these individual units.

The focal point of formal microeconomic analysis since its nineteenth-century origins has been the market. Accordingly, Part II looks at selected problems in the marketplace. Topics include problems of agricultural supply and demand, consumer market behavior, environmental economics, firm size, government regulation, income distribution, and government finance. Each topic presents some important dimension of market performance; each has been selected for its representative qualities in developing a broadened understanding of microeconomic problems within the contemporary American economy.

# Responding to Market Outcomes

## Competition or Protection for American Agriculture?

Farmers should raise less corn and more Hell.
*—Mary E. Lease, Kansas, 1890s*

We produce too much food in this country.
*—Marty Strange, farmer advocacy group, 1982*

Because farmers are provided an incentive to make cropping decisions according to program rules rather than market signals, the [farm] programs reduce the responsiveness of U.S. agriculture to changes in world market conditions and reduce its international competitiveness.
—Economic Report of the President, 1990

For eighteen years, the price of food has not kept up with the cost of farming.
*—Don Taus, South Dakota farmer, 1998*

## The Problem

The teaching of economic reasoning usually begins with a general examination of the market model and, more particularly, with a consideration of
how the market determines production, pricing, and resource allocation
under conditions of pure competition. Such an introduction to economics
presents the beginner almost immediately with a confusing irony. On one
hand, markets for agricultural goods would seem to be especially appropriate for illustrating the general conditions of competition because they are
dominated by many small producers selling virtually identical products to a
very broad range of consumers. Thus, agriculture should be a marvelously
useful example of the market forces of supply and demand at work, and
introductory textbooks invariably use wheat, corn, or some other farm
product when they begin constructing simple analytical models.

In the real world, on the other hand, agricultural markets illustrate a quite
contrary tendency. Here we do not find competition and free-flowing market forces, but rather some of the most elaborate efforts ever devised to
insulate an industry from the market and to employ government intervention to promote private objectives. Agricultural output and pricing decisions
actually are directly affected by a federal price support program that has been
in place in one form or another for sixty years. Meanwhile, a variety of government agencies provide emergency aid of staggering proportions. In fact,
annual payments of emergency loans and other funds in excess of $30 bil-
lion or more per year were not uncommon a decade ago, as net farm income
(in real dollars) hovered near the levels of the Great Depression.

The condition of American agriculture has not always been one of unre-
lenting crisis, but the farm problem was around, on and off again, for most of
the twentieth century. The rhythm of farm fortune and misfortune has been
like this: First, World War I created an exceptional demand for American farm
products to feed soldiers and starving European civilians. With rising prices
resulting, farmers increased their output, but in the 1920s and 1930s, after
production increased, foreign demand for American farm products declined
and prices plummeted. The deepening depression after 1930 soon transformed
the growing agricultural crisis into a full-blown catastrophe. With the coming
of the New Deal in 1933, the federal government introduced numerous market interventions aimed at artificially raising or maintaining prices. These interventions included establishing a price support system in which government
guaranteed paying farmers the difference between the market price and an
established *parity* (fair) *price* for their crops, as well as efforts to hold up the price

Figure 1.1 **Net Income of Farm Operators from Farming, 1970–2002**

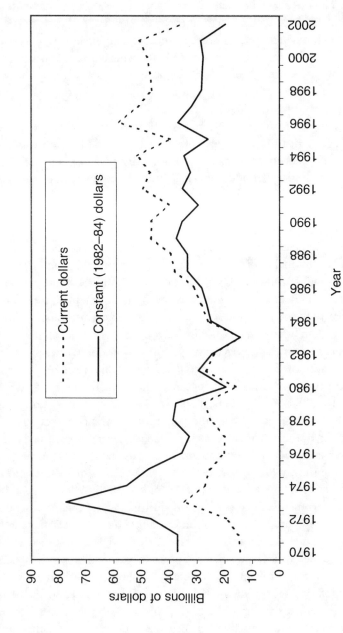

*Source:* Data from *Economic Report of the President* (Washington, DC: Government Printing Office, 2004).

of farm goods by paying farmers for taking some of their land out of production. These actions laid the economic and political foundations for what was to become a long-term, if not actually permanent, government intervention in agricultural markets. World War II pumped up demand and farm prices, but peace again brought tumbling prices and reliance on government support programs. Several Russian grain deals in the 1970s returned good times for a few years; however, farmers were soon caught up in new problems—a few of which were of their own making. Figure 1.1 illustrates the roller coaster ride that American farm income has taken since 1970.

As farm exports rose in the mid-1970s and farm prices and income followed, American farmers developed a false sense of security. Planting "fencepost to fencepost" became common. Many farmers undertook considerable acquisitions of additional land and new equipment, swelling their mortgage and loan obligations. Farm debt tripled between 1973 and 1983. At first, few farmers paid much attention to the fact that interest rates on their new loans were high and rising during most of this period. The farm mood was upbeat, and many farmers thought they had finally escaped from the traditional boom-bust cycle of the agricultural economy.

But throughout the 1970s until bottom was hit in the 1980s, American farmers experienced a lot of bust and very little boom. First, inflation got in its licks, as the general price expansion of the late 1970s pushed up fuel, machinery, and borrowing costs. Unable to pass these costs on in the form of higher prices, because overseas agricultural production was increasing and the prices of foreign food products were falling, American farmers saw their profit margins and net incomes squeezed. Throughout the 1970s and into the 1980s, American farmers' overseas sales declined, and cheaper foreign agricultural goods began to penetrate domestic markets.

However, by the mid-1990s, even in the face of several years of bad weather that adversely affected American agriculture, the hard times seemed to be lifting. When a new, Republican-dominated Congress took its seat in 1994, it promised to "get government out of farming." Briefly, it looked as though the old government strategies of levying tariffs on imported goods, operating marketing boards, paying subsidies, setting output quotas, making payments for letting land lie idle, and much else that had become American farm policy suddenly would be washed away by congressional opponents of agricultural protection. But in the Federal Agriculture Improvement and Reform Act of 1996 (also known as the Freedom to Farm Act), the final phasing out of agricultural support and subsidy programs was not to take place until 2002. Scarcely two years after the act's passage, opposition was building among farmers and farm groups to the entire philosophy of the Federal Agriculture Improvement and Reform Act of 1996. Moreover, by 2001, federal farm subsidies paid to farmers still stood at about the same levels that existed before passage of this act. The 1996 statute was replaced by the Farm Security and Rural Investment Act of 2002, which marked a return to government supports, manipulation, and protectionism for American agriculture.

The debate over agricultural policy remains an important issue and a profoundly significant theoretical question, since it goes to the very foundation of American economic belief; namely, do free and competitive markets work, or do they need constant repair and support by means of government intervention? Exactly how divided economists are on this question becomes apparent when we look at the policy alternatives proposed by our three paradigms.

## Synopsis

The Conservative position holds that the free operation of supply and demand is the correct and most effective determinant of agricultural prices. Liberals most frequently argue that an agricultural market left to itself is subject to wild cyclical fluctuation; thus a variety of government interventions are necessary to maintain reasonable order. Radicals see the American farm problem as a case of government being manipulated by agribusiness, with the result that government intervention has harmed both small farmers and ordinary consumers.

---

## Anticipating the Arguments

- Why do Conservatives believe that most government efforts to help farmers by artificially raising crop prices actually hurt both farmers and consumers?
- What is the historical and economic foundation to the Liberal argument that farmers cannot depend on unregulated farm markets?
- Why do Radicals believe that most farmers have been losers under both regulated and unregulated agricultural production in the United States?

## THE CONSERVATIVE ARGUMENT

Discussions of the American farm problem almost always begin with a mistaken identification of what the problem really is. Most agricultural observers, including many economists writing on farm issues, suggest that there is something inherently unstable about American agriculture. Somehow, agriculture is presented as proof that the market economy simply does not work, that the free market forces of supply and demand break down. Conservatives agree that there is indeed a farm problem; however, that problem begins and remains in Washington, D.C., not in the corn and wheat fields of the Midwest or the commodities markets in Chicago. In other words, the American farm problem is not the result of some basic failure of the market, but rather the failure of federal policy to allow the market forces to work.

### Policy Failure in Times of Surplus

Although many politicians and some economists may believe and act to the contrary, supply and demand remain the only effective determinants of prices and resource allocation. Of course, it is possible to contrive desired prices and output through a manipulated agricultural policy, but regardless of short-run success, such policies must produce serious misallocations and costs in the long run.

For a considerable period of time, at least since World War I, most economists have seen the American farm problem as a matter of rising productivity with comparatively stable or modestly increasing demand. The result in the marketplace was a general and persistent downward pressure on farm prices. The economic options under such conditions were either to let prices fall to whatever level they might reach or to maintain prices artificially. Due largely to political pressure from the farm lobby in the depressed 1930s, the government devised a potpourri of farm programs to keep prices up and supposedly guarantee a living income to the American farmer. Tariffs were slapped on foreign farm products. Certain basic farm products were guaranteed a government-paid parity price well above the going market price. Bureaucrats worked out production controls and acreage allotments, with the curious economic aim of paying producers not to produce.

These tinkerings with the market forces of demand and supply, however, did not produce order in agricultural markets. Each intervention, regardless of its noble intentions, increased agricultural dependence on government price-setting efforts and, at the same time, heightened market instability. For their own part, farmers paid less and less attention to production signals from the marketplace and relied increasingly on the government to bail them out whenever farm income showed signs of falling. With the government establishing minimum price levels (using either parity price or target price mechanisms) and standing ready either to buy surplus production (before the 1970s) or, more recently, to provide loans secured by surplus output, there has been little incentive to pay attention to market forces. Except for two brief interludes—during World War II, when America virtually fed the world, and after the early Russian grain deals in the 1970s—farm prices and the income of most farmers have been held up only by government manipulation of crop prices.

## The Price of Failure

### The Cost to Consumers

The benefits accruing to the farm lobby from government intervention have only recently become recognized as costs to the general public. Americans have paid for government subsidies, tariffs, and production controls in two ways. First, the price of food in general has been higher than it would otherwise have been in a free agricultural market. For most Americans over most of the past sixty-five years, this higher price presented few problems. With the steady rise in American standards of living, the artificially higher food prices seemed quite tolerable, and as food expenditures declined as a share of total consumer purchases during the post–World War II years, the farm lobby met little resistance in its efforts to expand market intervention. Not until the inflationary 1970s did Americans show signs of balking at rising farm prices, and even then most of their anger was aimed at grocery chains and other middlemen.

Second, Americans, in a sense, must pay for their food *twice*. Consumers are also taxpayers, and as such they are obliged to shoulder the cost of expensive government subsidies—direct payments and low-cost loans—to farmers. Moreover, they have had to pay for the maintenance of an elaborate bureaucracy developed to administer the various farm programs. As with the higher farm product prices, this hidden second price was for a very long time ignored by most taxpayers, a cost buried in the federal budget. However, with pressure growing recently to reduce government spending and to reverse the growth of government debt, this previously concealed second charge for food became more obvious. By 2000, federal price support and other income programs for farmers were costing the average American family more than $365 per year—for an agricul-

tural program aimed in the first place at keeping tabletop food prices artificially high. The 2002 Farm Act is estimated to cost Americans $190
billion in taxes over ten years. Additionally, the provisions of the law are
expected to inflate food prices paid by consumers by $271 billion.*

*Inability to Sell Overseas*

Historically, American farm prices have closed off U.S. food products
from world markets. Due to climate, soil, technology, and agricultural
science, American agriculture has had an enormous advantage over the
rest of the world in food production. Programs aimed at keeping domestic prices relatively high frittered away this advantage, and the export
income it would have created. Precisely at a time when the United States
faced a worsening balance of international payments (after World War
II), the government pursued an agricultural program that denied the nation earnings it could have been making by exporting food.

The Russian grain deals of the mid-1970s brought a dramatic but brief
reversal in agricultural export habits. In 1972, the Russians negotiated the
purchase of 19 million metric tons of grain. For a number of years, Soviet
leadership had been yielding to consumer pressure to produce more meat
protein. Of necessity, this meant providing greater amounts of grain for
beef in feeding lots. When the 1971 and 1972 crops failed to reach expectations, the Soviet leaders decided not to slaughter their beef herds or tell
their people to eat potatoes and beets. They chose instead to buy U.S.
grain and to allow their "protein program" to continue.

To growers and sellers, the discovery of the Russian market was a
critical new direction for American agriculture, putting an end to the
long era of chronic excess production, depressed prices, and dependence on government subsidy programs. By selling the equivalent of
one-quarter of the 1972 crop, the Russian grain deal literally emptied American storage bins and grain elevators. This additional demand drove the prices of wheat from $1.70 per bushel in mid-1972
to $5.00 in 1973.

The trouble was, however, that commitment to free agricultural markets was unfamiliar, and when net farm income began to tumble in 1977

---

*Riedl, Brian M., *The Cost of America's Farm Subsidy Binge: An Average of $1
Million Per Farm*, Backgrounder #1510, December 10, 2001 (www.heritage.org/
Research/Agriculture/BG1510.cfm).

as the combined result of increases in production (a natural reaction to the increase in worldwide sales), a deepening worldwide recession, and worsening domestic inflation, farmers returned to their old habits. When the Food and Agricultural Act of 1977 was renewed, the farm lobby succeeded in setting target prices (the prices government would guarantee farmers through subsidies regardless of the going market prices) at about 25 percent higher than the existing world prices for most key crops. The free market experiment was over.

Insofar as government agricultural policy continues to aid farmers by artificially raising farm prices, farmers will be unable to exploit their efficiency and natural advantages in world food markets. Indeed, American farm prices are high enough to invite threats of excessive agricultural imports.

*Maintaining Production Inefficiencies*

Before taking up the question of production inefficiencies resulting from interventionist farm policies, we need first to square with reality the myth of the lonely and hardworking individual agriculturist. The myth of the independent family farm is deeply ingrained in American popular belief and Liberal political posturing, and is the foundation of American farm policy. The irony is, however, that the small family farm has ceased to be an important supplier of foodstuffs. Figure 1.2 tells the story very quickly.

The farm population has fallen to less than 2 percent of the total population (compare this to its 1950 level of 15 percent), while the number of farms has declined by more than half and average farm size has more than doubled over the same period. Figure 1.3 makes the point quite clearly: At present, 87 percent of the value of farm production is produced by just 18 percent of all operating farms. Moreover, about 1 percent of all operating farms produce 42 percent of our food production.

The myth of the disadvantaged, independent farmer is the basis for government subsidies—an effort to provide an income floor for the very poorest of farmers. The effect is to subsidize the least efficient farm producers at the very bottom of the agricultural ladder (two-thirds of government payments go to small farms that produce only one quarter of the nation's output) and very large farms that do not need it. This expensive agricultural welfare system has discouraged the exit of marginal agricultural producers who might better shift their resources to other productive pursuits. Worse still, subsidies paid to large and effi-

44

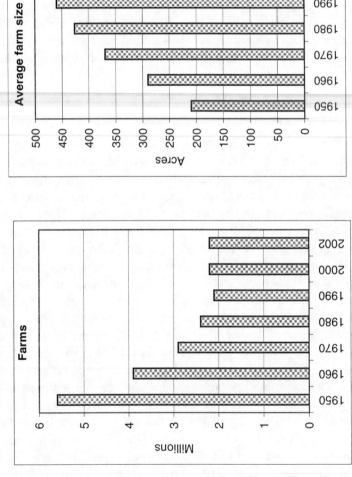

Figure 1.2  Changes in Farming, 1950–2002

*Source*: U.S. Bureau of the Census, *Statistical Abstract of the United States* (Washington, DC: Government Printing Office, 2003) and data from the U.S. Bureau of the Census.

Figure 1.3    **Shares of Total Farm Sales by Farm Size, 2002**

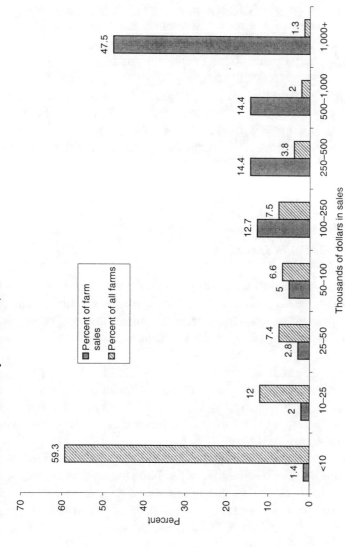

*Source:* U.S. Department of Agriculture, *2002 Census of Agriculture*, vol. 1.

cient farm producers act as restraints on improving their existing efficiency and productivity. Another argument against such subsidies is that
farmers are not clearly the beneficiaries of agricultural supports. Rather,
it is *owners* of farmland who experience the capitalization of price supports into the value of the finite amount of land available for farming.
Meanwhile, governmental sponsorship of generous crop insurance provides farmers the preposterous incentive of allowing crops to fail on
alternating years without serious financial penalty.

So long as we approach the farmer as if we are protecting a rare bird
from extinction, we will not benefit from the practical forces of the
marketplace. We will sustain at great economic cost farmers who should
stop farming and, at the same time, hold back the application of business management methods and technological advances among the farm
enterprises most capable of exploiting new techniques. We must recognize that farming is a business and, mythology notwithstanding, should
be open to the forces of a production-for-profit economy, just like the
manufacture of automobiles or personal computers.*

### Toward a New Policy Direction

A Conservative program for dealing with the nation's chronic agricultural problem is easily stated: *Let markets work.* This means ending all
subsidies, special loan arrangements, crop control programs, target pricing, and other arrangements aimed at setting selling prices above free
market prices.

The Federal Agriculture Improvement and Reform Act of 1996 was
on its way to restoring sanity to American agriculture. The phasing out
of government pricing efforts by the year 2002 was intended to reduce
agricultural prices and bring to an end the old and costly protectionist
approach to American farming.

Falling agricultural prices (or at least a halt to their artificial rise)
would have a number of salutary effects. First, it would be a direct benefit to American consumers. Second, it would expand American markets overseas. Lost revenues from lowered prices would be more than
offset by expanded total sales. Third, the resulting emphasis on efficient

---

*Indeed, we should recognize the growing importance of business corporations in
American agriculture. By the 1990s, 50,000 corporate farms, amounting to about
1 percent of all farms, produced more than one-fifth of farm output in the United States.

and innovative use of productive resources in agriculture would create a strong, self-sufficient, and highly productive agricultural sector where the market actually directs resource inputs.

To be sure, reliance on the market would not be without some adjustment problems. Critics would be quick to point out the effect of short-term cycles in agriculture on production and prices: This year's high prices cause next year's production to rise, increasing next year's supply faster than demand increases. The resultant lower prices lead to a reduction of supply in the next year and to a rise in prices, which in turn stimulate an increase in supply. According to many critics, this price instability perpetuates adverse effects alternately visited on consumers and then on farmers. The trouble with the argument is that no one has ever shown market-priced agricultural products to exhibit greater instability than most other goods priced according to market forces of supply and demand. In fact, demand for agricultural goods is much more stable over time than demand for steel, automobiles, or even personal computers. Moreover, a good deal of the volatility on the supply side is actually the result of government tinkering. There is a high probability that farm prices would fluctuate under a free market mechanism, but it is wrong to conclude that such fluctuations are undesirable. They are simply the market at work.

Regrettably, the Farm Security and Rural Investment Act of 2002 re-establishes the long tradition of agriculture's dependency upon government price rigging. The policy established by the 1996 Farm Act of phasing out subsidies and loans is reversed in favor of the continuation of fixed payments without regard to the crops planted or their prices. "Countercyclical payments" for specific crops to compensate for price declines are introduced. A system of "nonrecourse loans" obligates the Commodity Credit Corporation to accept agricultural commodities as payment for loans, effectively providing grants to farmers if commodity prices fall.

Because price fluctuations posed problems for farmers long accustomed to prices rigged by the government, American agriculture lobbied for a return to the security of government intervention. The less efficient will nonetheless find survival difficult, but the resumption of support programs prolongs the agony at considerable cost to consumers and taxpayers. On the other hand, efficient family farms and farm corporations are back to being deterred from applying the best production methods and determining output decisions on rational calculations of past *and* present market trends. Badly designed policy once again as-

Table 1.1

**U.S. Agricultural Productivity, 1800–1950**

| Crop | 1800 | 1880 | 1920 | 1950 |
|---|---|---|---|---|
| Wheat | | | | |
|    yield/acre (bu) | 15 | 13 | 14 | 17 |
|    labor hours/100 bu | 373 | 152 | 87 | 28 |
| Corn | | | | |
|    yield/acre (bu) | 25 | 26 | 28 | 39 |
|    labor hours/100 bu | 344 | 180 | 113 | 39 |
| Cotton | | | | |
|    yield/acre (bu) | 147 | 179 | 160 | 283 |
|    labor hours/bale | 601 | 318 | 269 | 126 |

*Source*: U.S. Bureau of the Census, *Historical Statistics of the United States*, Series K 83–97 (Washington, DC: Government Printing Office, 1960).

sures that income will be redistributed in their favor despite the average income and net worth of farm households being much greater than that of nonfarm households. Nostalgia for preserving the family farm may have its virtues, but it cannot be trusted for efficient allocation of resources and optimal pricing of outputs.

## THE LIBERAL ARGUMENT

Conservatives are quite right in stating that the American farm problem has been largely one of gains in production consistently outstripping increases in demand. Throughout most of this century, food demand was essentially a function of domestic population increase. Until recently the United States has exported large quantities of food abroad only in time of war. Meanwhile, steady advances in agricultural technology and science have produced greater output and reduced human labor needs. Table 1.1 puts these gains in perspective.

Gains in farm productivity continued to be impressive throughout the last half of the twentieth century. Output per unit of farm labor increased more than eightfold.

### Rising Production and Growing Crisis

Each unit of land has been producing greater yields as a result of new fertilizers and hybrid strains. At the same time, the application of greater capital has reduced substantially the number of worker-hours needed in production. By the 1930s, American farmers were the most productive in the world—and were going broke the fastest. It is easy enough for the Conservative devotee of the laws of supply and demand to say, "Leave things alone and let the devil take the hindmost." The fact is, excess agricultural production and falling prices affected people—a great number of people.

In 1930, about 44 percent of the U.S. population was classified as rural. About 57 million people still lived on farms or in small towns dependent on agriculture. At least 31 million were full-time farmers. To adopt the Conservative proposal of letting these human resources drop out of farming if it did not pay and find alternative employment would have been inhumane and stupid. In the Great Depression decade, there was no alternative employment. The exodus from farming (which did reduce the farm population to less than 10 million by 1972) would have been faster and would have created even greater employment problems for the general economy.

With this in mind, the New Deal policies of reducing farm migration through price supports, direct payments, and other subsidies (easy credit, electrification, and so on) were created. To be sure, these programs *did* artificially hold up farm prices and, in terms of subsidy costs, *did* pass on the cost of the farm program to taxpayers at large. But they also brought a degree of order to the agricultural sector and improved the income distribution inequities between farmers and nonfarmers. For example, 1934 farm income was only about one-third that of nonfarm income ($163 per year per person compared to $469 per year per person, respectively). By 1964, after nearly thirty years of New Deal–type tinkering, annual farm income per person stood at $1,405 and nonfarm income at $2,318. By 2002, average household income for farm operators stood at $65,757 while the U.S. average household income was $57,852.

Moreover, the supposed costs of federal farm subsidy programs have been vastly overstated. For instance, subsidies and support payments paid to farmers annually amount to less than 9 percent of all federally paid subsidies to the private sector.

It must be conceded that past American agricultural policy has had its failures. For instance, the improved income level of the farm sector, a noteworthy achievement, masks some other problems. The farm programs of the 1930s, 1940s, and 1950s could not halt the eventual decline of the family farm or the regional small farm in the Northeast. With greater application of technology and changes in farm production, farm employment (mostly family workers) fell from 7 million in 1960 to barely 2.9 million in 2001. Although average farm income has improved relative to nonfarm income of the 1960s and 1970s, maldistribution of earnings within the farm sector increased. Large farms (those with annual sales of $100,000 or more) increased their share of agricultural markets from 17 percent in 1960 to almost 89 percent in 2002.

We easily can conclude, then, that the few big farms have been getting bigger, but that most remaining farmers still earn very modest incomes. In such a situation, it is quite likely that past farm subsidy programs and payments to forgo production have provided the greatest gains for the large farm producer. However, even with these shortcomings, the earlier farm policies are defensible. They did raise and maintain average farm earnings above what a purely laissez-faire solution would have produced, thus strengthening agriculture in general. They mitigated the impact of the Depression on many farmers, and when farm out-migration did occur after World War II, the displaced farmers were more easily absorbed into a growing economy. The Conservatives' laissez-faire policy would have emptied rural America sooner, encouraged the growth of only the largest farms, and led to unacceptable human costs.

While past Liberal farm policies are historically defensible, it is apparent that America has moved into a new agricultural era demanding policy changes. The capital-intensive nature of agriculture is everywhere apparent, and the day of the *small* family farm is past, but the country is still heavily reliant on the family farm. At the same time, the long-run future growth in world food demand is undeniable. The free market advocates, however, misunderstand these trends.

### Failure of Market-Based Programs

Between 1972 and 1975, agricultural prices generally rose, and price supports and any effort to restrict output were unnecessary and ill advised. However, as the Agriculture and Consumer Protection Act of 1973 anticipated, high prices paid to farmers in the 1970s would not hold permanently. The 1973 act introduced the concept of *target pricing*. Under this arrangement, the government announces a target price on a specified list of commodities. If the market price is below the target price, the government pays farmers the difference between what they would receive for selling their goods in the market and the targeted figure. According to such a plan, consumers would still enjoy the benefits of the lower market price, but farmers would be guaranteed a reasonable return on their crops. To prevent the very large producers from tapping the public treasury for outrageous subsidy payments, the 1973 law specified that no farmer should receive more than $20,000 in payment for any crop.

Although subsequent agricultural acts have raised this per-farmer ceiling, the ceiling never was a very significant restriction because the larger farmers learned early on to divide their holdings among their relatives, with each smaller farm qualifying for the maximum payment. Very small farmers were virtually unaffected by the restriction on payments and continued to fail in large numbers. However, the target pricing and payment program did provide an important cushion for the middle-sized farms that are still the backbone of American agriculture.

If such payment programs, along with various loan programs, had not been in place in the middle and late 1980s, the disaster that struck American farming regions would have been much greater. More free market would have meant more farm agony. The experiment in the early 1970s with reliance on supply and demand had introduced "fencepost-to-fencepost" planting and encouraged farmers to expand debt and mortgage obligations to heighten production. Meanwhile, the collapse of demand for American farm products could be only partly blamed on high agricultural prices and the strong U.S. dollar. Quite simply, even in a hungry world, effective demand for food did not keep pace with the growth in world food supply. It should be remembered that the high interest rates and rising costs confronting farmers in the early 1980s were neither the farmers' fault nor the fault of farm policy. They were the outcome of a number of *supply shocks* (e.g., rising oil prices) that generated inflationary pressures. It was the Federal Reserve's decision to fight this inflation with a *tight money* policy that drove up interest rates and forced massive bankruptcies in American agriculture. Without standby government payments and credit and loan programs, many more than the estimated one-third of American farmers would have been facing bankruptcy in the late 1980s.

## What the Market Cannot Do

Curiously, the cyclical swing of agricultural fortunes through the 1970s and 1980s was forgotten by policy makers by the 1990s. With the passage of the 1996 Farm Act, the nation adopted a farm policy that would have eliminated price supports, target pricing, and virtually all other safety nets that had evolved to protect agriculture from the violent short-run fluctuations that forever attend agricultural markets. The promise of the 1996 act after half a dozen years proved to exceed its reality. Precisely as the 2002 date for ending government support programs was to kick in, agricultural profitability stood at its lowest level in two decades. Thus, it is not surprising that agricultural policy would simultaneously switch course.

The Conservative focus on long-run trends in agricultural markets is misleading, and their argument for free agricultural markets is too simplistic. A long-run trend is nothing more than the average of a cycle of short-run highs and lows. If short-run fluctuations are extreme, especially the lows, the agricultural sector will be torn apart. Resources forced out of agriculture in bad periods will not return quickly when prices later rise. A farm is not an enterprise that can be worked for a few years and then briefly retired until a boom naturally reappears. The land blows away if it is not cultivated, and the equipment rusts and becomes obsolete. Neither the farmer nor the consumer, who would face violently fluctuating prices, should be subjected to the severity of short-run market readjustments. The laws of supply and demand, in fact, can be regulated to improve market outcomes.

Price support programs provide stability at a minimum cost. This, however, is not all that is required. Congress and the president came to grips with the failure of the 1996 Farm Act by enacting the Farm Security and Rural Investment Act in 2002, introducing a more sophisticated agricultural policy. For example, the Conservation Reserve Program has the U.S. Department of Agriculture (USDA) negotiating long-term contracts to pay farmers to refrain from cultivating land to "improve the soil, water, and wildlife resources." Wetlands preservation and other environmental quality incentives have found their place in American agricultural policy because farmers are the country's natural experts on stewardship of the land. When supplied with the proper financial incentives through markets and with the assistance of government to compensate for the uncertainties owing to markets and weather, the nation's farmers earn a fair return for their efforts while securing a stable supply of food for domestic consumption as well as for export.

## THE RADICAL ARGUMENT

When conventional economics textbooks reach for an example in discussions of how supply and demand sets prices or how competition works, agricultural markets are usually cited. In the idealized models, at least, there are many small producers and consumers of homogeneous products who haggle and bargain until a fair and equitable price is established. For anyone vaguely familiar with the real-world conditions of American agriculture, the irony is heavy—nothing could be further from the truth. Perhaps because we start with such subtle deceptions when we talk about agricultural markets, we continue to deceive ourselves when we look for solutions to real farm problems. American agricultural affairs are dominated by a comparatively small number of giant producers, not by many small equal-sized farms, and prices are more the result of market power or government intervention than of the free market at work. For example, in 2000, Cargill, Archer Daniels Midland, and Zen-Noh accounted for more than 80 percent of corn exports. A similar pattern of four-firm dominance is found in beef packing, soybean crushing and exporting, flour milling, and terminal grain handling. Agriculture, as much as any sector of the economy, reveals the conflict between the professed ideal of a modified, production-for-profit system and the reality that a few benefit at the losses of many. The losers, of course, are small farmers and consumers in general.

### The Old Policy: Help the Big Guys

While most farm programs from the 1920s forward were supposedly aimed at protecting the family farm and supporting the agricultural sector in general, they failed utterly to halt the concentration of agriculture into fewer and fewer hands. Programs of price supports and payments for not producing stimulated this concentration, since small farmers could not possibly reap many gains from them. Between 1930 and 1990, land under cultivation actually increased, but the number of farms declined from 6.5 million to 2 million. At the same time, acreage per farm rose. Although Liberals reluctantly note this tendency, they do not understand that it has meant higher prices to consumers, with few, if any, benefits to most individually owned farms.

The market power of individual farmers, never very strong anyway, was eroded further during the 1950s and 1960s as marketing procedures were increasingly affected by the entrance of large business corporations into agriculture—*agribusiness*. Food chains bought orchards and feedlots and integrated their operations all the way from planting and slaughtering to the store checkout counter. Cereal producers, dairy products firms, baking companies, and other farm purchasers became more concentrated. At the same time, suppliers of farm machinery became increasingly integrated and powerful such that the price of farm equipment rose relative to crop income. As a result, the real cost of farming inputs increased while farmers had to sell their produce to comparatively few buyers. Thus, it is not surprising that the share of food purchases going to farmers declined from about 40 percent in 1900 to 10 percent by the end of the twentieth century. On the other hand agribusiness was quick to exploit the most profitable linkages upstream and downstream of farming, namely input supplies, transportation, processing, and marketing.

Meanwhile, agriculture also was being "discovered" by the large industrial conglomerates. Agribusiness grew and matured as ITT absorbed Wonder Bread and Smithfield Hams, Ling-Temco-Vought took control of Wilson Meats, Greyhound joined with Armour Packing, and other similar mergers took place. Basically, this phenomenon extended and accentuated the "price taker" situation of American farmers, even large farmers. Whether selling to the government, grocery chains, or General Foods, farmers had long been accustomed to dealing with buyers who set their own prices. The consumer, however, would feel the real power of this new and rejuvenated agribusiness, as well. The new conglomerate middlemen in food production and distribution had the potential capacity to extract enormous profits. The structure for increasing food prices and middlemen's profits had been established. The Russian grain deal represents a historical example of the corruption of agricultural policy. In 1972, the United States and the Soviet Union secretly negotiated the sale of 19 million metric tons of American grain. Ironically, this sale was completed precisely as the United States was mining Haiphong Harbor in North Vietnam and bombing rail lines north of Hanoi in an effort to stop the flow of Russian goods into the war zone. Although critics were to attack the sale as the "Great Grain Robbery," Secretary of Agriculture Earl Butz defended it as a boon to the American farmer. When accused of being willing to trade with the devil if it meant a profit, Butz replied, "If he has dollars."

### The New Policy: A Failed Attempt to Keep Prices Up

The Russian grain deal of the 1970s, though it may seem to be ancient history, remains an important instructional example of how capitalism really works. Conventional economists love to talk about "the market" as if it were a perfectly neutral abstraction. The Russian grain deal puts the lie to that argument. The sale of American grain to the USSR actually reflected a highly calculated effort to create super profits out of the anguish of farmers and the general public. Since the government itself lacked the legal authority to export goods, the grain sales had to be consummated by some half-dozen leading American grain trading firms. The steps in the selling process were something like this: First, the harvest came in and could not be altered by farmer action. Second, the USDA's Commodity Credit Corporation (CCC) granted the Russians exceptionally favorable credit arrangements. Third, the grain traders purchased the wheat owned and stored by the government in CCC bins and sold it to the Russians at a price significantly below the prevailing domestic price. Fourth, the grain traders, over and above their sales fees, received millions in subsidies from the government (the difference between the domestic price and the sale price).

The effects of the grain sales were injurious to practically all Americans except the grain companies and a few insiders who were able to make extraordinary profits by speculating on grain futures. Farmers were unable to take advantage of the resulting rise in wheat prices, since most had sold their grain to the government at the going market price. The American grain reserve was eliminated. Wheat prices and prices of substitute products went up, and so did the prices of beef and bread, both dependent on grain prices. Restive consumers were told it was just the law of supply and demand.

The Conservative prediction that growing world agricultural sales would eventually bring prosperity back to farming, although creating some hope in 1973 and 1974, had turned to ashes by 1978. Four years after agriculture secretary Butz promised a new era for farming by opening American agriculture to the world, farmers had become dependent on world demand to get rid of two-thirds of their wheat, one-quarter of their corn, and half of their soybeans. While American overseas grain sales remained fairly high, world grain prices (indeed, most world agricultural prices) tumbled.

And how did American consumers fare as agricultural prices fell? With large food corporations and agribusiness controlling the final goods prices for most U.S. food consumption, lowered per-unit farm prices meant higher profits, not lower prices at the grocery store. Food processors and distributors (who receive on the average 65 cents of every food dollar) saw their revenues and profits soar as farmers groaned and consumers cursed. Consumers blamed farmers. Farmers blamed unions for rising equipment costs and Arabs for higher energy and fertilizer bills. Almost no one placed the responsibility where it really belonged—with the grain trading companies and their agents at the USDA and with agribusiness monopolies, which were well represented in Washington.

### What Strategy to Deal with the Problem?

From the Radical perspective, the farm problem has a number of different and troublesome dimensions. First, the chronic tendency toward overproduction and falling prices followed by underproduction and rising prices simply reflects the instability and irrationality of free markets. The vicious cycle that sometimes brings prosperity and sometimes brings crisis can be mitigated only by an effort to plan output and control prices. The trouble is that past control efforts have been biased toward helping the large farmer and agribusiness at the expense of the small farmer and the consumer. The share of government support payments going to giant enterprises has been growing. Farms with sales over $40,000 per year received 54 percent of all government payments in 1975. By 1995, they received 90 percent. Moreover, while most farmers do not receive any subsidies, the biggest farms have been garnering an ever-growing share of total subsidy payments. For example, of the $114 billion in agricultural subsidies disbursed by the USDA between 1995 and 2002, the top one-tenth—about 289,000 recipients—received 71 percent or almost $81 billion in subsidies.

Such a payment schedule encourages increased production among the large farms while at the same time pushing the small producer to the wall. By and large, it has been the small and middle-sized farmers who are going broke, not the large farmers or farm corporations. In terms of our agricultural policy, that was precisely what was supposed to happen. Shifting the direction of payments toward smaller farmers would equalize income but also encourage inefficient farm producers to continue operations. The Gordian knot can be untied only if we develop an output and pricing program that humanely moves inefficient agricultural producers out of production while curbing the ability of the giant farm enterprises to set output and prices for their own—but not the consumer's—advantage.

The USDA continues to release stylized statistics that emphasize the prevalence of small, family-operated farms while sidestepping any reference to their true economic circumstances or calling attention to the misdistribution of agricultural support in the direction of large operators. The plain fact is that a few vertically integrated transnational corporations such as Archer Daniels Midland, ConAgra, and Cargill have come to dominate *all* aspects of food production not only in the United States but worldwide as well. Moreover, joint ventures with biotechnology firms such as Monsanto and Novartis have resulted in "food chain clusters" that have furthered their hegemony in the agriculture marketplace. For example, the Cargill/Monsanto cluster has produced a "terminator gene" that causes their seeds to become sterile after a single growing season. Such technological advances will only ensure more sales for Cargill, which were about $55 billion in 2002 and "supported" with about $10 million in USDA subsidies. Even several *Fortune* 500 corporations—not well known for their agricultural products—including Chevron, Dupont, Caterpillar, and the John Hancock Mutual Life Insurance Company also received above-average crop subsidy payments from the USDA in 2002. Silly data from the Census of Agriculture about demographic diversity among farmers are prominently publicized presumably for appeal as a human interest story rather than any serious attempt at rationalizing that the market system or agricultural policy are in some mysterious and positive way influencing the numbers of female or minority farm operators.

Most Americans take eating for granted. Prices may affect our diets from time to time, but most of us have little concern about the general availability of food. This is true even though probably not one in fifty of us have the slightest knowledge of how to grow the food we eat. And so it is, of course, that we are not inclined to think very deeply about our national agricultural policies. From a Radical perspective, this is a matter of considerable shortsightedness. The emerging concentrated and centralized food production system can only result in higher food prices for consumers, lower prices paid to small farmers, and further subsidies by taxpayers to obscenely profitable agribusinesses.

In summary, the Radical agenda for agricultural reform calls for a major shift away from the support of big agribusiness, genetically engineered foods, patented life forms, and heavy pesticide and chemical use. Agricultural policy must be refocused on encouraging agricultural cooperatives through price supports, subsidies, and loans that adequately compensate farmers for production costs. Basic foodstuffs and fiber production should be emphasized along with crops and animal husbandry that yield alternative fuels.

# Consumer Welfare

## Is It Necessary to Protect the Consumer?

Consumption is the sole end and the purpose of all production; and the interest of the producer ought to be attended to, only in so far as it may be necessary for promoting that of the consumer.

*—Adam Smith, 1776*

The upshot of consumer protection, when it succeeds, is simply to hold industry to higher standards of excellence, and I can't see why they should object to that kind of incentive.

*—Ralph Nader, 1967*

Let me emphasize: competition does not protect the consumer because businessmen are more softhearted than bureaucrats or because they are more altruistic or because they are more generous, but only because it is in the self-interest of the entrepreneur to protect the consumer.

*—Milton Friedman, 1978*

Make no mistake: no one wants to roll the clock back on environmental, health, or safety regulations.

*—John F. Smith Jr., Chairman, CEO, and President*
*General Motors Corporation, 1998*

## The Problem

Our survey of American agricultural policies illustrated the outcome of efforts to correct the market on behalf of certain producers of goods. We now turn to an example of market intervention on behalf of consumers. Just as we found that there is no free lunch when government acts to protect and promote certain sellers of goods, we now find that protecting buyers also exacts costs. While the existence of costs associated with such intervention is not a matter of much disagreement among economists and economic observers, there remains much disagreement on whether the costs are justified by the direct benefits obtained.

For ordinary citizens, consumer protection today is far less turbulent a debate than twenty to thirty years ago. The comparative calm is explained by the greater acknowledgement and acceptance of government's involvement in the more prominent concerns posed by consumer protection efforts. Consumers have come to expect protection from exposure to injury or death when purchasing and using products and services. Government has increasingly assumed the role of compensating for incomplete knowledge on the part of consumers, policing health and safety matters, and generally assuring that markets are a fair game for consumers. However, the appropriateness and extent of government intervention on behalf of the consumer remains a source of considerable controversy.

The time-honored doctrine of *consumer sovereignty* maintains that the final authority in determining production and prices is the consumer. The consumer, according to this doctrine, always is aware of *caveat emptor* (buyer beware) constraint as he or she makes consumption decisions. Consumers vote with their dollars in the marketplace. Their decisions are expressed by their final selection and willingness to pay for goods. In theory, at least, consumer sovereignty further presumes that buyers' tastes are given and unchanging, that buyers are expert and fully informed about products they are purchasing and the range of alternative products they might buy, and that prices are efficiently set in fully competitive markets. In the real world, however, many economists view such expectations about buyers' knowledge to be unrealistic. Consider that a consumer's attempt to acquire the necessary knowledge to act expertly involves sampling foods and drugs that in fact could prove fatal. Thus, as early as 1906, the federal government passed the Pure Food and Drugs Act to protect consumers from adulterated food and unsafe drugs.

The publication of Ralph Nader's *Unsafe at Any Speed* in 1965, an effective muckraking attack on a popular General Motors car, the Corvair, marked the beginning of a full-blown consumer protection movement. Nader argued persuasively that the sporty rear-engine auto had a number of defects, among them a dangerous habit of flipping over when turning corners, even at low speeds. He also claimed that General Motors engineers and managers knew about the car's engineering deficiencies but had kept quiet about them. Corvair sales dropped after Nader's attack, although General Motors disputed his influence. The company made its last Corvair in 1969.

Spurred by Nader and his activists and by the sobering fact that auto fatalities had grown by about 40 percent since 1960, Congress enacted the National Traffic and Motor Vehicle Safety Act in 1966. This legislation required that the auto industry begin to install certain specific safety features in all new cars. The first requirements (which went into effect in 1968) specified seatbelts for all occupants, energy-absorbing steering columns, increased windshield resistance, dual braking systems, and padded instrument panels. Over the years, additional safety requirements have been mandated by the National Highway Traffic Safety Administration.

Fast forwarding to the present, the public attitude toward consumer protection and safety has undergone a major transformation: safety sells products. Airbags, antilock brakes, and comparative crash testing data are high in the minds of consumers when purchasing automobiles. The National Highway Traffic Safety Administration has the expanded role of testing the effectiveness of safety devices such as airbags and children's car seats.

The consumer protection movement expanded beyond automobile safety with the passage of the Consumer Protection Act of 1972 and its creation of the Consumer Product Safety Commission. The commission claims authority to regulate the safety of some 15,000 products, including household appliances, toys, household products, and recreational products. By 1980, more than four hundred separate units in forty different government agencies were operating to advance consumer interests or protect consumer rights.

Most Americans believe that an active consumer-protection effort by their government is proper public policy. Certainly the general popularity of the government's recent assault on the tobacco industry and the drift toward criminalizing smoking supports such a conclusion. Regardless of the economic consequences or the various contradictions involved, most citizens expect their government, at least to some degree, to "protect" them from the consequences of consumer sovereignty. However, consumer protection is not a free item. As producers are aware (and consumers *should be*), consumer protection increases production costs. And sometimes protection can cause *real* pain as millions of users of the painkiller Vioxx discovered in late 2004 when—under pressure from the Food and Drug Administration—the manufacturer removed it from the market.

## Synopsis

Conservatives argue that consumers are best able to determine for themselves what they should buy and that efforts to improve on consumer rationality diminish satisfaction, raise prices, and lower economic efficiency. Liberals maintain that consumers do not have enough strength to protect themselves from the manipulative power of giant enterprises. Radicals go beyond mere consumer protection, raising questions about uncritical consumption as an end in itself.

---

### Anticipating the Arguments

- How do the Conservative, Liberal, and Radical views differ regarding the consumer's rationality and ability to choose freely and intelligently?
- In what ways do the Liberal and Conservative views of calculating the cost of goods differ?
- Why are Radicals suspicious of all efforts to protect consumers in a production-for-profit economic system?

## THE CONSERVATIVE ARGUMENT

Early seeds of the consumer movement were planted at the start of the twentieth century, when a variety of state and federal laws aimed at maintaining the purity of food and drug products were passed. A second thrust developed in the 1930s with the passage of disclosure legislation that was intended to protect consumers from mislabeled or fraudulently labeled merchandise and false advertising. In the late 1960s and throughout the 1970s, consumer protectionism developed along a third line: specifying product standards for the alleged purpose of making all consumer products safer. Taken together, these three efforts, as they have developed over the past eighty years, constitute the contemporary American consumer protection movement.

Obviously, the consumer protection movement is neither a passing nor an inconsequential attempt by social engineers to correct and improve on the workings of the market. In fact, few efforts at market intervention have been so assiduously nourished as the belief that government is better able to protect and advance the interests of the consumer than anyone else—naturally enough, better than business, but even better than consumers themselves. Indeed, this idea sounds so sensible to many citizens that the irony of the last sentence will be lost entirely on many readers. Consumers have been abused to a much greater extent in the name of consumer protection than is generally appreciated.

### Free Markets and the Freedom to Choose

To understand the Conservative position in the consumer protection debate, recall that all Conservative arguments start from the presumption that each individual's economic and political freedoms must be preserved—that free men and women making their own rational choices in the production and consumption of goods in free markets is the ideal social condition. While the exercise of individual freedom of choice may not always produce perfect economic and social consequences, free market conditions are ultimately preferable to those that arise in regulated or protected markets. Consequently, the underlying logic of Liberal consumer protectionists must be rejected out of hand since it rests on the view that individuals are not capable of making free choices affecting their own lives, or that if they do make such choices, there will be disastrous results. Such a dim view of people's abilities to reason and to choose, of course, inevitably leads to the conclusion that more thoughtful individuals must act to protect the ignorant majority. It is on such a rock of authoritarianism that Liberals build their arguments on behalf of social tinkering of all types, whether in the area of consumer affairs or in other realms of economic behavior.

Having said this, however, we must qualify our position in the case of consumer protection. Conservatives believe that sellers of goods, free though they may be, do not have the right individually or collectively to undertake conscious actions intended to do harm to consumers. Indeed, fraudulent sellers of shoddy products may be held responsible for damages resulting from their products, and damaged individuals must be able to recover losses resulting from sellers' fraudulent activities. Conservatives also recognize that the complexities of products present the modern consumer with problems in rationally evaluating and choosing among goods offered for sale. Consumers will be well served if a hidden hazard is brought to their attention, either by the government or by private agencies, so they can make purchases based on rational risk calculation, such as in the case of potential side effects of certain medicines. As Milton Friedman has accurately observed: "Insofar as the government has information not generally available about the merits or demerits of the items we ingest or activities we engage in, let it give us the information. But let it leave us to choose what chances we want to take with our own lives." Such a two-pronged effort on behalf of consumer protection goes a long way toward redressing the possible market imperfections that adversely affect consumers without destroying the market in the process. The freedoms of individual consumers to choose from among a broad range of alternative goods will not be impaired, as they invariably are under a Liberal protectionist scenario. The Conservative solution also avoids the unnecessary restrictions that excessive consumer protectionism ultimately produces. After all, it takes little imagination to see that government efforts to insulate us from all risks associated with goods we might voluntarily choose to consume must require the elimination of a wide range of useful or pleasurable goods—from stepladders to bicycles—that even in their ordinary use might cause us harm.

### The High Cost of Safety

The Conservative approach is simple and rational, but it has not been the strategy adopted at a national level. Over the past eight decades or more, Americans have come to accept the philosophy and practices of an ever-growing body of consumer protection legislation, apparently on the premise that more protection will lead to fuller, more satisfying lives. The premise, however, fails on a number of grounds. The level of consumer protection we have been drifting toward imposes very heavy costs not fully appreciated by consumers. The costs of protection are levied in two ways. First, as taxpayers we must absorb the administrative overhead of operating numerous consumer protection agencies.

A second cost burden, and one of monumentally greater proportions, is the higher price of products, caused by the increased production costs that consumer protection efforts produce. For instance, the Consumer Product Safety Commission (CPSC), with jurisdiction over fifteen thousand products, requires manufacturers to keep detailed records on the performance of all products and even more substantial records of testing and evaluation on any product that may be deemed to "create a substantial risk of injury"—a category that has come to include everything from power mowers and stepladders to bathrobes and infant back carriers. The CPSC also has the power to recall products, demand their redesign, and, ultimately, to ban them altogether. The manufacturer absorbs all these costs. To these costs, arising in extreme but not uncommon cases, firms must add the ordinary costs of keeping abreast of the blizzard of CPSC paperwork and hiring professional safety experts, recall managers, public relations specialists, and the like. Of course these business costs are then passed along to consumers. Incidentally, these costs may be spread among a whole array of a firm's products; consequently, certain products not directly affected by consumer protection activities or made safer by protection may actually bear some of the protection costs associated with other goods.

How large the final bill is for consumers is uncertain, but one study of auto safety requirements legislated between 1968 and 1982 placed direct costs at about 10 percent of manufacturers' total costs (and this does not count another 13 percent of production costs required to cover mandated environmental protection measures).

### Is It Worth It? The Cost-Benefit Question

Liberals justify the high and escalating costs of consumer protection by appealing to cost-benefit analysis. This conventional method of economic analysis justifies protectionist endeavors as long as the net money amount of social gains or benefits exceeds all private and social costs resulting from such requirements. (Or, to put it in the stricter terms of economic jargon, up to the point where marginal social costs equal marginal social benefits.) Nowhere has this technique of calculating the gain from required safety been so extensively applied as in auto safety. Needless to say, the protectionist advocates have been able to prove to their own satisfaction that the money value of safety costs is but a small fraction of the money value of social gains obtained from safety requirements.

The key, however, to any cost-benefit analysis is the calculation of benefits and costs. Benefits roughly equal the private and social outlays that would have to be made if the degree of protection required *was not* required. Naturally, benefits look impressive when lost earnings, property damage, medical costs, and the like, attributable to a presumably preventable hazard, are estimated quite high and less impressive if lower estimates are applied. The problem is that benefit and cost estimations are not an exact science, and the estimates or the use of the estimates can be self-serving.

The controversy surrounding the use of cellular phones while driving provides a compelling example. The Harvard Center for Risk Analysis issued studies in 2000 and 2002 concerning the cost-effectiveness and benefits of banning cell phones while driving. The first study rejected cell phone restrictions as premature and inefficient compared to other safety measures such as mandatory seatbelt use and daytime running lights. The net cost to society of cell phone prohibition was estimated to be about $23 billion.* The subsequent study in 2002, presumably using better data and methods, concluded that banning cell phones while driving would cost society roughly $43 billion (the economic value of banned calls), which was approximately equal to the benefits of a ban (averted property damage, medical costs, pain, suffering, and death). **

The newer estimate increases the justification for states to criminalize talking on a cell phone while driving because the benefits realized at least match the costs imposed upon society. This is easily construed to mean that such extreme measures are worth it. Yet, the monetary estimates in these studies are divined from a wide range. That is, the benefits could be as low as $9 billion or as high as $193 billion. On the other hand, costs are between $17 billion and $151 billion. This imprecision did not deter Liberal interventionists from acting upon their routine assumption that the individual should be safeguarded from his or her own shortsightedness, lack of agility, potential lapses in judgment, inattentiveness, or sloppy driving skills to the greatest extent possible by government. New York enacted the first cell phone ban in 2001. New Jersey and Washington, D.C., followed in 2004. Several other states have partial bans, most banning school bus drivers and persons with learner permits (inexperienced drivers) from using a cell phone. No one knows if

---

* K.S. Lissy, J.T. Cohen, M.Y. Park, and J.D. Graham, "Cellular Phone Use While Driving: Risks and Benefits," in *Risk in Perspective*, vol. 8, no. 6 (Boston, MA: Harvard Center for Risk Analysis, 2000).

** Joshua T. Cohen, and John D. Graham, "A Revised Economic Analysis of Restrictions on the Use of Cell Phones While Driving," in *Risk Analysis*, vol. 23, no. 1 (Blackwell Publishing, 2003).

the highways are safer as a result, but we do know that another revenue stream from the citizen's pocket to the state coffers has been established through the traffic citations issued.

One should not lose sight of the fact that each mandated safety cost is an *opportunity cost*—dollars diverted from other potentially higher valued purposes. For instance, what if the billions of dollars spent by automakers to meet safety standards (and presumably passed on to auto buyers) were spent on driver education? Would the social benefits be greater or less? No one really knows—most certainly not the Liberals who use cost-benefit analysis to justify, rather than to objectively evaluate, consumer safety actions.

For Conservatives, quite apart from the challenge of calculating social costs and benefits, cost-benefit analysis fails for more fundamental reasons. It simply defies the logic of the free market, replacing it with political value judgments. Accordingly, cost-benefit method is an instrument of presuppositions and fraught with statistical uncertainties. The results, therefore, can be inefficient and unfair. Individuals, rather than purchasing units of *safety* according to their preferences and willingness to pay, are forced to pay for levels of safety they do not want or need. Rational suburbanites who keep their fingers out of their lawnmowers must pay for protection devices they do not need. Although mental midgets who might, out of perverse curiosity, put a finger into the mower blades are protected (thus providing some alleged social gain), the thoughtful operator who gains nothing must pay more. In effect, efforts to obtain an uncertain, elusive degree of greater social benefits require that private cost-benefit considerations—the very heart of free markets in operation—be disregarded.

The search for greater net social benefits may actually produce the opposite—people acting against their own interests. For instance, higher-priced but safer cars may force some consumers to drive older, unsafe ones. But, most important, such an approach toward consumers attacks the fundamental freedom of choice and therefore compromises the liberty —even the liberty to act foolishly—that Conservatives consider so essential to a free society and a free economy.

## THE LIBERAL ARGUMENT

The classical economic assumption—that buyers and sellers bargain equally in the marketplace and that buyers, acting with restraint and

wisdom, are sovereign—falls into the same intellectual category as belief that the world is flat. As in the case of the flat-worlders, a great
many compelling reasons can be mustered in an attempt to prove the
argument, but they fly in the face of virtually all available evidence.

## The Need for Intervention

From the Liberal viewpoint, protectionist interference in the private production of goods is justifiable and necessary for several reasons. First
and foremost, products have become more complex. They present potential risks and hazards that consumers are simply unprepared to evaluate and act on rationally. If a product simply fails to function as promised
in its advertising and labeling, the loss is limited to its purchase price
plus whatever incidental expenses were associated with acquiring it. But
sometimes the product is risky to use or outright dangerous. The consumer may not have sufficient expertise to judge the risk or may be
completely unaware of the hazards inherent in certain products. Without government intervention, how would we have learned of thalido-
mide causing birth defects or the cancer risks of red dye no. 2, cyclamates,
certain pesticides, and other commodities that have been removed from
the market or restricted in their use? Dangerous products pose the threat
of injury or death. Such losses are colossal compared to those associated with a defective ballpoint pen or a washing machine that does a
poor job of cleaning clothes.

Second is the matter of *external costs*—costs paid by society that
may not be accounted for in the selling price of a good. Conservatives
emphasize the private cost of goods: in the case of an automobile, how
much an individual must pay in the marketplace for a minimally
equipped transportation vehicle. Additional costs for safety features
are seen as purely private purchasing decisions: Buy safety if *you* want
it. This misses an important point in understanding real costs. Social
costs go beyond merely the production, assembly, and sales expenditures and the expected profits of the automaker. The private decision
to drive an unsafe but cheaper car or to be distracted by a phone conversation imposes upon society the additional costs of automobile accidents, injuries, and fatalities. In turn, this leads to higher insurance
rates, greater court costs, and heavier expenditures on roads, accident
prevention, and enforcement. Nor are injuries or deaths simply personal matters. These human losses mean the loss of present wage earn-

ings and the loss of productive workers (now and in the future). Thus, insufficient attention to safety results in an unnecessary burden to the whole society in the form of social costs.

The Conservatives' argument against safety standards on the grounds that they unfairly raise consumer costs is misguided. Higher-priced autos, and many other commodities, are necessary to cover all the costs certain goods generate. As we shall see, it is still a good bargain.

### Restraining Sellers

The extraordinary growth of giant enterprises over the past century, along with the development of huge advertising budgets and sophisticated selling techniques, has created immense power on the sellers' side of the market. Economic concentration has given producers great freedom in establishing and maintaining their own price and quality standards. Mass advertising, meanwhile, has moved well beyond an informational function to one of actually creating and manipulating consumer wants. In such a situation, it is essential that government intervene on behalf of consumers to protect them from false advertising and poorly made or dangerous merchandise.

The efforts in automobile safety since the 1966 National Traffic and Motor Vehicle Safety Act demonstrate how governmentally supported consumer protection actions can improve the quality of an important consumer good. With 95.7 million cars on the road in 1966, the country saw more than fifty thousand fatalities from auto accidents and an accident rate of five and one-half per 100 million miles traveled. By 2003, the National Highway Traffic Safety Administration estimated that fatal accidents had dropped to 43,200 and the accident rate had fallen to one and one-half. Impressive gains in auto safety prevailed despite the fact that there were now 230 million registered vehicles.

Government and its protection agencies led to the development of more crashworthy vehicles, mandatory safety belt use, airbags, bumper improvements, window defrosters, stronger glass, and the like. Careful monitoring of autos has led to massive recalls to remedy specific safety deficiencies. And, of course, the CPSC's and Food and Drug Administration's monitoring in other product areas has similarly contributed to the improvement of product quality and consumer safety throughout the economy.

## The Savings from Safety

Government safety requirements have no doubt added to the price of what we buy, although much less than Conservatives have argued. Safety belts, for instance, which (when used) have radically reduced serious injuries in collisions, add less than 1 percent to the price of a $20,000 automobile. The problem, of course, is to measure the increases in costs to consumers against the savings to society from reduced auto hazards. It is a distortion to stress only increased auto prices in a survey of auto safety costs and benefits.

Literally dozens of cost-benefit studies have been undertaken since the early 1970s in an effort to compare actual costs paid by the consuming public for auto safety devices and the actual benefits thereby obtained. No reasonably thoughtful study has ever demonstrated that the aggregate private safety costs exceed the aggregate social and private safety benefits obtained. Practically all studies indicate that a dollar in safety outlays produces at least two dollars in benefits, with most showing a vastly larger ratio of benefits to costs. The benefits are measured principally by calculating the reductions in lifetime or short-term earnings and associated medical costs that would have been lost in auto fatalities and injuries but were saved by the employment of auto safety devices. To these actual dollar losses, we could also add—if a figure were actually calculable—the value derived from the psychological satisfaction a driver or rider obtains from knowing (even if they are never involved in an accident) that theirs is a safer automobile.

To say, as Conservatives do, that such a cost-benefit argument is Liberal hooey is nonsense. Proof of that fact can be discovered by looking at one's own auto insurance policy. Quite simply, insurers would not provide the specific premium discounts they do for optional safety items if such items did not in fact reduce injury claims against the insurer.

Manufacturers may complain that enforced recalls of cars to remedy defects constitute an assault on their profits, and there is probably some truth to this. The answer, however, is better workmanship and engineering on the industry's part, not relaxed consumer protection. The cost for shoddy construction must be borne by industry, not by society at large.

If there is any serious defect in the government's efforts to protect consumers, it is that not enough has been done. The National Highway Traffic Safety Administration, for instance, operates on a yearly budget of about $430 million and employs a staff of about 660. The Consumer

Product Safety Commission is expected to regulate safety on everything from toasters to lawnmowers to roller coasters with 480 employees and a budget of just $60 million. That is a very small bureaucracy indeed to watch over safety standards in a broad swath of the nation's largest consumer-oriented industries.

The recent trend toward deregulation and reducing government interference in business decision making will cost the nation dearly if it continues. Conservatives are right in saying that withdrawing safety and consumer protection standards (and environmental and job safety standards as well) could lead to lower priced goods or, more realistically, greater industry profits. But these are cruel and false gains obtained only through creative accounting—by shifting the social or external cost of goods onto certain groups in the society. Greater efforts in consumer safety are essential. Consumer protection will not be attained until *caveat emptor* (let the buyer beware) is replaced by *caveat venditor* (let the seller beware) as the dominant motto of the marketplace.

## THE RADICAL ARGUMENT

The relevant issues in the controversy over improved consumer safety are rarely raised. Conservatives approach the question as a matter of maintaining free markets and free choice while Liberals argue for the improvement of market conditions and the protection of buyers; but these are really evasions of what the consumer safety question highlights. Why, in an advanced and supposedly civilized society such as ours, is consumer safety a problem at all? Is it that we lack the resources and technology to manufacture safe products? On the contrary, we all know that technology has nothing to do with the problem. Unsafe autos, like unsafe food and dangerous drugs, are just "there." They are part of our economic and social systems—to be tolerated or, when things get bad enough, to be reformed. They are the necessary but unwanted effects of an irrational social order.

### Why "Consumer Sovereignty" Does Not Exist

Capitalist economic systems are organized to make profits, not to make people happy or to make life safer. For a capitalist enterprise to make large profits, it has to sell in great quantity, and must obtain as great a surplus over costs as possible. Obviously that calculation nowhere contains any estimate of social costs and benefits. Insofar as the production-for-profit system is concerned, satisfaction is maximized simply if we have *more*. Irrespective of the time-honored tradition of consumer sovereignty, it is not really the consumer's power to choose among goods that is important. In fact, capitalism has succeeded in focusing people's attention on their relationships with goods rather than with other people. Owning and consuming the "right" goods is advertised to raise social status, win friends, improve sexual performance, and so forth.

The populace is turned into walking billboards of corporate logos and trademarks, with mass consumption as the arbiter of social relations and economic well-being. What is important is consumption, period. Citizens in a capitalist society are taught from birth to accept uncritically that the object of life is to obtain goods: the more goods, the better their lives.

Looked at this way, it is easy to see why modern capitalism periodically becomes absorbed in such developments as the consumer protection issue. The social costs of the mass consumption of dangerous products as well as private concerns about safety have finally developed to a point where reformist action must be taken. The auto safety movement, for instance, is merely another step in the long progression of product reform movements. It differs very little from the public outcry against adulterated food and unsafe or ineffective drugs that resulted in the passage of the Pure Food and Drugs Act in 1906 and the eventual establishment of the Food and Drug Administration. The FDA certainly improved food cleanliness; just as the modern consumer movement has made cars safer to drive (or at least we all believe so). However, the *success* of such reforms deflects us from questioning the reasonableness of an economic system that sells poisoned food or hazardous vehicles in the first place.

Conservatives and Liberals may bicker over whether consumer sovereignty is best expressed in free or regulated markets, but both are committed to encouraging high levels of essentially irrational consumption. No traditional economist has ever proposed that the users of goods define consumer sovereignty as the rational, coordinated control of production. That, of course, would lead to the abolition of the capitalist system. No matter how strongly Conservatives and Liberals seem to disagree on the extent of government interference with production, both hold firmly to the principle of maintaining high levels of output as well as the primary goal of production for profit.

## *The Self-Serving Use of the Safety Idea*

Americans have been misled about the high costs of safety. Conservatives emphasize that safety features increase product prices. Liberals admit that price increases are an outcome but that the costs are worth it given the social benefits obtained. The thrust of both arguments is that safety costs money—and corporations have not missed their cue. With a public prepared by the media and the economics profession to accept higher prices as the cost of greater protection, business has used the safety argument to push product prices ever higher. Back in 1977, as extensive safety requirements were being built into American autos, General Motors reported a record-breaking net income of $4 billion on sales of $55 billion. At the same time, this firm, supposedly racked by the costs of expensive safety features, managed to rank thirty-seventh among the top five hundred American corporations in income as a percentage of shareholders' equity. And paid earnings per share were two-thirds higher than stockholder earnings a decade earlier, in preconsumerist 1966. Ford and Chrysler also ranked in 1977 among the top two hundred firms in earnings ratio, with their earnings-per-share record better than a decade earlier (Ford's had increased almost 100 percent). Such evidence seems to suggest that, initially at least, the safety boom of the 1970s may have been a ploy for digging even deeper into consumers' pockets and, of course, hiding the action.

Only later, as the economy stagnated in the late 1970s and early 1980s, did corporate management begin to push energetically against many previously accepted safety mandates. Faced with declining domestic demand and rising imports of foreign-made products, it became expedient to use safety costs as a contributing factor in the profit squeeze felt by many American firms. In the auto industry especially, consumer, environmental, and job safety programs *and* workers' salaries were obvious targets. Automakers quickly mounted a highly successful public relations and political lobbying effort to "take back" on all these fronts. Once a boon to profit making, auto safety was now depicted as a threat to profits as well as to the continued strength of a basic American industry. In the new political and economic setting, many consumers even became convinced that we could no longer afford rigorous auto safety standards. Accordingly, during the 1980s and early 1990s, many previously approved safety and environmental requirements for automobiles were rolled back.

## *Putting the Debate in a Radical Perspective*

No doubt the Radical position seems hopelessly negativistic and irrelevant to the specific question of protecting the consumer; indeed it is if Radicals are expected by conventional economists to offer long-run remedies that do not consider the underlying philosophy and social organization of consumption activities in a capitalist society. Radicals understand that capitalism is propelled by the private search for profit and that profits increase, *ceteris paribus*, either by increasing sales or by keeping costs down. Profits by themselves are not tied to intrinsic social concerns about safety—unless, of course, safety can be used as a gimmick to raise prices. Similarly, Radicals understand that Liberal efforts to improve product safety, regardless of their posturing on behalf of consumers, cannot seriously assault the profit prerogatives or the rights of capitalists in a production-for-profit economy. Liberal actions on behalf of the abused in a production-for-profit system can never be so massive that they damage the basic profit-maximizing arrangements. The failure of the FDA to seriously test and monitor pain relievers that later proved to induce heart attacks and strokes is a perfect example of regulation based on corporate rather than social interests.

Given the constraints of a system that depends on private profit making, on one hand, and, on the other, requires the political pretense of repairing the more egregious functional shortcomings and social atrocities resulting from such a system, Radicals are inclined to ask a broader philosophical question: *Why is it that we do not have a more rational approach toward the production and use of goods?* Such a question requires one of Radical outlook to approach the issue of consumer welfare in a very different way than Liberals and Conservatives. First, from a Radical perspective, it is immediately obvious that consumer behavior (aggregate or individual) is not disconnected from the realities of consumer incomes. The chief determinant of what goods an individual consumes is, of course, that individual's level of income and preexisting wealth. American income distribution is examined in Issue 6; suffice it to say at this point, however, that *American consumers are not equal when they enter the marketplace.* Consumers with lesser incomes are excluded as purchasers of certain goods (a fact of free market economic life that does not trouble Conservatives) and they are afforded fewer of the consumer protections Liberals have successfully advocated. Safer automobiles and roads, lead- and asbestos-free housing, truth-in-lending laws, and electric shock- and fire-resistant appliances are luxuries mostly unknown to the poorest 25 percent of Americans.

However, the obvious fact that Americans have unequal access to either consumer sovereignty or consumer protection pales before an even larger problem: The mix of goods the nation chooses to consume—regardless of whether the goods are safe or not—is, from a social perspective, wasteful. For instance, in the case of the privately owned automobile and the enormously expensive system of roads and ancillary services needed to make auto ownership feasible, most Radicals see an incredibly irrational, polluting, and wasteful transportation mode. Accordingly, Radicals view the debate over private automobile safety and the virtual absence of any discussion about devising an environmentally friendly, efficient system of mass transportation as a good example of how we never address the basic questions in our analysis of consumer behavior.

Mere recognition of the broader questions of what and why we consume is not part of the present economic agenda. Radicals, in addressing the current consumer protection problem concretely, embrace most protectionist objectives: the maintenance of quality and purity in product manufacture, the accurate dissemination of information about a product's uses and limits, the recall of dangerous products, and the ability of the consumer to gain redress for damages and defrauding. *Caveat venditor* (seller beware) is an acceptable short-term strategy, but it scarcely goes to the root of our problems as long as production for profit drives the nation's economic and political engine.

# Dealing with Externalities

## How Can We Save the Environment?

These pollutants originate in the Midwest, eastern Canada, and western New York State; rain and snow wash them out of air passing over the state [of New York] to fall on our forests, lakes, and cities. Because some of these air pollutants become sulphuric acid, nitric acid, and other acids when dissolved in the precipitation carrying them to earth, this whole process has been dubbed "acid rain."
— *John Hawley*, The Conservationist, 1977

When we calculate all the costs to everyone, on balance, we will save money when we pass this [the Clean Air] bill.
— *Senator George Mitchell, 1990*

Kyoto is, in many ways, unrealistic. Many countries cannot meet their Kyoto targets. The targets themselves were arbitrary and not based upon science. For America, complying with those mandates would have a negative economic impact, with layoffs of workers and price increases for consumers. And when you evaluate all these flaws, most reasonable people will understand that it's not sound public policy.
— *President George W. Bush, 2001*

Prices at the pump are skyrocketing; jobs are being lost to countries with lower natural gas costs. And through it all, some in Washington still continue to stubbornly ignore the potential of a vital domestic source of energy: Arctic National Wildlife Reserve.
— *Gale A. Norton, Secretary of the Interior, 2004*

## The Problem

They began to notice the problem in the Adirondack Mountains of up-state New York more than two decades ago. Plant and aquatic life in many of the region's lakes began to undergo a significant change, reflecting a general degradation of lake water quality. Within a few years the problem rapidly worsened as dozens of lakes became dead—virtually void of fish and plants. The cause, at least as far as New Yorkers were concerned, was acid rain. Precipitation containing high levels of sulfuric and other acids was altering nature's balance, not only killing lakes but showing signs of damaging the trees and ground cover as well. The source of the acid rain was, to most scientists, easily explained: The burning of fossil fuels un-leashed sulfur dioxide, nitrogen dioxide, and other chemicals and particu-lates into the atmosphere. These returned to earth with falling rain and snow and, combined with water, became highly acidic. Since northern New York had no significant fossil fuel burning, the source of the problem was determined to be the industrial Midwest. There, manufacturing plants and electric generating facilities belched large quantities of chemicals into the air from high smokestacks, to be carried northeastward and deposited by the prevailing wind and weather systems.

In general terms, economic theory offers both a theoretical explanation and a potential remedy to the problems posed by acid rain and other types of environmental pollution. The theoretical tool employed is the concept of *externalities*. The analysis runs like this: Under free market conditions, the interaction of all individual sellers (supply) and all individual buyers (demand) establishes a market price for a product. Yet the market price may not reflect all the incidental costs or benefits associated with the good. For instance, a student may value (in terms of his or her estimated private benefits) a college education at around $80,000 or $90,000, but society in general may derive benefits of much greater value from individuals who obtain college educations. A better-educated public may be more creative, more efficient, and harder working, thus producing a larger economic pie for everyone, not just the solitary student. These additional gains are spillover or external *benefits* (sometimes called *external economies*) beyond the actual market price paid for the commodity.

Acid rain or pollution represents spillover or external costs (also known as *external diseconomies*). In a market economy, output decisions are based on calculations of direct production costs. Air, water, and even the land itself may be viewed as free goods in the production process. Insofar as the atmosphere and the earth are free sewers and dumping grounds, the producer enjoys lower production costs by polluting. Society, living in a dirtier world, however, is saddled with the social costs of pollution. The market price of the good does not reflect the social costs of manufacturing the good. Obviously, to be efficient prices of goods need to accurately incorporate all costs, both private direct production costs and social costs. The objective of an efficient environmental policy is to internalize the social costs of pollution in the price of the goods so that preventive or remedial action is included.

However, the step from theory to practice is big. From the viewpoint of New Yorkers (and New Englanders and Canadians, too, who have been living with acid rain for some time), it is essential to attack acid rain at its source by restricting Midwestern industrial emissions. At the same time, naturally enough, Midwesterners have an interest in keeping their industries operating at low costs and in obtaining cheap coal-generated electricity.

Maintaining environmental quality has been a highly popular social priority with Americans for more than three decades, but acid rain has been a tough problem. Unlike most pollution, which affects the immediate surroundings of the polluter and usually inspires community pressure on the polluter, acid rain's apparent source and its effects are a thousand miles and many state lines separated from one another. In fact, the general problem of air pollution and global climate change is now widely regarded as an issue of international proportions. A United Nations convention grappling with the threat of greenhouse gas emissions resulted in the Kyoto Treaty of 1997, the enactment of which has been stalled by its rejection by several key countries, including the United States.

Just as conflicting regional interests make it difficult to comprehend any solution to the acid rain problem below the federal level, the transnational consequences of all sorts of pollution have commanded that solutions be sought on an international scale. Just as resolution at that national level infers that the Environmental Protection Agency's powers would have to be increased in scope and application, efforts to address international pollution problems such as greenhouse gas emissions infers the use of mechanisms and enforcement presiding above the discretion of sovereign nations. But beyond the politics of maintaining environmental safeguards, there remain important economic questions. How, precisely, does one determine the social cost of pollution? How is its source to be pinpointed? And even if the cost and the specific polluters are identified, what means should be undertaken to internalize the social cost?

Conservatives, Liberals, and Radicals come to quite different policy conclusions in answering these three questions, even when they start from an
agreement about the existence of pollution, its threat, and its source. The
issue, of course, is not simply acid rain or greenhouse gases, but a strategy
that will be effective in dealing with all environmental problems.

## Synopsis

Conservatives recognize the *neighborhood effects* of pollution and advocate a
cost-benefit technique in determining the amount of environmental cleanup
outlays. They favor use of market mechanisms such as emissions fees and
cap-and-trade programs as the best way to allocate cleanup costs. Liberals
place less trust in market-based schemes and favor direct government controls or even the use of a subsidy policy to clean up the environment.
Radicals argue that most efforts to protect the environment are doomed to
failure since actual environmental damage is always underestimated. Production-for-profit systems simply do not find it to their advantage to undertake truly effective actions to protect the environment.

---

## Anticipating the Arguments

- On what grounds do Conservatives favor market-based approaches
  over direct government controls in eliminating pollution?
- On what grounds do Liberals believe that emissions fees and cap-and-
  trade schemes are insufficient in dealing with pollution problems?
- Why do Radicals believe that conventional market-directed or
  government-directed efforts are likely to be insufficient in protecting the environment?

## THE CONSERVATIVE ARGUMENT

The debate over pollution and acid rain raises a somewhat different set
of economic and theoretical questions from those considered in the earlier discussion of consumer safety. Owning and wearing seatbelts is (or
at least should be) a purely voluntary matter directly affecting no one
but the party involved. Pollution, on the other hand, focuses directly on
third-party effects—damage done to individuals who have no economic
stake in the polluting action and who can exercise no voluntary control
over the effects of pollution.

According to Milton Friedman and most others who have looked at the pollution issue, there is a neighborhood effect that must be calculated and accounted for. According to Friedman:

> A . . . general class of cases in which strictly voluntary exchange is impossible arises when actions of individuals have effects on other individuals for which it is not feasible to charge or recompense them. This is the problem of "neighborhood effects." An obvious example is the pollution of a stream. The man who pollutes a stream is in effect forcing others to exchange good water for bad. These others might be willing to make the exchange at a price. But it is not feasible for them, acting individually, to avoid the exchange or to enforce appropriate compensation.*

## Neighborhood Effects and the Role of Government

Clearly, in this situation, it is appropriate to expect the community to establish some technique for determining the costs that one individual imposes on another and to develop a mechanism for allocating the costs. Admitting to such occasional needs to remedy market failures, however, should not be construed as a total condemnation of the market or as a license to introduce all manner of "benevolent" tinkering with the market. Indeed, it becomes quite important that the community action chosen to deal with neighborhood effects be as neutral and nonbureaucratic as possible. Quite simply, the object is to develop a policy that makes a firm internalize all of its costs (social as well as private) in its production decisions.

In our time, magnificent government structures have been created in the name of protecting the innocent from the polluters. Yet society's gains from expensive and creative antipollution efforts have been few—and often obtained only at an unacceptable burden to everyone's voluntary rights and to economic well-being and efficiency in general. Consider the ruthless application of antipollution standards in the 1970s. With the creation of the Environmental Protection Agency (EPA) in 1970 and the passage of the Clean Air Act in the same year, the EPA was given authority to (1) determine national air quality standards; (2) set emission levels for old and new plants; (3) set motor vehicle emis-

---

*Milton Friedman, *Capitalism and Freedom* (Chicago: University of Chicago Press, 1962), 30.

sion standards; (4) establish which fuel substances may be burned in motor vehicles; and (5) establish standards in emergency situations (including the power to close down industrial polluters presenting an immediate danger to public health).

With great zeal and little contemplation of the consequences, the EPA wrote standards and enforced them vigorously. Murray Weidenbaum of the Center for the Study of American Business has estimated that between 1979 and 1986, public agencies and private firms spent nearly three-quarters of a trillion dollars in efforts to meet the EPA requirements. Looking at the data another way, Weidenbaum estimates that meeting EPA direct control standards absorbed 14 percent of the paper industry's capital outlays and 20 percent of the steel industry's new investment. Before the Reagan administration began to relax EPA direct pollution controls in the early 1980s, nearly two hundred plants employing over two hundred thousand workers had closed as the direct result of imposed pollution abatement costs.

Did such antipollution costs produce benefits? The answer is a qualified yes. National urban air quality has improved fairly steadily since 1974. The Great Lakes and the Far West have experienced significant environmental improvements. The expected national rate of environmental damage that would have occurred without pollution controls has slowed, with actual damages falling in recent years. However, it is a matter of some debate whether the benefits, in dollar terms, came anywhere close to the dollar costs imposed by the EPA.

The problem in dealing with acid rain and other pollution problems lies in establishing a method for bringing costs of control and benefits into balance. It is patent nonsense to argue, as Radicals and some Liberals do, that an absolutely clean environment is essential *whatever its cost.* To begin with, there is no technically feasible way to return the environment to its unspoiled, pre–fossil-fuel-era condition regardless of the cleanup outlays that might be undertaken. Given that some level of environmental damage is inevitable, society must establish reasonable cleanup expectations that are based on (1) the value of real benefits actually attainable and (2) the community's willingness to pay the cost of obtaining such benefits. Government-imposed cleanup costs vastly in excess of antipollution benefits that the community deems reasonable lead to a serious misallocation of resources, resulting in closed plants, inadequate new capital investment, failing world competitiveness, lost jobs, and other consequences.

## The Possibility of Private Approaches

From a Conservative perspective, the most useful techniques for abating pollution employ minimal social tinkering and a greater reliance on forces of the market to bring social and private benefits into line with social and private costs. Although reliance on the market to deal with neighborhood effects has its limitations, two private (nongovernment) means of assigning the costs of pollution to polluters are possible: negotiation among affected parties and setting specific liability rules.

Negotiation of pollution costs between polluters and damaged parties is feasible where one person's property rights are clearly damaged by a second party's polluting—for instance, a city's loss of its water supply or added costs in preparing its drinking water because of a single identifiable upstream polluter. The damaged party may sue in court, which gives an incentive to the polluter to clean up its emissions. In fact, the polluter and the damaged party may sit down and bargain rather than go to court. Presumably, the pollution fee or the extent of cleanup agreed upon reflects both parties' balancing of benefits and costs.

Failing negotiation, liability rules depend on use of the courts to establish private costs resulting from pollution. Once the court sets particular damages for polluting actions, the firm must calculate such damages as a fairly certain cost of any production having polluting side effects. If the firm pollutes more, it pays more; if it pollutes less, it pays less. The incentive—without any government directives—is on the side of reducing pollution.

The obvious difficulty with relying on negotiations and liability rules is that they do not work well when the specific effects of a specific polluter are uncertain or where specifically damaged parties are either hard to determine or have difficulty establishing clear property rights. How, in fact, does a New York fisherman establish the level of personal damage from acid rain and determine who actually caused the acidity in the first place?

## Collective Action

Given the shortcomings of purely private approaches to environmental issues, collective action is the sole alternative. Collective action comes in three general forms: direct controls, emissions taxes (fees) or permits, and subsidies.

Conservative opposition to direct controls was already noted. When government sets specific emissions standards backed with the force of fines or the power to close plants, government wields a dangerous degree of power. Even if used cautiously, there is no certainty that this power will produce the desired effect of balancing cleanup costs and benefits. As a matter of practice, government has tended to overvalue the benefits of halting or slowing pollution while underestimating the costs of attainment. To a considerable degree, direct controls reflect imperfect pollution-measuring standards that vary widely from firm to firm, industry to industry, and region to region.

Most important, however, direct controls provide little monetary incentive for the marginal polluter (at or just below the accepted emission standard) to reduce pollution at all. Direct controls can, at best, establish only an acceptable minimum; they have no effect in bringing about a general improvement in environmental quality as a function of a market economy's constant drive to lower costs.

Subsidies paid to firms as inducements to installing antipollution devices may sound attractive but are hopelessly inefficient. Like direct emissions controls, government-imposed problem solving looks better than it really is. Subsidies provide no market-based inducement for firms to take antipollution actions; they do not cause firms to internalize the social costs of polluting. Ironically, they simply lower polluters' costs, possibly increasing levels of pollution in the long run. If the government installed scrubbers in the smokestacks of Midwestern coal-burning plants, which are allegedly the source of acid rain, the effect would be to lower production costs (in terms of the alternative of the firm's internalizing its own pollution costs). This might encourage more coal burning, wholly offsetting the initial clean air gains.

A more acceptable method for repairing the neighborhood effects of pollution is levying an emissions fee. The fee is levied on polluters to offset the environmental damage they are causing. Relying on the firm's desire to maximize profit, cleaning up its emissions will lead to reductions in its pollution fee burden. Firms most able to adapt to antipollution requirements will respond most quickly, thus holding down their expenditures on fees. On the other hand, inefficient or poorly managed enterprises that do not act to reduce emissions will find their profits adversely affected by having to spend greater amounts on emission fees. The emissions fee essentially requires firms to pay a price for each unit of pollution emitted. Government regulators can cause a reduction in emissions by raising the fee.

cy of benign neglect. And with the arrival of the George W.
istration in 2001, the White House obtained an occupant
ctive of his rhetoric, clearly was not a dedicated environ-
he Bush administration made certain that they wrestled fund-
EPA in 2004 down to the 1999 level of $7.6 billion. Whatever
ents to the contrary, Conservatives have shown themselves
ess concerned about neighborhood effects than about relax-
mental regulations.

the Bush administration's environmental stance looks like a
he Reagan years. There is a zeal for opening public lands re-
r habitat preservation to mining and oil and gas exploration.
to the ecosystem seems to be sidelined in favor of obtaining
sil fuels to burn, which is the principal source of air pollution
nhouse gases. At the same time, the Bush administration has
to endorse the Kyoto Treaty, which is aimed at averting a global
change disaster, citing that the costs of reducing greenhouse
re too high for the United States to bear.

## Intervention versus Emissions Taxes

, emissions fees and creating a market for emissions permits have
he the rage among many economists. Supposedly, metering a firm's
arges and then taxing the firm on the basis of its measured pollu-
creates a neutral fee mechanism that internalizes the external costs
seconomies. The fee becomes another cost of production that the
t-maximizing firm will seek to avoid by introducing emission con-
. Even in the most ideal scenario—efficient fees and rational firms
rating in competitive markets—emissions fees and tradable allow-
es are a slow process for forcing change in pollution habits.
Direct intervention, if seriously undertaken, promises a quicker short-
solution. When the government sets emission standards and enforces
m with stiff fines or the threat of plant closure, a firm has an immediate
centive to introduce emission controls. If a carrot were preferred over a
ck in inducing industry compliance with environmental standards, di-
ct subsidies, either to pay for the cost of pollution control or as cash
centives to firms that voluntarily reduce emissions, could be paid. Di-
ect controls also offer regulators the advantage of specifying the best
methods and technologies that firms should use to abate pollution—the
public has an interest in seeing pollution controlled in the *right* way.

Technical problems remain in metering the amount of an individual firm's emissions and translating this into a dollar value of social damages that would be the basis for estimating the correct fee level to deliver the optimal reduction in pollution. Nevertheless, emissions fees are more attractive than direct intervention and rely on the firm's basic incentive to maximize profits and minimize costs to make environmental protection work.

The question of how an emissions charge should best be levied remains a matter of some debate, but Conservatives favor the use of *marketable emissions permits.* Under such an arrangement, a scientific determination of the environment's capacity to absorb pollutants over a given area would be determined. Then a responsible public authority would auction off pollution permits totaling the permissible annual volume. Firms with high abatement costs (the costs of cleaning the air or water affected by their operations) would be inclined to pay higher prices for an emissions permit sold at auction. Those with low abatement costs might find it cheaper to do their own cleanup—as they would be required to do without acquisition of an emissions permit. Once issued, the permits would develop their own market, with firms buying and selling permits among themselves according to which is least expensive: paying their own abatement costs or buying a permit that allows a specified quantity of annual emissions from their manufacturing sites.

In practice, the EPA administers a cap-and-trade system to control acid rain. A nationwide cap is set on the sulfur dioxide ($SO_2$) emissions and enforced by the issuance of a limited number of emission permits called emissions allowances by the EPA. One emissions allowance is required to emit one ton of $SO_2$. Plants that find it easier to reduce output of $SO_2$ can sell unused allowances to plants that are less able to abate pollution.

The market-based approach to reducing pollution by requiring polluters to buy the right to pollute establishes incentives to curtail emissions at lower compliance costs than with command-and-control regulation. The cap-and-trade program for $SO_2$ has been so successful that other nations have adopted similar approaches, and a mechanism of international emissions trading worked its way into the Kyoto Protocol for reducing greenhouse gases.

The merits of marketable emissions permits are clear. Government intervention is kept to a minimum. And everyone relies on market signals rather than social control in the everyday direction of resources toward a cleaner environment. This system avoids the inefficiency and inequity of direct controls.

## THE LIBERAL ARGUMENT

Although Conservatives may seem reasonable enough in their concession that pollution involves neighborhood effects that the community has the right to regulate, their actual track record with regard to environmental protection is a poor one. Their less-than-enthusiastic embrace of federal government action to control pollution stems from their blind commitment to a free market. Moreover, the pollution problem goes a long way toward demonstrating that free markets may not always ensure society's well-being.

### The Failure of the Market to Allocate Externalities

As noted earlier, externalities arise when, beyond the market price of a good, there is either a calculable *external cost* (detrimental externality) or *external gain* (beneficial externality) to the individuals consuming the good or to society as a whole. Externalities are not, as Conservatives might suggest, merely interesting exceptions to the theory of markets in which the free play of supply and demand establishes prices and allocates resources accordingly. Instead, they reflect a serious market failure and are ample justification for the Liberal assertion that the market can very often be improved upon.

Externalities reveal two types of problems in allocating resources purely according to market dictates. First, there is the problem of external benefits or economies. A firm that perhaps inadvertently supplies substantial benefits to a community—say, by laying out attractive park-like playgrounds around its production site—has little monetary incentive to continue such investment in this site because it receives no gains in sales from such activity. Although the community derives esthetic and health benefits, there is no market incentive for the firm to allocate resources to such objectives (hence it is not surprising that many places of production are so drab). Second, there is little incentive to invest in good things that produce no private market gains, but there is considerable incentive to spin off certain costs onto the community rather than internalize them as part of the firm's own production costs. Thus, the rivers and the air have been viewed as free sewers by firms spewing

chemicals out into the com
market's allocation of resourc
eficial externalities and many

In developing a useful econ
quires modification and redirec
environmental problems it poses
ment action.

### The Need for a National Environ

As a general rule, Conservatives
from the federal level. They prefer t
vention as more democratically resp
case of acid rain demolishes their arg
tive to lower the acidity of New York's
consideration for voluntary agreement
parties is a flawed argument. Since Nev
persuade Ohioans to voluntarily reduce
economic advantage for the polluters to
these distant and differently motivated pa

Nor does the prospect of enforcing prop
in the courts seem more probable. While
polluters are technically possible, the legal
ing tactics. Moreover, individuals as damag
possibility of financing long legal battles aga
financed Midwestern corporations.

Given the shortcomings of voluntarism an
the acid rain problem, it becomes quickly evid
eral intervention provides a possible solution.
argument, despite basic opposition to broad coll
this point—at least theoretically. The Conservati
ertheless demonstrates a different view in practic
office in 1981, the Reagan administration began
mental protection and preservation. Administrators
nesses' (read: "polluter's") needs began to wind do
programs developed during the 1970s and opened
commercial ventures. Few new efforts to exert federa
vironmental protection emerged.

During the 1990s, the Republican-controlled Congr

Reagan lega
Bush admir
who, irresp
mentalist.
ing for the
their argun
markedly
ing enviro

In fact,
rerun of t
served fo
Damage
more fos
and gree
refused
climate
gases a

**Direct**

Lately
becor
disch
tion
or di
prof
trols
ope
and

rur
the
in
st
re
i

The Conservative argument against direct controls and subsidies maintains that they are inefficient, creating greater total social and private costs than the value of the benefits obtained. This supposedly results from compelling too much antipollution activity too fast. While it may not be possible to restore the environment to pre–industrial-era conditions, indulging in excessive cost consciousness may produce a "rational pro-environment strategy" that does nothing at all for the environment.

## THE RADICAL ARGUMENT

Over the past three decades, a noteworthy social awareness has developed about various market failures and their effect on the quality of life under a capitalist system of production. With fairly substantial popular support in the 1970s, a number of collective efforts were launched to deal with such issues as consumer protection, occupational safety, developing new sources for energy and other scarce resources, and, of course, environmental protection. Yet two points are worth remembering: First, it was erroneously believed that more government intervention to correct any market failure was all that was needed. Second, the few timid gestures undertaken produced very limited benefits, and, in fact, the past twenty years have been a march away from the minor victories of the mid-1970s. The problem is that "market failures" are not seen for what they really are: the market working precisely as it is supposed to work under a production-for-profit system.

### *Capitalism and the Environment*

Profits, of course, are merely the revenues obtained by the capitalist after all production and distribution costs have been subtracted. To maximize profits, the rational capitalist must minimize costs. Insofar as it is cheaper (more profitable) to emit sulfur and other particulates into the atmosphere than invest in antipollution devices or nonpolluting production, acid rain and other environmental horrors are a quite rational and expected by-product of a production-for-profit system. Viewed this way, it becomes apparent that whatever the advantages to people in general from a clean environment, there are no advantages to a firm to undertake antipollution activities voluntarily. And this is also true of other socially directed objectives such as consumer protection and occupational safety.

The record of capitalist destruction of the earth, its atmosphere, and ultimately its inhabitants is obvious enough. The degradation of the land through clear-cutting hardwood timber in the nineteenth century to obtain nothing but tannic acid for boot making, the mid-twentieth-century practice of strip-mining coal, and the modern crises of acid rain, greenhouse gas emissions, habitat destruction, and radioactive waste from a vast number of nuclear production sites illustrate that the search for private profits stands in open opposition to environmental, and hence human, concerns.

### The Failure of Past Environmental Efforts

Liberals and Conservatives (who, after all, cannot deny the evidence of environmental decline) concede the need for some proenvironmental activity. Liberals tend to favor direct control mechanisms implemented by a benevolent and all-seeing state, whereas Conservatives prefer the use of neutral emissions fees and marketable emissions permits that "induce" firms to reduce their polluting. Will either approach work?

The Liberal reliance on government direct controls or subsidies presumes, of course, that government is neutral—that government can determine environmental targets and develop and enforce rules that might directly threaten business enterprises' profits or continued operations. Yet the supposed neutrality of government in the marketplace has proved an illusion in practice. Even under Liberal administrations, the Environmental Protection Agency has shown softness in forcing businesses to pay cleanup costs. Effectively using their lobbying power, firms have successfully pointed out that cleanup efforts that are too energetic can lead to lost profits, diminished ability to compete abroad, and loss of workers' jobs. In fact, even the unions have joined private enterprise in going slow on acid rain and other pollution problems. Accordingly, in the last years of the Carter administration, the EPA introduced *pollution offset* programs in which newly established firms and plants could emit pollution so long as they could induce (pay) other firms to reduce emissions or, within their own company, reduce emissions elsewhere by an equal amount. Meanwhile, using a bubble concept, existing firms were given general permissible emissions limits over each plant, with the firm choosing where and how it would cut total pollution within the plant to meet the limits—more in the water and less in the air, or vice versa, if it was profitable. Such actions reflected concerns that too strenuous an antipollution policy could damage firm profitability. At best, they slowed the rate of pollution buildup without recognizing the need to undo the crimes of the past as well as the present.

Conservatives showed their practical lack of concern for pollution problems during the Reagan-Bush years. While talk of emissions taxes and the sale of emission permits characterized the writings of Conservative economists, when they actually addressed the pollution problem, no national emissions tax program was put in place. In fact, the EPA even pulled back from the limited level of effectiveness that characterized the Carter years. Meanwhile, although the avowedly Liberal administration of President Clinton showed more interest in environmental problems and, occasionally, showed more backbone in standing up to certain polluters, it did not produce a new and wide-ranging environmental effort.

To be perfectly blunt, even though surveys show that most Americans believe the environment must be protected whatever the cost, and even though the public's environmental awareness is now well over three decades old, no effective national environmental program has emerged or seems likely to emerge soon.

### The Need to Get Beyond "Cost-Benefit"

For some, the Radicals' discounting of Liberal and Conservative environmental proposals will be interpreted as silly obstructionism. As in the case of consumer protection, the Radical opposition at first seems contradictory—that Radicals somehow oppose serious efforts to make safer products or to clean up the atmosphere. Such an inaccurate perception stems from a failure to grasp the basis of the Radical argument.

From a Radical perspective, failure to deal with environmental issues is not merely a capitalist oversight or some accidental consequence of a market-dominated society; it is directly traceable to capitalism's dominant feature—*the drive for profits*. Furthermore, it is not possible for capitalism to be itself (searching for profits) and to be better than itself (taking actions that reduce profits) at the same time. Capitalist (Conservative or Liberal) discussions about halting acid rain or cleaning up pollution in general are therefore nothing more than seductive deceptions.

The point becomes obvious when we peel back the Conservative and Liberal arguments to examine their real content. Both rely on a cost-benefit measurement of the extent of pollution as a problem and as an indicator of how much antipollution activity should be undertaken. The ultimate determinant of the extent of antipollution activity is, according to conventional theory, established by the point at which marginal social costs equal marginal social benefits (in other words, where the last dollar spent on cleaning up the environment is at least equal to a dollar's worth of gain from the actual cleanup). On the surface, this seems rational enough until we consider how costs and benefits are calculated. *Social costs* are seen as the sum of all private costs plus any governmental outlays for reducing pollution as determined by market-established prices. *Social benefits* are the sum of dollar benefits accruing to all individuals affected by the reduction of pollution. The bias of such an approach is always to overestimate costs and underestimate benefits, since costs are comparatively easily calculated in market terms while only a portion of benefits can be assigned a particular market value. A $10 million outlay for a scrubber (whether paid for by the firm or by tax dollars) is easily perceived as a cost. However, what is the benefit of not killing a lake? A lake is only partly a commodity to which a market value can be assigned as a piece of real estate lost to its owners for personal or business use. A lake, a stream, or, more pointedly, a sunset has a certain intrinsic value that is not calculable in current market terms.

Cost-benefit discussions under capitalism are always limited to property and commodity relationships. The *neighborhood effect* of Conservative theoreticians (and used also by Liberals) rests on calculating damages to individuals' property rights as the beginning point for offsetting spillover costs. Hence the estimated value of social benefits—which in discussions of external diseconomies are nothing more than the sum of estimable private property or market value gains—will always be lower than the real benefits to society of ending pollution.

Marauding global capitalism has turned environmental problems into a global concern. Developed countries that would have to be key players in any international attempt to address the environment predictably resorted to benefit-cost calculations that struck down the Kyoto Treaty. Other polluting nations sought exemptions from the greenhouse gas reductions contemplated by the treaty. The charade about "efficient pollution control" has simply moved to the international level with the same failed results experienced on the domestic front in the United States.

Recalling the issue of consumer safety, once it was stripped to its basics, the conventional debate over consumer protection was off target and avoided the real issue of socially irrational production and consumption choices being the natural outcome of a production-for-profit system. No remedy to irrationality could be found within even a modified capitalist system. Likewise, no remedy is forthcoming from efforts alleged to offset the market failure of external diseconomies resulting in acid rain or other pollution. Remedial antipollution actions of any consequence will take place only when social policies reflect real human needs, not the requirements and values of a commodity-dominated society. Ending pollution and maintaining a safe and humane environment, now and for the future, is a social goal that must be understood as having no ultimate cost limits with regard to what must be paid for its attainment. From a Radical perspective, society is more than the sum of each of its individual members. Society, or humankind, also has a historical dimension. We at the beginning of the twenty-first century have no right to limit the potential and blight the lives of human beings who will follow with acid rain, global warming, mass extinctions of species, and other environmental degradation. The simple fact remains that capitalism is incompatible with rational stewardship of the environment.

# Imperfect Competition

## Is Big Business a Threat or a Boon?

People of the same trade seldom meet together, even for merriment and diversion, but the conversation ends in a conspiracy against the public, or in some contrivance to raise prices.

*—Adam Smith, 1776*

Every contract, combination in the form of trust or other-wise, or conspiracy, in restraint of trade or commerce . . . is hereby declared to be illegal. . . . Every person who shall monopolize, or attempt to monopolize, or combine or conspire . . . to monopolize . . . shall be deemed guilty of a misdemeanor.

*—Sherman Anti-Trust Act, 1890*

Microsoft does not have monopoly power in the business of developing and licensing computer operating systems.

*—Bill Gates, Chairman and CEO*
*Microsoft Corporation, 1998*

Moreover, over the past several years, Microsoft has comported itself in a way that could only be consistent with rational behavior for a profit-maximizing firm if the firm knew that it possessed monopoly power, and if it was motivated by a desire to preserve the barrier to entry protecting that power.

*—Thomas Penfield Jackson*
*U.S. District Court Judge, 2000*

## The Problem

On any list of contemporary economic problems that captures the American public's interest, *bigness in business* does not rank very high. That said, however, it would be incorrect to infer that corporate size and the business practices of giant corporations are unimportant economic issues. Indeed, in an economy preponderantly organized around free market principles, the size and power of the participants in any market must be matters of perpetual concern.

Conventional market theory distinguishes between competitive market structures and numerous imperfectly competitive alternatives (monopolistic competition, oligopoly, and monopoly). Moreover, conventional theory demonstrates that society reaps greater benefits under pure competition: Maximum output is assured, prices are lower, and excessive profit making is avoided, with all firms reacting to the dictates of a free market as *price takers*. Under imperfectly competitive conditions, firms are able to exercise some degree of *price making,* controlling prices and output for their own profitable advantage. In a textbook situation, there is little disagreement among economists about such generalizations. The trouble develops when we move from textbook examples to the real world.

A seemingly paradoxical situation appears when we examine the existing structure and organization of American business enterprise. On one hand, the official ideology of American capitalism espouses a competitive ideal of many smallish producers, no one of which can materially affect price or output. On the other hand, everyday experience tells us that most markets are dominated by a comparative handful of very large firms. Exactly how much bigness might alter or eliminate desired competitive conditions has long been a concern in American capitalism. Since the passage of the Sherman Antitrust Act in 1890, a considerable body of law has been enacted to protect competition. The essence of these accumulated laws may be summarized as follows:

1. It is illegal to enter into a contract, combination, or conspiracy in restraint of trade or to monopolize, attempt to monopolize, or combine or conspire to monopolize trade.
2. When the effect is to lessen competition or create a monopoly, it is illegal to acquire the stock or assets of competing companies, to discriminate among purchasers other than what can be justified by actual costs, or to enter into exclusive or tying contracts.

3.  Under all cases, whether the effect is to monopolize or not, it is
    illegal to serve in the directorships of competing corporations, to
    use unfair methods of competition, or to employ unfair or decep-
    tive acts or practices.

Despite the thrust of law and prevailing economic theory, the tendency
toward larger market structures has persisted since the closing decades of
the nineteenth century. Although bigness has sometimes been occasioned
by a firm's own individual production and sales efforts, by far the most
popular route to increasing corporate size is through merger and combination. The earliest merger efforts of the late nineteenth century were largely
*horizontal mergers,* which combined side-by-side competitors in the same
industry. Very shortly, there followed *vertical mergers,* combining suppliers
and purchasers of goods involved in the same chain of production. United
States Steel, General Motors, and the American Tobacco Company came
into existence following the former path. The National Biscuit Company
and Standard Oil (which also used horizontal combination) grew in size
and influence using the latter strategy.

Three eras of horizontal and vertical mergers are easily identifiable: the
1890s, the 1920s, and the period immediately following World War II. Until
comparatively recently, horizontal and vertical merger activity had slowed,
in part because the really juicy combinations had already taken place and in
part because antitrust law impeded greater concentration and growth of
market power by existing giants. Merging, however, did not cease. Beginning in the 1960s and continuing to the present, firms have increasingly
undertaken *conglomerate mergers,* uniting enterprises where no horizontal or
vertical market advantages are present.

In recent years, the annual estimated value of mergers and acquisitions has increased from about $44 billion in 1980 to $1.2 trillion in 2003.
Despite this tremendous rise, not all consolidations have resulted in either increased market share or profitability. Large industrial conglomerates such as General Electric and General Motors earn a growing share
of their profits from financial and other nonmanufacturing operations.
Other corporations such as AT&T and ITT were forced to downsize or
sell off divisions they acquired but on which they could not generate an
acceptable rate of return. That noted, however, we cannot fail to recognize that in the past couple of years there have been some truly gargan-
tuan mergers including JP Morgan Chase and Banc One, Cingular Wireless
and AT&T Wireless, Travelers-Citicorp, and Time-Warner and AOL.

Moreover, further combinations in the airline and technology industries clearly indicate that we are in the middle of a new and important period of corporate combination.

Since the election of Ronald Reagan, government policy toward big business has focused on promoting competition through the deregulation of industries and markets, especially where there are only a few competitors or perhaps none. Market forces, rather than government-initiated policies and antitrust litigation, have been viewed as the quickest and most efficient means for ensuring adequate price competition and consumer sovereignty. These policies have led to a significant curtailment of prosecutions by the Justice Department for price fixing, price discrimination, and other antitrust violations. Whether or not such policy might undergo change is a matter of debate.

What is the significance of growing business concentration? To what extent are large firms able to act as price makers, setting excessive prices, restricting output, and creating market inefficiency? To what degree do antitrust law, foreign competition, and other economic developments offset or negate the trend toward bigness?

While no economist, regardless of ideological preference, denies the existence of big business, there is widespread disagreement as to whether modern corporate size and increased merger activity represent a serious monopoly threat to the economic and social organization of American society.

## Synopsis

The Conservative argument asserts that there are sufficient market and legal checks to make certain that big business does not act in an exploitative way but actually improves our economic well-being. Liberals accept the fact of bigness but maintain that government intervention is essential to control potential monopoly exploitation. The Radical argument holds that monopoly is the logical historical development of capitalism and that there is no way to halt this tendency without abolishing the production-for-profit system.

---

## Anticipating the Arguments

- How do Conservatives argue that bigness in business is not proof of growing monopolistic power?
- What role do Liberals propose for government in dealing with the

rise of giant enterprises, and how does their view differ from the Conservative approach?

- How do Radicals support their claim that the growth of alleged monopolistic business behavior in the United States is merely the logical progression of capitalist development?

## THE CONSERVATIVE ARGUMENT

American public policy toward big business tends to be cyclical, in some periods reflecting a strong antibusiness bias (the early 1900s and the 1930s, for instance) and in others tending to be more tolerant of large-scale enterprise. During the past couple of decades, with a few exceptions, public policy makers have shown reasonable restraint in their antitrust pursuits. The result has been beneficial to both American business and the American public. But federal judge Thomas Penfield Jackson's 2000 determination that Microsoft was a monopolist demonstrated that the unreasoned fear of bigness in business could reassert itself anytime. Accordingly, it is well to remember why such fears can lead to dangerous economic policy making.

In general, fear of bigness rests on gross misunderstandings of the structure and performance of American business. Foremost among these is the confusion of bigness with monopoly, and the resulting corollary that big is bad. The anti–big-business attitude that emerges from these views is always a serious threat to the American economic system. Far from leading to the rebirth of a competitive business society, most anti-monopoly efforts erode free enterprise itself. Ironically, an attack on big business boils down to an attack on business of all kinds. More than they realize, the owners of mom-and-pop grocery stores and the like are themselves threatened by assaults on business giants.

### Bigness Does Not Equal Monopoly

Bigness in and of itself is not proof of monopoly power. Of course, there is no denying the existence of *dominant firms* in certain American industries and of the concentration of market share and capital in the hands of a few firms in others. However, a variety of real-world market forces come into play that negate or significantly diminish the price-making powers that economic theory suggests these business giants might possess. The point here is to get beyond monopoly theory and look at the world as it is. For instance, there are many cases of interindustry competition among different highly concentrated industries. Glass, aluminum, steel, paper, and plastic producers, for example, all battle each other for the food-container market. Nor should international competition be forgotten. While tariffs and shipping costs may offer some protection to American firms, the protection is not absolute—witness the 30 percent share of the auto market seized by foreign carmakers. The point is simple: Big business, far from ending competition, has heightened it. The solitary village blacksmith, barrel maker, or flour miller of a century ago had far greater monopoly power over price, quality, and output than does his present-day big business counterpart.

Those who worry about excessive monopoly power should consider one further point. In a market society, the great check against price gouging, by Microsoft or by a barrel maker, is consumer demand. If prices go too high, sellers simply cannot sell their products—or enough of them to make a profit—and prices will come down. If we can get beyond the silly but appealing logic of the "big is bad" argument, we might truly understand that the opposite is much more nearly correct: Big business has been good for America.

### In Defense of Bigness

The primary reason for merger and combination among enterprises in the past has been to obtain technical *economies of scale* that lower production costs—in other words, cost reductions deriving from enlarged output. To be sure, there have been examples of firms attempting to exploit their market power as monopolistic price makers; however, such mergers are rare indeed, and when detected (as they easily are), antitrust law and civil law provide ample protections to society at large. In the meantime, big business has been the major vehicle for economic and technical advance in the United States. Few can deny that product progress and relatively falling prices for most consumer and producer goods since the beginning of the twentieth century have been the result of expensive technological advancements; these could have resulted only from the great capital concentration and large-scale marketing strategies of big enterprise.

Recently, Liberal and Radical critics of business enterprise have directed their wrath against the newer conglomerate mergers. Such attacks are also threats to business growth, since conglomerate mergers presently account for about three-quarters of all combinations. This strategy is an extension of the "big is bad" argument; however, it fails to consider that conglomerate mergers may also provide consumer benefits. By strengthening inefficient and costly businesses through improved management techniques and by providing badly needed capital, prices will be lowered. Moreover, the conglomerate merger often increases competition by resuscitating firms that otherwise would fail. And strong firms are strengthened by acquiring many diverse operations that permit the firm to avoid putting all its eggs in one basket. In this era of immense and swift technological and product change, diversification is an important strategy to manage business risk for a large enterprise.

The size and scale of the truly large American firms become a bit less threatening if two factors are considered: (1) the threat posed by giant foreign enterprises and (2) the health and abundance of small enterprises in the United States.

A policy aimed at weakening large firms simply because they are large will not protect the American consumer—and certainly not the American worker. A host of foreign giants stands ready to flood American markets with goods should large American firms fail to maintain their vitality and profitability. Indeed, the relative slippage of American producers in world competition is an important argument on behalf of reducing constraints on the size of American business.

In any case, bigness is vastly overemphasized. Of America's 17.6 million businesses, more than 99 percent of employer businesses qualify as small businesses, according to the Small Business Administration (SBA). Regardless of the size of the giant enterprises, no other economy can boast this proportion of small, independent enterprises to the entire population. The SBA reports that small business employs about half the private nonfarm workforce and accounts for about 60 to 80 percent of net new jobs created annually. Given these characteristics of American business enterprise, it becomes obvious that big business, even if it were a problem, gets undue attention from Liberals and Radicals. Smallness and competition remain the dominant characteristics of American enterprise.

Singling out big business is unfair and misleading. Even if business bigness were demonstrably bad, why isn't the same logic applied to big government or big labor unions? Those who cry "monopoly" in the business sector rarely apply that argument against the United Auto Workers or the Teamsters, nor do they see the bureaucratic state management of pricing—from hospital rooms to agricultural products—as analogous to the imagined monopoly power of big enterprise.

## The Promise of a New Approach by Government

The record of government enforcement of antitrust law has, since the beginning of the century, been inconsistent and contradictory, tending always to reflect the political ideology of the current occupant of the White House. Naturally enough, the intensity of antitrust action heightens with Liberal occupancy. However, even under Conservative administrations, there remained a troublesome ambivalence about how to deal with giant enterprises. Frequently actions were initiated by both Conservative and Liberal administrations against firms purely on the grounds that they were big or too profitable. Such an approach works against the development of dynamic and thriving firms. It is rather like punishing the winning runner in a race because she ran too fast. The profitable business is not the only loser, however; so is the society that has benefited in jobs and lower product prices from the large firm's efficiency. However, two landmark antitrust cases of the 1980s restored some reason to our public policy toward big business.

In the 1982 dismissal of a government action against IBM for monopolizing the mainframe computer industry, the Justice Department agreed that despite IBM's size and its share of the market, there was no proof that the firm had acted monopolistically. The decision should stand as an important legal landmark against those who would penalize a firm thoughtlessly simply because it has been successful. In the AT&T case, decided at the same time as the IBM case, the Justice Department affirmed the doctrine of competition. AT&T's monopoly power in the buying and selling of communications equipment and services was ended. AT&T was proved guilty of using its power (provided by government as a regulated monopoly) to exclude competitors from the data and electronic transmission market. AT&T was compelled to divest itself of its purely "public utility" local phone operations and join battle fairly with competing firms in the long-distance and information systems markets. A sensible antitrust policy was put in place: *Bigness itself does not prove collusion or unfair price setting, but when such activities are proved, they will be halted.*

Paralleling and complementing the IBM and AT&T cases has been a relaxation at the Justice Department of vigorous opposition to large corporate mergers. This, of course, has sparked criticism from some Liberal critics who fail to see the advantages obtained from most of these mergers. Far from being a submission to business pressure, the more passive approach toward mergers and bigness in its many forms is a recognition of the economic gains from size that provide important benefits to the entire society, not the least of which is an improvement of American firms' ability to compete with foreign giants.

The initial determination in 2000 that Microsoft was a monopolist seemed at the time to portend a worrisome throwback to the antitrust era born out of the Alcoa decision of 1945, where the possession of a 90 percent market share was regarded as *proof* of monopoly. Fortunately, the recent resolution of Microsoft's 2001 antitrust settlement with the Justice Department will now allow the company to focus on its main problems: growth and innovation. Unlike bureaucrats, financial markets are much better judges of market power: Microsoft's four-year stagnant stock price unambiguously reflects its market weakness, not market prowess. Antitrust enforcement must get beyond confusing innovation, growth in market share, and business success with the evils and abuses of monopoly. The Microsoft settlement indicates a return to sanity at the Antitrust Division of the Department of Justice.

Conservatives do not deny the existence of monopoly abuse when it is real. Very clearly, the exercise of monopoly power is unjustifiable and injurious to individuals. It prevents efficient allocation of resources. However, aside from those cases of monopoly initiated or encouraged by the government and occasional conspiratorial endeavors by individual enterprises, the monopoly problem is mostly a phony issue. Liberals use it as a pretext for urging massive social or governmental interference with the market, while Radicals find it convenient as an excuse for their revolutionary assault on the entire system. Both groups would use the issue in a self-serving fashion to extinguish individualism and private property rights.

## THE LIBERAL ARGUMENT

Traditional economic analysis since Adam Smith has argued that the "great regulator" for business activity is the market. Here, small, competitive firms struggle against each other to sell goods and gain customers. Prices and the possibility of exploitation are always regulated by what Smith called the *invisible hand*—the market interaction of supply and demand. Although we may nitpick over whether this type of pure competition ever existed outside of economists' minds, it certainly does not exist in the United States today. Just two thousand businesses in all areas of the economy produce over half of our gross domestic product; the highly visible fist of corporate power has largely replaced the invisible hand.

## The Problem of Policy Selection

While most modern-day Conservatives equivocate on the issue of big business, preferring not to see any monopoly problems except in the rarest of cases, Liberals face the problem directly. *Business concentration does exist in the United States.* The scale and intensity of efforts to increase concentration through merger is growing. Nor are all merger efforts benign conglomerate combinations. The policy issue, then, is not a matter of recognizing the obvious but of determining how to deal with it.

The most rudimentary analysis of monopoly behavior tells us that, all things being equal, monopolistic firms tend to charge higher prices and produce less than might otherwise be expected under competitive conditions. They employ fewer workers at lower wages and generally foster resource misallocation. Moreover, the greater the degree of monopoly power, the greater the consumer exploitation.

The implications of this line of economic analysis are clear. The return of competition is apparently the only way to return to economic virtue. In a policy sense, this might mean the enforcement of a vigorous antimonopoly policy, leading to the restructuring of some industries into greater numbers of similar-sized units of production. Liberals are not in total agreement on this point, but most would oppose a grand breaking up of giant enterprises. First of all, the practical application of a literal "break them up" policy is not politically or legally feasible. We long ago passed the point of being able to return to some romantic eighteenth-century concept of the marketplace. This is not to say that stimulation of competition in certain industries might not be desirable or possible through the application of antitrust laws. In fact, the Justice Department must always be prepared to initiate antimonopoly legal action, but this could not be carried out on a broad scale without weakening our legal and economic structures. Second, there is no solid evidence that pure competition, enforced indiscriminately, would be beneficial, even if it could be attained without seriously wrenching society.

What these observations mean in a practical context is that Liberals approach the question of bigness in American business quite pragmatically. The degree of concentration varies from industry to industry, and concentration alone does not tell the whole story about abuses of market power. Accordingly, concentration in the oil industry might be approached differently than concentration in the auto industry. Domestic automobile production is effectively limited to just three firms, with General Motors (GM) producing about 50 percent of American output. Some years ago, GM's size and share were so large that, in the minds of many Americans, the firm appeared to be a logical candidate for "break them up" antitrust action, a situation not unlike the one in which Microsoft later found itself in the personal computer software industry. Charges that GM has worked effectively in the past as a price leader are difficult to question. However, that was a long time ago, when GM effectively controlled 70 to 75 percent of the American car and truck market. In any case, even if this sales practice still existed as an option for GM, price leadership would not necessarily mean consumer exploitation. Nor would breaking up GM necessarily lead to social improvement. Even though GM's size has probably pushed it well beyond what is necessary for attaining efficiency from the point of view of *economies of scale,* there is no assurance that forty or even a dozen smaller GMs could produce a product of similar price and quality and hire the workforce that the present firm does. And, at any rate, the once-dominant position of GM has been severely eroded by the extensive penetration of the American auto market by foreign carmakers. In this case at least, most Liberals will agree with Conservatives that concern over national concentration ratios and domestic firm size must be weighed against the realities of world competition. On the other hand, the oil industry, with less actual concentration than the auto industry, conspired during the 1970s energy crises to force up the prices of gasoline and natural gas by withholding supplies.

The point is that there are different types of giant enterprises, some highly predatory and exploitative and others reasonably responsible to the public interest. Concentration alone is no justification for applying a vigorous antitrust action against members of the American auto industry. But the behavior of the oil industry in the 1970s is the worst kind of monopolistic activity. There are no easy monopoly tests. Each case must be taken on its own merits.

Having rejected the rigid competitive argument, we are left to accept the reality of modern corporate concentration. However, though Liberals realize that bigness itself need not be proof of monopoly abuse, they do not subscribe to the policy advanced by Conservatives. The quest for greater market power is not always enlightened; it may, in fact, destroy business itself, as large firms act consciously or unconsciously to protect and expand their influence. Certainly, the current merger mania in American business has had a negative effect because it diverts funds into takeovers rather than capital investment and absorbs the brightest business minds in short-run profit objectives rather than long-run production planning.

Meanwhile, unrestrained business power may lead to the domination of government by narrow business interests and the subversion of the rights of the many for the benefit of a few. Thus Liberals believe the creation of a clear public policy toward mergers and bigness in business is essential to protect the balance of pluralistic interests in an open society. An equitable balance of labor, consumer, and capital interests must be the philosophical cornerstone of any intelligent policy toward business.

Through fair and calculated government intervention, big businesses can be made compatible with the social objectives of economic order, reasonable prices, high quality, and technological advancement. Government actions, depending on the situation, must go beyond mere antitrust enforcement. They may take the form of selective tax and subsidy arrangements, under certain circumstances exercising direct controls over pricing, hiring, and capital investment policies, and sometimes exerting some degree of intervention in the international operations of business. Monopoly policy, moreover, must not be separated from general public policy objectives directed at inflation control, maintaining full employment, and encouraging economic growth. Some people will argue that this external imposition of social objectives on the private sector is pure socialism, but they miss the point.

### Social Control Is Not Socialism

Pragmatic social control of big business is not the same as social ownership. Corporate ownership today is widely dispersed and far removed from the day-to-day management decisions of American business. Excessive concern over *who* owns the productive property only clouds the important business and public issues at stake. *How* the privately owned property is performing is the really important question. Even though privately owned, most large businesses are already social institutions with social responsibilities. To put the point simply, GM, or even Microsoft, does not have the right to fail any more than they have the right to conspire against the public. To demand social responsibility is perfectly consistent with the real-world structure of business and the economy, and it does not challenge private ownership in any serious way.

Businesses, moreover, are more responsive in the area of social responsibility than is generally understood. Social concern on their part is not purely altruism but good business. Flagrant monopolistic behavior invites government scrutiny and public outrage. The old era of "the public be damned" is past. Few firms, whatever their size and market power, want long and costly antitrust litigation. Even consumer boycotts and public pressure for legislative intervention are sizable threats and induce thoughtful constraint. Moreover, there is significant pressure within the business community to police itself. Abuse of economic power disrupts markets and creates economic instability; this situation, while perhaps favorable to one or a few firms, interferes with general business activity. Social responsibility, finally, is not an ethical question but a matter of profit and loss.

These points should not be misunderstood. The Liberal fully understands that big business may indeed be a threat in its pricing, labor, international, and other policies. But big business does not *have* to be a threat to the economic system. It can be brought under social control.

Public policy toward big business, then, remains a matter of directing private enterprise toward social objectives that include reasonable prices, efficiency, high employment, and adequate profit return while also taking into consideration such broad concerns as ecology, resource conservation, and the overall performance of the economy. The creation of such a policy must be the responsibility of an enlightened federal government. Government must act as an unbiased umpire, attempting always to balance the diverse economic and social interests of the nation. Such intervention need not abridge basic property rights (which is what Radicals want). But it would set social priorities above the pursuit of selfish individualistic goals (so feverishly defended by Conservatives).

## THE RADICAL ARGUMENT

One of the great evasions of economic theory is its idealized portrayal of competition as a process devoid of conflict, power, and politics. Indeed, the existence of *any* market power is defined strictly in technical terms: If market prices are observed to be above marginal cost, then actual competition is falling short of its standard of perfect competition. Microeconomic theory aside, it is well understood by citizens and CEOs alike that the tendency for businesses to become both more centralized in control and concentrated in sales and assets is, and has been, a persistent outcome of capitalist competition. Today, large corporations dominate most markets, and it is through their control of economic resources that they can command such a disproportionate and deleterious impact on American society. While both Conservatives and Liberals oppose monopoly power, neither group wants to recognize that political power has become concentrated in a relatively small capitalist class that now seeks to dominate the political process through its unchallenged economic power.

All mainstream economic theory is loath to recognize not only that firms seek to grow but that their objective is to dominate both a particular industry and the economy and greater society as well. To achieve these goals, it is crucial that a firm have the strength to impose its own price on the market in order to increase its profits. To do this, a business must have the capacity and power to engage in price gouging as well as sustain a ruinous price war. Competition cannot be managed, democratized, or negotiated—corporations are fundamentally authoritarian organizations driven by the imperatives of growth and profitability. Thus, the Radical position can be easily distinguished by its understanding of a relatively simple business strategy that *all* capitalist firms must obey: Grow or die. Unpalatable as it may be, small firms do not play a major role in the U.S. economy and also tend not to persist. Either they evolve into large units of production and distribution (whatever the product) or they are eliminated. In the final analysis, if the state truly wants to tame and manage big business, it has to change the terms and conditions under which large firms exist and operate.

### Monopoly Capitalism: What Went Wrong?

Prior to the late 1970s, most economists—including many Radicals—believed that capitalism had entered a new stage where the cutthroat, predatory price competition that characterized the nineteenth-century economy would no longer be appropriate for large modern corporations. The new post–World War II era of *monopoly capitalism* was one where profitability would be ensured by collusive or monopoly pricing arrangements. Because there was little micro or macro evidence of persistent price declines, economists of all stripes had come to believe that firms no longer competed on the basis of price. Furthermore, though economists were loath to acknowledge it, an uneasy but workable arrangement between management and workers prevailed: Labor would subordinate its demands for higher wages and benefits if capital allowed living standards to rise. Indeed, inflation-adjusted income for workers generally rose from about 1950 to 1973, largely due to labor's ability to impose its demands upon capital through unions and political organizing. However, in the early 1970s most of these gains were reversed. The average real wage peaked in 1973 at about $14 per hour and has failed to recover to that level after nearly thirty years. Workers in capital-intensive manufacturing industries were especially hard hit as capitalists shifted production overseas or invested in more profitable, nonindustrial sectors. By the 1990s, so-called white-collar occupations that were thought immune to economic adversity were now facing layoffs, downsizing, and widespread job insecurity. What went wrong? Why could monopoly capital not maintain its pricing power and guarantee high levels of production and employment?

For one thing, by the early 1980s the political consensus that had held the economy together was over. Deregulation and globalization created a dog-eat-dog economy with rampant job insecurity and declining living standards for the vast majority of wage earners. These reactionary policies were actually initiated by Democratic president Jimmy Carter but were fully unleashed under the Reagan administration. While workers bore the brunt of these reactionary policies, there was a battle being fought within the capitalist class. First, industrial capitalists who had become complacent with their dominant market positions were quickly supplanted by nimbler and more efficient foreign competitors. This was partly the result of years of underinvestment and managerial incompetence and arrogance, but it also reflected the end of unchallenged military and economic dominance by the United States.

A second problem faced by capitalists was how to tame the unprecedented inflation that gripped the U.S. economy from about 1968 through the mid-1980s. Financial capital sought to reestablish profitability in their industries by breaking the back of persistent price increases and inflationary expectations. Once again, Jimmy Carter—a liberal Democratic president—rescued financial capital by appointing a conservative banker, Paul Volcker, to head the Federal Reserve Board. Volcker's high-interest-rate policies, combined with rampant deregulation of financial markets, brought about a decisive victory for the financial sector. Smoke-stack industries such as autos, steel, and heavy manufacturing could not survive the simultaneous onslaught of a stagnating economy, widespread inflation, foreign competition, and disaccumulation. The subsequent period of deindustrialization and disinflation that destroyed the indus-trial heartland set the stage for what has turned out to be the greatest increase in the value of paper assets in U.S. history.

### Persistent Concentration, Persistent Competition

If firms have little choice but to grow or die, it should come as no surprise that success in the marketplace necessarily entails having a large scale of production and sizable market share. Growth, however, can be achieved in any number of ways, such as by increasing sales or by gobbling up a competitor. Since 1998, businesses have spent an astounding $12.2 trillion either to merge with or to acquire other firms. While capitalists and their apologists claim that combinations serve to cleanse the system of inefficient producers, in actuality much of this money will be used to transfer ownership from one capitalist to another. For workers, mergers and acquisitions typically result in plant closings and layoffs rather than new investment in factories and technologies. Even Microsoft announced in 2004 that it expects to cut $1 billion in expenses, especially in employee health care costs and benefits over the next year. In recent years, deregulation and global competition have undermined the largest firms' traditional strategies of price fixing and production limits in their efforts to ensure profitability. Nevertheless, large multinational corporations now seek to acquire both resources and their competitors in order to better withstand the increasingly dy-namic and turbulent competitive environment. Earning high rates of return has become dependent on access to large pools of financial, technological, and human resources.

To gain some perspective on the degree of centralization in the Ameri-can economy, let us examine Table 4.1, which shows the number of firms and sales receipts in the major sectors of the American economy with assets of at least $250 million (based on corporate federal income tax returns). It is clear that the distribution of receipts is profoundly unequal across sectors. In almost every sector, less than 1 percent of the

Table 4.1

**Corporations with $250 Million or More of Assets in 2000**

|  | Number (tax returns) | Receipts (millions of dollars) | Percentage of industry's firms | Percentage of industry's receipts | Percentage of total receipts |
|---|---|---|---|---|---|
| Agriculture, forestry, and fishing | 19 | 8,764 | 0.01 | 7.48 | 0.07 |
| Mining | 161 | 111,505 | 0.49 | 70.30 | 0.89 |
| Construction | 137 | 151,642 | 0.02 | 14.42 | 1.21 |
| Manufacturing | 1,595 | 4,371,728 | 0.55 | 76.15 | 34.93 |
| Transportation and warehousing | 124 | 300,790 | 0.08 | 57.06 | 2.40 |
| Utilities | 158 | 720,404 | 1.98 | 95.19 | 5.76 |
| Wholesale and retail trade | 714 | 2,324,349 | 0.07 | 43.07 | 18.57 |
| Finance, insurance, and real estate | 5,773 | 2,563,781 | 0.77 | 81.37 | 20.49 |
| Information | 479 | 780,284 | 0.41 | 80.68 | 6.23 |
| Management of companies and enterprises | 1,170 | 650,184 | 2.46 | 93.76 | 5.20 |
| Totals | 10,883 | 12,514,715 | 0.22 | 60.74 | 100.00 |

*Source:* U.S. Bureau of the Census, *Statistical Abstract of the United States*, table no. 741 (Washington, DC: Government Printing Office, 2003), 501.

firms garner more than three quarters of all receipts; for utilities and management companies and enterprises, less than 3 percent of firms control well over 90 percent of industry sales. Overall, about 0.22 percent of all firms took in almost 61 percent of the 12.5 trillion in total receipts in 2000.

As mergers and acquisitions continue and concentration of sales and assets in many industries increases, large corporations will attempt to reassert their power in the market by using a variety of strategy and tactics. Rather than being a new era of manageable capitalism, we have returned to the nineteenth century, where unbridled competition wreaks havoc on anyone who works for a living. Reducing the labor content in each unit of output is the dominant objective in the internationalization of production. For example, multinational clothing manufacturers and retailers are able to achieve incredible profits by paying their overseas workers 50 cents per hour while simultaneously charging so-called competitive prices—between $20 and $100—for a pair of jeans or sneakers sold in the U.S. market. Meanwhile, the overseas workers toil under oppressive working conditions that would be illegal under U.S. labor law. Nike, Gap, and Disney have become unconscionably profitable by producing and pricing their products in this manner.

Domestic service industries are also trying to significantly reduce wage costs while seeking to grow through the development, acquisition, and consolidation of integrated delivery networks. Because it is more difficult to use foreign cheap labor in the production of services (e.g., a haircut or a heart transplant), capitalists employ a different but equally effective strategy. Initially, the goal is to quickly gain market share by offering a service well below the actual cost of production. Low prices in turn generate significant volume growth as the customer base rapidly expands. Managed health care companies, airlines, cable television, and online computer service providers have been singularly successful in pursuing this type of strategy. Once market dominance is achieved in a region, prices can be increased with little retaliation from either competitors or the government. In fact, all of these industries are subject to some form of regulatory oversight; yet there is little political will to control predatory market conduct for fear of losing valuable campaign contributions from corporate donors. What's more, the Justice Department has shown little interest in prosecuting corporations for unfair pricing policies. The relatively low inflation rates of the 1990s have also helped to shield large corporations from scrutiny of their pricing power. Nevertheless, it is quite evident that competition both within and between industries will intensify, which surely will lead to lower wages and benefits while capital acts to consolidate its position and seek to create conditions where it can continue to dominate the American economy.

### Big Capital and Politics: Change the Rules

As concentration and centralization grow and industries invade each other's territory, corporations will not only use the political system to repress worker demands, but, more important, will use legal and governmental authority to gain competitive advantages. Historically, big business has always maintained legions of lobbying organizations to press their demands before legislators. While it is difficult for big business to win at the ballot box, it has had little problem in getting politicians to create fiscal and regulatory policies that are favorable to its

interests. The rash of scandals related to campaign finance irregulari-
ties involved many large corporations seeking preferential treatment
and/or governmental contracts. Moreover, the $350 billion settlement
with the tobacco industry and the $100 million penalty paid by Archer
Daniels Midland indicate the scale and depth of capital's resources to
withstand any pressure from the state. Campaign contributions continue to be an extremely cost-effective method for businesses to obtain
favors, preferential tax treatments, contracts, and a host of other benefits from the government. As voters become increasingly dissatisfied
with the political process, corporations will wield greater power over
federal and state legislatures.

The solution to the seemingly unstoppable power of big business does
not lie within the framework of conventional economic analysis and
policy. While worker control over investment, production, and employment is the only long-term solution to rein in big business, in the short
run more specific measures are required. In particular, what is needed is
a strategy to undercut corporate power by changing the legal status of
corporations so they lose their privileges of unlimited longevity, due
process, and limited liability granted to them under federal and state
laws. Historically, courts have ruled that corporations are "individuals,"
entitled to all the rights and protections guaranteed under the U.S. Con-
stitution. Following the Reconstruction Era (1865–70), corporations
shrewdly used the due process clause of the Fourteenth Amendment
(ratified by the states in 1868) to overturn limitations placed upon them
by state governments. Rulings by state regulatory agencies and legislatures were continually overturned by the federal courts, which in effect
defended the rapacity of nineteenth-century robber barons by arguing
that state controls deprived a corporation of property without due process. While some states fought to limit corporate power, other states
(such as Delaware) actively courted corporations by exempting them
from taxes and granting them perpetual charters.

Limiting longevity and the ability to transfer risk will significantly
curtail the capacity of a corporation to grow and achieve market dominance. Corporate managers will be very wary of undertaking illegal actions since their liabilities will not be limited to their equity holdings.
While Karl Marx forcefully argued that capital would never accede anything to labor without a fight, he also recognized that capitalism depends upon specific juridical and legal institutions, especially property
rights. Changing the legal status of a corporation would be a strategy

both bold and politically practical, with a realistic chance of limiting the power of big capital. However, changing the status of corporations will not be sufficient to change the economic and social relations between labor and capital. As competition further winnows the ever-shrinking number of large firms and democracy withers under the oppression of a tiny number of megacorporations, it will become evident to all citizens that social control and ownership of the economy's asset base is the only viable solution. Planning by and for the needs of all citizens—not corporate planning—will become central to ensuring and fulfilling the political economic ideals of American society.

# Economic Regulation

## Which Path: Deregulation or Reregulation?

The committee has found among the leading representatives of the railroad interests an increasing readiness to accept the aid of Congress in working out the solution of the railroad problem which has obstinately baffled all their efforts, and not a few of the ablest railroad men of the country seem disposed to look to the intervention of Congress as promising to afford the best means of ultimately securing a more equitable and satisfactory adjustment of the relations of the transportation interests to the community than they themselves have been able to bring about.

*—U.S. Senate Select Committee*
*on Interstate Commerce, 1886*

Railroads were totally regulated for almost a century. Obviously it will take time for railroads to learn all of the things that can be done in a freer climate. It will also take shippers time to learn this as well. But already it is apparent that both can use deregulation to their respective advantages.

*—Association of American Railroads, 1982*

No reasonable person will lament the passing of the Interstate Commerce Commission.

*—George Will, ABC News commentator, 1996*

Since WorldCom's public announcement on June 25, 2002 that the company misstated its earnings for 2001 and the first quarter of 2002, there's been an understandable outpouring of anger from every quarter of American society. While the misdeeds we uncovered occurred before I became CEO, I want to apologize on behalf of everyone at WorldCom. And I want to underscore that WorldCom's new management team—and our more than 60,000 employees—share the public's outrage over these events.

*—John Sidgmore*
*President and CEO of WorldCom, 2002*

Despite the major financial collapses and growing evidence of market failure, the critics of regulation steadfastly maintain their commitment to the goal of free markets and their resistance to economic regulation.

*—Harry M. Trebing*
*public utilities regulation economist, 2004*

## The Problem

Public policy with respect to the operations of American business enterprise traditionally has rested upon two very different strategies: antitrust law and economic regulation. The objective of antitrust law and its enforcement, as discussed in Issue 4, is to maintain an acceptable degree of competition in most markets. The second type of government intervention in the structure and performance of markets rests on the assumption that certain markets perform best under less-than-competitive conditions, which are strictly regulated by government agencies. In these regulated industries, a kind of "monopoly bargain" is struck whereby one firm, or at most a few, is granted various protections from competition in return for surrendering to a regulatory agency power over pricing, output, and other production, financing, and marketing decisions.

The most common example of a regulated industry and a regulatory agency has been a regional public utility (a gas and electric company or a regional phone company) regulated by a state public service commission. Historically, the concept of public regulation has been applied much more broadly than just to public utilities. The first federal venture into direct regulation came with the Interstate Commerce Commission (ICC) in 1887 (three years before federal antitrust law was laid down in the Sherman Antitrust Act). The ICC was charged with restoring order to the nation's ailing railroads, an industry long characterized on one hand by periodic episodes of financial collapse resulting from vicious rate wars and on the other by the very worst type of monopolistic practices. Over the next century, more than a dozen independent federal agencies and commissions were erected to bring a measure of government regulation to everything from banking to the airwaves to nuclear power.

The logic of insulating certain industries from the forces of the market rested on two economic considerations: (1) that there existed the economic advantages of lower costs (*economies of scale*) resulting from a single producer or a limited number of producers and (2) that a discernible *public interest* would be served by exempting the industry from competition and by establishing government regulation of price, service, and output. As the years passed, these two criteria were stretched, modified, and sometimes neglected altogether as the extent of government regulation expanded in many directions. The idea of "regulating private industry in the public interest" was a peculiarly American experiment. Elsewhere in the world, state ownership has been the preferred technique for dealing with public interest questions. In the course of European economic development, postal services, railways, telecommunications, and electric and gas utilities were generally state owned. In the United States, the postal service is the only industry ever entirely owned and operated "in the public interest."

For most of the past century, industrial regulation enjoyed a high degree of public support, with most practicing economists nodding their approval at the work of regulatory agencies. The regulatory high-water mark was reached in the early 1970s. However, in the economy of the late 1970s, troubled by inflation, recession, unemployment, energy crises, and growing federal budgetary problems, regulatory activity was placed under greater scrutiny.

Most Liberals, who had long been supporters of the "regulation in the public interest" philosophy, defended the practice. Conservatives, sensing the direction of a new ideological wind that was blowing, were quick to attack federal regulation of industry. Never strong supporters of regulatory efforts, most Conservatives identified the regulatory link as among the weakest in the chain of Liberal interventionism in the economy. Their attack was direct enough: Regulation produces greater costs to society through creating and maintaining market inefficiency than any benefits it might provide for the public interest. By the mid-1970s, a new buzzword had entered academic and political discussions of the regulatory process: *deregulation.*

Beginning in 1978, the deregulators (which now included a fair number of Liberals as well as most Conservatives) began a campaign that succeeded in eliminating most regulation of airlines, buses, trucking, radio broadcasting, and natural gas and electric power production and distribution. Considerable relaxation occurred in the regulation of railroads, television and cable broadcasting, and banking and financial services. Meanwhile, the splitting up of the Bell telephone system in 1984 as the result of federal antitrust action opened much of the previously highly regulated phone system to market competition. The deregulatory mood spread during the Reagan presidency to a variety of government agencies charged with overseeing broad areas of social regulation, such as the Department of Consumer Affairs and the Federal Trade Commission.

The deregulation movement lost some momentum when the financial shock of a 500-point decline in the stock market on October 19, 1987, brought forth calls for greater regulation of the securities market by the federal government. This shock was followed quickly by a monumental solvency crisis in the savings and loan industry that seemed to be the direct outcome of excessive deregulation of banking institutions. In the airlines industry, formerly hailed by antiregulation advocates as the model for successful deregulation, the initial consumer benefits of increased competition and lower fares seemed to be ebbing in favor of greater monopoly power and higher prices. At the same time, deregulation of the television industry seemed to be pointing toward a decline of over-the-airwaves television and the potential loss of a long-held American "right," that of free television programming. Such developments began to generate second thoughts about deregulation.

Yet if there were serious second thoughts about deregulation, they did not produce a marked redirection of public policy. The Interstate Commerce Commission Termination Act of 1995 eliminated the ICC. Regulatory functions were scaled back and transferred to the Department of Transportation's newly created Surface Transportation Board (STB).

New technologies in the form of broadband Internet access through cable, power lines, and wireless fidelity (Wi-Fi), and cellular phones posed new competition for conventional telecommunications providers. It is now feasible to sidestep old-fashioned hardwired telephones by using wireless communications and the alternative of voice-over-internet to complete phone calls. The forward progress of technology is an invitation for local phone service to join long distance as deregulated, but public policy has not yet caught up with technology.

The long economic boom of the 1990s also helped stifle doubts over deregulation: Good times rarely author policy redirections. However, by the summer of 2001, Californians and many other Americans braced themselves against rolling blackouts and rising electricity and natural gas prices in the new deregulated public utility environment. A huge failure of the electrical power grid in the Northeast and Midwest in the summer of 2003 led people to ponder the notion that more government regulation and intervention was needed, not less, to ensure public health, safety, and convenience. Conventional industry regulation was about to intersect with the regulation of both the financial sector of the economy and the accounting profession. The physical failure to deliver electricity was paralleled by the high-profile bankruptcy of the Enron energy corporation in 2001. Defects in the deregulation of electricity markets, relaxed accounting oversight, and apparent criminal activity had contributed to the second largest bankruptcy in U.S. history, rivaled only by the debacle surrounding telecommunications and Internet giant WorldCom in 2002.

WorldCom's operational problems were disguised by improper accounting. The result was the largest bankruptcy in U.S. history, dragging down the market value of the telecommunications sector across the board. Asset values plummeted, telecom bankruptcies rose, retirement accounts were decimated, and many jobs in the industry were wiped out. Much of the blame was laid at the doorstep of corporate governance and flawed regulatory oversight of the accounting profession. The response was the Public Company Accounting Reform and Investor Protection (Sarbanes-Oxley) Act of 2002. The act established the Public Company Accounting Oversight Board to better regulate auditors of public companies and required new Securities and Exchange Commission rules demanding that chief executive officers and chief financial officers of public companies "certify" the truthfulness and accuracy of financial reports. Clearly, the deregulation debate is not yet over.

### Synopsis

Conservatives argue that regulation is counterproductive, producing more costs than benefits to both the regulated industries and the public. Accordingly, they support the drift to deregulation and advocate more. The Liberal argument defends the general performance record of most regulated industries and maintains that many recent experiments in deregulation are dangerous to the economy. Radicals see the historical development of regulation as essentially a prop to monopoly privilege and recent deregulation efforts as merely a smokescreen for doing away with what business now considers the less attractive aspects of serving the public interest.

---

### Anticipating the Arguments

- What are some of the counterproductive results of regulation that Conservatives see, and how would their plan for deregulation end such problems?
- On what grounds do Liberals defend at least limited regulation over complete deregulation?
- Why do Radicals reject regulation and instead call for public ownership and operation of previously regulated industries?

### THE CONSERVATIVE ARGUMENT

The Conservative position on regulation is based on two sturdy and now familiar principles. First, regulation—or any interference with the market—tends to create resource misallocation, inefficiency, and, ulti-

greater costs to the community. Second, left alone, the market is capable of more rational decisions about the success or survival of a firm or industry than is the voting public or its representatives and bureaucrats.

## The Failure of Regulation

Except for the very limited and infrequent situations where a *natural monopoly* exists, there are no justifiable conditions for regulating industry. A natural monopolist, such as a local supplier of electric power, enjoys the advantages of large-scale distribution that can provide all of a market's output at lower unit costs than could exist if there were a number of power distributors. In such a situation, the community can obtain the lower costs only if it restrains the monopolists' natural propensity to maximize profits by setting prices at whatever the market will bear. The problem with the American application of this regulation principle, however, is that regulation has mostly been applied in situations where some degree of competition actually exists or where competition should be encouraged. The result has been that the community gets a regulated monopoly or a tight oligopoly when it would have been better served by creating and maintaining competitive conditions. Even the regulation of so-called natural monopolies has had its problems because of inefficient rulings on pricing and service by the regulatory agency, usually in the name of protecting the public interest.

Recounting the experience with the first effort at using an independent regulatory agency to supervise an industry—the ICC—is instructive. As the oldest U.S. regulatory agency, the ICC accumulated the longest list of classic regulatory errors and is a good example of all the debilitating effects age brings to commission activity. Its goal was to protect the public from railroad price collusion and to protect the railroads from one another. By the mid-1930s, ICC power extended to all surface commercial transportation in the country: rail, trucking, and barges. Specific ICC controls covered rate setting, mergers, financial issues, abandonment, and service discontinuance, as well as carrier layoffs of labor. There was virtually nothing that a rail carrier or any other carrier regulated by the Interstate Commerce Commission could do without first obtaining commission approval.

The ICC followed a narrow, two-sided strategy: first, to maintain a competitive balance between and among the different modes (trucks and railroads) of surface transportation that provided each carrier with an adequate return on its investment, and second, to provide a level of service that would accommodate broad public interest objectives and to do so at a cost that also served those objectives.

In misguided efforts to maintain competition among different transportation modes, the ICC long followed the strategy of *umbrella ratemaking,* a practice of setting a rate high enough to allow less efficient modes of transport to earn a profit on specific services. This provided a special handicap to railroads, which lost traffic to other modes simply because they were not allowed to set lower rates (prices) and use their greater efficiency in the movement of certain goods. In protecting trucks and water carriers, the ICC directed business away from the more efficient railroads. At the same time, shippers and consumers absorbed higher-than-necessary transport charges in their purchases.

Similar anticompetitive outcomes resulted from the ICC's opposition to rail mergers. This led to costly balkanization. The line-haul railroads were unable to combine to increase freight exchange and coordination and to strengthen their financial structures. By denying the industry access to these economies of scale, service remained expensive and inefficient. The ICC also prohibited intermodal mergers: Railroads were not allowed to consolidate with trucks and other carriers to improve their overall efficiency.

Meanwhile, in search of the will-o'-the-wisp "public interest," the ICC also acted to raise transport costs and reduce rail efficiency by maintaining redundant routes and little-used spurs. Permission to abandon low-density or loss-producing operations was difficult to obtain from the commission, and railroads were compelled to pour millions of dollars into expensive routes that generated only a few dollars in traffic.

By prohibiting railroads from setting their rates freely, denying them the right to develop joint rail-truck transportation companies, and demanding that they continue to operate costly and inefficient services and schedules, the ICC rendered the railroads' competitive situation virtually hopeless. ICC decisions on rates, abandonments, and mergers were presented as proof of the agency's commitment to the public interest. In point of fact, its action harmed rather than protected the nation's welfare.

The general ICC strategy was applied by other regulatory agencies with not much better success. Whether we look at railroads, airlines, long-distance telecommunications, broadcasting, trucking, or banking, we see the same dismal results from the era of public regulation. First, regulation encouraged cartel pricing. This usually meant setting a price floor that was high enough to allow the least efficient member of the cartel to survive. The industry price was usually higher than the price that would have existed under competitive conditions. Second, in the absence of any effective price competition in the industry, competition could only emerge in nonprice areas. Banks emphasized "special services." Airlines promoted themselves as "friendlier" or as offering more sumptuous in-flight meals. Few regulated firms were likely to introduce new services that produced real benefits or savings to customers. New ways of doing business were always seen as posing elements of risk and instability that neither the regulated industry nor the regulators wanted. Meanwhile, new investment and modernization lagged in regulated industries. Third, industries in a regulated cartel developed a special inertia at the management level. In fact, as deregulation became an increasingly popular idea in the 1970s and 1980s, many of its strongest opponents were the very industries that were to be deregulated.

### The Market Alternative

Efforts to introduce a market alternative to regulation have posed and will continue to pose special problems. Not only are government bureaucrats unwilling to destroy their own jobs, but a number of regulated firms and many of their customers have also shown some fear of living in a free marketplace. What, in fact, can unregulated markets do better than regulated ones?

The first advantage the consuming public usually enjoys is falling prices. Except in cases where certain consumers experienced benefits from price discrimination, competitive market prices will be lower than those established for regulated cartels. Airline passengers, for instance, have learned to enjoy these benefits on long-distance routes since the start of the 1980s. However, some short-distance (and very high-cost) flights have gone up in price to reflect real rather than administered pricing conditions. Meanwhile, the downward pressure on prices caused by competition among existing firms and the entry of new firms into the market (limited if not impossible under regulated conditions) will compel enterprises to improve operating efficiency. This will spark new investment among firms that are vital and capable enough to undertake the outlays; it will also act as euthanasia for firms and industries that are inherently inefficient or historically outmoded. With market profitability now directing resource usage, the application of labor and capital in production operations will require efficient resource allocation. The artificial wages and job protections unions possessed in certain industries such as railroads and airlines will, of course, come to an end.

Meanwhile, bad business habits and indefensibly uneconomical managerial activities will cease under competitive operations. The old regulated industry mentality of avoiding anything that smacks of newness will have to be replaced by a more innovative and entrepreneurial managerial philosophy. The habit of counting on the regulatory agency or the government to bail out financially troubled firms through rate increases or direct subsidies, such as the rail industry long enjoyed, will end.

Under regulation, price discrimination was common. Usually referred to as *cross subsidization,* it appeared whenever certain customers were, with regulatory encouragement, charged considerably in excess of costs for the same service that other customers received at less than cost. In the telephone industry, before the AT&T breakup, cross subsidies existed when long-distance charges were artificially inflated to underwrite losses on local service. The result was to discriminate against business customers primarily and in favor of most residential phone users. In this case, deregulation has meant higher prices for residential phone users (but lower prices for all long-distance users). As with airline pricing, ending cross subsidies produces winners and losers. Only the shortsighted will oppose ending official price discrimination, for unless actual costs are the major determinant of rates and prices, we are employing a pricing system that is inefficient *and* unfair.

Finally, of course, a market-directed system explodes the fiction of the public interest. The notion that some bureaucratic authority can determine a transcendent public interest and then act to implement it belongs more to the realm of metaphysics than to that of sensible economic reasoning. To return to our earlier discussion of the ICC and America's railroads, we might speculate that, left to the dictates of a free market (and without an ICC), a national transportation mix might have emerged that would have allowed each transport mode to develop its inherent strengths. Instead of the artificial competition created "in the public interest" that pitted trucks and railroads against each other but provided no way of determining their relative efficiency, each form of transportation could have exploited its own advantages, dropping out of markets where it had none. The market is indeed the best determinant of the public's best interests.

## Evaluating Deregulation to Date

The final test for the effectiveness of deregulation is not logic but actual performance, and here deregulation has proved an important spur to the American economy. A look at the record should be convincing enough.

The Airline Deregulation Act of 1978 was the first important effort to dismantle a regulated cartel and return it to competition. Under this law, air carriers were granted greater ratemaking freedom and greater freedom of entry and exit from airline markets. Accordingly, the Civil Aeronautics Board (CAB) (which went out of business in early 1985, the first major regulatory agency so abolished) allowed airlines to fly on a "first come, first served" basis to most American cities. The action ended the old, inefficient practice of granting virtual monopoly power to certain carriers over certain routes. As a result, dozens of existing companies altered their routes (both expanding and contracting service on specific routes). At the same time, more than a score of brand-new long-distance carriers suddenly appeared. Meanwhile, the market, rather than the CAB, was allowed to determine most airline rates. The new approach brought most long-distance airfares down. Loss-producing routes were abandoned to new specialized commuter lines, or fares were adjusted upward by the larger carriers to reflect real operating costs. The new market freedom allowed the airlines to price and operate according to actual supply-and-demand conditions and permitted passengers to enjoy the price benefits of competition.

Two years after the deregulation of the airlines, the Motor Carrier Act of 1980 brought gradual deregulation to the trucking industry (regulated by the ICC since 1930). Again the approach was the same: to allow greater freedom in ratemaking by individual truckers and the easing of entry restrictions into long-haul, interstate trucking. The benefits to the public came quickly. More than 5,200 new trucking firms entered the industry in the first eighteen months of deregulation; 20,000 new route applications were filed with the ICC; and average freight bills went down 10 to 20 percent.

In 1980, the Staggers Rail Act gave railroads some relief from ICC control. In particular, they were freed to make most rate changes without prior ICC approval and were given permission to contract directly with shippers at less-than-market rates for long-term, bulk shipments. Previously, approval for rate changes had cost the railroads up to $1 billion a year as the ICC delayed adjusting rates for inflation, and special shipper-railroad contracts had been held to be an illegal form of rebating. The Surface Transportation Board has calculated that rail rates (adjusted for inflation) fell by more than 45 percent from 1984 to 1999, and this resulted in annual savings to consumers in 1999 of $31.7 billion.*

The gains from deregulation have not been limited to transportation. The deregulation of long-distance telecommunications has produced consumer savings and a more vibrant industry. In banking and finance, most restrictions have been lifted on branch banking, bank mergers, and overseas banking operations. There is more freedom to offer greater variety of financial options to customers. The elimination of artificial limits on the operations and functions of banks and other financial institutions has promoted increased competition among commercial banks, thrifts, credit unions, brokerage firms, and insurance companies in funds markets, raising investor earnings possibilities and lowering customer charges.

Those interested in *reregulation* will doubtless cite the recent California public power crisis as evidence that deregulation does not work. Likewise, blackouts caused by unreliable power transmission are erroneously blamed on deregulation or the absence of other forms of government intrusion. According to their view, California's experiment with partial deregulation of energy prices (the separating of power generation from public utility distribution and the introduction of free market conditions in the pricing of wholesale purchases of natural gas and electric power) led to the state's energy shortage *and* to the bankrupting of the public utility deliverance of gas and electricity. It is true, of course, that the wholesale prices of gas and electricity rose after partial deregulation. *They had to.* California (like other regulated states) had for too long maintained artificially low wholesale prices under its regulated system. This was done so consumers could pay below-market retail prices. But a low return on energy supplies (even when these supplies were owned by the public utilities themselves or by the State of California) discouraged the development of new sources of supply precisely as the artificially low cost to consumers pumped up the demand for energy. Long before deregulation of energy supplies took place, California was headed for a train wreck—one caused by the regulators themselves.

* "Rail Rates Continue Multi-Year Decline," Office of Economics, Environmental Analysis and Administration, Surface Transportation Board (December 2000).

To argue that California's rolling blackouts and rising consumer prices were the result of price gouging by suppliers is simply not true. The price of energy had to go up one way or another. There can be no free lunch. Either California taxpayers would pay (to build state-operated or subsidized power sources) to close the gap between fixed, below-market prices and rising wholesale energy costs or, sooner or later, California consumers would have to pay. In any event, while deregulation of wholesale energy prices in California will lead to somewhat higher retail prices, higher rates will also invite more suppliers into the energy market. In the long run, prices will settle in at an acceptable level *and* California will no longer face the energy deficit that regulation forced upon the state.

Regulation and reregulation advocates continue to stake out policy positions that retard the development of new markets, curtail benefits to consumers, and extend the monopoly power of regulated firms. For example, innovations in wireless and Internet communications really obviate the need for rate regulation of wire-based telecommunications, but the Federal Communications Commission continues to regulate pricing policies and attempts to manage competition among different modes.

Those who now see certain shortcomings with deregulation forget that the gains of market-directed economic activities are not possible without occasional risks. Avoiding such risks through regulation may produce a desired orderliness, but only at an exceptionally high cost. Overall, the economic costs of regulation impose a much greater burden on society than any risks associated with market competition.

## THE LIBERAL ARGUMENT

Regulatory agencies are the logical outcome of the need to improve market conditions in certain industries. Direct regulation is not essential to all markets, but in certain cases—mainly where natural monopolies tend to develop or should be encouraged—regulation by government agencies can maximize the benefits to both the consumer and the affected industry. Antitrust action, as we have discussed, is employed in cases of conspiracy to attain a socially undesirable monopoly advantage in the market, but direct regulation is a ratification of monopoly power. In exchange for this recognized monopoly position, a firm submits to close political and economic supervision.

## The Rules of Regulation

Under regulation, business firms are guaranteed certain rights. For example, their property rights are legally protected, and confiscation is not a serious possibility. They are entitled to receive reasonable prices and a fair rate of return on their capital. In the specific geographic area in which it operates, a regulated firm is given partial or total protection from competition. A firm can challenge in the courts any regulatory decision made by the relevant commission.

Regulated firms also have certain obligations. Their prices and profits must not be excessive. Prices should be established that offer the greatest possible service without compelling a company to forfeit its capital through continuous losses. Moreover, the regulated firm must meet all demand at the established prices. Any change in the quantity or quality of service must be approved in advance by the regulatory agency. The final decision in such cases as petitions for abandonment of service must balance two conflicting objectives: the firm's operational benefits and the public interest. Finally, all regulated industries must be committed to high levels of performance with the highest possible standards of safety to the public. The key to regulation philosophy, developed over ten decades of experience and through sixteen independent agencies, is this: a balance of public and private (corporate) interests.

## The Public Interest Revisited

The deafening roar of the Conservative crowd cheering on the recent drift toward deregulation has drowned out reason. While theoretical arguments are developed with considerable elegance to "prove" that regulation does not work and that a return to market competition for previously regulated industries would improve economic efficiency and well-being, the real issue has been papered over. What we have forgotten in our rush toward deregulation is to ask ourselves why Americans introduced the regulatory experiment in the first place. Surely regulation did not just happen accidentally. What, then, were its antecedents? It began with the long-held view that certain public interest objectives could never be well served in unregulated markets.

In the current rewriting of American economic history, Conservatives fail to recall that most ventures into regulation by independent regulatory commissions were not simply unconscious evasions of a market-dominated economy. A survey of previously or presently regulated industries shows that regulation evolved only after consistent evidence of market failure under conditions of competition.

The creation of the ICC in 1887 and its development of real regulatory power over the next twenty years came only after the excessive and irrational building of the American railroad network had brought about cutthroat competition that destabilized the industry. Periodically, bloody rate wars would break out among the giants as each tried to gain a larger share of the restricted transportation market. Consequently, there were frequent bankruptcies and breakdowns in service. Because of their critical place in the economy, as railroads went, so went the nation. Every major financial panic and recession after the Civil War—in 1873, 1884, and 1893—started with railroad bankruptcies. Attempts at private rate fixing and cartels, even before the Sherman Antitrust Act established their unconstitutionality, almost always failed. Even so, these expedients harmed farmers and other shippers. This, then, was the situation when the ICC was created. The free market operation of the rail industry could no longer be tolerated. This view was widely held by bankers, farmers, shippers, and railroad management.

Eventually all commercial surface transport enterprises came under ICC jurisdiction. The accretions of power in every case were responses to the failure of competitive market operations in the transport industry. It is important to recognize that elimination of the ICC in 1996 did not *eliminate* surface transportation regulation. Essential regulatory authority was moved to the Surface Transportation Board in practical recognition of the fact that the transportation industry's stability depends on government oversight.

The story was similar elsewhere as public regulation was employed to offset a variety of problems rooted in an overly competitive economic system. The regulation of the airwaves in the 1920s by the FCC made it possible for radio listeners to interpret the chatter coming from radios. Competitive stations had operated without license or assigned frequencies, and the public was ill served. The building of the Federal Reserve System in 1914 (following passage of the Federal Reserve Act of 1913) came after a hundred years of unregulated and chaotic competition. Banks, usually operating with the skimpiest of reserves, showed a dangerous tendency to fall off into periods of panic, which in turn drove the nation into episodes of economic depression. The Securities and Exchange Commission was created in the 1930s after the overzealous actions of securities firms and banks played a central role in the financial collapse of 1929.

The list of regulatory responses to the market failures of a purely free and competitive economy goes on and on. Regulation reflects not a situation where the nation has *not tried* competition, but rather one where it has been tried and found wanting, where the disadvantages of competition have shown themselves to be greater than the community wishes to shoulder. Conservatives attack the concept of regulation in the public interest without admitting that the public was badly served by an unreliable and frequently bankrupt transportation system, by dangerous if not fraudulent banking practices, by unscrupulous investment bankers and brokers, and by an unregulated use of the airwaves. When railroads fail and banks close or when unregulated energy prices close industries and chill homes, the nation is not simply faced with some readjustment of markets but with a threat to its very survival. Accordingly, it has been understood that certain basic sectors of the economy have responsibilities that go beyond private interest, that in fact serve a broader public interest even if they are privately owned. Europeans generally chose to deal with this conflict of interests by nationalizing or operating as public enterprises those industries that had broad public interest responsibilities. Public regulation was a less extreme response to this problem.

Another dimension of the "public interest approach" is the commitment to maintaining *universal service.* Under this philosophy, regulatory agencies frequently employ cross subsidization to ensure that certain customers who might not otherwise have obtained service if charges were based solely on costs do in fact have reasonable service. Essentially, an ability-to-pay principle is applied, with those with greater carrying capacity subsidizing those whose costs are high but capacity to pay is low. So it was that rural rail and trucking services were subsidized by long-distance shippers and that elderly, fixed-income phone users had part of their costs paid by large corporations. To Conservatives, this is price discrimination, pure and simple; however, they make no attempt to explain how society's interests would be better served if small communities atrophy for lack of reasonably priced transportation or if low-income families are left without phone service.

Finally, on behalf of the public interest, it is appropriate for the government to allocate scarce resources. For instance, regulating prices and limiting exploitation of natural resources, with a view toward rationing their use, are appropriate public policy objectives that transcend any narrow profit interests.

To be sure, regulation in the public interest is not without its costs. The costs, however, are not really the alleged costs of inefficiency so frequently cited by Conservatives. They are the costs of creating market stability and equity that would not otherwise exist. Supplying reasonably priced phone service to all users may mean higher costs for some users. A safer banking system costs more to operate than a dangerously weak and speculative one. These costs are more than offset, however, by the long-run gains achieved for the entire society. Deregulation, meanwhile, stresses only the benefit of short-run savings (profits, really) from relaxing our concern for the public interest.

### The Deregulation Balance Sheet

Deregulation as an effective economic policy is now more than a quarter century old. Evidence is abundant enough to make an evaluation, and, contrary to the cheery Conservative assessment, it is not all that supporting.

In the transportation industries, the results are at best mixed. Railroads generally have benefited at the expense of the less efficient trucking competitors and of hundreds of communities that have lost rail service. Accordingly, some shippers—those able to use railroads—have gained, while others have lost. In the airlines industry, the early pricing benefits obtained by consumers under greater competition were quite temporary. Very quickly the opening of new routes and markets was followed by a wave of mergers that reduced the number of competing air carriers and consequently increased monopolistic control over passenger traffic at each of the major hub cities. Characteristically, airfares began to rise and passengers noticed a steady deterioration of service.

Although not the specific result of dismantling a regulatory agency but certainly the outcome of other public policies running in that direction, the breakup of AT&T does not stand out as a shining example of deregulatory success. The ending of cross subsidization translated directly into high and rising phone bills for virtually all residential customers. Meanwhile, the alleged benefits of competitive long-distance service seem lost in the confusion of phone bills and the selecting of one's long-distance carrier. Most average users of the telephone regularly report in opinion surveys that they feel costs have risen and service has declined since the breakup of Ma Bell.

The extent to which deregulation can produce truly catastrophic costs for society is best illustrated by the banking and finance industry. With thrifts (savings and loan associations, mutual savings banks, and credit unions) freed in 1982 to compete with commercial banks and other financial intermediaries, they found themselves compelled to pay fairly high interest rates to attract funds. Indeed, the exceptionally high interest rates of the time would have caused problems regardless of deregulation. However, now freed of earlier restraints that confined the savings and loan activities almost exclusively to mortgage markets, thrifts ventured into high-return—and high-risk—lending. Loans to speculative real estate ventures, solar energy companies, windmill farms, and the like had very high failure rates in the early 1980s. Accordingly, many banks drifted toward and finally into bankruptcy.

With depositors' savings insured, government was obliged to "socialize" the costs of the thrifts' zeal in seeking high-return investments. Some will argue that this was a unique situation, largely the result of government insulating financial institutions from market discipline by insuring their fiduciary responsibilities. However, it does not take an overactive imagination to consider that the socialization of deregulatory costs is not necessarily limited to financial markets. Should conditions resulting from deregulation demand it, government bailouts of airlines, telecommunication companies, public utilities, and the like are not unthinkable.

Of course, some criticisms of regulatory agencies—especially regarding their inflexibility in the face of changed economic and technological conditions and their habit of becoming too cozy with the very firms they regulate—are quite valid. Some regulatory agencies have outlived their usefulness. The passing of the ICC in 1996 was scarcely noticed by anyone. However, regulatory weaknesses are not causes for abandoning regulation altogether. The tumult produced by haphazard deregulation of electrical generation combined with insufficient regulation of the accounting profession resulted in severe disruptions and the largest corporate bankruptcies in history. That recent lesson calls for a reasoned and longer view of deregulation and its effects. Dismantling regulatory machinery has reintroduced the old problems that were the impetus for regulation in the first place. Liberals see little benefit from having to learn again that unregulated capitalism produces serious market failures and imperfections that must sooner or later be offset by government intervention.

## THE RADICAL ARGUMENT

History readily shows that the natural inclination of production-for-profit enterprises is to acquire as much price-making power as possible. Therefore, the long-term outcome of competition is invariably the development of some degree of monopoly power. Yet monopolistic power is not always easily attained. It often requires enlisting the apparatus of the state in its behalf to be effective. Accordingly, public regulatory commissions were organized in the United States to ratify the existence of monopoly. Regardless of the intention of reformers who championed their development, regulatory agencies worked primarily on behalf of the industries they regulated. The creation of independent regulatory agencies and their performance do not support the Liberal claim that public interest is a major element in regulatory action. Neither do they support the Conservative charge that regulation has been antibusiness.

Curiously, however, the deregulation movement also has advanced the objective of creating monopoly—but, of course, not in an obvious way. From a Radical perspective, the oscillations in public policy from free market to regulation to deregulation (and recently) to reregulation are not a cycle at all, as conventional economists suggest, but are variations on the same monopoly capitalist theme. Such an argument will be unfamiliar to many non-Radicals and may initially appear to be contradictory. To make the Radical position a bit clearer, we will examine one regulatory case in considerable detail rather than undertake a broad survey of American regulatory activities. The Interstate Commerce Commission's regulation of surface transportation in the United States is an excellent representative example.

### Regulation as a Creature of Industry: The Case of the ICC

Progressive-era legislative and regulatory actions, rather than being single-minded efforts to find a compromise between parties on either side of a particular market (as the then-current political rhetoric maintained), were really efforts to bring order to highly disrupted and overly competitive markets. But order was achieved on terms that supported the principles of private property and corporate profit seeking, terms that replaced competition with official recognition of limited monopolistic power and cartelization.

The ICC from its very beginning was an attempt to create an official cartel in rail transportation. This policy was steadily enlarged and elaborated on by the industry. Eventually, it also was applied to other modes of public transportation (buses, trucks, water carriers, and pipelines under the ICC and air carriers under the Civil Aeronautics Board). The development of the ICC was not a haphazard abandonment of high principles; it was the unfolding of a planned and rational policy. (It was rational at least in the sense that it consistently pursued clear ends, even though these goals might ultimately result in economic and social loss to the nation.)

Although many economic interests favored the creation of a federal railroad regulatory agency in the late 1880s, one of the most influential groups consisted of railroad leaders themselves. The closing decades of the nineteenth century had witnessed costly rate wars and other competitive difficulties, resulting largely from the enormous excess capacity built into the industry. These conflicts could not be handled through private efforts at cartelization, partly because these efforts usually collapsed of their own enforcement weaknesses and partly because other economic groups challenged such blatant attempts to build monopoly power. The railroads, therefore, turned to the federal government for official sanction of cartel creation. Progress toward this end began with passage of the Interstate Commerce Act of 1887; over the next twenty years, in the ICC and in Congress, railroads obtained important recognition as a cartel. Indeed, the Elkins Act (1903), which ended the hated competitive practice of paying rebates to certain shippers, was written in the legal offices of the Pennsylvania Railroad. The Hepburn Act (1906), which enlarged the ICC's power, supposedly at the expense of the rail monopolies, had considerable management endorsement.

"Community of interest" (informal domination of all rail operations in a region by a few large railroads) and other plans formulated to integrate rail properties for the purpose of gaining greater monopoly power were frustrated for a time, but railroads emerged from World War I, after their ignominious operational collapse and more than two years of government control, with the Esch-Cummins Act of 1920. This law, as interpreted by the ICC and the courts, firmly established the principle of railroad cartelization. The old competitive situation within the industry no longer existed and the rail network was reduced to a limited number of essentially noncompetitive systems. Most state regulatory powers over finance and operations were abolished. The old ambition of industry pooling and rate bureaus was nourished during the Depression. Throughout the disastrous 1930s, the government, at Franklin Roosevelt's insistence, officially recognized the Association of American Railroads as the industrywide policy-making body. It was a powerful lobby and a tool for encouraging collusion within the industry. At the behest of rail leaders, the government moved in 1935 to control competition from the hated trucks and buses by placing them under ICC regulatory control. Finally, with the passage of the Transportation Act of 1940, the federal government officially declared an end to any pretense of maintaining "costly competition," either between railroads or among competing transport modes.

None of these regulatory and legislative successes by the railroads could, however, insulate the industry from competition or the structural and demand dislocations that persistently wreaked havoc with railroad balance sheets through the 1950s and 1960s. The decline was not halted even by the hastily drawn Transportation Act of 1958, which took away the last effective regulatory power of the states over passenger trains, nor by the ICC's growing willingness to approve almost any kind of merger or abandonment. The railroads had succeeded in getting themselves established as a protected cartel. Though they were not totally free to undertake whatever was in their interest, the official commitment to maintaining railroads as a privately owned industry meant that railroad legislation and regulation were loaded in their favor. The industry had to be kept going—on its own terms. For society, this translated into the reduction of rail service and the steady deterioration of service that remained.

### The Deregulation Phenomenon

In many respects, the emergency legislation efforts to deal with the rail crisis in the Northeast corridor reveal the actual content, past and present, of our transportation and regulatory policy. Under the 1976 Railroad Revitalization and Regulatory Reform Act, six bankrupt northeastern railroads were organized into Conrail. Two points are noteworthy in this development. First, Conrail, although federally organized, was to become a private production-for-profit corporation after it had been reconditioned by a massive infusion of government funds and by a ruthless reduction in its trackage. Second, Conrail was devised to rescue the funds of the bankrupt railroads' investors. Although the government's initial estimate of the scrap value of the bankrupt railroads was set at $621 million, the owners claimed their deteriorated rolling stock and rusting rails to be worth at least $7 billion. Under pressure from banks, insurance companies, and other holders of railroad securities, Conrail was initially granted $2.1 billion in federal funds to acquire the nearly worthless financial paper of these railroads. The prospects of monetary gain from Conrail were evident to the investors in the bankrupt lines, many of whom spoke glowingly of government ownership. There was little talk of such actions being socialistic, but economist John Kenneth Galbraith has correctly called it "socialism for the rich."

The Motor Carrier Act of 1980 and the Staggers Rail Act of the same year put the finishing touches on what had been started four years earlier. The former deregulated trucking, and the latter gave broad ratemaking and other freedoms to railroads. Deregulating surface transportation can only help the railroads, just as regulation helped in an earlier stage. With the end of ICC pricing strategies that protected the less efficient long-distance trucking industry, deregulation gives railroads a chance to utilize their major cost advantage over trucks. Regulation previously protected railroads from competition between themselves and the highly subsidized truckers. Now, with the railroad industry highly concentrated (and few new railroads likely to be built), intermodal competition will likely create rail domination of trucking. The less concentrated trucking industry is already feeling the effects as its profits fall and rail profits rise. In the railroad-truck competition, giant transportation firms can be built on the railroad stem as railroads expand trailer-on-flatcar (TOFL) and container service on long-distance routes and add their own trucking facilities at either end of their rail routes. For a while there may be an illusion of competition (more truckers, more rate freedom, etc.), but the competition only masks the development of new monopoly power in the transportation industry.

The surface transportation industry scenario, which we have examined in detail, reflects the case of other industries undergoing deregulation. Among the deregulated airlines, despite the early appearance of new entrants in the market, recent mergers are increasing the likelihood of greater concentration among long-distance carriers. Caught up in the deregulation mood of the times, the Federal Communications Commission has permitted several giant mergers and a very large number of small ones in the radio and television industries. These mergers have narrowed the number of independently owned radio and television stations and created several absolute giants in broadcasting. Deregulation in banking has meant the building of giant financial-service enterprises that combine banking and nonbanking functions as well as the enlargement of already huge banks by reducing restrictions on branch banking and interstate banking. Such developments in no way support the Conservative claim that deregulation is restoring competition. Deregulation only continues the cartelizing of certain industries that commenced in the now discredited era of regulation.

Deregulation, whatever its immediate short-term gains to particular industries, can never be a long-term strategy. The destabilizing effects of excessive monopoly power—the direct result of deregulation—must be corrected to maintain economic and social order. The potential for abuse by deregulated but monopolistic railroads and air carriers provokes pressure for reregulation from the public and from commercial shippers. Similarly, the destabilizing of American banking and finance cannot be permitted. The banking industry requires reregulation to provide orderly financial markets. The 2001 price gouging affecting California's electricity consumers is only the latest example of the destabilizing effects of deregulation. The recent appeal of controlling and cartelizing deregulated industries, while appearing to be a new public policy direction, is merely a return to the old strategy of creating officially protected cartels.

As deregulation pressures wind down and give way to calls for reregulation, we should learn this lesson: *Social ownership and control of predominantly public interest industries offers the only viable alternative.* Public ownership and operation of transportation, banking, telecommunications, and the like is a means of establishing the collective control that regulation initially promised but could not achieve and that deregulation directly opposes.

# Income Distribution

## Does America Have an Income Inequality Problem?

Like all other contracts, wages should be left to the fair and free competition of the market, and should never be controlled by the interference of the legislature. The clear and direct tendency of the poor laws is in direct opposition to these obvious principles: it is not as the legislature benevolently intended, to amend the condition of the poor, but to deteriorate the condition of both poor and rich; instead of making the poor rich, they are calculated to make the rich poor.

—*David Ricardo, 1821*

It is not to die, or even to die of hunger, that makes a man wretched; many men have died, all men must die. . . . But it is to live miserable we know not why; to work sore and yet gain nothing; to be heart-worn, weary yet isolated, unrelated, girt in with a cold, universal Laissez Faire.

—*Thomas Carlyle, 1853*

Here's the bottom line: welfare reform worked because single mothers left welfare and went to work in unprecedented numbers. Good for them. Good for their children.

—*White House News Release, 2002*

## The Problem

In August 1996, Congress passed the Personal Responsibility and Work Opportunity Reconciliation Act (PRWORA) in order to "end the dependence of needy parents on government benefits by promoting job preparedness, work, and marriage." The legislation transferred much of social welfare policy making and program development to the states. Congress also imposed several new mandates including stricter work requirements and time limits on benefits. Cash payments to impoverished families are now administered under the Temporary Assistance to Needy Families (TANF) program and funded by federal "block grants" administered by the individual fifty states. The block-granting of funds to the states seemed to mean the repeal of an old covenant between the federal government and the nation's needy that could be traced all the way back to the New Deal of Franklin Roosevelt. To others, it was less a reneging on an old promise than a matter of coming to terms—"getting real"—with the mess that the nation's previous welfare system had become. For example, TANF now requires that 90 percent of a state's welfare recipients be moved into work or work-related activities within two years and there is a five-year time limit on most benefits. At its core, TANF transformed cash assistance to poor people from a right to a privilege, contingent upon the ability to perform work.

Welfare as a right was, in fact, a comparatively new idea in the United States. Its origins could not be traced back beyond the 1930s, and, some would argue, not really beyond the late 1960s. In the distant past (before the twentieth century), any welfare that existed was mostly provided by private charitable activity, sometimes by churches but most frequently by the largesse of compassionate friends and relatives. As late as 1902, combined federal, state, and local outlays for public welfare totaled only $41 million, and practically all of this came from local governments. This amounted to 0.2 percent of gross domestic product (GDP).

Until the 1930s, public assistance was always intended to address short-term instances of unemployment or poverty. Ordinarily, the recipient was required to work at some public-sector job for the assistance received. Indeed, Franklin Roosevelt followed that long-accepted pattern with his make-work Works Progress Administration (WPA) welfare programs in the 1930s. In 1934, in the depths of the Great Depression, public welfare outlays by state, local, and federal governments totaled about $1 billion, or about 2 percent of GDP. Still, public assistance was seen as a short-term measure. Unlike Great Britain, where the poorhouse and the dole had persisted for more than a century as a way of life for the truly poor, no similar arrangements were constructed in the United States to deal with chronic poverty. However, the notion that citizens had a right to public assistance began to take shape with certain New Deal programs—Aid to the Aged, Aid to the Disabled, and Aid to Dependent Children (later to be known as Aid to Families with Dependent Children, or AFDC). In the late 1960s, President Lyndon Johnson's War on Poverty efforts left no doubt that access to public assistance was a right for all needy citizens.

By 1978, with the federal government having essentially taken control of most public assistance programs (although the states still exercised some influence over the level of certain in-state payments), means-tested (or income-based) public assistance programs accounted for more than $63 billion in federal outlays and $20 billion in state outlays. Such programs included Medicaid, AFDC, Supplemental Security Income, food stamps, child nutrition, and housing assistance and opportunity grants. By the mid-1990s, federal and state cash and in-kind assistance and Medicaid had grown to more than $225 billion. Large as such a figure seems, it was still only a bit over 3 percent of GDP.

In any case, in the emerging debate about the nation's welfare program, the actual size of the public assistance outlay was always secondary to another question: What exactly was the nation buying with its welfare outlays? Even the welfare system's defenders took little pride in what had been created. True, by the mid-1990s, public assistance was only a temporary stopping spot for most of the 10 to 12 percent of the nation who were poor; but almost half of the poor, about one in every twenty Americans, were caught in chronic poverty. Among this group, public assistance, for whatever reason, had become a permanent condition. All too frequently it was accompanied by an ugly social pathology of broken families, unmarried mothers, educational failure, joblessness, high rates of substance addiction and crime, and, always, abiding personal despair.

By the 1990s, amidst an increasingly conservative political climate, the old American opposition to providing a permanent dole had resurfaced with a vengeance. Politically speaking, there was no way to oppose the growing national will to abolish welfare as a right and to place stringent restrictions upon it as a privilege. The political mood doubtless had been buoyed by the good economic times of the 1990s in which it became easy to believe that most poor people should be able to work themselves out of welfare.

While it is too early to give a definitive answer about the ultimate success or failure of the current experiment with welfare reform, certain trends are not disputed. Since 1996 there has been about a 50 percent decline in the number of families with children who receive cash compensation from public assistance. Moreover, while there was much concern over the effect of a recession on workfare participants, recent Census Bureau data suggest only very modest increases in child and female-headed household poverty rates, while the poverty rate for African American children reached an all-time low in 2001. Employment rates among TANF recipients have remained relatively stable while labor force participation rates for unmarried mothers exhibited a persistent and notable increase after 1996.

Nevertheless, the precise reasons for these changes cannot be easily disentangled from the larger economic picture. First, individual states such as Wisconsin had already been transforming their social welfare policies and programs from needs-based to work-based requirements well before federal reforms. Second, significant state-level economic growth between 1995 and 2000 reduced welfare rolls and freed up TANF funds for additional welfare benefits, especially for day care, health insurance, education, and job training. Third, the broader ten-year economic expansion generated significant gains in inflation-adjusted wages, especially for low and unskilled workers. Unemployment rates among high-school dropouts were cut in half and reached all-time lows for African American and Hispanic workers. Finally, the minimum hourly wage rose to $5.15 in 1997 while the Earned Income Tax Credit (EITC) made an additional contribution to after-tax wages through tax rebates to minimum-wage workers with children.

The significant decline in the number of families receiving public assistance since 1996 was likely due to a combination of both strong employment growth and welfare policy changes. The transformation of welfare policy continues to incite broad disagreement about its long-term effects. With the success of welfare reform hinging in a large way upon the economy's performance, the practical questions remain about financing and sustaining income security for the poor. Yet, such questions are deceivingly ordinary because the deeper ideological passions range from questioning the necessity of income redistribution to an avowed commitment to equal distribution of income.

### Synopsis

Conservatives are profoundly skeptical of social welfare programs, arguing that efforts at redistributing income are bound to produce a drag on economic performance. Liberals contend that a distribution of income based upon markets is bound to generate inequitable results that can be offset only through governmental manipulation of taxes and transfers. Radicals express deep-felt rejection of capitalism's exploitative mechanism of distributing economic rewards and would make a first step in rectifying matters through aggressive redistribution of income and wealth.

---

## Anticipating the Arguments

- On what specific grounds do Conservatives condemn the view that welfare is a right that should be guaranteed to all needy citizens?
- While Liberals may agree with Conservatives that past uses of the welfare system have failed to help the poor, how do their proposals for dealing with poverty differ from the Conservative view?
- Radicals maintain that we have attempted to get rid of welfare support only for the needy but not for the well-to-do. What do they mean by such an assertion?

## THE CONSERVATIVE ARGUMENT

From the perspective of American Conservatives, the contemporary dismantling of the nation's welfare system is an undertaking that is long overdue. Whatever the good intentions of several generations of welfare advocates, their efforts placed a heavy burden on the entire society, perhaps the heaviest of all on those citizens whom they sought to help. The current shift in American social policy toward dismantling the dole and bringing the nation's poor and less fortunate population into the mainstream of economic life is to be lamented only because it took so long for common sense to be translated into actual practice. Since Congress enacted the most sweeping welfare reform program in seventy years in 1996, welfare rolls have plummeted while formerly welfare-dependent Americans have become gainfully employed. The emancipation of the nation's poor from the tyranny of the welfare state has put them firmly on the path to becoming mainstream Americans.

### The Sources of the Welfare Problem

The sources of modern America's welfare problem are not difficult to determine. They reside amidst the rubble of the general economic collapse of the 1930s—the Great Depression. Poverty, of course, did not make its first appearance in the 1930s, but it was in the 1930s that America began to institutionalize poverty. Up to this point in the American experience, poverty and the joblessness that was its primary cause had been viewed as a temporary situation. Given time and their own hard work, the poor could sooner or later put the episode behind them. Indeed, by the 1920s, the record was rather clear on this. Most of those who came to America voluntarily came poor and, within a generation or two, managed to escape the clutches of poverty. Only African Americans, devastated by their experiences first with slavery and then with sharecropping, moved out of poverty slowly. But even among this group of citizens on the eve of the Great Depression, there was noticeable upward economic movement.

Whether or not the Great Depression had to be as deep or prolonged as it was is a matter of debate. Conservatives, of course, hold the view that this great rupture in American political and economic life was really worsened by the Liberal response it initially brought forth (see Issue 8). In any case, with unemployment hovering at about 25 percent, the matter of providing relief for the unemployed and the poor was an important underlying issue in the presidential contest that year between President Herbert Hoover and New York governor Franklin D. Roosevelt. The Republican and philosophically conservative Hoover took the correct but unpopular position that any federal provision of emergency funds to the needy would establish a precedent that would eventually destroy the long-held American commitment to individualism. Roosevelt won, and the die was cast for the growth of the American welfare state.

Interestingly, even Roosevelt had reservations about establishing a permanent womb-to-tomb welfare system. As late as 1935, a couple of years after introduction of his WPA make-work relief program and his Aid to Dependent Children program, Roosevelt observed: "The lessons of history, confirmed by evidence immediately before me, show conclusively that continued dependence upon relief induces a spiritual and moral disintegration fundamentally destructive to the national fiber. To dole out relief in this way is to administer a narcotic, a subtle destroyer of the human spirit. It is inimical to the dictates of sound policy. It is a violation of the traditions of America. Work must be found for able-bodied but destitute workers."

No Conservative could have stated the case any more forcefully than Roosevelt did. However, putting the toothpaste back in the tube was politically impossible. Once the Liberal solution to poverty—providing a dole for any who chose to demonstrate need—became understood as an American right, it would not be a right quickly surrendered. This became even more the case as the extent and amount of public relief continued to grow in the 1960s and 1970s. More than half a century would pass after Roosevelt's public lament before a Conservative Congress could put an end to this awful Liberal experiment in social engineering.

## Toward a Just System of Rewards

As the American welfare system grew, especially in the 1960s and 1970s, so did the notion that the nation would be better served with a more equal distribution of income. More than is generally realized, this idea legitimized the expansion of the welfare system and obscured real understanding of the terrible outcomes that welfare dependence was producing. Accordingly, it is important at this point to understand where Conservatives stand on the entire matter of income distribution before taking up the particular issue of current welfare reform.

A unifying feature of all Liberal and Radical programs for the past hundred years has been the call for egalitarianism in income. The "Robin Hood" illusion is the very beginning of any collectivist's social dream. In the United States, income redistribution efforts in this century have appeared in two general forms: (1) a highly progressive income tax structure aimed at piling the expense of social spending on the upper-income members of society, and (2) a vast giveaway of these appropriations to the poor and the nonproductive groups within the nation. Both schemes rest on serious errors of economic and social thinking that deserve fuller elaboration and criticism.

Distribution of income should be governed by the simple and equitable principle that all members of a society should receive according to what they, or whatever they own, are able to produce. The abilities, tastes, and occupational interests of individuals vary. People value work and leisure differently. Some individuals are willing to forgo an assured lower income in favor of taking a risk and possibly earning more than the guaranteed level. Enforced equality of income utterly fails to consider these possibilities. It presumes that greater social satisfaction is attained by income parity rather than by letting people make their own valuations of what money means to them.

Consider, for instance, a person who is quite content to live on $500 a week. From this person's point of view, needs are satisfied and the right balance between leisure and work has been achieved. To transfer to this person one-quarter of the wages of another person who makes $1,000 a week will hardly increase the first person's welfare or happiness. At the same time, it subtracts much satisfaction from the second person, who is willing to work hard enough to earn the $1,000 wage. If we now added up the relative satisfactions of the two workers, it would be lower after redistribution than before. In other words, proof is lacking that a more equal income distribution actually maximizes community satisfaction.

At another level, egalitarianism leads to more serious troubles. Enforcing equal distribution of income penalizes the industrious and inventive and subsidizes those with less initiative. If the industrious fail to obtain rewards for their talents and work, they will naturally slacken their efforts. As a result, the total productiveness of society is lessened. In the subsequent egalitarian redistribution, everyone gets less than before. Just how far the detrimental effects of income equalization can go in destroying a society became evident in Great Britain by the 1970s. Subsidies for idleness and confiscation of earned income had lowered British output and put the nation at considerable disadvantage in world trade. The best minds and the nation's capital were fleeing overseas. A shabby equality and a culture of mediocrity enveloped the domestic economy. Only the reversal of the old welfare-state policies by the Conservative government of Margaret Thatcher in the late 1970s and early 1980s saved Britain from social and economic collapse.

While the discussion so far has been mostly concerned with individual labor, it also applies to individuals' command over capital and wealth. Appropriating the wealth of one person to support another denies the individual's right to property and will lead to inefficiency and economic contraction in the whole society. (Whether the wealth is inherited or has been earned by the individual is irrelevant.) This is not just an economic matter. Seizures of wages and property are violations of freedom. It is not such a big step from telling people what their income will be to telling them what work to do or what ideas to think.

### The Basic Problems with Welfare

Conservatives have long understood that their attack on welfare is often depicted as a Scrooge-like heartlessness. In a nation of abundance and opportunity, it is natural for there to be much popular support for charity aimed at the "deserving poor." But charity involves a number of costs.

First of all, there is the cost to the giver. In the growing national economy of the 1960s, the expansion of a variety of welfare programs—AFDC, for example—provoked little taxpayer response. The programs seemed relatively small, and because the nation was enjoying an impressive annual growth in its gross domestic product, few Americans doubted that this was a charity we would someday not be able to afford. However, after thirty years of failed government welfare policies, a lot of working Americans began believing that charity should start at home. No doubt this self-concern was sharpened by the new realities of American labor markets. Corporate downsizing meant that many American workers had to take considerable pay cuts as they scrambled about for new jobs. In the new employment environment, a growing friction emerged between those choosing to work, even at considerably reduced wages or with the prospect of reduced wages, and millions of welfare recipients choosing not to work at all. That the former should continue to support the latter comfortably made less and less sense to many hard-working citizens. By the mid-1990s, public opinion polls no longer indicated that the majority of Americans supported the nation's welfare experiment.

There was also growing recognition of a second type of cost that welfare exacted, this one borne by its recipients. Aid to Families with Dependent Children, given only to mothers and children in the absence of a working father, was from its very beginning—although well-intended welfare advocates generally ignored the fact—constructed so as to fracture the families of the poor. It also encouraged out-of-wedlock childbirth. Accordingly, millions of children were denied the opportunity to grow and thrive within a conventional nuclear family. Generally, cash-assistance welfare programs required that eligible recipients have no earned income or that any earned income be subtracted from welfare payments received. Fortunately, the welfare reform of 1996 has begun to correct these destructive policies.

The overall effect of America's former welfare program was easily summarized: It created a strong disincentive to work and discouraged people from improving themselves. Recipients not only had to be poor to qualify for welfare protection but they had to remain poor to keep getting it. Thus our welfare system created a vast, permanent subculture of the disadvantaged. And, of course, overseeing this mess was a monumental welfare bureaucracy utterly lacking in incentives to solve the welfare dilemma, because their paychecks depended on the problem's continued existence. It is hard to imagine that such an irrational system could have been defended, and thereby permitted to exist, for so many years.

### The Results Are In: Workfare Works!

There is no doubt that the welfare reform legislation enacted by Congress in 1996—especially the TANF program—has been an unqualified success: workfare works! Data gathered by both federal and state authorities confirm that the policy changes are achieving unprecedented results. Welfare rolls have been cut in half since 1996 and former recipients are finding gainful employment. Detailed studies from forty states show that on average most mothers leaving welfare find gainful employment. Labor force participation among unmarried mothers has increased since 1996 and Census Bureau data confirm a dramatic increase in income from wages for the bottom 40 percent of female-headed households while income from welfare declined. Finally, the objective of promoting marriage and decreasing nonmarital births is slowly being realized. This is because states have been given greater flexibility to use federal resources to reduce nonmarital and teenage births, especially through abstinence education programs and improving child support enforcement. There is ample evidence to suggest that if impoverished single mothers married the biological father of their children, most poor families would be lifted out of poverty. While Conservatives do not harbor a philosophical predisposition anchored in marital relations, from a practical standpoint encouraging and promoting marriage has proven to be a sound policy for ending welfare dependency.

Given the success of these changes in social welfare policies, Conservatives readily acknowledge that circumstances may arise from time to time that make it impossible for some citizens to find work. To the extent that an individual is disabled and unable to work at all or is too young to work, we recognize that society bears a responsibility to provide for the basic needs of those so affected. But when an individual is capable of working, it is not a cruel act by society to require that person to provide some useful labor on behalf of those providing his or her support.

Conservatives are particularly enthusiastic about welfare reform efforts that encourage welfare recipients to seek private sector employment. Restoring a sense of self-worth to former welfare recipients by means of their finding jobs is the only long-term cure for the welfare problem. However—and this is an important point to keep in mind—successfully engaging former welfare recipients in the ordinary economic life of the nation requires more than a little job training here and a little career counseling there. As a nation, we should be very careful that some of our economic initiatives—often actions that seem to have nothing to do with the welfare problem—do not work against solving that problem. For instance, the simple act of raising the legal minimum wage may seem to be a fairly benign undertaking aimed only at raising the living standards of a few million low-wage workers. In fact, such an action, or any others that raise an employer's cost in hiring additional workers, will shrink the employment opportunities of current welfare recipients and may even be the cause of a new round of joblessness and a resurgence of the old welfare cycle. Moreover, there is much that remains to be done in welfare reform: half the TANF caseload is still sitting idle while the food stamp and public housing programs are completely unreformed.

Remember, from a Conservative perspective, welfare dependency emerged in the first place as the result of undesirable tinkering with a market economy. We can reform welfare as much as we like, but the usefulness of such reforms depends ultimately on our commitment to permitting the economy to operate freely and openly, with as little social and economic interference as possible.

## THE LIBERAL ARGUMENT

Conservatives are on the right track when they attack redistributive programs, but not for the reasons they present. The failure of public policy efforts is not due, as Conservatives believe, to some collectivist utopia in which a massive Robin Hood program takes from the rich and gives to the poor, simultaneously trampling on property rights, reducing work incentives, and lowering overall economic efficiency and national economic growth. Liberals maintain that public policy actually *has* failed in its professed efforts to close the gap between those at the very bottom of the income distribution and those at the top.

Conservatives are by no means troubled by this aspect of public policy failure and indeed perceive inequality as in some way incentive-inspiring and a normal outcome of well-functioning competitive markets. Liberals question the disincentives and adverse effects upon economic growth that Conservatives assert are the by-products of an oversized welfare state. Moreover, the Liberal view challenges the ability of the market mechanism to generate socially acceptable results with regard to income distribution. Conservatives turn a blind eye to the potential contagion of social problems that accompany poverty. Liberals criticize Conservatives' methods of reforming welfare as overridingly motivated by the goals of reducing the influence of central government and curtailing redistribution under the guise of cost savings—all the while chanting the popular mantra of efficiency.

Liberals are receptive to reforms that reduce costs and improve efficiency, but are realistic in our evaluation of income distribution and aware of the limitations that poorly functioning markets impose upon economic opportunity. Consequently, while adhering to the notion of personal responsibility and self-reliance, Liberals maintain that government's role in welfare can never be as small as Conservatives would hope.

### Examining Income Distribution

As Table 6.1 illustrates, shares of money income received by various American income groups showed some movement toward greater equality in the New Deal era of the 1930s. The distribution was markedly stable from the 1940s to the mid-1970s. Thereafter the distribution began to exhibit greater inequality. Moreover, the quintile figures mask the fact that the share of income going to the top 5 percent climbed from under 16 percent in the 1970s to over 22 percent by 2001. Economists have also adopted another measure of aggregate income inequality, the Gini ratio, which was developed by Italian statistician Corrado Gini (1884–1965). This index measures the gap between an equal income distribution (where each share of the population has an equal share of national income) and the actual income distribution. A Gini ratio of 0 indicates zero inequality or *perfect equality*. A value of 1 is interpreted as 100 percent inequality or *perfect inequality* in the distribution of income. For example, if the column values in Table 6.1 were all equal to 20 percent, the United States would have had a Gini index equal to 0. Historically, the Gini ratio peaked around 1932 and then rapidly declined through World War II and stayed relatively flat until

Table 6.1

**Share of Aggregate Income Received in Families in Each Income Quintile, 1929–2001**

| Income quintile | 1929 | 1936 | 1947 | 1960 | 1970 | 1980 | 1990 | 2001 |
|---|---|---|---|---|---|---|---|---|
| Lowest    . |      | 4.1  | 5.0  | 4.8  | 5.4  | 5.3  | 4.6  | 4.2  |
| Second      | 12.5* | 9.2  | 11.9 | 12.2 | 12.2 | 11.6 | 10.8 | 9.7  |
| Third       | 13.8 | 14.1 | 17.0 | 17.8 | 17.6 | 17.6 | 16.6 | 15.4 |
| Fourth      | 19.3 | 20.9 | 23.1 | 24.0 | 23.8 | 24.4 | 23.8 | 22.9 |
| Highest     | 54.4 | 51.7 | 43.0 | 41.3 | 40.9 | 41.1 | 44.3 | 47.7 |

*Source*: U.S. Bureau of the Census.
*Lowest and second quintile combined.

1968. Figure 6.1 shows the actual Gini index for the United States beginning in 1970 when income inequality began an almost uninterrupted increase. Thus, both sets of data strongly suggest that the economic situation of those at the bottom of the income distribution has not appreciably improved. Since the late 1960s, individuals in the highest quintiles in the income distribution were claiming an even larger share of money income. Clearly, such evidence does not support the Conservative suggestion that we have been on a long and dangerous slide toward egalitarianism.

Liberals concede that the sources of the rise in income inequality are numerous and elusive. Experts cite the impact of technological change that has handsomely rewarded particular types of skills, adverse effects of international competition that happened to be more pronounced for those at the bottom of the income distribution, decline in the purchasing power of the minimum wage, lower levels of unionization in the labor force and weakening of union influence over wages, and an influx of low-skill, low-wage immigrants who shrink the income share figures at the bottom of the distribution. However, these explanations have little to do with the Conservative assault upon government's efforts to redistribute income via the welfare system. And despite these explanations, one must bear in mind that the principal focus of redistributive efforts has not been to significantly alter the distribution of income. Specifically, the evolution of welfare programs has been a response to the inadequacies of a market system and the experiencing of the actual consequences of those inadequacies.

148

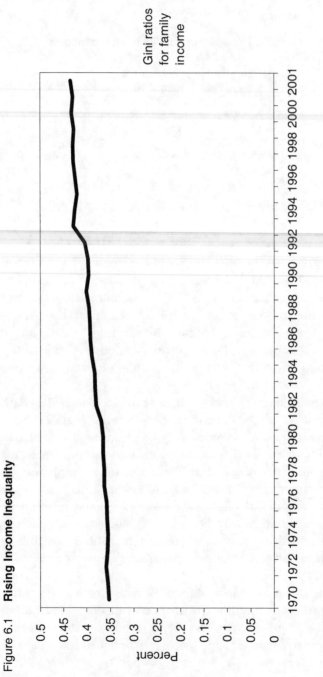

Figure 6.1    **Rising Income Inequality**

Gini ratios for family income

*Source:* Data from the U.S. Bureau of the Census.

### Belief versus Reality

In its strictest embodiment, the Conservative view has a terribly difficult time reconciling the predictions of its most honored models with
actual phenomena. This is particularly true when models of competitive
markets are compared against real-world results. While acknowledging
that theoretical models of *perfect* markets suffer from a strained relationship with their real-world counterparts, Conservatives are reluctant
to acknowledge that the problems of monopoly power, the absence of
complete information—or the presence of distorted information—for
consumers to make intelligent choices, and the serious failures of markets (as in the case of pollution) are serious enough to warrant much
intervention on the part of government. Likewise in the cases of poverty
and income inequality, Conservatives are unwilling to find the justification for government intervention.

Experience finds this perplexing. The depths of the Great Depression
motivated Franklin Roosevelt, a fiscally and ideologically conservative
president, to discard Conservative claptrap in favor of Liberal policies
that might at the very least finesse the problem. Similarly, the enviable,
burgeoning production economy of the United States was tormented in
the post–World War II period by a legacy of high poverty rates, in excess of 20 percent. These rates began to fall with the onset of a combination of economic growth and redistribution policies—both instilled
through government intervention—that improved the economic lot for
not only the citizenry at the bottom of the income distribution but everyone else as well. On the subject of economic growth, both Conservatives and Liberals agree: The best way out of poverty is a job. However,
the contingency is economic growth. Here, as on other matters, Liberals
must part company with the Conservatives.

### The Basis for Intervention

Although the landscape of reasons is expansive and can become highly
detailed, the Liberal argument for intervention and income maintenance
programs rests mainly upon the following foundations:

- Competition in markets is not universal, and the existence of monopoly
  power and other market imperfections necessitates government corrective action on several fronts, including redistribution of income.

- Private markets fail and cannot insure people against the uncertainty of economic downturns that throw people out of work and into poverty.
- Egalitarianism is not at odds with economic growth.
- Government policies should be crafted to fight poverty and promote fairness in the income distribution—not just to unload or shift around the financial burden of paying for the nation's poor.

## Market Imperfections

Theories of competitive product markets and resource markets presume certain ideal conditions that dodge practical complications. Conservatives maintain that such models strongly represent economic reality, and Radicals reject them outright. Liberals reside in between, with well-founded concerns about the magnitude of imperfections in real-world markets. These imperfections are bound to influence the fairness of the game and, therefore, the fairness of the results. Recognize that Conservatives do not perceive imperfections as a very large problem and that Radicals believe the game is rigged.

The competitive model promoted by Conservatives is countered by the existence of monopoly power in product markets and the results must be reflected in the income distribution. In short, the monopolist gets rich at the expense of society as whole.

Likewise, inequality in bargaining power in labor markets places the employee in a weaker position relative to the employer when striking the wage bargain. Other imperfections such as geographic and sociological immobilities impair the performance of labor markets by denying people ready access to improved economic opportunities just because they are unaware, too far away, or can be had only after insurmountable personal adjustments. Other citizens experience lack of opportunity and access to proper education, training, and experience—what economists call *human capital*. Hence, insufficient investment in human capital yields paltry returns in the form of income earned in the labor market, which in turn leads back to low investment, trapping the poor in a vicious circle of poverty.

Poverty and inequality are further cultivated by circumstances that are beyond the control of individual choices and relative efforts in the labor market. Some may suffer from the limitations imposed by disabilities. Others are the victims of accidents and misfortune. Still others must tangle with labor market discrimination. Certainly society could not be intent upon ignoring or punishing these people.

## *Welfare as Social Insurance*

Conservatives are well aware that economic activities for certain sectors of the economy would be greatly retarded or nonexistent were it not for the development of insurance. Insurance offsets the discouraging effects imparted by random accidents, bad weather, fire, flood, or other adverse events where, based upon past experience, an insurer can estimate the expected frequency and severity with which such events will occur. Private insurance works quite well within a particular domain. However, private insurance markets do not provide adequate (or any) insurance against the uncertainties of the business cycle and consequent unemployment. Nor have private insurance markets found it financially feasible to extend coverage to the chronically ill or to develop income security insurance for low-wage workers with spotty employment histories. The development of social insurance programs, including antipoverty programs, is a response to this particular failure of markets.

## *Egalitarianism, Incentives, and Growth*

Liberals do not subscribe to Conservatives' reasoning about the adverse impact of income redistribution upon economic incentives and economic growth. Conservatives' assertion that taxes levied upon productive efforts and transferred to unproductive individuals are a disincentive to being productive seems to make sense. However, this proves to be a matter of degree or the *threshold* at which extremely high taxes and bountiful welfare benefits truly discourage work effort, saving, and investment. In fact, there is no discernible, systematic relationship to support the idea that greater equity is accompanied by a pronounced loss of economic efficiency. Many European countries engage in far more vigorous tax and transfer efforts than the United States. Yet this does not seem to impinge upon economic progress. Greater economic security may actually improve the outlook for economic growth! Consider the examples of less developed countries with highly unequal distributions of income, coupled with marked inefficiency and abysmal records of economic growth. Indeed, income redistribution does confront society with a dilemma. However, the trade-off is not so pointed that we must agonize about whether future economic growth is dangerously jeopardized by trying to help the poor.

### Throw Them Overboard?

Liberals advocate government policies to fight poverty and promote an equitable distribution of income. This overarching objective does not obstruct exploring the most expeditious and inexpensive means of dealing with the poverty problem. However, Conservative prescriptions for cost cutting and efficiency are worrisome. When likened to the allegorical overcrowded lifeboat, Conservative policies seem bent upon shrinking the size of the boat and heaving passengers overboard.

Although the Conservative agenda may be honestly dominated by the desire to shrink government and its influence, there is certain mean-spiritedness to their methods. Liberals are, therefore, skeptical of efforts that merely shift the responsibility for, and burden of, the poverty problem from one level of government to another. Historical experience with the failure of "poor laws" that held local governments accountable for providing for their resident indigents is instructive: The approach was to make it legally difficult to be poor *and* be a resident, or for governmental provision for the poor to be parsimonious. The purpose of this strategy was to chase the undesirables into some other political jurisdiction where tolerance and provision for the poor were greater.

Inequities are certain to grow if each state establishes its *social minimum*. In the 1930s, some states denied voting rights to those on public assistance. In the 1950s, welfare in some Mississippi townships consisted of $75 and a one-way bus ticket to Detroit. Inevitably, local governments would be prompted to adopt in common the worst of restrictions and frugality lest they be overwhelmed by legions of paupers. Understanding the problem of ceding responsibility to local authority prompts reasoned caution about policy reforms—especially if they reverse decades of progress in reducing poverty.

### Success in Reducing Poverty Rates

Figure 6.2 shows the trend in poverty rates since 1959. There are some cyclical ups and downs because poverty rates rise during economic contractions and fall during periods of prosperity. The rate of economic growth is clearly a powerful force in determining poverty rates. A rising tide of economic growth lifts all boats—or nearly all. Conservatives are fierce advocates of work rather than welfare. However, suf-

Figure 6.2 **Poverty Rates, 1959–2002**

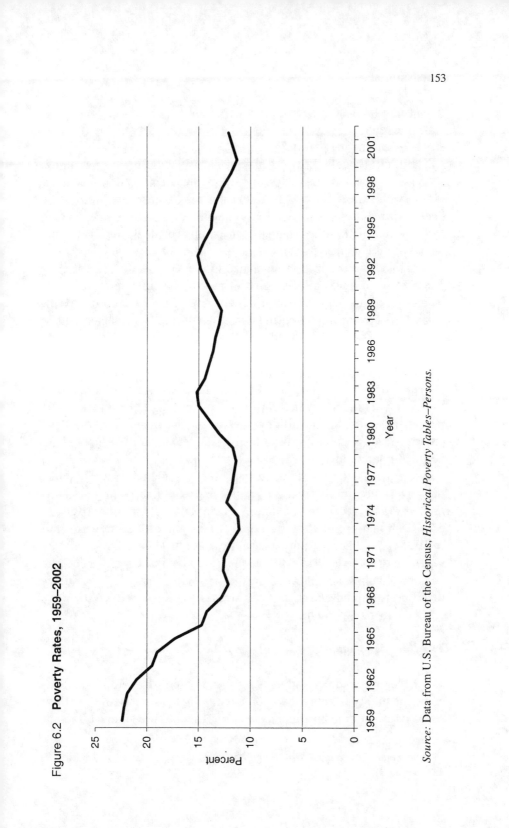

*Source:* Data from U.S. Bureau of the Census, *Historical Poverty Tables–Persons.*

ficient employment opportunities depend on the economy's performance. Even then, growth has never been a foolproof remedy for poverty and income inequality.

The 1960s brought the onset of expanded social insurance programs, which had impressive results. Propelled by President Lyndon Johnson's vision of the Great Society, poverty rates took a nosedive, from more than 22 percent of the population to slightly more than 11 percent by 1973. Much of the improvement can be attributed to more generous Social Security benefits and the creation of Medicare in 1965, providing medical and hospitalization insurance to the aged. A companion program, Medicaid, was also initiated to pay the health care costs of the indigent. Social Security, Medicare, and even Medicaid, to the extent that it pays for nursing home and home health care for the elderly, have escaped the notoriety of being "welfare." The beneficiaries, many of Conservative persuasion, fervently refuse to allow that *they*, with *their* transfer payments from government, bear any resemblance to the recipients of payments from AFDC or food stamps. While older Americans could claim victory in the War on Poverty, beginning in the 1970s poverty rates rose at an alarming rate for persons under eighteen. Poverty continued to exhibit a disparate impact upon minorities and female heads of household.

Nonetheless, the overall poverty problem would be far worse without government redistribution programs. In the *Economic Report of the President, 1997,* the president's Council of Economic Advisors estimated that cash transfer payments held the official poverty rate in 1995 to 13.8 percent; otherwise, it would have been 21.9 percent! Furthermore, the effect of the Earned Income Tax Credit (EITC) as discussed below and the value of *in-kind* transfers (such as subsidized housing and health care services) effectively reduce the poverty rate to 10.3 percent.*

### The Liberal Agenda

The Liberal agenda for addressing the problems of poverty and income inequality is not based upon attempting to preserve the "welfare state" or the welfare bureaucracy. Rather, Liberals are guided by sound

---

*\*Economic Report of the President* (Washington, DC: Government Printing Office, 1997), 186.

principles of where and when government should intervene as well as the desire for a humane and civil society. Let us translate that into a plan of action.

### Increase the Minimum Wage

A straightforward way to raise income and encourage work is to raise the minimum wage and index it to automatically rise with consumer prices or in tandem with other wages in the economy. The inflation-adjusted value of the minimum wage is 24 percent lower than it was in 1979. Conservatives who argue that minimum-wage laws restrict the demand for labor cannot claim it is due to its lower real cost: The number of workers demanded should increase as its price falls. If the minimum wage had simply kept up with inflation since 1968 when it was $1.60, it would stand at $8.46 in 2003.

### Maintain and Expand the Earned Income Tax Credit

The Earned Income Tax Credit permits low-income families to receive as much as 12.5 percent of earned income as refundable tax credit, depending upon family size. The EITC is a version of a guaranteed annual income (GAI) or negative income tax (NIT) for the working poor. Even Conservatives such as Milton Friedman have advanced some support for a GAI or NIT. The EITC is not a full remedy, but it can be credited with greatly increasing employment among unmarried mothers (34 percent increase from 1992 to 1996) and lifting 4.1 million individuals (including 2.3 million children) out of poverty in 1999.*

### Fostering Economic Opportunity and Personal Responsibility

Welfare is not the real solution to poverty or income inequality. Programs designed to pacify the poor create a permanent poor. Federal programs must attack the root of the problem through job creation, training, and education. Although Liberals are not fully enthralled with workfare as an alternative to unrestricted grants to the poor, it is the only viable long-run strategy for eliminating chronic poverty. Since the enactment of the 1996

---

*Economic Report of the President* (Washington, DC: Government Printing Office, 2001), 200.

welfare reform there has been a decline in both welfare caseloads and poverty rates. Nevertheless, whether this was due to a change in welfare policies or a booming economy is unclear. The Federal Reserve Bank of New York evaluated the progress and prospects of the 1996 legislation.* A critical question was whether a strong economy, by itself, "pulled" the most "job-ready" welfare recipients off the welfare rolls, but left the least-skilled recipients behind. Alternatively, a decline in the welfare caseload could also be due to the indiscriminant "pushing" off of indigent citizens from the welfare rolls by cold-hearted caseworkers.

From a Liberal perspective, the recent changes to reform the welfare system should be commended. Unfortunately, disadvantaged recipients remain in large numbers—primarily women with very young children—who have experienced significant hardship after leaving the welfare system. Therefore, the Liberal program still requires devoting additional resources to the pursuit of eliminating poverty. Not all of these resources need to be marshaled by government. However, private enterprise cannot sit idly by regarding this social problem as principally one for government to solve. Private businesses profess a strong interest in reforming welfare and must participate as a quintessential partner to that end. Alas, Liberals must concede that the Conservative program to reform the welfare system has had some success; however, much more support is needed to build on these limited gains. The Liberal approach is predisposed to what Conservatives would call social engineering, *but there is no other way.*

## THE RADICAL ARGUMENT

The welfare reform bill that was passed by Congress and signed into law by President Clinton in 1996 codified and justified a brutal attack waged by the right wing on the poor and working class of America. Conservatives have been phenomenally successful in implementing their agenda to criminalize poverty and stigmatize the poor in order to eliminate any and all remaining social protections such as unemployment insurance and Social Security. While Senate and House Republicans are unabashed and unapologetic about implementing these changes, Liberals are somewhat more cautious regarding their likely success. Nevertheless, both view poverty as a *personal* failure of character or circumstance. To the Conservative, a

---

*Welfare Reform Four Years Later: Progress and Prospects, Economic Policy Review,* vol. 7, no. 2, Federal Reserve Bank of New York, September 2001.

low income or the absence of any income at all reflects the market-determined value of an individual's talents and initiative. Defects of character and skill of the poor themselves are the root cause of their poverty. To the Liberal, poverty is partly the result of failing to behave in an economically responsible manner and partly the result of forces outside an individual's direct control such as racial discrimination, insufficient education, or other characteristics. Conservatives, of course, are content to let the poor struggle out of their condition, whereas Liberals are quick to apply moderately redistributive tax and transfer programs and other social-policy Band-Aids for the economically disadvantaged. By focusing only on the personal characteristics of the poor, albeit in different ways, neither Conservatives nor Liberals recognize that poverty and extreme income inequality are inherent outcomes of the capitalist system.

## Demoting the General Welfare

The debate over welfare reform has been almost entirely defined and discussed in profoundly moral terms. Poverty is generally assumed by both Conservatives and Liberals to be the result of an individual's inability to adopt market-friendly habits and attitudes, rather than the persistent failure of an economy that is equally proficient at producing extreme wealth *and* destitution. The Personal Responsibility and Work Opportunity Reconciliation Act (PRWORA) of 1996 began by moralizing that "marriage is the foundation of a successful society" and then went on to blame the growth in poverty, crime, and general social decay since the 1960s on the increase in single motherhood. Left unchallenged was any notion that the lack of employment opportunities and financial resources causes crime and poverty, rather than the reverse. Nor did the legislation acknowledge that white married-couple families were twice as numerous among the poor as families headed by an African American mother. Politicians find it much easier to moralize about the sanctity of marriage than to acknowledge the crushing impact that their so-called welfare reform will have on the economic prospects of the poor.

Under the guise of getting the incorrigible and indigent to adopt behaviors and attitudes that fit into capitalist labor markets, workfare has served a punitive function to lower overall wages and working conditions and break the power of unionized workers. The "successful" meeting of TANF mandates by states (e.g., that half of all single parents and 90 percent of two-parent families have to work thirty hours per week) is glowingly cited by both Conservatives and Liberals. Since areas of high unemployment tend to also have high poverty rates, some states have "privatized" many functions by firing state workers and replacing them with TANF recipients in order to comply with federal workfare requirements. But this is only one of several destructive results from so-called "welfare reform." Profound problems with both the 1996 welfare reform statute and TANF are ignored by the mainstream. First, Congress has fixed the nominal value of total TANF funding for the foreseeable future. Freezing cash benefits at their 1996 value of $16.5 billion guarantees that future job training, childcare, and other discretionary TANF spending will disappear over time due to inflation. Second, the five-year TANF-mandated time limit on benefits has been particularly onerous on poor families and promises only to become more punitive. The previously cited Federal Reserve Bank of New York report on welfare reform stated: "Many studies have shown that a significant portion of the [welfare] caseload spends more than sixty months receiving benefits (the maximum time limit specified under PRWORA), although many states have opted for shorter time limits." Finally, even Conservatives and Liberals admit that the depth of poverty—as measured by families who are 50 percent below the poverty line—has been steadily rising. In 2002, this population increased by 600,000 to about 14 million people. Thus, the "poverty gap" continues to grow rendering the poorest Americans worse off than at any time in the past quarter century. In short, the federal government has not only succeeded in abrogating its responsibility to guarantee some minimum standard of living for *all* its citizens, but states can now balance their budgets on the backs of the poor as they continue to cut social spending with impunity.

While workfare is clearly an attack on the poorest citizens, it also serves to undermine the wages, benefits, and employment conditions of all American workers. By destroying the economic safety net for those at the bottom, welfare reform has ensured that low-wage workers will remain docile with respect to demands for higher compensation and organizing activities. Even higher-paid workers will lower their expectations about pay and job security as they watch workfare recipients replace unionized workers.

In sum, the pacification of the American poor and working class is just one of many consequences of the new welfare reform bill. These changes are not just about economics and government efficiency; they are also about exploiting antagonisms among and between the working poor and the middle class, between whites and minorities, and males and females. Ultimately, this program will serve to polarize and immiserate American society while consolidating and expanding the power of the corporate elite and their minions.

## The Legacy and Reality of Wealth Inequality

Reforming the welfare system only serves to draw attention away from the fundamental problem of capitalism's inability to produce an equitable distribution of market outcomes. Adam Smith believed that since growth was an intrinsic feature of capitalism, over time the rewards of the market would spread throughout the economy. While Smith recognized the potential for social conflict, he claimed that competition would prevent the concentration of economic resources and political power. Marx, who very much admired Smith's analysis of capitalism, agreed that capitalism was the only social system capable of generating unparalleled growth; however, it also produced unmatched poverty and inequalities in wealth and income.

While growth in aggregate income, output, and employment has been touted as a long-term feature of American capitalism, inequality in wealth and personal income has also persisted. In fact, with the exception of the early colonial era (through about 1800) and the periods during and around World Wars I and II, American society has been fairly polarized with respect to the distribution of both income and wealth. Although the Depression of the 1930s ushered in a time when incomes at the bottom and in the middle actually rose, since the mid-1960s inequality has steadily increased (see Figure 6.1). Not only do mainstream economists regard this as necessary to spur personal initiative and corporate investment, but each year the business press gloats over the richest people in America. For example, Forbes magazine compiles a list of the four hundred wealthiest people in America. In 2003, you needed a net worth of at least $500 million to qualify ($5 billion would have placed you only in thirty-third position). In addition, in 1982, the combined net worth of the Forbes 400 was "only" about $92 billion, but in 2003, that figure was ten times higher—a net worth of $955 billion. Finally, it should be noted that rather than being a bunch of Horatio Algers or self-made billionaires, a significant number of the Forbes 400 inherited most of their wealth.

While these figures only illuminate the wealth of the super-rich, it is quite evident that the overall distribution of wealth and income remains highly unequal. Table 6.2 provides data on the distribution of wealth, debts, and income based on the Federal Reserve's Survey of Consumer

Table 6.2

**Distribution of Assets, Liabilities, Income, and Net Worth***

|  | Bottom 90 percent | Top 10 percent |
|---|---|---|
| Assets | 30.1 | 69.9 |
| Home | 62.9 | 37.1 |
| Auto | 76.2 | 23.8 |
| Bonds | 4.2 | 95.8 |
| Stocks | 11.9 | 88.1 |
| Liabilities |  |  |
| Home mortgage | 75.1 | 24.9 |
| Other real estate | 44.4 | 55.6 |
| Other liabilities | 78.8 | 21.2 |
| Net worth | 30.1 | 69.9 |
| Income | $47,097 | $270,000 |
| Average net worth | $133,360 | $2,766,673 |

Source: Federal Reserve Board, *Survey of Consumer Finances*, 2001.
*Figures are percentage shares, except where dollar amounts are indicated. Percentage shares may not sum to 100 percent because of rounding.

*Finances* for 2001. As Marx would have predicted back in the late nineteenth century, wealth is far more concentrated than income in capitalist America: While the bottom 90 percent garnered a little more than two-thirds of total income, it held less than one-third of total wealth. Moreover, while their net worth was only slightly greater than their income, for the top 10 percent it was more than eleven times as great.

The data also show that the top 10 percent—about 10 million households—owned 90 percent of stocks and 96 percent of bonds (either directly or as part of a mutual fund). On the other hand, it is painfully obvious that the vast majority of Americans have nearly all their assets in a home or car—resources that are not easily deployable to either capital markets or a new business. In fact, the top tenth of households owned over 92 percent of assets held in the form of businesses and well over two-thirds of real estate and other assets.

Rather than showing an evolution toward a more democratic economy, the data underscore how a small class of elites increasingly controls the financial resources that will determine the future livelihoods of most Americans. Moreover, while most of the rich were raised in wealth, more than one in five American children continue to grow up in poverty. Not only does poverty deprive children of a decent standard of living, it also cuts their lives short. Poor children also have a much greater likelihood of dying from diseases and accidents, but even as adults, their longevity is likely to be curtailed by inadequate access to health care.

While "welfare queens" are vilified in the media, little attention is paid to the fact that social service expenditures also subsidize the rich and well-to-do. Welfare dollars buy the goods and services of corporate America. They underwrite the medical-industrial complex that includes hospitals, doctors, drug companies, health maintenance organizations, and a host of suppliers and providers. For example, Medicaid fraud is almost always committed by doctors, hospital administrators, insurance companies, and other well-paid health care professionals. Rarely does an indigent patient ever benefit from such crime. In fact, government expenditures on the truly needy (where income eligibility tests are required) are less than 5 percent of total federal outlays and have been steadily declining for several years. Meanwhile, the wealthy elite and corporations continue to obtain special tax breaks from Congress, which further undermines the revenue base to fund social programs.

### A Radical Program to End Inequality

The federal welfare reform program is doomed to failure, especially for those living in states with mean-spirited social policies. As workers and middle-class people continue to be ignored and disaffected by the political system, state and local politicians will continue to hack away at the social safety net. Unchallenged by any threat from either workers or the poor, welfare benefits no longer need to serve the system's need to quell social discontent or legitimate an increasingly inequitable economic system. While AFDC payments and other welfare programs grew after the urban unrest of the 1960s, the current absence of political pressure from the poor and disenfranchised will allow the state to continue to ignore their demands and needs. Meanwhile, following the passage of their welfare reform agenda, corporate interests and their representatives in Congress are actively attacking middle-class entitlements such as Social Security, education subsidies, veterans' benefits, and a host of other programs that benefit both the nonindigent and nonrich.

What can be done to curtail these reactionary social welfare policies and bring about a more equitable distribution of wealth? In the short run, it is crucial that the bottom 90 percent of income earners realize that they must band together with the poor and mobilize around a new political agenda that puts their economic interests ahead of those of the rich. Such action also requires a new political party that can nullify capital's dominance of the current political system. Second, there must be a radical renovation of the tax structure such that taxes on inheritances above about a million dollars would become confiscatory. Third, only *earned* income below a certain threshold, perhaps $40,000, would be free from all taxes. Also, *all* income—from whatever source—would be subject to Social Security taxes. This would allow for a dramatic decline in the payroll tax rate for all workers and insure permanent solvency of the Social Security system. Fourth, social welfare programs would be designed to help families in the most direct manner possible: the government would pay parents to stay home (if they choose) to raise their children. The Scandinavian countries and other Western European nations offer similar benefits to parents irrespective of income. Furthermore, since economists agree that goods and services produced at home are nonmonetary forms of value, such a program would actually have the effect of raising the nation's gross domestic product. Finally, the federal government must get directly involved in providing employment opportunities to the poor and indigent that will be both meaningful and productive *and* pay a living wage. Given the numerous tasks that remain unmet or poorly provided by the free market—such as child and elder care, health care, new infrastructure, pollution reduction and cleanup, along with many other needed goods and services—the federal government will find ample demand for the labor now in their employ.

All of these steps, even though they fall short of the goal of public ownership of capital, would still be unacceptable to the leaders and defenders of the capitalist system. However, the system's failure, indeed its inability, to achieve and sustain some equitable measure of income distribution, along with its chronic problems of joblessness, discrimination, and poor economic growth, must eventually erode popular acceptance of existing arrangements. To be sure, the American dream of equal and unlimited opportunity for everyone has remained a powerful myth promoted by corporate propaganda, and it always has constrained the emergence of a truly Radical political and social movement in the United States. However, as the conflict between the dream and everyday reality sharpens, Radical alternatives to conventional social and economic measures will become matters of public debate and discussion. Just as America has used the promise of equal opportunity as the social glue to hold the nation together, the actual drift toward greater inequality becomes the device that undoes the entire production-for-profit system.

# Financing Government
## What Is a Fair System of Taxation?

In the most advanced countries, the following will be pretty generally applicable: . . . A heavy progressive or graduated income tax.

—*Karl Marx*, The Communist Manifesto, *1848*

The flat tax is a deeply moral system. Purchase of tax privileges through political influence would end. We accept this social contract: a single tax rate and *no* tax breaks beyond the personal exemption. We will not try to increase government at someone else's expense. Every taxpayer will have to contribute.

—*William Poole, 1996*

This tax relief plan is principled. We cut taxes for every income taxpayer. We target nobody in, we target nobody out. And tax relief is now on the way.

—*President George W. Bush, 2001*

Deficits over the next decade are now projected to be enormous in size. . . . Despite the deteriorating fiscal outlook and the historically low corporate revenue collections we already face, Congress nonetheless seems poised to shower more tax breaks on corporations that would cause deficits to grow substantially larger over time.

—*Center on Budget and Policy Priorities, 2003*

## The Problem

In the spring of 2001, the new administration of George W. Bush took up its premier campaign promise: obtaining the largest tax cut ever enacted by the federal government—a ten-year, phased-in reduction of approximately $1.5 trillion, stimulated by the prospect of continued federal budget surpluses. Bush pledged "to give the people back their money." Following the terrorist attacks of September 11 and continued job losses, the White House engineered two more tax cuts in 2002 and 2003 to stimulate a lackluster economy.* However, the combined effects of the tax cuts, declining employment, and growing costs associated with the Iraq war, led to an exploding federal deficit. Despite the tide of red ink, the Bush administration remained steadfastly committed to reducing taxes, especially the dividend and capital gains tax rate. However, the complete impact of the three consecutive tax cuts is a source of controversy. Many of the tax cut provisions in the 2003 legislation that mainly benefited the highest income bracket would not become effective for several years. The use of tax "loopholes" to avoid paying corporate income taxes, including excess depreciation write-offs, offshore tax shelters, and industry-specific subsidies has reduced the corporate tax burden as a share of national income to an all-time low. Thus, the distribution of the tax burden in the face of ever-growing federal deficits and how Americans will pay for mandated tax cuts remains a critical issue. Persistent budget deficits may generate pressure to rescind or reverse the tax reductions.

Whether or not the tax cuts and their consequences will be borne equitably by all Americans is debatable. Indeed, the larger question of whether or not the entire system of American taxation is fair remains a matter of considerably divided opinion. However, before turning to that question, a few general comments on the development of the nation's tax policy are in order.

The American passion for fairness in matters of taxation is a well-established historical fact. Indeed, the very birth of the nation is traceable to this outlook. Taxation without representation, an eminently unfair idea from the perspective of many colonists, led to the famous "tea party" in Boston Harbor in 1774 that directly defied the authority of the British

---

*Economic Growth and Tax Relief Reconciliation Act of 2001, Job Creation and Worker Assistance Act of 2002, and Jobs and Growth Tax Relief Reconciliation Act of 2003.

colonial administrators. That spark was soon fanned into the flame of the American Revolution and, eventually, the birth of the United States of America.

At least through most of the nineteenth century, with the probable exception of the Civil War era (1861–65), the individualistic and anti-central-government temperament of most Americans meant a close eye was kept on the size of the federal government. Indeed, as late as 1902, the federal government's total spending amounted to only $485 million, or about one-third of all governmental outlays in the United States. Reflecting the outlook of Americans toward government in general, local government accounted for nearly 60 percent of all government spending. In any case, government spending of all kinds was equal to only about 7 percent of the nation's gross domestic product (GDP) in 1902.

Events of the twentieth century would greatly alter the anticentrist approach to government and governmental finance. Two major wars and an emerging redefinition of "appropriate" government responsibilities in the economy and social life of the nation not only ballooned the size of governmental outlays in general, but exploded the federal share to nearly two-thirds of total outlays. Such a spending explosion also required a commensurate increase in revenue sources to finance it. Throughout most of the prior century (with the exception of the Civil War years), most federal revenue was obtained from tariffs on goods entering the nation and from sales of public land.

The development of a federal income tax system occurred relatively late in the nation's history. After brief use of an income tax to help finance the Civil War, it was not until 1913—with the enactment of the Sixteenth Amendment—that Congress actually acquired the "power to lay and collect taxes on incomes, from whatever source derived, without apportionment among the several states, without regard to any census or enumeration." The requirements of apportionment and enumeration had restricted the federal government to the option of imposing head taxes—which would have limited the capacity to raise revenue and introduced difficult issues about fairness.

When the new federal income tax was initially levied, the personal exemption was quite generous, such that people earning below $4,000 (about $75,676 in 2004 dollars) did not pay any tax. Beyond incomes of $4,000, the federal income tax was mildly progressive, with tax rates rising in increments of less than 1 percent on those with incomes between $4,000 and $15,000 to a 6 percent rate on all income over $1 million. With family

Table 7.1

**Marginal Federal Income Tax Rates on Taxable Income, for Selected Years** (in percentages)

| Year | $1,000 | $5,000 | $15,000 | $50,000 | $100,000 | $1,000,000 |
|------|--------|--------|---------|---------|----------|------------|
| | | | | Income class | | |
| 1913 | — | 0.4 | 0.8 | 1.5 | 2.5 | 6.0 |
| 1919 | — | 4.8 | 11.9 | 22.3 | 35.2 | 70.3 |
| 1929 | — | 0.3 | 1.9 | 8.5 | 14.9 | 23.1 |
| 1934 | — | 2.8 | 7.6 | 17.4 | 30.2 | 57.1 |
| 1944 | 11.5 | 22.1 | 32.9 | 55.9 | 69.9 | 90.0 |
| 1951 | 8.2 | 19.3 | 30.2 | 53.5 | 67.3 | 87.2 |
| 1962 | 8.0 | 18.9 | 29.7 | 52.8 | 66.8 | 87.0 |

*Source*: "Historical Statistics, Series Y," pp. 319–332 as cited by Albert W. Niemi in *U.S. Economic History* (Chicago: Rand McNally Company, 1975), 121.

income averaging less than $2,000 in 1913, few Americans, even before exemptions and deductions were considered, saw the new income tax as much of a threat. Only 357,000 Americans filed federal income tax returns for 1914. However, as Table 7.1 shows, tax rates soon rose for all levels of income, and they rose quite sharply for higher income levels.

During World War II, the government instituted automatic payroll deductions for federal taxes using a *graduated* schedule in which the tax rate rose with income. At that time, the government also reduced the personal exemption, which had the effect of widening the tax base to include middle- and lower-income classes. *Marginal tax rates*—the rate applied to successively greater increments of earned income—remained relatively high throughout the 1950s. With rising incomes and low inflation during these years, most Americans accepted the *ability-to-pay* principle of taxation. Under this approach, those with higher incomes would be taxed at a higher rate. In reality, however, because of the availability of numerous tax deductions and legal loopholes, few wealthy Americans ever paid the then-existing top statutory rate of 91 percent.

John F. Kennedy, following his election in 1960, undertook the first major change to the federal income tax structure. Faced with a sluggish economy, President Kennedy was counseled by his economic advisers to jump-start macroeconomic growth by lowering income tax rates and granting investment tax credits to the private sector. Although initially reluctant, Kennedy, an astute politician, realized that by tinkering with the tax system he could increase his popularity with both voters and the business community. While some Kennedy advisers believed that manipulating fiscal spending policies rather than taxes was a more effective and equitable means of managing the economy, more conservative advocates of tax cutting prevailed.

The federal income tax system did not change a great deal through the rest of the 1960s and 1970s. Following Kennedy's proposed reduction of the top marginal rate from 91 percent to 70 percent, which was enacted in 1964, not much changed for the average taxpayer. It was not until the early 1980s, following the election of Ronald Reagan, that Congress significantly altered the federal income tax system. First, the Economic Recovery Tax Act of 1981 cut the top rate from 70 percent to about 50 percent. Second, the number of tax brackets was dramatically reduced, and third, many tax loopholes were supposedly closed. Another round of rate changes was undertaken with the Tax Reform Act of 1986, simplifying the rate structure to two basic rates of 15 and 28 percent with the provision that the rate went to about 33 percent for high-income taxpayers.

While the federal tax system remains essentially *progressive*, state and local governments typically use *proportional* and *regressive taxes*. A proportional or flat tax is one that takes a *constant* percentage of income. For example, Pennsylvania has a proportional state income tax. A regressive tax is one that takes a *declining* share of taxpayer income as income rises. Retail sales taxes are regressive because they are mostly levied on consumption items, which tend to claim a larger share of a poor person's total income compared to a wealthy individual. User and registration fees, excise taxes (especially on gasoline), filing fees, and other types of lump-sum payments are all examples of taxes that are effectively regressive. It can also be argued that the Social Security tax is regressive because it applies a 12.4 percent rate (6.2 percent imposed on both the employee and employer) only to wages and salaries under $90,000 (for 2005). Income above this threshold, plus all unearned income (e.g., from dividends, interest, rents), is not subject to the Social Security tax.

In contrast, progressive taxes, as we have seen in the case of the federal income tax, take an *increasing* share of income from higher-income classes. The federal income tax is progressive in that higher tax rates apply to higher income. For example, in 2003 there were six different rates that applied to a single taxpayer: 10 percent on income up to $7,000; 15 percent on additional income up to $28,400; 25 percent on the next slab of income up to $68,800; 28 percent on subsequent income up to $143,500; 33 percent on each dollar of income greater than $311,950; and 35 percent on income above this amount.

Table 7.2

**Federal Government Receipts 1950, 1960, 1970, 1980, 1990, 2000, and 2003** (in percentages)

|  | 1950 | 1960 | 1970 | 1980 | 1990 | 2000 | 2003 |
|---|---|---|---|---|---|---|---|
| Current tax receipts |  |  |  |  |  |  |  |
| Personal current taxes | 28.6 | 34.3 | 36.0 | 37.5 | 34.7 | 39.5 | 32.9 |
| Taxes on production and imports | 34.8 | 33.2 | 31.9 | 25.2 | 24.9 | 22.7 | 26.2 |
| Taxes on corporate income | 27.1 | 16.9 | 12.0 | 10.6 | 8.2 | 8.2 | 7.2 |
| Taxes from the rest of the world | 0.0 | 0.1 | 0.1 | 0.2 | 0.2 | 0.2 | 0.2 |
| Contributions for government social insurance | 8.3 | 12.2 | 16.2 | 20.8 | 24.0 | 22.5 | 25.8 |
| Other sources | 1.2 | 3.3 | 3.9 | 5.7 | 8.0 | 6.9 | 7.7 |
| Total | 100.0 | 100.0 | 100.0* | 100.0 | 100.0 | 100.0 | 100.0 |

*Source:* U.S. Department of Commerce, National Income and Product Accounts
*Does not add to total due to rounding.

One final point on the federal tax system needs to be made: It has increasingly become a system in which the tax burden falls directly and immediately on *individual* taxpayers. A little over fifty years ago—as Table 7.2 illustrates—taxes collected from corporations accounted for more than 27 percent of all federal tax revenues; by 2003, their share had dropped to about 7 percent. Alternatively, taxes on individual's incomes and employee and employer contributions to Social Security had risen to nearly 59 percent of federal tax revenues. Since deficits are expected to become cumulatively about $5 trillion over the next decade, then the burden borne by individual taxpayers must increase.

It is obvious that the type of revenue system a government chooses to employ—regressive, proportional, or progressive—necessarily says a lot about a nation's sense of fairness. Most economists agree, and have agreed for a long time, that if all taxes paid by all persons to all governmental units in the United States were aggregated, the American tax system could best be described as moderately progressive. Whether a moderately progressive tax system is *fair,* however, remains a matter of debate.

## Synopsis

Conservatives generally favor levies on consumption or other activities that will not distort an individual's decision to work or save. On the other hand, Liberals assert that since the level of income and wealth best reflects a person's ability to pay for governmental functions, a proportional or graduated income tax is the fairest system of taxation. Radicals argue that the long-term increase in the share of income borne by wage earners directly reflects the power of business elites to purchase congressional votes to ensure the passage of laws that will lower their share of the tax burden.

---

## Anticipating the Arguments

- Why do Conservatives argue against progressive taxes as a means of financing government?
- What reasoning is employed by Liberals to justify progressive taxes as equitable?
- Why do Radicals advocate a steeply progressive tax on all sources of income?

## THE CONSERVATIVE ARGUMENT

Ever since the economist Adam Smith specified the role for limited government interference in a market economy, most Conservative economists have recognized the need for a small public sector. However, the government sector in most advanced capitalist societies has expanded well beyond what Smith ever expected. To Smith, the state should provide for the national defense; educate citizens; administer justice; pay for "public works and institutions for facilitating the commerce of society"; sustain the indigent, old, and infirm; and "support the dignity of the sovereign." Furthermore, government should pay for its provision and administration of goods and services by imposing taxes in an *equitable* and *consistent* manner. Thus, the overall goal of government tax policy should be to (1) devise a system that is fair to all citizens and (2) help stimulate market forces that promote growth and capital formation.

Since the adoption of the federal income tax in 1913, the U.S. tax system has failed to adhere to these two basic principles. Instead, the income tax has been used to redistribute income from productive, hardworking taxpayers and businesses to government programs that support unproductive economic activities or unprofitable ventures. Moreover, onerous redistributive income taxes encourage individuals to avoid paying taxes by either working "off the books" or by seeking employment in the underground economy. The current tax system undermines the work ethic by significantly lowering after-tax wages. This causes workers to reduce their labor effort supplied to the market, often to the point where they choose to avoid work altogether and become dependent upon government welfare. Finally, the design and enforcement of the tax code is unnecessarily bureaucratic and intrusive, and imposes high costs of compliance.

Rather than adhering to Smith's maxim of an "equitable, certain, convenient and efficient" system of taxation, the U.S. government continues to confiscate an increasing share of taxpayers' incomes. Progressive income tax systems are based on the fallacious assumption that wealthy individuals do not gain as much satisfaction from an extra dollar of earnings as do those with lower incomes. Therefore, the government erroneously believes that it is actually improving society's well-being when it taxes away a "hardly missed" dollar from a high-income person and spends it on public goods or redistributes it to the lower end of the income distribution.

Little regard is given to the central role played by the savings and investments of thrifty individuals who provide the funds that ultimately drive growth and job creation. Moreover, since the poor tend to consume all their income, free markets crucially depend upon society's net savers to fund the enterprises (and some government activities) that put people to work. By taxing investors, the government only encourages savers to consume their surplus earnings, invest overseas, seek out unproductive tax shelters, or engage in other tax-avoiding activities.

## The Savings Crisis

Adam Smith was one of the first economists to understand that capitalism cannot thrive without the accumulation of a financial surplus for investment. The U.S. economy's ability to provide gainful employment and adequate income for all able-bodied workers is fundamentally determined by its savings rate. American capital markets must be able to harness the surplus funds of households, corporations, and foreigners and deploy them to the private sector for the purchase of new plants, property, and equipment. Thus, it is clear that without savings, the capital stock cannot expand and labor productivity cannot rise, which will ultimately result in a lower overall standard of living.

Unfortunately, the savings rate in the United States has been falling since about 1970. The decline in the personal savings rate is illustrated in

Figure 7.1. Battered by higher personal income tax rates enacted by the Clinton administration, the personal saving rate went into free fall after 1992. In 2002, the savings rate was 2.3 percent—placing the United States on a par with the savings rates of the poorest of lesser-developed nations.

The long-term consequences have been unambiguous: A decline in the savings rate has choked off domestic capital formation, which constrained the growth in overall labor productivity and thus reduced both income and mobility for numerous working people. Economies that cannot sustain an adequate rate of capital accumulation are destined to decline. Moreover, with heightened global competition for limited financial resources, new demands for investment capital can be expected to divert the savings of foreigners (who currently provide about one-third of our domestic savings) from the American economy. Given these dire trends and circumstances, it is essential that federal tax policies be designed to increase capital formation by eliminating taxes on all forms of savings.

## The Failure of Progressive Income Taxes

The legacy of progressive taxation has not been good. Since the early 1960s, when the top marginal tax rate was more than 90 percent, both the savings rate and labor productivity have steadily deteriorated while the share of taxes raised from personal income has steadily increased. Efforts to reverse this trend were helped with the passage in 1981 of President Reagan's tax reforms, which were designed to increase federal tax revenues by reducing the top marginal tax rates and by simplifying the federal tax code. The success of supply-side economics is supported by the fact that federal revenues increased by almost 50 percent from 1982 to 1988. While Ronald Reagan's tax policies generated higher revenues, the savings rate has continued to languish because Congress subsequently raised tax rates on the highest-income groups and steadfastly refuses to eliminate taxes on capital gains.

Although Liberals claim that the progressive income tax system helps to reduce income inequality in America, both disparities between income classes and the overall poverty rate steadily increased during the 1970s. This is because our tax laws stifled personal initiative by penalizing those who seek to better themselves. At its core, the old tax system only benefited the very poor—who are exempt from paying taxes—or the very rich who have already amassed their fortunes. For example, a graduated income tax often discourages risk taking by reducing an

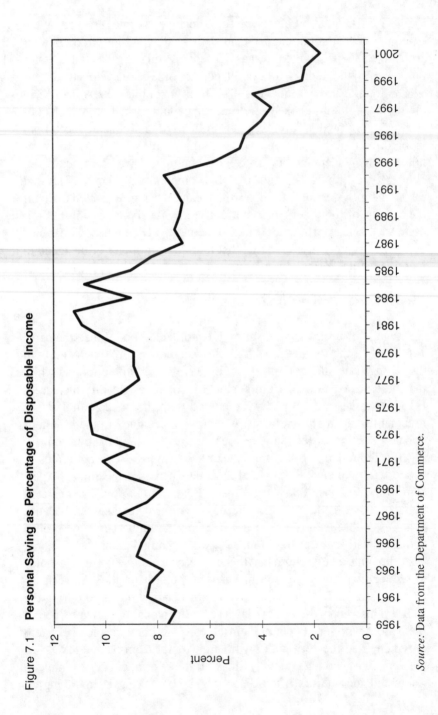

Figure 7.1   **Personal Saving as Percentage of Disposable Income**

*Source:* Data from the Department of Commerce.

entrepreneur's net return. This in turn chokes off innovation and competition while acting as a powerful deterrent to others who have the capacity to undertake new business ventures but choose not to for fear of seeing the fruits of their labor taxed away by the state. Furthermore, wealthy individuals living off a flow of unearned income will avoid risky investments in order to cover their ever-increasing tax liability.

Finally, the progressive income tax system is particularly onerous for families with two wage earners. When considered individually, a working husband and wife might not make very much money. However, when their incomes are combined, they are quickly pushed into the highest income tax bracket. In the case where one spouse earns most of the household's income, the less-compensated husband or wife often pays more than half their income in taxes.

Put simply, the prior tax system undermined the free market system by creating powerful disincentives to work, save, or invest. President George W. Bush began to reverse many of these damaging policies with his tax program designed to bolster capital formation and savings. The three tax packages proposed by the administration and quickly enacted by Congress between 2001 and 2003 provided a successful short-term stimulus to the economy while significantly improving the longer-term prospects for growth. The president's strategy of lowering marginal income tax rates, significantly increasing child tax credits, and cutting dividend taxes all resulted in higher inflation-adjusted after-tax income. In addition, business profitability and labor productivity increased as the cost of capital fell assisted by accelerated depreciation rules and a reduction in the capital gains rate.

Despite these short-term successes, the federal income tax code is much too complex, cumbersome, and fundamentally inequitable. Some Conservatives endorse a proportional or "flat tax" on income, which is attractive from the standpoint of practicality and certain equity considerations. However, the superior long-term solution is to adopt a consumption-based tax system.

### The Solution—A Progressive Consumption Tax

The Conservative argument for a progressive consumption tax is embedded in the notion that the economy remains fundamentally constrained by insufficient savings on the part of individuals. Moreover, an intrusive and overly complex federal tax system has created perverse incentives that diminish or misdirect investment activities, lowering productivity and encouraging profligate consumption. A progressive consumption tax would simultaneously address issues related to fairness and consistency that plague the current tax system.

Under a progressive consumption tax system, taxpayers would be allowed to deduct *all* funds that are saved or invested from their gross income. Money borrowed or taken out of savings would be included in taxable consumption. Since consumption is defined as income minus savings, computing an individual's tax liability from his or her paycheck would be a relatively straightforward process. There would be no need for investment tax credits or a capital gains tax since the government would allow a single, comprehensive loophole for all earnings not consumed—no matter what the source of those funds. Lobbyists would be banished from the halls of Congress because there could be no gain from trying to get special tax breaks for specific kinds of investments or business activities. Complicated tax formulas to account for inflation, depreciation, and a host of other problems related to capital accounting would be eliminated, as all income from savings and investments would be treated exactly the same—they would *all* be exempt from taxes.

Fairness would improve because tax rates on consumption would increase with higher levels of consumption. This would capture more government revenue from conspicuous and profligate consumption by wealthy individuals. Less affluent taxpayers would have more of an incentive to save because (1) there would be a lower tax rate on the last dollar consumed, and (2) they would gain the benefit of tax-exempt interest earnings. Business people would find it much easier to start new firms because all investments would be made in a tax-free environment. With a greater supply of savings forthcoming, the cost of capital would decline, and riskier and more innovative investment projects would be undertaken. Companies would be much more willing to start up new ventures and/or expand existing operations, thus leading to the hiring of more workers and an overall increase in output, income, and employment.

## THE LIBERAL ARGUMENT

Political ideologues of either the Right or Left will eventually come to understand that an optimal system of taxation can never be achieved. Neither a program of "soaking the rich" nor one that primarily taxes consumption can ensure that the collective responsibilities we entrust to government will be funded. Economists have learned that there is no single tax system that can simultaneously achieve an equitable distribution of income, stable growth, high productivity, low unemployment, and a myriad of other policy goals. While economic theories may purport to prove the superiority of a particular tax structure, tax systems—like all governmental undertakings—are *political* institutions that embody social and other noneconomic considerations. This fact cannot be evaded.

Most people would agree that the strength of the U.S. economy and society is largely due to the heterogeneous and pluralist nature of its population. This diversity enables individuals who possess a broad range of talents and abilities to harness America's resources for the betterment of all. However, wealth and skill are not evenly distributed throughout society, so that every individual cannot be expected to succeed solely on his or her initiative and skill. Nor is the private sector capable of insuring society's citizens against uncertainty and calamities of various sorts. Thus, an advanced capitalist economy requires its citizens to pool resources via government in order to offset and ameliorate income and job losses arising from recessions, foreign competition, technological unemployment, disease, natural catastrophes, and a host of other accidental and unforeseen factors. Put simply, the state must find a pragmatic method to raise money in order to undertake the necessary expenditures and projects required to hold a free market society together. The primary problem is to decide how best to obtain the funds needed for the provision of public goods and services.

While Adam Smith was correct in calling for the equitable taxation of those with roughly equal means, the question of how to tax *disparate* incomes is a more vexing issue. For example, a poor taxpayer and a rich taxpayer both receive the same amount of protection from the provision of defense services by the armed forces. Nevertheless, the question remains: Should the wealthy person still pay more for national defense because he or she has more to lose in the event of social unrest, war, or invasion? Alternatively, if a poor person lives in an area with a higher crime rate, should her tax liability be higher to pay for increased police protection? Even if we acknowledge differential abilities to pay, apportioning the appropriate benefits and costs to particular taxpayers cannot be guided by some fixed rule or principle.

Despite these ambiguities, it is quite evident that government revenues should be acquired in such a way as to maximize tax compliance and minimize avoidance and administrative costs. The development of both an efficient and an equitable system of tax collection should be the prime concern of lawmakers, even though the federal income tax system has grown in scope and complexity since its inception in 1913. While tax simplification would likely increase compliance with current tax statutes, the government could also significantly increase its revenues—without raising taxes—if it simply collected all that it was owed. In 2004, the IRS estimated a "tax gap" equal to about $311 billion, a figure equal to approximately one-half of the federal budget deficit. The problem has also been compounded by the persistence of many tax loopholes despite recent tax reform measures to close them. For example, corporations have avoided paying billions of dollars of federal income taxes through the use of various types of domestic and offshore "tax shelters." The Internal Revenue Service estimates that such "abusive" tax shelters are costing taxpayers well over $50 billion per year in lost revenue. Moreover, continued inequities in the incidence and distribution of many state and local taxes have heightened taxpayer frustration.

Nevertheless, the primary justification for the federal income tax rests mainly upon equity considerations. That is, a taxpayer's income is the best indicator of his or her ability to pay for the costs of government. On the other hand, those who are below some minimum income level can be easily excused from paying income taxes. In a similar vein, only the income tax is flexible enough to adjust an individual's personal circumstances to their tax liability. For example, suppose a family incurs substantial medical bills or loses a house to a fire or storm in a given tax year. In the first case, because the family "consumed" a substantial portion of their discretionary income in the form of medical goods and services, that family would now have a substantial tax liability. Moreover, replacing a home or car lost in a fire or accident would also subject a person to substantial consumption taxes. Finally, while many grumble about paying taxes each April 15, taxes fund many activities with significant benefits to all, including police and fire protection, schools, hospitals, sports stadiums, and museums.

## The Success of the Progressive Income Tax

While few would dispute the complexity of our federal tax system, it has in fact accomplished its main task of raising government revenues in a generally equitable and efficient manner. Contrary to what Conservatives claim, the top marginal tax rate is one of the lowest among the industrialized nations. Indeed, these same "overtaxed" nations have for the most part reported greater long-term efficiency and growth compared to the United States, thus disposing of the Conservative charge that our "soak the rich" tax strategy is a major cause of our recent sluggish economic performance. We should also remember that we pay taxes other than federal income taxes, for instance, state and local sales, income, property, and use taxes; and, of course, corporate income and other business taxes are to some extent pushed onto consumers in the form of higher prices. When the effects of all of these taxes (many of which are highly regressive) are considered, the alleged "burden" of our progressive tax system is just not true.

What is true, however, is that our federal income tax system has been quite successful in distributing the tax burden: Those with higher incomes *do* pay a greater share of federal income taxes. In 2004, for example, those with incomes exceeding $96,700 pay almost 60 percent of total federal, state, and local taxes. In fact, a key reason why President Clinton was able to achieve a balanced federal budget—without slowing the economy—was that the progressive tax structure permitted a slight tax increase on those with high incomes to generate a greater-than-proportional rise in tax revenues. Unfortunately, President Bush's tax cuts to the wealthiest taxpayers and giveaways to large corporations have caused the federal deficit to escalate at a rate that alarms many Americans. The Bush administration has reintroduced the country to the use of "supply-side" tax cuts to increase tax revenues—a cornerstone of economic policy from the Reagan administration of the 1980s. The balanced budgets by President Clinton during the 1990s should have put an end to this fiction. Thus, instead of accomplishing President Clinton's objective to pay off the entire federal debt by 2010, the Bush administration's tax cuts will likely add $5 trillion to the debt by that year. Although some economists claim that taxes distort an individual's choice to work, consume, or invest, the evidence suggests that only very high marginal income tax rates actually discourage such behavior. Doctors, lawyers, accountants, and stockbrokers continue to supply just as many hours to the market, irrespective of any tinkering that Congress might undertake with regard to the federal income tax law.

A progressive personal income tax also acts as a built-in stabilizer for the overall economy. During business expansions, it allows the government to collect relatively more revenues as output and incomes expand and proportionately less during recessions. Ronald Reagan used tax cuts to stimulate the economy during the 1981–82 recession. Unfortunately, the federal deficit exploded because he did not raise taxes on upper-income individuals, nor cut defense expenditures. This is exactly what is happening again as a result of Bush's tax policies. Nevertheless, fiscal and tax policies—when applied in a reasonable and judicious manner—can be an effective means to maintain a stable balance between the growth of savings and income. While the current federal income tax system is far from perfect, it is clear that it satisfies the range of goals demanded by society.

## THE RADICAL ARGUMENT

The development and workings of the American tax system must be understood in the context of its impact on wage earners as opposed to those who obtain their livelihood from unearned income in the form of profits, rents, interest, and dividends. Since the inception of the federal income tax on personal income in the early part of this century, most economists agree that wage earners have increasingly borne a higher share of the national tax burden. Given this trend, mainstream economists either argue for tax simplification—via a single tax rate—or emphasize the need to strengthen tax collection efforts at all levels of government. Alternatively, Radicals analyze the question of a fair tax system by whose interests are being served. For example, lucrative tax credits and esoteric tax deductions were not designed for wage earners who file the standard "EZ" tax form. Rather, our complicated federal tax system and attendant tax laws directly reflect the efforts on the part of rich people, corporations, and other monied interests to reduce their tax burden. The fact that the federal tax liability of capital has steadily *declined* for the past forty years only underscores the success of the richest 1 percent of income earners in shifting the costs of government onto the backs of the vast majority of working people.

### Taxes and Accumulation

It has become an unquestioned premise of mainstream economic analysis that savings is the primary determinant of growth and accumulation. According to the Conservative paradigm, government attempts at taxing savings necessarily imply less growth in output, employment, and income. In addition, when the state runs a deficit, not only does it have to raise taxes in the future, but also in the short term it increases the overall cost of capital by bidding up interest rates to attract savings that would normally be allocated to private capital markets.

The logic of the Conservative argument suggests a strong inverse correlation between the top tax rate and the share of income devoted by an economy to investment. However, the economic data for successful advanced capitalist economies do not support this argument. Moreover, the high marginal tax rates of more egalitarian economies do not seem to have a punishing effect on investment spending and savings rates.

The bleating of the "overtaxed rich" is belied by reality, and their seemingly contradictory tolerance for government taxes to fund expenditures for warfare over those to enhance human welfare and dignity cannot be ignored. The federal income tax system initially taxed capital and upper-income individuals while granting generous exemptions to those further down the income ladder. The top marginal income tax rates have remained above the current top rate for most years since the inception of the federal personal income tax in 1913. However, since that time, personal exemptions for most taxpayers have been significantly reduced, as has been the minimum income threshold where one begins paying taxes. Moreover, since 1935, funding the Social Security system has always been borne by workers whose earnings rarely exceed the salary ceiling beyond which no more payroll taxes are due ($90,000 for 2005). Thus, it is no surprise that the Social Security tax is the most highly regressive of all federal income taxes because it is capped at 6.2 percent of salaries up to $90,000. For a person earning $100,000 the Social Security tax is just above 5.5 percent; at a salary above $200,000 the rate drops to about 2.8 percent. Finally, since about 1942, the federal government has reached further and further down the income distribution to find needed revenues. While the exigencies of World War II necessitated emergency taxes and debt financing, the government never returned to the prewar tax schedules that were much less onerous for working-class taxpayers.

### The Problem with Flat Taxes

Since the passage of California's Proposition 13 in 1978, the "taxpayer revolt"—primarily against increased property taxes to fund municipal services, especially public schools—has spread to other states. Politicians at the national level have responded to taxpayer frustrations by proposing several changes to the current federal income tax system. Unfortunately, many plans to create a more simplified tax system also include many regressive features that will continue to foster an increase in the share of taxes borne by lower-income workers. There are currently several proposals in Congress to change the current federal income tax system. Most prominent among the Republican initiatives is a *progressive consumption tax*. Let us briefly examine the problem with each of these tax schemes.

Presidents and lesser politicians have often enshrined their names in the history books not by noble deeds but by tinkering with the federal income tax code. The original federal income tax statute enacted in 1913 taxed unearned income (dividends, interest income, and the like) at a higher rate compared to earned (wage and salary) income. In contrast to the current climate, which favors capital income, the first national tax scheme exempted almost all wage earners from federal taxes and permitted more generous personal exemptions. The top marginal personal income tax rate was first lowered by John F. Kennedy from 90 percent to 70 percent in 1964. Ronald Reagan lowered it to 50 percent in 1981 and even further to 33 percent in 1986. In addition to cutting the tax rates, lobbyists and other special interests have spent millions of dollars to induce Congress to include special rules that exempt particular businesses from federal taxes. Over the years, a vast and complicated system of tax laws and administrative rulings has created an unwieldy and highly inequitable tax system. The net result has been a decline in the share of federal taxes paid by large corporations and a notable increase in the tax burden of working people and small businesses.

The Conservative plan for a progressive consumption tax is a clever proposal to reconcile the inherent regressivity of consumption taxes with the current system, which taxes higher incomes at an increasing rate of taxation. To demonstrate its tenability, Conservatives appeal to the logic contained in the following mathematical example: Suppose an individual who makes $50,000 per year is taxed at a rate of 10 percent but also saves $5,000. A tax rate of 11.1 percent on an individual's consumption would be needed to raise the same amount of revenue because taxable income is reduced by the amount saved ($5,000). Though the example appears to be eminently reasonable, a problem arises as we move to higher incomes. Under current law, an individual taxpayer earning $10 million owes about $2.5 million in taxes (an average tax rate of 25 percent). Even if a very wealthy individual could consume $2.5 million of goods and services per year, the consumption tax rate would have to equal at least 100 percent to raise the same amount of revenue obtained from the current income tax structure. The point is that consumption tends to be a rather stable proportion of income for all individuals; however, wealthy people tend to consume a much smaller proportion of each dollar increment of income they earn. Short of forcing rich people to consume more, a consumption-based tax structure is inherently less burdensome for the wealthy compared to those with much less income.

### A Return to Progressivity

In recent years, it has become quite unfashionable to argue for a tax system where the rate increases as an individual's income rises. Though Radical policy proposals are rarely put forward with any historical consistency or consensus, Marx and Engels argued for "a heavy progressive or graduated income tax" in their *Communist Manifesto* in 1848. Even Liberal economists have traditionally advocated a progressive income tax system based on the idea that an extra dollar of income for a middle-class or wealthy income earner provides diminishing satisfaction, and thus can be taxed at a higher rate compared to earnings below a mandated threshold. Adam Smith also believed that defense expenditures and education should be funded from "general contributions" and courts, roads, and other social infrastructure should be supported by tolls or fees. Smith also wrote in the *Wealth of Nations* that taxes should be levied in an equitable and consistent manner, *primarily* based upon an individual's ability to pay.

Nevertheless, since about 1981, cutting the top income tax rate while broadening the income range that applies to each rate has reduced the progressivity of the federal income tax system. The net effect of these changes has been to significantly reduce the percent of taxes borne by the upper-income groups. A recent analysis by Citizens for Tax Justice shows that Bush's tax cuts have lowered the overall federal, state, and local tax burden on the richest 1 percent of taxpayers—earnings above $978,000—by 12 percent. The ostensibly small reduction in the top bracket translates into a phenomenal windfall in absolute dollars for those in the top 5 percent of the income distribution. The *Forbes* 400 listing of the richest people in America, whose huge collective wealth multiplied into a megafortune in the last six or seven years (see Issue 6), will beget still greater incomes, now at more favorable tax rates.

While the federal income tax system has become less progressive, state and local tax schemes have also become less equitable. After the Reagan tax cuts of the early 1980s, many states simply adapted the federal tax brackets to their respective tax schedules. Furthermore, most local governments rely upon *regressive* property and sales taxes to fund most municipal activities. Property taxes are regressive because all incomes usually pay the same rate of tax, but the property valuation of the poor, in contrast to the wealthy, is often above its actual market value. Meanwhile, sales taxes are inherently more burdensome to the poor because they tend to spend a higher portion of their income on taxable consumption items. Since property taxes are the major source of funding for public schools, it is obvious why richer communities always seem to have outstanding public school systems, irrespective of governmental tax policies and/or fluctuations in the general economy. Conversely, it is not surprising that poorer communities generally have inferior public schools, particularly when their communities are faced with permanent economic decline.

The Conservative desire for a consumption-based income tax system is part and parcel of their broader program to end all collectively funded social programs. In their view, an individual's ability for pecuniary gain should be the *sole determinant* of personal worth in society. Accordingly, any effort on the part of government to encumber private income is illegitimate and leads to a misallocation of scarce resources. It is only a short leap of Conservative logic to demonstrate how *any* income tax leads to the downfall of capitalism.

A Radical program for a more equitable tax system would start with a steeply progressive income tax system on *all* income. Those who earn less than a government-guaranteed income—say, $40,000 for a family of four—would automatically be exempt from all taxes. Second, most tax loopholes would be eliminated, inheritance taxes would be substantially increased, and a flat tax on all stock market transactions would be imposed. While long-term investors would not be taxed as heavily as short-term speculators, all capital gains would be subject to a highly progressive income tax structure. Under this tax system, no one would be prevented from accumulating wealth; however, wealth would not become the source of dynastic power for those who did not create it.

Finally, all income—both earned and unearned—would be subject to a *progressive* Social Security tax. This would make the Social Security system solvent and eliminate all the inequities existing under current financing methods—especially since about three-quarters of all taxpayers pay more in social security taxes than federal income taxes. Moreover, aggregate demand would grow much faster if payroll taxes on low-wage workers were drastically reduced or temporarily suspended to raise income and stimulate consumption. For far too long, rich corporations and wealthy individuals have been able to use the political system to reduce their tax burden. It is time for the vast majority of Americans to direct their anger not so much at the tax collector but at a Congress that is wholly incapable of creating a fair and equitable tax system. Ultimately, the vast majority of working-class Americans must band together to ensure that there will be an end to taxation without representation.

# Problems of Aggregate Economic Policy

Part III focuses on issues that are primarily *macroeconomic* in origin. In other words, our attention will be directed to issues affecting the economy as a whole and to variables affecting its aggregate economic performance. Specifically, we shall examine such problem areas as business cycle behavior, stabilization policy, the federal deficit, unemployment, inflation, international trade and monetary policy, and the changing demographics of the nation's population. Part II examined problems of specific economic units—households, firms, industries, labor groups, and the like. As one economist described the difference between microeconomics and macroeconomics, the former examines the trees, while the latter studies the forest.

# Macroeconomic Instability

## Are We Depression-Proof?

We have nothing to fear but fear itself.
*—President Franklin D. Roosevelt, 1933*

This is a unique moment in U.S. history, a time of unrivaled prosperity and progress, with few internal crises or external threats. We have the responsibility to use our good fortune wisely. If we maintain our current economic strategy, we can sustain our prosperity, expand the circle of opportunity, meet the long-term challenges of this new century, and provide our children the chance to live their dreams.
*—President Bill Clinton, 2001*

The economy of the United States has been through a lot. If you really think about it, it's pretty remarkable to be able to stand up and say to you that our economy is strong and getting stronger, that we're witnessing steady, consistent growth. After all, we've been through a recession, a national emergency, a war, corporate scandals.
*—President George W. Bush, 2004*

In world market crisis, the contradictions and antagonisms of bourgeois production break through to the surface. But instead of investigating the nature of the . . . catastrophe, the apologists content themselves with denying the catastrophe itself.

*—Karl Marx, 1867*

## The Problem

Fluctuations in the general level of economic activity have long been one of the more prominent features of the macroeconomy. Throughout the nineteenth century and the first third of the twentieth, the cyclical pattern of national economic performance was more or less accepted as the normal state of affairs: first a period of boom and expansion, then a stage of general contraction (until the 1930s usually called a "panic"), followed by a recovery that culminated in yet another boom, and, sooner or later, another contraction. Always a matter of some interest to economists, public interest in the business cycle varied inversely with the ebb and flow of business conditions. Not until the long contraction of the 1930s did the business cycle become a matter of serious and enduring discussion among ordinary citizens. The dreary decade after the stock market crash in 1929 directed almost everyone's attention to efforts to understand the causes of economic fluctuations. This was especially true because the Great Depression was, by most past standards of cyclical behavior, exceptionally deep and protracted. Although the Great Depression is no longer a part of recent American history, and is remembered only dimly by a comparative handful of living Americans, its impact on our economic thinking and reflexes remains extraordinarily strong.

That Americans might have a special concern about severe business downturns is not surprising when the severity of the "Great Rupture" in American history is recalled. Between 1929 and 1933, the gross domestic product (the nation's annual output of goods and services) was sliced almost in half. Unemployment, which had averaged about 3.2 percent in 1929, soared to 24.9 percent by 1933. Unemployment for 1933 totaled 13 million men and women, but this figure was deceiving because several times that amount, perhaps 65 percent of the labor force, suffered some unemployment or could obtain only part-time work. On the business side, before-tax corporate profits fell from a record $11 billion in 1929 to an operating loss of $1.2 billion four years later, and industrial production declined by more than 45 percent.

Historians have documented the wrenching effect of the Depression on institutions and values. However great the changes in modes of American thought and behavior, none were more profound than those in economic thinking and practice. Before Black Tuesday's stock market collapse on October 29, 1929, and the crisis that followed, conventional economic wisdom unashamedly espoused the virtues of laissez-faire. The economy was to operate freely. Although this meant the periodic toleration of bad times as business activity occasionally slowed, these downturns were offset by succeeding periods of expansion and prosperity. Left alone, economic analysis held, the economy would right itself and, over time, move upward to new, higher levels of output, employment, and real income.

But recovery was not spontaneous, and for good or ill, the orthodox belief in the self-regulating business cycle fell from favor. Ruminating in England on the worldwide depression, John Maynard Keynes concluded it was time to clear the intellectual stage of all the old furniture of economic orthodoxy. In 1936, his *General Theory of Employment, Interest, and Money* proclaimed that capitalist economic institutions were not self-balancing mechanisms but instead tended toward chronic stagnation. This situation required action by governments through fiscal and monetary policy to forestall collapse. The solution: Raise aggregate demand for goods through massive government spending, thereby putting to work unemployed people and idle factories. Not given to modesty, Keynes correctly warned his readers that his ideas would change the way people thought about modern capitalist economies. And they did, as Keynes's "New Economics" became the dominant wisdom in economic matters.

For most of the first three decades after World War II, Keynesian orthodoxy reigned. The Keynesian view that periodic slumps in the economy could and should be offset by government efforts to stimulate the demand for goods went virtually unquestioned, and many economists began to think and act as though fluctuations in business activity were only a feature of the past, pre-Keynesian era. With the new economic logic maintaining that depressions were unnecessary and could always be headed off by appropriate use of public policy, a good many Americans came to believe in the 1960s that we were now "depression-proof." However, events in the mid-1970s prompted a reexamination of the New Economics. Although no depression developed, the economy did suffer through stagflation as economic growth slowed, unemployment rates rose, and price inflation gnawed deep into the economy.

Meanwhile, the general economic uncertainty that prevailed during and after the 1970s had reopened old debates among contending economic philosophies about what were the appropriate and most effective strategies for dealing with business fluctuations or any impending depression. Liberals had to reexamine their earlier claims that the business cycle had indeed been brought under control through demand-management policies. While not abandoning their view on the inherent instability of production-for-profit economies, modern Keynesian Liberals have accepted more modest countercyclical targets, no longer arguing so vigorously that the economy can be sustained on a permanent expansionary course by simply fine-tuning levels of aggregate demand. For Conservatives, the stagflationary epoch provided first visibility (which had all but disappeared during the era of "High Keynesianism") and then a high degree of respectability. In the new economic setting, it was appropriate to challenge the Keynesian explanation of the Great Depression as well as Keynesian policy making in general. For Radicals, the stagflationary crises of the 1970s and early 1980s were seen, at least in the short run, as a vindication. They had always viewed the 1930s as proof that unregulated capitalist economies were inherently self-destructive, and the economic problems of the 1970s had shown that regulated capitalism did not work either.

Then, along came the economic boom of the 1990s. Its durability was such that a great many ordinary citizens became inclined to believe that the Great Depression and its consequences should be consigned to the trash bin of "forgettable historical events." Of course, not many thoughtful economists believed that the good times of the nineties were *proof* that the business cycle had been repealed. Most, if pressed on the question of whether or not another Great Depression was *possible,* would have responded with a cautious affirmative answer: *Possible but really unnecessary as long as we responded to a downturn "intelligently."*

By early September 2001, the evidence indicated that the boom was over and the nation had descended into recession—but a recession of ordinary and tolerable dimensions. However, the terrorist attacks on the World Trade Center and the Pentagon on September 11, 2001, and the resulting commitment of the United States to a "war on terrorism" caused considerable professional reconsideration about the prospect of a "normal recession." The New York Stock Exchange's biggest one-day loss of value in its history (although the loss was overcome in the following three weeks), the particularly heavy blow to transportation and entertainment industries, the American consumer's decision to reduce current spending, and the resulting cut back on employment and investment outlays by business dealt the sagging economy a heavy blow.

Although the 2001 recession officially lasted only nine months, as of June 2004, employment still remained below its prior peak level. Though the economy is not likely to slide down a precipice resembling the Great Depression, the last recession was notable for the breadth and duration of unemployment—especially among college-educated workers. Perhaps this will be a new feature of the American business cycle where employment prospects in recessions are not that much different from expansions. The prospects of another Great Depression may be greatly muted, but they have not been silenced.

### Synopsis

The Conservative position maintains that depression and protracted economic stagnation are not central to capitalist economic systems and that the business cycle downturn after 1929 was worsened, not moderated, by government intervention in the economy. Liberals argue that only through vigorous, active countercyclical policies by government can the economy's natural propensity toward recession and depression be controlled. To Radicals, crisis and depression are quite natural to production-for-profit systems, and although crises may be delayed by governmental actions, they cannot be eliminated in the long run.

---

### Anticipating the Arguments

- On what grounds do Conservatives argue that Liberals and Radicals have failed to prove their case that capitalism naturally tends toward protracted periods of economic stagnation? How do they account for economic downturns?
- In what ways did the Keynesian critique depart from the conventional wisdom of the 1930s?
- How does the Radical scenario of capitalism's chronic tendency toward crisis differ from the Liberal Keynesian view?

### THE CONSERVATIVE ARGUMENT

The classical economic tradition from which most Conservatives draw their analytical perspectives and their strength of purpose holds to a simple proposition: *When free human beings operate freely in free markets, this necessarily will lead to optimal economic and social outcomes.* This view is not limited to microeconomic (individual market) operations, but extends to an aggregate or macroeconomic analysis of economic activities. Left to operate freely, the aggregate economy, like an individual market, will be self-correcting over time, setting optimal output, price, and employment conditions to avoid excessive long-term swings in business activity.* Business fluctuations over the short term are, of course, not surprising since an economy must from time to time adjust to changing conditions. But long-run or violent contractions are essentially the result of unwarranted interventions by government or others seeking to *improve on* market outcomes.

For a long time this point of view did not enjoy extensive currency among economic reasoners nor much practice by Western political leaders. The long Depression of the 1930s signaled a decline in classical economic modes of thought that was not reversed until the late 1970s. Given the long economic boom of the 1980s and the record-breaking expansion of the 1990s, however, it is easy to forget the economic past. Yet two important points need to be recalled lest we repeat, in our forgetfulness, our past errors. First, we need to understand the real causes and effects of economic events in the era that came to be known as the Great Depression. Second, we must comprehend how our errors in understanding these events led to the development of economic doctrines and policies that produced the near catastrophic economic crises of the 1970s. Much mythology surrounds these questions, but also much danger if we are not historically and factually accurate in our understanding of the past seven decades of economic history.

To put matters directly, most of what is believed about the causes of the Great Depression is wrong. More important, the body of economic policy developed to make us depression-proof was dangerously irrelevant, constructed to deal with a problem that never existed. Alas, the cumbersome structure of government intervention in the economy through countercyclical fiscal and monetary policy has been unnecessary. Indeed, government intervention has been more of a threat to stability than a bulwark.

## On Misreading the Significance of Causes of the Great Depression

Contrary to popular economic beliefs, the initial business downturn between 1929 and 1930 was not in itself a unique event. As most econo-

---

*This principle, sometimes called Say's law after the French economist Jean-Baptiste Say, who formulated it in 1803, is, of course, directly challenged by Liberals and Radicals.

mists know but sometimes overlook, the general economic performance of the United States, both before the Great Depression and after (even with the tools of the New Economists), has followed a cyclical course. Indeed, the expansion/contraction rhythm of economic affairs had fascinated many students of business cycles long before the 1930s. Business contractions had appeared at intervals of about eight to twelve years, each eventually succeeded by a counteracting stage of growth and prosperity. Economists offered a variety of explanations for such cyclical behavior, including new inventions, changes in investment or consumer behavior, and even sunspot activity. But before the 1930s, few, except perhaps Marxists committed to the destruction of the system, held that business contraction could become a permanent state of affairs. Just as surely as the business cycle turned downward, it would sooner or later turn upward.

This pattern, however, did not occur in 1929–30. To obtain a clearer understanding of modern-day economic tendencies, we must ask why. According to the zealots who quickly snatched up John Maynard Keynes's ideas and perverted them for their own uses, the depression of the 1930s was not merely a periodic movement within the business cycle. Instead, it was a problem of chronic *stagnation,* a situation in which the economy could no longer maintain high levels of employment and output because of the inadequacy of business investment. In short, depression had become a permanent state of affairs.

Such a situation, according to Keynes's followers, demanded firm action. First, the economy would have to be managed by government since the Treasury and monetary authorities could no longer count on the natural bottoming out of the depression. Second, government would have to act to *stimulate demand*—by undertaking efforts to increase consumer spending and business investment. Third, this demand stimulation would probably have to come from enlarged state expenditures, purposely unbalanced budgets and deficit spending for public goods, and transfer payments to business and individuals.

Thus began the modern period of economic thought. The epoch of laissez-faire was to be closed, with government replacing private accumulation and private instincts as the driving force of the economic system. Never mind the past spectacular performance of the private and open economy in building the nation. Never mind the implied assaults on individual economic freedom and choice that were the underpinnings of political freedom in the United States. Lord Keynes and his followers had determined that these now were outmoded beliefs and that only through massive government intervention in the economy could survival be assured.

## A Better Interpretation

Ordinarily, the best test for a hypothesis that interprets a set of events is to ask whether the hypothesis adequately explains the situation and is the best explanation possible. Applying this rule to the Keynesian critique, we find it wanting.

There is no evidence to support the idea that the Great Depression was, at its beginning in 1929, exceptional or that it differed markedly from past business downturns. Therefore, there is nothing to support the Keynesian belief that depression had become a permanent, congenital economic condition by the 1930s. What we do know, however, is that the depressed business conditions were worsened by the money policy actions of the Federal Reserve Board (the Fed), the government authority charged with maintenance of the nation's money and banking system. The Fed succeeded in transforming the difficulties of an excessively careless epoch of stock market speculation, coupled with an ordinary downturn in the business cycle, into an economic catastrophe of the first magnitude.

Lowering interest rates had always served to bring forth new investment and stimulate recovery in past downturns. However, reacting to the speculative bull market, the Fed had pursued a tight money policy even when it was apparent in early 1929 that a business downturn was forming. With high interest rates discouraging new business borrowing and reducing the stock of money (the money supply), business investment and consumer buying sagged even before the stock market collapsed. This was the Fed's first mistake. Its second came in December 1930 when the Bank of the United States in New York City closed its doors. Although it was an ordinary commercial bank, many people believed it to be an official government bank, and panic set in. Depositors in New York City and elsewhere rushed to withdraw their savings. Bank after bank faced liquidity crises. Unable to meet depositors' demands, banks began to fall like a line of dominoes. Meanwhile, the Fed, created in 1914 for just such an emergency, failed to take any action to improve bank liquidity. In fact, its next action was simply disastrous. In September 1931, as economic and financial problems spread worldwide and more and more gold was drained from the United States, the Fed raised interest rates in an attempt to stop the flow of gold overseas. Banks, now unable to borrow from the Fed (because of the high interest rates), had insufficient funds to meet their customers' demands and had to fold. Fourteen hundred closed their doors in three months, and the nation's money supply (consisting largely of *demand deposits* held in the form of checking accounts) fell by 12 percent. Meanwhile, on the business side, high interest rates discouraged new investment, and consumer spending fell as the money supply contracted. An ordinary depression had been transformed into an unprecedented financial crisis and, in turn, a near-complete prostration of business.

One other misguided economic action deserves special note: passage in 1930 of the protectionist Smoot-Hawley Tariff Act. Under pressure from businesses seeking to protect domestic markets from foreign competition, the Hoover administration, caught up in the anxiety following the market crash, encouraged Congress to pass a tariff that established the highest duties on imported goods in American history. Predictably, our protectionism was quickly matched by similar actions by our trading partners, and while we were protected from imports, we soon found it impossible to sell our products overseas.

The foregoing analysis differs sharply from the Keynesian stagnationist approach. While the Keynesians are partially correct that the Depression did finally become a matter of insufficient aggregate demand that happened only after and as a result of the failure of the Federal Reserve System and the passage of Smoot-Hawley. Rather than the economy manifesting some sinister and fatal stagnationist flaw, the evidence suggests that the Great Depression was largely accidental. That being the case, there is no proven analytical foundation for the Keynesian prescription that only through massive government intervention can free enterprise economies be kept afloat. Ironically, when we focus on the critical failures of monetary and tariff policies between 1929 and 1933, we find the reverse of the Keynesian analysis to be true: that government actions (through the Fed and the Smoot-Hawley Tariff) in fact caused the Great Depression.

The worsening and deepening of the Depression after 1933 was also the result of government activity. Liberal defenders of Franklin Roosevelt like to depict the New Deal as an experimental, pragmatic program to *prime* the economy. Not yet convinced by the Keynesian arguments, Roosevelt is usually presented as doing too little with countercyclical policy to get things going (until the government spending boom of World War II). This interpretation of the New Deal period of the Great Depression is guilty of a serious error of omission.

Roosevelt's antidepression strategy, Keynesian or not, was antibusiness and antibanker. The president's public addresses identified these two groups as both the cause of the Depression and the reason why his own policies had not turned the economic tide. Roosevelt's attempts to increase regulatory agency power, to insert government in the pricing mechanism, to reform the banking community, and especially to reform the Supreme Court when it threw out key pieces of his interventionist legislation created considerable business uncertainty. Within such a charged political atmosphere, business expectations, key to the undertaking of new investment and critical to recovery, remained essentially negative. Thus the interventionist policies of the New Deal tended to deepen and broaden the already crucial business depression.

### The Painful Legacy of the Depression

The passing of the Depression did not signal the passing of Keynesian ideas; indeed, it only marked the beginning of a long era of wrongheaded economic thought and policy. The victory of the Keynesian analysis led to the building of ever more elaborate theories to justify the enlargement of the government sector. The size of federal spending grew, and the extent of fiscal and monetary manipulation of business activity was expanded. For decades, beginning students of economics were taught, as if it were received religious truth, that deficits do not matter, that the growth of the public sector is healthy, and that the macro performance of the economy can be insulated from depression and *fine-tuned* to produce desired levels of output, employment, and price stability instantaneously as well as in the long run.

By the 1970s, however, the basic flaws of such an analysis were becoming uncomfortably evident as the nation slipped into a decade of inflation, unemployment, and disappointing growth. The Keynesian emphasis on *maintaining demand* meant neglecting and even restricting the production or supply side of the economy. As we shall see in subsequent issues, it led by the 1970s to an explosion of the federal debt, which in turn triggered an inflationary spiral that discouraged savings and slowed business investment. Incorrectly deciding that business had caused the Great Depression led, naturally enough, to forgetting that business was the very foundation of the economy. The situation was a bit like concluding that the health of the goose that laid the golden eggs would be improved by increasing the demand for eggs.

Looking back over the years of Keynesian dominance, with its patch-work of countercyclical and income-redistribution programs, George Gilder has observed:

> When government gives welfare, unemployment payments, and public service jobs in quantities that deter productive work, and when it raises taxes on profitable enterprise to pay for them, demand declines. In fact, nearly all programs that are advocated [by Keynesian economists] . . . in actuality reduce demand by undermining the production from which all real demand derives. . . . This is the essential insight of supply side economics. Government cannot significantly affect real aggregate demand through policies of taxing and spending.*

At best, the demand-side management efforts of the Keynesians amounted to a zero-sum game, merely shifting the earnings of some to others. At worst, as we shall see in the next issue, Liberal Keynesian fiscal and monetary policies drove the economy downward. The growing political, professional, and even popular reaction against Liberal economic and political policies, which commenced in the late 1970s and has continued to grow, is heartening.

### Are We Really Depression-Proof?

Turning to the original question of whether or not another Great Depression is possible, the Conservative position, although similar to the Liberal Keynesian position in giving a negative response, should be seen in light of its own assumptions. First, a massive depression is not the natural outcome of a free enterprise economy. Second, the elaborate policy tools developed in an effort to insulate the economy from depression are both unjustified and inherently dangerous. Third, the fact that we have not experienced a serious depression since the 1930s should not be accepted as proof that Keynesian macro policy ever worked. Rather, it might just as easily prove that the private economy is basically durable and adaptable—even with Keynesian roadblocks thrown in its way.

Thus we can conclude that another Great Depression is not inevitable unless, of course, we continue to rely on mistaken interpretations and cures in the formation of public policy. The "cures" we learned from the

---

*George Gilder, *Wealth and Poverty* (New York: Bantam Books, 1981), 62–63.

last depression are a far greater menace to future stability than anything else on the horizon.

## THE LIBERAL ARGUMENT

Riding the crest of a relatively less volatile business cycle since the mid-1980s, Conservatives have found it expedient to rewrite American economic history. Accordingly, they dismiss the significance of the Great Depression and the elaboration by John Maynard Keynes and his followers of modern macroeconomic theory and policy making. It is necessary, therefore, to go back and set the record straight. The exercise will be helpful in putting our subsequent examination of contemporary macroeconomic issues in a proper perspective as well as addressing the immediate question of whether or not we are *depression-proof.*

At the outset, however, it must be conceded that the *stagflation* of the 1970s with its high rates of inflation, slow economic growth, and high levels of unemployment—events that helped propel Conservative economic reasoning back onto center stage—did demonstrate that a too narrow Keynesianism has limitations in dealing with *all* the problems of the modern economy. However, the events of the 1970s should not be misread and used as dismissal of all that we have learned over the past sixty years or so. The stagflationary problems of high unemployment *plus* inflation did not prove the essential Keynesian critique to be in error. The absence of self-adjusting and self-regulating mechanisms in a laissez-faire capitalist economy is just as true today as in the 1930s. Similarly, the tendency of mature capitalist systems toward stagnation remains as much a characteristic as ever (as the current anemic employment growth confirms). Whatever the benefits of emphasizing the production side of the economy—and most Liberals would admit that some benefits have been obtained from the *supply-side* debate of the past several decades—this does not amount to a proof that Keynes's basic analysis should be abandoned in favor of a return to the discredited laissez-faire assumptions of a bygone era.

### The Collapse of Orthodox Ideas in the 1930s

The prevailing economic view in 1929 was that the economy was a natural, self-adjusting mechanism. Wages, interest, and rents were paid to individuals according to the value of their contributions to national

output. Such payments were, over time, equitable and just rewards for work and risk. The general mode of economic activity was assumed to be pure competition. Interference in the economy, whether by government, labor unions, or collusive business practice, was condemned. The economy was thus described and analyzed theoretically in terms of an open laissez-faire system. To be sure, periodic downturns in the national economy were possible, just as periodic stickiness in wages, savings, and business investment was possible. However, the focus was on the long haul, and over time, such deviations were thought to be self-correcting.

Within this general economic structure, traditional economists based their analysis of the national economy on a four-cornered foundation. First, there would be no long-run overproduction of goods (or, to look at it from the other side, no long-run underconsumption). This was true because payments to producers, labor, business, and so forth were always equal to the value of the goods produced. As the nineteenth-century French economist Jean-Baptiste Say put it in what has since come to be known as Say's Law, "Supply creates its own demand."

Second, and following from the first point, there could be, again in the long run, no such thing as involuntary unemployment. With flexible wages and prices, there would always be sufficient work at any given wage level to employ all those willing to work at that wage. Individuals who chose not to work at a particular wage (supposedly because they valued leisure more) were not "unemployed" at all.

Third, through free and flexible interest rates, private savings would be just enough to meet the investment (or borrowing) needs of businesses. If business sought greater investment, interest rates would rise, people would choose to save more, and funds would become available for business expansion. This, in turn, would create jobs, raise wages, and stimulate balanced economic growth.

Fourth, the level of prices in the society was determined by the rate of growth of the money supply. An increase in money would stimulate spending and demand for goods, which would raise market prices. A decrease in money would lower prices.

To the orthodox, these theories offered policy solutions to the periodic downturns in the economy. If business output exceeded consumer demand, just wait! Prices would fall to clear the market of goods. Wages would fall, and the number of workers seeking employment would be reduced until an equilibrium wage was reached. Interest rates would

fall, and individuals would shift savings to consumption. With lower interest rates and increasing consumption, business would again invest. Public policy within such a self-balancing economic order could be described quite easily: *Do nothing.*

As the international economy continued to inch downward after 1929, John Maynard Keynes began to rethink the orthodox analysis and reach his own conclusion on the evidence at hand. First of all, he observed that the automaticity of Say's Law was unfounded. Indeed, it was possible for overproduction or underconsumption to develop if individuals held money rather than saved it (lent it to borrowers). Second, wages were not, in the real world, freely flexible. Business could and did keep prices up and laid off workers while awaiting the sale of inventories. The alternatives available to workers were not lower wages or leisure but simply increased involuntary unemployment. Third, lowered interest rates did not induce business investment at a time of overproduction. With goods on hand, business would be unlikely to produce more goods even if the cost of borrowing was near zero. Finally, businesses will neither invest nor hire additional workers without the *expectation* of future sales.

Thus in Keynesian analysis, the allegedly *short-run* business fluctuations of the economy could become very long indeed. The self-correcting nature of the economy was an incorrect premise. And squaring with the real evidence that continued to build after the early 1930s, it was possible to have a continuing low level of output that left large numbers of workers and factories idle. Indeed, it was not only possible, it was quite natural in an unregulated economic system.

### The Keynesian Solution

Keynes's objective in his *General Theory* was to lay out the path to a high-employment economy. His approach emphasized aggregate economic performance rather than the microeconomic aspects of orthodox analysts. First, he explained, aggregate levels of employment depended on the total demand for goods, including consumer purchase of goods and services and business investment as well as government spending. Second, the primary culprit in the cyclical downturn of an economy was the activity of businesses because changes in investment outlays most directly affect changes in total demand for goods and services. Consumer spending, he maintained, was a fairly constant function of total income, with consumer outlays rising and falling directly as national

income fluctuated. Government spending was small, and in depression conditions it tended to get smaller as governments tried to live within the orthodox doctrine of annually balanced budgets.

Keynes's position was that only through artificially induced higher levels of aggregate demand would it be possible to attain full employment and full utilization of plants and equipment. The course was clear: Business investment had to be stimulated, government spending had to be inflated, or, more likely, some combination of both had to be tried. The combined effects of expansionary fiscal policy (greater government spending and/or tax cuts usually accompanied by a budget deficit) and expansionary monetary policy (lower interest rates and easier money) were to produce enlarged aggregate demand and diminished unemployment.

## The Victory of the New Economics

Although Keynes quickly gained academic adherents for his ideas, he made little headway in Washington during the Depression. For all his alleged fiscal profligacy, Franklin Roosevelt, with his pump priming and "ABC" government agencies, never grasped the Keynesian analysis and never embraced massive federal spending until he was forced—during World War II.

There was enormous federal spending during the war (with government spending in 1944 nearly twice the GDP of 1933), which produced a rapid growth of demand that was restrained only by rationing and price controls. Simultaneously, there was an equally rapid growth in the federal debt. When the war ended, many economists still feared the economy would drop back into depression. Instead, the stored-up wartime demand became the engine for a long postwar boom. Even before the inadvertent Keynesianism of World War II proved to be effective, however, the United States had rung down the curtain on the laissez-faire era. On February 20, 1946, President Truman signed Public Law 340, better known as the Employment Act of 1946. This act committed the federal government to the three objectives of (1) providing high levels of employment, (2) maintaining stable prices, and (3) encouraging economic growth. The groundwork had been laid for countercyclical fiscal and monetary policy.

The lessons of World War II fiscal expansion and the license for government fiscal and monetary intervention in the economy granted by the act of 1946 opened American economic thinking to the New Economics. Although Presidents Truman and Eisenhower showed only passing interest in the new doctrines and the new possibilities for public policy, university economists were quickly won over.

With the election of John Kennedy in 1960, Keynesian theory became policy. Coming to office during the third Eisenhower recession (1960–61), Kennedy introduced a fiscally experimental program. With an investment tax credit worth $2.5 billion to businesses in 1962 and a proposal for an $11 billion general tax cut in 1963, the Kennedy agenda offered sound Keynesian medicine. Lyndon Johnson continued and elaborated on the Kennedy theme. For almost eight years the economy moved forward, and Americans learned (although they were soon to forget) that economic crisis, whether periodic or inherent, need not be the nature of the economy.

### Is the Keynesian Analysis Still Relevant?

There is little denying that the simultaneous appearance in the 1970s of high unemployment, slow growth, and raging inflation was very unkind to Keynesians. Displaying a propensity to throw the baby out with the bathwater, many economists (including some previously ardent Keynesians), politicians, and ordinary citizens incorrectly identified Keynesian thinking and policy making as the cause of the stagflationary crisis. True, the Keynesian focus had not prepared the nation for all economic crises—it had not anticipated the severe *supply shocks* of the 1970s. Moreover, Keynes's original critique had emphasized an economy caught up in severe and pervading depression. It saw this chronic contraction as the result of insufficient private spending and argued that correction required massive offsetting government spending. While, as we have seen, the events of the Depression and war seemed to prove Keynes correct, it was discovered by the late 1960s that Keynesian demand-management efforts did not work well when the focus of policy attention was on a nearly or fully employed economy.

Although some of Keynes's followers argued for *fine-tuning*—simply turning on or off the demand spigot as conditions dictated—events soon showed that closing the spigot, when such anti-inflationary actions were called for, was painful and unpopular. The short-run benefits of expansionary economic policies were quickly perceived by politicians, as were the politically suicidal effects of contractionary policies that required raising taxes and reducing government spending. Indeed, as much as anything else, it was this politicization of Keynesianism that transformed what was mostly a technical shortcoming into a near catastrophic deficiency.

Keynesian ideas, however, did not disappear even though the limitations of fine-tuning and anti-inflationary policy were exposed. Based simply on a survey of the content of the average college introductory economics text, as well as the op-ed pages of the *Wall Street Journal,* it becomes obvious that most economists still use the Keynesian identities and causalities in setting up the framework of macroeconomic analysis. Most texts retain the Keynesian view that production-for-profit economies still tend naturally toward periodic stagnations. They still outline the potential uses of government policy to remedy such situations, although these exercises are decidedly more theoretical than policy-oriented, reflecting the constraints imposed by the experiences of the 1970s. However, those accepting the Keynesian framework (whether they actually use the label or not) pay a great deal more attention now than in the past to the role played by private investment in the long-run maintenance of high levels of employment.

While Conservative economists like to claim credit for ending inflation, their cures were little more than an application of Keynesian principles. How was inflation finally halted in the 1980s? The Federal Reserve closed off investment and consumer spending by raising interest rates and bringing on the worst recession since the 1930s. How was the long period of peacetime growth after 1982 achieved? The tax cut of 1981 and enormous defense outlays produced a tripling of the national debt—to $3 trillion by 1990—that provided sufficient demand stimulation to keep the boom going (although the boom was quite moderate by past standards).

In a perverse and economically dangerous way, Conservatives were applying Keynes's aggregate demand analysis without giving appropriate credit or understanding the long-term consequences. The administration of President George W. Bush has rerun the tired fiscal policies of the Reagan-Bush period of the 1980s. The large tax cuts of 2001–3 (see Issue 7) and significant increase in defense expenditures are a mixed message, with demand-side and supply-side stimuli reasoning tossed together with a plea for "tax fairness" that principally benefits only the wealthy.

As a result (as we shall see in the following issues), the economy remains plagued by serious fundamental problems. During the 1990s there was a significant increase in the share of national income going to the top 20 percent of households, while the vast majority of nonsupervisory production workers experienced growing indebtedness and inflation-adjusted wages remained below their early 1970s all-time peak. The destruction of the World Trade Center, the attack on the Pentagon, and mail distribution of potentially deadly anthrax delivered a shock to an economy already caught in the tightening grip of a slowdown. Policy makers responded with a visibly Keynesian slant, relying upon expansionary fiscal and monetary policies. To be certain, Keynesian economics is as relevant as ever to the task of macroeconomic stabilization. Indeed, Liberals may not possess *all* the answers, but at least they understand the question when asked: Are we depression-proof?

## THE RADICAL ARGUMENT

For both Conservatives and Liberals, albeit for different reasons, the imminent or future collapse of the American economy is not an inevitable event. Their views, of course, are not very startling. That defenders of varieties of capitalism believe the system has a future should be expected; however, the evidence, if looked at closely, points to a different conclusion. Contrary to the cheery Conservative view that free enterprise economies suffer only periodic and inconsequential business downturns, it is apparent from both historical and recent perspectives that crisis is part of the nature of production-for-profit economies. The Liberal contention that the countercyclical use of fiscal and monetary policy can insulate us from depression enormously understates the systemic roots of economic crisis and fails to comprehend the costs and effects of the tools of countercyclical policy.

### *The Chronic Tendency Toward Crisis*

Economic crisis and instability are not peculiar to capitalist societies alone. However, with the dawn and maturity of capitalism, crisis (or what we presently might call depression) took on a new dimension. In precapitalist societies, economic contraction resulted largely from wars, plagues, crop failures, or other natural disasters. The granaries were empty, people starved, and there were shortages of goods of all kinds. Crisis was associated with underproduction. Paradoxically, in the capitalist era of crisis, this situation has been reversed. Capitalist contraction usually appears after an era of growth in the productive forces of a society. With excess goods on hand and no market, producers reduce current output, unemployment rises, and wages and prices fall. In short, capitalist crises usually begin when the granaries are full.

To be sure, the periodic panics and depressions that strike capitalism have usually been followed by recoveries. For many years before the appearance of Keynes's work, the periodicity of boom and bust (especially boom) allowed Conservatives to describe economic contractions as "mere disturbances" that would go away and therefore did not merit very serious analytical study. No effort was made to see stagnation as fundamental to the capitalist order. Nor has this view changed much among modern Conservative economists. Keynesian Liberals, meanwhile, have accepted the fact that underconsumption generally leads to depressions in modern capitalism, but they hold that the tendency is easily manageable through the tools of modern public policy.

From the Radical perspective, however, economic crises are both fundamental to capitalism and beyond capitalists' capacity to resolve in the long run. As Karl Marx pointed out long ago, the crises are inherent in the capitalist system of production. In their perpetual search for expanded profits, capitalists must create *surplus value*—that is, they forever attempt to maximize the difference between the higher price for which goods sell and the lower price of the labor involved in production. To acquire greater profits, the capitalist must enlarge surplus value through the introduction of greater amounts of capital equipment, through the direct exploitation of labor, or through some combination of the two. The object is to produce greater output per unit of wage labor paid. As capitalists endeavor to produce more and more at greater profit, the capacity of the workers (consumers) to purchase this output declines. Although the people may *need* the goods, they do not have the *effective demand* to obtain them. Overproduction and underconsumption create periodic gluts of goods, which in turn cause crises wherein production ceases, capital is destroyed or left idle, and human beings starve.

As capitalism progresses, Marx argued, its productive capacity constantly enlarges. The possible depths and duration of production-consumption crises are heightened, and the ultimate end of the system is brought that much closer. Nineteenth-century Marxists observed the growing incidence of capitalist crises and predicted, a bit prematurely, early collapse.

While the capitalist system has not collapsed, this does not mean that

Marx's analysis is wrong or outdated. In fact, Marx foresaw several sources of macroeconomic instability that are easily observable today, including the accelerating pace of labor-displacing technological change, increasing financial fragility, growing income and wealth inequality, continued corporate concentration and centralization (through ever-larger mergers and acquisitions), and the ongoing conflict over global trade. Looking a little closer at two of these current trends will underscore the continuing relevance of Marx's arguments to the Radical position.

As was noted, profitability is crucially dependent on the ability of capitalists to extract as much surplus value per unit of output as possible from employees by working them harder or longer and/or by equipping them with better machines. Unfortunately for capitalists, there are legal constraints in most advanced industrialized countries that limit the length of the working day. While firms can try to evade or change these laws, there can be penalties as well as intangible costs such as loss of goodwill. Moreover, a worker's physical capacity to labor at a given task is limited by the need for rest and sleep. Thus, the only substantive way to increase the rate of profit is to mechanize and automate production such that fewer workers are required for a given level of output. The present *new economy* strategy of wringing labor costs out of any product or service is central for understanding the surge in profitability over the past several years. While mainstream macroeconomists rejoice at the recent growth in labor productivity, it is clear that these gains have been obtained by the continual displacement, deskilling, and degradation of occupations as diverse as mining, engineering, farming, teaching, and medicine. The macroeconomic consequences of persistent job destruction and diminishment are clear: lowered living standards, greater income and wealth inequality, more indebtedness, and economic insecurity for the vast majority of workers.

A second source of current macroeconomic instability identified by Marx, is the ever-increasing income gap between rich and poor. Despite the smug and self-congratulatory tone of Conservatives and Liberals over *productivity-led* growth and prosperity during the 1990s, real wages and working conditions for most Americans have not shown much improvement. For example, the inflation-adjusted income of the bottom 40 percent of households grew much more slowly during the last decade compared to the 1970s and 1980s. Thus, the vaunted acceleration in productivity of the New Economy did *not* translate into higher wages or reduced work hours for most Americans. In fact, the number of hours it would take a worker who is paid the average wage to earn the average family income is about 3,700

hours per year (a seventy-one-hour workweek). It is painfully obvious to working American families—despite admonitions to acquire more education and improve their work ethic—that capitalists and their high-paid functionaries have appropriated most of the productivity dividend. Thus, it is no surprise that both the share of national income going to capital and the aggregate profit rate (20.2 percent and 8.0 percent, respectively, in 2002) have returned to levels last seen in the 1960s.

Finally, it should be noted that capitalist societies have adopted policies —such as a progressive income tax structure, free public education, and an end to child labor—that Marx recommended in the *Communist Manifesto*. While Marx never developed his ideas about the role of the state in the economy, he understood, like Keynes, that government could be a stabilizing (albeit only temporary) force. In particular, the state could foster or sanction monopoly behavior, mitigate the effects of labor exploitation and unemployment, and act directly to absorb the surplus production through government purchases (especially during war) and transfer payments. Yet, such efforts to "rationalize" capitalism by temporarily disguising or hiding its self-destructive propensities cannot eliminate capitalism's chronic tendency toward crisis.

## The Collapse of 1929

The expansion of overseas markets and sources of cheap labor and resources, the increasingly monopolistic behavior of business enterprises, and the enlargement of government protective actions held back the breaking of the dike before 1929. It did not, however, stop serious leaks.

In the case of the United States, seven major business cycles can be identified between the panic of 1893 and the beginning of World War I. Each downturn lasted longer and became more pronounced. As the United States entered World War I and a wartime business boom, unemployment stood at about 10 percent. The Roaring Twenties were not much better. Probably the worst depression in U.S. history to that point occurred in 1921–22, and throughout most of the decade unemployment was higher than 4 percent. Meanwhile, real wages moved upward only slightly. Only the phenomenal expansion of consumer debt buoyed the economy. For those who wished to see the evidence or could at least understand it, it was apparent that the dike would soon collapse.

The crisis after 1929 was a near-classic example of Marx's overproduction-underconsumption scenario. Moreover, it precipitated a general international collapse. The mature capitalist economies had exhausted their markets for goods. Overseas, the underdeveloped economies had little capacity to absorb output. At home, warehouses bulged because consumers lacked effective demand. As the first signs of crisis appeared, the banking and financial system, which itself rested on the capitalists' ability to realize their surplus, tottered and collapsed: first the Wall Street crash, then New York bank failures, then European bank failures. Full-scale industrial contraction followed.

### The Old Economics in a New Package

The Keynesian response to the deepening depression was to accept the essential outline of the older Marxist critique of capitalism: Overproduction and crisis were endemic to the system. However, the Keynesians neatly evaded the Marxian conclusion. According to their analysis, insufficient business and consumer demand could be either manipulated by fiscal and monetary policy or supplemented by government spending that would raise the level of aggregate demand. In Marxian terms, government now became the vehicle to realize surplus value.

Much has been made of this new thinking on the problem of the capitalist system. The "Keynesian Revolution" came to describe dominant economic opinion; however, it was no revolution at all. Keynes and his followers have sought not to end capitalism but to save it. The central features of capitalism—private property, production for profit, wage labor, the business system, and all the rest—were retained. Indeed, as business leaders came to appreciate the profit (surplus value) possibilities of increased government spending during World War II and the trial-and-error Keynesian years after the war, corporate America enthusiastically accepted the New Economics. The frequent Liberal posturing against big business should be recognized as pure political rhetoric. In the 1964 Johnson-Goldwater presidential election, big business showed its colors by rejecting the Conservative, laissez-faire Republican in favor of the big-spending Democrat from Texas. Giant corporations poured millions of dollars into Johnson's campaign.

### The Keynesian Mirage and Back to Reality

Through the 1960s and most of the 1970s (remember that even Richard Nixon had proclaimed himself a Keynesian), the New Economics seemed to be just what capitalism needed. The old capitalist business cycle of roller-coaster ups and downs simply disappeared as the economy underwent continuous expansion. In silly self-congratulation, economists wrote and talked of "no more depressions" while they enjoyed a place never before reserved for them in the public's esteem.

With the Vietnam War and other government spending growing and an easy monetary policy usually operating to encourage private borrowing, high levels of demand kept factories operating at near-peak utilization rates and kept unemployment rates low. Yet these signs of success through the 1960s were actually danger signals, for in capitalism success invariably sows the seeds of doom. The basic problem, as with all expansionary phases of the capitalist business cycle, was that expanding demand put serious pressures on business by causing rising costs, which in turn squeezed profits. With unemployment at very low levels, workers—unionized and nonunionized alike—enjoyed a seller's market for their labor. Real wages rose as businesses bid against each other for needed employees. Between 1960 and 1973, real (adjusted for inflation) after-tax weekly earnings rose by 35 percent. Since this exceeded productivity (output per worker-hour) growth, it translated into rising per-unit costs for producers. To make matters worse, resource costs worldwide began rising, the principal source being rising energy costs resulting from the Arabs' opting to challenge their former colonial and neocolonial masters.

At any rate, after-tax corporate profits peaked in 1965 (at about 10.4 percent on investment) and fell thereafter (to about 5.9 percent in 1974). With profits falling, businesses continued to reduce their investment outlays through the late 1960s and into the 1970s. At first the decline was scarcely felt as demand remained high for a time, but in the late 1960s, unemployment began to edge upward. By the early 1970s, regardless of expansionary fiscal policy efforts to offset the trend, unemployment grew as profits fell. Prices, meanwhile, began to rise, producing the new phenomenon of *stagflation* (rising unemployment *and* rising prices). Inflation took hold simply because demand, fueled by government and private borrowing, remained high. Without an expansion of business production facilities and with productive efficiency falling as the investment base got older and more outmoded, the high levels of demand caused price increases rather than output expansion. Meanwhile, the high levels of demand had few salutary effects on employment since profits remained low and business actually reduced its rate of investment. The outer limits of runaway Keynesianism had been reached.

There remained only one solution, the old solution: recession. Through the mid- and late 1970s, under enormous pressure from rising prices, government fiscal policy turned less expansionary. Predictably, unemployment crept upward. Inflation, however, was not significantly slowed until Conservative Ronald Reagan supported a bone-chilling tight money policy that shut off private borrowing. The immediate result was the recession of 1981–82, which produced Great Depression levels of unemployment.

Although Conservatives crowed about their victory over inflation and enjoyed pointing out that Keynesianism had proved itself a failure, they, as we shall see in the next issue, understood little about what had happened. They offered no new solution to the capitalist system. However, as we shall see in subsequent issues, the Conservatives have enjoyed a considerable measure of popular support during their recent return to policy-making power.

The dislodgement of the Republicans from the White House in 1992, after the brief recession under George H. Bush, did not bring a return of traditional Liberal political economy. Although President Clinton leaned toward a Liberal position during his first two years in office, the election of Republican majorities in both houses of Congress in 1994 was a fair measure of the popular ascendancy of Conservative political and economic outlooks. Clinton quickly adapted to the new realities, winning reelection in 1996 after allowing that the era of big government was over and more or less conceding to the Conservative insistence that fiscal policy should be subordinated to the necessity of balancing the federal budget. In all this, both Clinton and Conservatism benefited from a long economic expansion through the mid- and late 1990s. Everyone seemed caught up in the boom.

Conservative burbling about a "new world economic order" in the aftermath of the demise of the USSR in 1992 and their growing praise for a technology-based New Economy were muted upon the predictable arrival of yet another recession in early 2001. Ironically, the crisis materialized just as the administration of George W. Bush unleashed an explosion of deficit-financed tax cuts for the rich.

To Radicals, the recent resurgence of Conservative antigovernment and probusiness ideology and practice, after a generation of Liberal as-

cendancy, is a matter of considerable irony. Marx, commenting on the ironies of history, once remarked that when history repeats itself, it first appears as tragedy and then as farce. However, to the more thoughtful, the idea of America returning to the "good old days" of Calvin Coolidge and Herbert Hoover is both farcical *and* tragic.

Yet, in a sense, that is precisely where we are. Indeed, production-for-profit capitalism, in any substantial sense, has never really passed much beyond the era immediately preceding the Great Depression. Is another great depression possible? *Very definitely.*

# Economic Growth and Stability

## Can We Maintain High and Steady Rates of Economic Growth?

We must recognize that only experience can show how far the common will, embodied in the policy of the state, ought to be directed to increasing and supplementing the inducement to invest.

*—John Maynard Keynes, 1935*

Is fiscal policy being oversold? Is monetary policy being oversold? . . . My answer is yes to both of those questions. . . . What I believe is that fine tuning has been oversold.

*—Milton Friedman, 1968*

Originating in a liberal effort to respond to the popular will and relieve the pressures of poverty, demand-oriented politics ends in promoting unemployment and dependency.

*—George Gilder, 1981*

Although the evidence is widespread that there really is something new about the economy, it is not clear just how much the basic parameters of macroeconomic performance have changed.

—Economic Report of the President, 2001

## The Problem

Conservative, Liberal, and Radical paradigms are strikingly divided on the matters of long-term growth and stability and the economic role to be played by government to best ensure rising living standards. The problems of short-term economic performance tend to attract the attention of the public, policy makers, and economists. In other words, more day-to-day concern is placed on the trim of the economic ship than on what might be done if it actually capsized. Looming in the background are larger and more spectacular questions about whether living standards can rise at an appreciable pace and if the economy is actually depression-proof. The issue can be conveniently divided between the maintenance of short-term macroeconomic stability and the subject of long-term growth. The two are intertwined, but in this issue we set our sights principally on the long-run outlook for sustained economic growth and rising living standards.

Since the passage of the Employment Act of 1946, the federal government has had the responsibility

> to use all practicable means consistent with its needs and obligations and other essential considerations of national policy, with assistance and cooperation of industry, agriculture, labor and State and local governments, to coordinate and utilize all its plans, functions and resources for the purpose of creating and maintaining, in a manner calculated to foster and promote free competitive enterprise and general welfare, conditions under which there will be afforded useful employment opportunities, including self-employment, production and purchasing power.

This rambling and wide-ranging statement has been interpreted over the years to mean that government is charged with three basic public policy objectives:

- Providing high levels of employment
- Maintaining stable prices
- Encouraging economic growth

For better or worse (the reader may already be anticipating in the arguments to come who might think it better and who might think it worse), the government had assumed some level of responsibility, albeit indistinct, over the great trinity of employment, prices, and growth.

Table 9.1 (see p. 216) shows how well the economy performed in the last half of the twentieth century with respect to the three objectives. The economy had enjoyed 120 months of economic expansion before the 2001 recession. The very length of the boom was impressive, but the period had also been impressive when compared to the previous boom of the 1980s and the dismal stagflationary years of the 1970s because of its uncharacteristically high rates of economic growth and correspondingly low inflation. Not surprisingly, Conservatives used the boom of the 1980s as proof of the errors of the earlier Keynesian heresy and evidence that a policy relying predominantly on market-directed forces is capable of maintaining both economic stability and growth. Liberals could counter that the 1960s and 1990s, under political leadership of closer affinity to their views, produced economic success that surpassed the Conservative heydays. Radicals would, of course, be unconvinced by either.

Thus, even during good economic conditions, the paradigms differ on why these events occurred, the principal forces that drive the operation of the macroeconomy, and how very similar policies affect economic performance. Conservatives tend to emphasize supply-side economics while Liberals place greater faith in the demand-management theories of Keynesian heritage;* Radicals assert that capitalist economies are fundamentally unstable and prone to long-term crises of underconsumption, overproduction, and accumulation. While achieving full employment and building upon the productive base of the economy are common objectives, the different sides possess very divergent opinions about how this is to be accomplished.

---

*The supply-siders' analytical critique of Keynesian theory can be fairly easily demonstrated. For supply-siders the inflationary episode of the 1970s was directly traceable to the Keynesian error of believing that increases in demand had only a salutary effect on output and employment and no impact upon prices. The supply-side argument is illustrated in Panel 1 on page 216. With aggregate demand (AD) and aggregate supply (AS), respectively, illustrating the total demand and total supply of goods at all possible combinations of gross domestic product (GDP) and price level, the economy is in equilibrium in Panel 1 where AD = AS. It can be noted at a low level of equilibrium output (Q), an increase in the total demand from $AD_1$ to $AD_2$ has a far greater impact in increasing GDP than in raising the price level. However, the shift from $AD_2$ to $AD_3$ has a far greater impact upon prices. This is because as the economy approaches full employment, the aggregate supply curve slopes upward more steeply reflecting higher resource prices that are caused by increased competition for scarcer resources. The solution to the problem is demonstrated in Panel 2. Actions should be taken to increase aggregate supply. This appears as the shift from AS to $AS_1$, resulting in higher GDP and a decrease in prices.

A second, but closely related, dimension of the problem is labor productivity growth. A slowdown in productivity growth started in the middle of the 1970s. Table 9.2 illustrates that the rate of growth in output per worker had assumed a slower long-term pace, dropping from an average annual rate of 3.1 percent between 1960 and 1973 to 1.6 percent between 1973 and 1995. Productivity growth accelerated to 2.7 percent between 1995 and 2003, largely due to widespread use of information technologies, more capital goods, and improved labor force skills, among other things.

Although an increase in labor productivity does not guarantee that society's economic well-being will be improved, there is general agreement that productivity is closely related to living standards. A rough-and-ready gauge of a country's standard of living is to look at output per capita, and this measure is closely connected to productivity, that is, the output per worker that in turn determines available output per person. Table 9.2 illustrates the connection between the rate of growth in gross domestic product (GDP) per capita and productivity growth. Recognize that even during periods of comparatively rapid GDP growth such as exhibited by the majority of years in the 1990s, rates of growth in productivity and living standards can be comparatively slow.

The data in Table 9.2 reveal that growth rates in productivity are more than a full percentage point higher in the period 2001–2003 than 1973–95. How important is a percentage point or so? The answer is found by turning to a rule of thumb known as the *rule of 72,* which permits a quick approximation of how long it will take something (such as living stan-

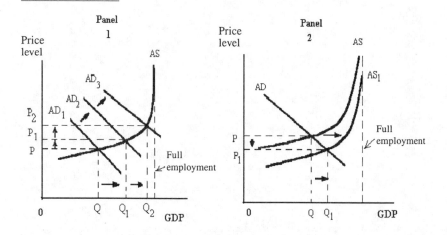

Table 9.1

**Economic Growth, Unemployment, and Inflation Rates, 1959–2003**

| Year | Annual percentage change in real GDP | Annual unemployment rate (percentage) | Annual percentage change in consumer price index |
|------|------|------|------|
| 1959 | 7.1 | 5.5 | 0.7 |
| 1960 | 2.5 | 5.5 | 1.7 |
| 1961 | 2.3 | 6.7 | 1.0 |
| 1962 | 6.1 | 5.5 | 1.0 |
| 1963 | 4.4 | 5.7 | 1.3 |
| 1964 | 5.8 | 5.2 | 1.3 |
| 1965 | 6.4 | 4.5 | 1.6 |
| 1966 | 6.5 | 3.8 | 2.9 |
| 1967 | 2.5 | 3.8 | 3.1 |
| 1968 | 4.8 | 3.6 | 4.2 |
| 1969 | 3.1 | 3.5 | 5.5 |
| 1970 | 0.2 | 4.9 | 5.7 |
| 1971 | 3.4 | 5.9 | 4.4 |
| 1972 | 5.3 | 5.6 | 3.2 |
| 1973 | 5.8 | 4.9 | 6.2 |
| 1974 | −0.5 | 5.6 | 11.0 |
| 1975 | −0.2 | 8.5 | 9.1 |
| 1976 | 5.3 | 7.7 | 5.8 |
| 1977 | 4.6 | 7.1 | 6.5 |
| 1978 | 5.6 | 6.1 | 7.6 |
| 1979 | 3.2 | 5.8 | 11.3 |
| 1980 | −0.2 | 7.1 | 13.5 |
| 1981 | 2.5 | 7.6 | 10.3 |
| 1982 | −1.9 | 9.7 | 6.2 |
| 1983 | 4.5 | 9.6 | 3.2 |
| 1984 | 7.2 | 7.5 | 4.3 |
| 1985 | 4.1 | 7.2 | 3.6 |
| 1986 | 3.5 | 7.0 | 1.9 |
| 1987 | 3.4 | 6.2 | 3.6 |
| 1988 | 4.1 | 5.5 | 4.1 |
| 1989 | 3.5 | 5.3 | 4.8 |
| 1990 | 1.9 | 5.6 | 5.4 |
| 1991 | −0.2 | 6.8 | 4.2 |
| 1992 | 3.3 | 7.5 | 3.0 |
| 1993 | 2.7 | 6.9 | 3.0 |
| 1994 | 4.0 | 6.1 | 2.6 |
| 1995 | 2.5 | 5.6 | 2.8 |
| 1996 | 3.7 | 5.4 | 3.0 |
| 1997 | 4.5 | 4.9 | 2.3 |
| 1998 | 4.2 | 4.5 | 1.6 |
| 1999 | 4.5 | 4.2 | 2.2 |
| 2000 | 3.7 | 4.0 | 3.4 |
| 2001 | 0.8 | 4.7 | 2.8 |
| 2002 | 1.9 | 5.8 | 1.6 |
| 2003 | 3.0 | 6.0 | 2.3 |

*Source*: Bureau of Economic Analysis, *Economic Report of the President* (Washington, DC: Government Printing Office, 2004) and authors' calculations.

Table 9.2

**Trend in Real Gross Domestic Product per Capita and Productivity**
(annual rates)

| Year | Growth in real GDP per capita (percentage) | Growth in output per worker hour (percentage) |
|---|---|---|
| 1960–1973 | 2.9 | 3.1 |
| 1973–1995 | 1.9 | 1.6 |
| 1995–2000 | 2.6 | 2.2 |
| 2001–2003 | 0.9 | 3.9 |

*Source:* Bureau of Economic Analysis and U.S. Bureau of the Census. Calculations by the author.
Note: GDP = gross domestic product.

dards, price levels, population, or output) to double if it grows at a specific percentage rate. For the example at hand, the percentage rate of increase in real GDP per capita is divided into seventy-two to yield the number of years it will take for living standards to double. The growth rate for the period 1960–73 would permit living standards to double in less than twenty-five years (= 72/2.9) By comparison, the rate of growth in GDP per capita had slowed to just under a 1 percent average annual rate for the period 2001–3. Were that rate to be sustained, it would take seventy-two years (= 72/1) for living standards to double.

The difference a percentage point can make is indeed profound. At the 1960–73 rate of growth in real GDP per capita, living standards could easily quadruple in one lifetime, whereas at the slower rate of the 2001–3 period, it takes most of a lifetime to experience a doubling of living standards.

Although output per worker hour is the usual basis for measuring productivity, it is obvious that the American productivity dilemma goes much deeper than the question of how hard the individual American works. After all, workers can be more or less productive if they have more or fewer capital goods (machinery) with which to work. An hour of work by a person equipped with a shovel will be trifling by comparison to an hour of work performed by a backhoe operator. This leads to another dimension of the issue: Is capital, even if it is of great quantity, being dedicated to its best purpose? Furthermore, we might ask: Is the available technology the best we are capable of producing? Overarching all of these components of productivity is the question of the management skill of American industry: Does it possess the qualities necessary to make the best decisions about what is to be produced, how much is to be produced, and under what production arrangements?

When evidence suggested that something was wrong somewhere within the labyrinth of economic forces that determine productivity, a long list of culprits was submitted. Depending on ideological viewpoint, government intervention, excessively powerful labor unions, poor business decision making, the "quick profit" motive, too much dependence by business upon government, a decline in entrepreneurship, deterioration in the work ethic, too many lawyers and not enough engineers, insufficient investment spending, decline in the quality of primary and secondary education, and so on were identified as causes of the productivity slowdown. The acceleration in productivity exhibited from 1995 to 2003 poses the challenge to explain whether something was *going right* at that time within the economic forces that determine productivity. The differing assessments of the productivity puzzle go to the very roots of the ideological differences among economic paradigms.

The robust expansion of the 1990s rebuilt American confidence but did not allay all trepidation about the future. Macroeconomic stability and growth had produced a minor miracle in employment opportunities and reduced rates of unemployment. Yet Americans realize that not all jobs are created equal. Full-time opportunities seem less plentiful, employment security is seemingly more tenuous, benefit packages are skimpy, and employees' urine is something that demands testing. The 2001 recession had a particularly harsh and lingering impact on college-educated workers who experienced lengthy periods of unemployment. The attention-grabbing, but falsely robust, recorded music industry actually experienced a collapse as the industry's value of shipments shrank by 19 percent between 1999 and 2003, eliminating thousands of jobs.* Collectively, these developments temper the typical exuberance or euphoria incited by economic booms. At the same time, America's confidence is probably not uplifted by past experience and recurring controversies with macroeconomic policy that reveal no clear consensus on the proper course.

Lackluster economic prospects are hard for Americans to accept, especially those generations conditioned by the unusually rapid gains of the long postwar boom. A longing for the "good old days" is not lost on policy

---

*Based on manufacturers' shipments data reported by the Recording Industry Association of America.

makers who understand that the citizenry wants a quick but long-lasting fix for productivity and living standards.

The twenty-five years of economic growth and dominance that America enjoyed following World War II were the consequences of unusual circumstances. While the New Economy was thought to be impervious to business cycles, the recession of 2001 refuted such hubris. Rather, it appears that the New Economy—despite its vaunted technological prowess and dynamism—is more akin to the nineteenth-century economy where economic opportunity went hand-in-hand with economic insecurity.

## Synopsis

Conservatives argue that efforts to stabilize the economy and foster economic growth have been ill fated in the past. They argue that such policy initiatives are actually the cause of poorer macroeconomic performance. They generally favor tax reductions, budget balancing, and smaller government as the means for returning the economy to the growth track. Liberals cite random shocks, over which economic policy makers had no control, and society's negligence of crucial areas in need of government investment and guidance as largely responsible for the economic difficulties that have beset the economy since the 1970s. They argue in favor of activism and contend that careful examination of the historical record of intervention indicates that the results have been quite favorable. If anything, the problem has been a lack of adequate and properly timed intervention. Radicals argue that Liberals are impelled to intervene in the economy's performance less out of social conscience than on behalf of business and ruling-class interests. The protracted trend of sluggish growth in GDP per capita and productivity reflects the deepening crisis of modern capitalism and presages worsening economic and social decay.

---

## Anticipating the Arguments

- What policies do Conservatives advocate to maintain macroeconomic stability and maintain rising living standards?
- If the economy is not delivering desirable results in terms of stability or growth in living standards, how would Liberals respond?
- Why do Radicals reject the idea that the economy can be managed by either the Conservative or Liberal prescriptions for stabilization and maintenance of economic growth?

## THE CONSERVATIVE ARGUMENT

Understanding the Conservative program for stabilization and growth requires recognition of the fact that consumption is at the center of economic life. Accommodating consumption necessitates production and the means for production. On the macroeconomic level, it is the production or supply side of the economy that is the source of income that permits consumption. It does not happen the other way around. The Conservative prescription is composed of two basic elements:

- Redirect fiscal and monetary policy from attention to the demand or consumption side of economic activity to the supply or production side. Ultimately, fiscal and monetary policy must be neutral. The government should perform only its most necessary functions and under the regimen of a balanced budget. Monetary authorities would set a rate of growth in the money supply that approximates the potential growth in the economy and spurn trying to manipulate interest rates in the interest of stabilization. Markets will be the workhorse and coordinator of economic activity, not the government or the central bank.
- Deregulate and eliminate various impositions and controls upon industry and labor markets. The government's imposition of regulatory costs and outright obstruction, which has hindered production, work incentives, innovation, and productivity growth, needs to end.

### The Errors of Demand-Management Economics

Until recently, conventional macroeconomics had acquired a one-dimensional perspective that had its origins in the Keynesian critique of an economy mired in the depths of the Great Depression. With large numbers of people unemployed and much of the nation's plants and equipment sitting idle, Keynes's logic in retrospect was nearly artless: Find the means to increase demand for goods and services, which would generate the demand for men, women, and machines to go back to work. The supply side could be taken for granted because of the sheer volume of idle resources. Demand would dictate the level of output with a near-instantaneous response from the supply side. The only constraint upon output is when full employment is reached. With an economy far from full employment, the Depression-built economics of Keynes was hardly concerned with the consequences of forcing the economy toward full employment.

The Keynesian remedy for the prostrate economies of the 1930s was seductively simple and painless: *Spend your way out of the Depression.* Moreover, it had even seemed to work during the late 1930s and during World War II, when massive government outlays did rejuvenate the economy. As an antidepression strategy, Conservatives will admit, Keynesian policies were—in the short term at least—a politically attractive alternative to simply allowing the business cycle to undergo a natural correction. However, their political appeal in no way made it sound economic policy. Worse still, their superficial success led to the eventual institutionalization of demand-management fiscal and monetary policies, reserved not for exclusive use to counter an economic depression but for persistently fine-tuning the economy.

The preoccupation with unemployment that had hung over from the Great Depression and the fact that the Keynesian contingent of the economics profession had expressed a theoretical and practical justification for government spending was simply too alluring for government policy makers. Now they had experts to support the implausible: Taxes could be cut, government spending increased, the money supply expanded, and perennial deficits incurred, all in the interest of improving macroeconomic performance. Yet, the agenda expanded beyond lowering unemployment. Grand expenditure and social engineering programs were introduced to advance President Johnson's vision of the Great Society. Simultaneously, America's growing involvement in the Vietnam War led to increased military spending.

It looked as if a holiday from economic reason had been declared. The old principle of a guns-versus-butter trade-off was placed in abeyance. More of both military and civilian goods could be attained. The cake could be eaten and had too!

Likewise, the ramifications of excessive government spending were blissfully ignored until the nation moved into the final years of the 1960s and made the transition into the awful decade of the 1970s. Demand-pull inflation appeared in the late 1960s. Then came the incongruous situation of *stagflation*—both high rates of unemployment and high rates of inflation. Growth rates faltered, the trend in rates of personal and gross saving flattened, and the climate for investment spending suffered as government deficits gobbled up loanable funds and inflation elevated interest rates and lowered after-tax capital income.

## Regulatory Burdens and Other Disincentives

While fiscal and monetary meddling proved a major force in fostering the long descent to slower progress in living standards and productivity, ample assistance in battering the nation's productive base came from other steps taken by the Liberal-leaning policy makers of the times.

- The economic inefficiencies of industry regulation were now to be hugely amplified through the social engineering measures of the 1970s that were aimed at consumer, environmental, and worker protection. This added to business costs at a time when general economic conditions were depressing profits. Investment and innovation were further stifled by the strictures of regulation. By some estimates, billions of dollars are transferred annually from productive purposes to the bureaucracy that was given life through regulation, and hundreds of billions are squandered on compliance costs.
- A "soak the rich and business" taxation mentality pervaded the thinking of the time. Of course, such policies appropriate resources from those who do the most saving, investing, and producing. Although Liberals ostensibly favor growth, their zeal about income equity seems to dominate.

The combination of inflationary fiscal and monetary policies, overzealous regulation, and punitive taxes was the formula that sank the economy in the 1970s and established a foundation for enduring hardship that has proven difficult to reverse. Economic policy from the period of high Keynesianism unwittingly worked to slow the growth of the nation's productive base—to kill the goose that laid the golden eggs.

## Reversing the Trend

Perhaps growth and productivity, more than any issue, have given historical legitimacy to the Conservative position. The 1980s ushered in the political administration of President Ronald Reagan and with it at least a partial reversal of demand management and social engineering. Although the Reagan policies were but rough and incomplete proxies for the Conservative agenda, their rapid success was striking. More progress was made in particular areas in the years to follow right up to the present. A brief summary is instructive.

- Conservatives focus on the supply side of the economy as the source of increases in output, employment, productivity, and living standards. Supply-side growth policy calls for greater incentives to work, save, invest, and engage in entrepreneurial risk taking. Punitively high tax rate brackets drove a *tax wedge* between before- and after-tax labor income, interest income from savings, investment income, and profit. Because a large share of the rewards associated with work, savings, investing, and entrepreneurship was forfeited to taxes, people were discouraged from these productive activities. The drag on production caused by high tax rates actually retards the growth in government revenue as well. The Economic Recovery Tax Act of 1981 and the Tax Reform Act of 1986 provided much needed relief from the tax wedge by greatly reducing income tax brackets. Thankfully, the three consecutive tax cuts proposed by the Bush administration and passed by Congress from 2001 to 2003 have all helped to reverse the higher tax rates enacted during the Clinton administration, restoring the focus on supply-side growth policy (see Issue 7).
- Conservatives also call for less government regulation and restrictions upon business investment and risk taking. Progress in this area advanced in the 1980s with an acceleration in industry deregulation that saw completion of the deregulation of airlines, elimination of price controls on most oil and natural gas, and inroads into the deregulation of trucking and railroads (see Issue 5). The result has been measurable cost savings and innovations in those industries as well as lower overall inflation. By the 1990s, it seemed as if the government was getting over its penchant for regulating business and fearing markets. This is exemplified by government auctioning off the electromagnetic spectrum for communications, the development of a market for pollution permits (see Issue 3), and reluctance (or perhaps its real inability) to regulate or tax the Internet.
- Economic growth and growth in living standards are best served by a global environment of free trade (discussed in detail in Issue 14). Fortunately, a strengthening trend of trade liberalization has come into vogue and the economy is reaping the benefits of that course.
- The nation's public education system is dysfunctional. American high school students are now routinely performing well below their counterparts in other industrially advanced countries and also, to our chagrin, some not-so-advanced countries. Privatizing the system or introducing competition through a voucher system that would

allow individuals the choice of what school to attend would instill the incentive to deliver high-quality education. This would strengthen the base of *human capital* that is essential to restoring productivity growth.

### Greater Acceptance of the Conservative Paradigm and Its Success

The Conservative paradigm has enjoyed greater acceptance in the last two decades because it successfully reversed the misguided policies of the past, placing America back on the track of economic growth and rising per capita GDP. Liberals' criticism of supply-side policies in the 1980s for not delivering immediate results has been increasingly muted as the course of lower taxes, deregulation, and reliance upon market forces set the stage for the significant economic boom that has since transpired. It took long-term adherence to the Conservative program to nullify the long downward slide caused by the policies of the past. A glance back at Table 9.1 confirms the impressive long-term response of GDP growth to Conservative policies that stimulated work, savings, investment, and enterprise; promoted freer trade; and trimmed government. The economy will continue to thrive if it is freed from the social engineering of affirmative action, government favoritism toward labor unions, and the propping up of ailing businesses.

The greater stability of GDP growth since the mid-1980s and unprecedented acceleration in labor productivity since 2001 conclusively demonstrate the superiority of Conservative policies to promote long-term growth and prosperity. This was accomplished in large part because fiscal policy manipulation of the macroeconomy was shelved. Unfortunately, just as the American economy is currently poised for continued growth the Federal Reserve System is resuming its monetary activism in response to a perceived threat of inflation. Their overreaction with a tight money policy was plainly responsible for the unnecessary recession in 2001. Frightened first by the slowdown they helped to create and then by the economic ramifications of the September 11 terrorist raid on the United States, the Fed radically reversed the policy with thirteen interest rate cuts in rapid succession. Now, the Fed is currently reversing that policy in favor of rate increases that can only foster instability. Conservatives can only hope for a return to a less activist monetary policy and continued shrinking of government involvement in the economy.

## THE LIBERAL ARGUMENT

It is wise to remember that the experience of the Great Depression and the shortcomings of classical economic thought gave rise to the Keynesian critique. Classical economists had no answers and no solutions. Their recommendation was to wait around until the economy corrected itself through the *automatic stabilization mechanism of markets*. After a decade of waiting for self-correction, the Keynesian prescription was by happenstance put to the test by the coming of World War II and the massive military spending it required. National defense budgetary outlays rose from $1 billion in 1939 to $81 billion by 1945, accounting for 82 percent of federal spending and absorbing nearly 40 percent of the nation's output. Although the principal purpose behind this effort was to defeat the Axis powers of Nazi Germany, Italy, and Japan, the economic results of rising output and employment served as confirmation for Keynes's proposition that we could indeed spend our way out of the Depression. Since then, we have come to understand and refine the analytic and policy tools necessary to manage the general level of economic activity. At the same time, our understanding of the productivity and growth problems has advanced, ensuring improvement in the management of those problems as well.

Conservatives, who do not believe in the efficacy of macroeconomic stabilization policy, are in fact long on theory and short on evidence. Their pessimism about government's role in regulating economic growth and in addressing the related problem of the slowdowns in productivity and GDP per capita growth illustrates not only a lack of faith but also a disregard for specific troubles that can be countered only by government intervention.

Having made this point, Liberals do acknowledge that possessing the tools of correction and using them properly are different matters. There was outright misuse of countercyclical policy during most of the 1970s, and indeed there were examples of overzealous regulation and some poorly conceived efforts at social experimentation. However, it was not so much these errors as it was unpredictable random shocks and structural changes in the economy that were mainly to blame for the economic crisis of the 1970s and its lingering effects. On the other hand, the assertion that Conservative-leaning policies in the 1980s and the continuing drift toward the practice of Conservative economic policy making have produced a great turnaround for America is simply unfounded.

## A Different View of the Economic Record

The general framework for policy making to counter the business cycle was in place by the beginning of the post–World War II period. Steps to end the Depression, wartime spending, and the legal commitment of the Employment Act of 1946 helped end the traditional government commitment to balance the budget. Nevertheless, between 1946 and the early 1960s, the political leadership of the nation showed little mastery of the new policy possibilities. Fiscal policy, as it was practiced, was unplanned and ill timed. Deficits or surpluses appeared at the wrong time or quite accidentally at the right time. Manipulative monetary policy was not practiced at all.

After inheriting a stagnant macroeconomy, President Kennedy sought recommendations from economic advisers who were schooled in Keynesian economics. A reluctant Kennedy was convinced to propose a discretionary tax reduction. In 1964, three months after Kennedy's assassination, Congress passed a bill to reduce personal taxes by $11 billion and corporate taxes by $2.6 billion. The results were quite good: By 1965, unemployment fell, the growth rate in output per capita nearly doubled from 1963 levels, and prices were stable. However, the Vietnam War, coupled with Lyndon Johnson's adamant stance that the economy could produce guns *and* butter, gave rise to excessive demand for goods and chronic inflationary pressures.

Elementary Keynesian economics would have called for a tax increase and a reduction in government spending. Neither of these, especially a tax increase, looked politically appealing to Johnson. His successor, Richard Nixon (a Republican), sidestepped that dilemma by invoking the extraordinary measure of wage and price controls.

Consequently, there is a relatively short period within which to evaluate countercyclical policy. However, the data in Table 9.3 show that the 1960s, the decade most affected by the judicious exercise of macroeconomic policy, stands out in terms of gains in living standards. Referring back to Table 9.1, generally impressive rates of economic growth prevailed.

Thereafter, the economy faltered, but not precisely for the reasons expressed by Conservatives. Economic policy making's expansionary bias was certainly not designed to counter the economic challenges besetting the economy in the 1970s. Inflation and the growth slowdown were exacerbated.

Table 9.3

**Average Annual Changes in Gross Domestic Product per Capita**

| Year | Change in real GDP per capita (percentage) |
|---|---|
| 1950–1959 | 2.3 |
| 1960–1969 | 3.1 |
| 1970–1979 | 2.2 |
| 1980–1989 | 2.1 |
| 1990–1999 | 1.9 |
| | |
| Entire period 1950–1999 | 2.3 |

*Source:* Bureau of Economic Analysis and U.S. Bureau of the Census. Calculations by the author.

## Random Shocks and Structural Change

The 1970s presented a confluence of problems found in no other period. Contrary to the Conservative view, Keynesian stabilization policy does not bear primary responsibility for the stagflationary malaise of the times. The real culprit was a series of random events and structural changes in the economy.

- By 1971, the American economy was faced with worsening balance-of-payments problems (which were caused mostly by Vietnam War spending). Simultaneously, the world began to doubt the sturdiness of the gold-backed dollar, and the collapse of confidence was confirmed when America suspended the conversion of dollars into gold on the international level. The dollar lost stature as an international reserve asset and had to be devalued by the Nixon administration in an attempt to correct the balance-of-payments deficits. While this made American goods less expensive to foreign buyers, prices of imported goods rose, contributing to inflationary pressure.
- In October 1973, the United States exported 19 million metric tons of wheat to the Soviet Union, reducing American wheat supplies to practically nothing. This resulted in higher food prices.
- In late 1973, the Organization of Petroleum Exporting Countries (OPEC) imposed a temporary embargo on oil exports to the United

States and began a long series of increases in the price of crude oil, which rose from less than $2 per barrel in 1970 to nearly $40 per barrel in 1981 (or about $50 per barrel in 2004). The rapid escalation in oil prices affected the costs of heating, transportation, chemical processing, plastic production, and virtually everything else. Price levels soared. Given that the price of oil is stated in dollars on the international market, each announcement of a price increase delivered an almost instant shock to consumer prices in America.

• Structural changes of various sorts that had quietly evolved were now exerting a downward pressure on productivity and economic growth. Inexperienced teenagers and women had entered the labor force in large numbers. The economy was prominently exhibiting a shift from manufacturing and agriculture (where productivity is rather readily observable) to services (where productivity gains are less obvious). Research and development spending (the engine of technological advancement) as a share of national output had been declining since the mid-1960s. The amount of capital per worker was in a state of decline as war had seized and wasted the best technology and capital, and evidence of poorer management and a diminished work ethic mounted.

The situation's complexity is but incompletely summarized above. The 1970s proved to be a tar baby for policy makers of any ideological stripe. Each use of the blunt tools of fiscal and monetary policy mired the economy more deeply than before. Nixon's mandatory wage and price controls (1971–74), Ford's WIN (Whip Inflation Now) buttons, and Carter's feeble efforts to maintain wage-price guideposts were a testimonial to bafflement.

### Supply-Side Paradox

It is difficult to understand why supply-side economists, with their attachment to tax cutting, see their policy efforts as uniquely different from the maligned Keynesian economics of the past. While income tax reductions may vary in magnitude, timing, and targeting, there is no solidly logical way to predict whether it is the demand side or supply side of the economy that is most affected by such actions. Economists have clearly determined that the Economic Recovery Tax Act of 1981 had little supply-side effect. Advocates asserted that it worked, but just as Keynesian stabilization efforts were not responsible for the lousy economic performance of the 1970s, the same could be said about supply-side economic policy's impact upon the improved performance in the 1980s.

Fortuitous circumstances gave the illusion of success: A tight money policy that had begun in August of 1979 wrung the inflation out of the economy by inducing a severe recession. The OPEC oil cartel lost unity and oil prices fell. Labor union membership as a percentage of the labor force went into major decline, perhaps relieving upward pressure upon wages.

Unemployment rates dropped, as they usually do, once the economy emerged from the recession of 1981–82. Ironically, the 1980s became the *go-go* years of stimulative fiscal policy, with seemingly unrestrained increases in annual federal deficits piling up federal debt and tripling the federal debt per capita. In the end, inflation-adjusted GDP per capita had not improved and labor productivity turned in a worse performance than in the 1970s (Table 9.3). The 1990s continued this trend with real per capita output slightly lower than the prior decade while labor productivity was almost half a percent faster. In retrospect, despite a sustained focus on supply-side considerations, the last two decades of the twentieth century were periods of below-average growth in real per capita output and productivity.

### What Is Wrong?

If the macroeconomy is performing well, what else needs to be in place to alter the course of productivity and GDP per capita? The fact is economic science has no exact answer. Differing perceptions of the main causal factors and what policies might work are at issue. Liberals maintain that neglect of pressing social and economic problems has helped to worsen the structural changes that resulted in the productivity slowdown and weakened growth in living standards.

For one thing, the rate of technological change may have slowed beginning in the mid-1960s. This was suggested by the lower percentage of GDP going to research and development spending. The market system tends to devote insufficient resources to research and development because the payoffs of such investments may be risky or uncertain, or hard to claim if competitors are swift and unobstructed imitators. Government can play a critical role in stimulating technological progress by offsetting the risks and uncertainty of research and development (R&D) spending through such measures as tax credits and subsidies. Government also establishes and lays the groundwork for enforcement of intellectual property rights through the patent system and copyrights—invention and innovation will be stifled if not protected from theft. Given that most of the productivity slowdown can be blamed on slower technological change, it is instructive to look at the late 1940s and the 1950s when productivity was speeding up. In this era, private sector business productivity was the beneficiary of a government-inspired surge in innovation. Government has to engage in planned peacetime encouragement of R&D spending to reverse or prevent productivity slowdowns. Indeed, government directly and indirectly subsidized research and development into computing and information systems technologies, which fed the productivity acceleration experienced from 1995 to 2000.

Although deficient investment in human capital cannot be identified as a major contributor to the slowdown, quite plainly a better-educated, more highly skilled, and healthier labor force is essential to maintaining and advancing productivity growth. Conservatives' obsession with shrinking the public sector and nonintervention is part of a deeper social and political agenda aimed at privatizing public schools and dismantling affirmative action. Again, the knee-jerk Conservative response is to prescribe a competitive market as the solution for nearly every complex problem. This ignores the fact that the real source of failure for public education is a starvation diet on which schools are supposed to thrive. The constraints imposed on public school budgets have decimated specialties such as foreign language and music education, and now threaten the basic fields of mathematics and science. Meanwhile, poverty rates among children have been allowed to climb, worsening preparation for learning and acquisition of human capital. The scaling back of affirmative action simply promises a return to the inefficiencies caused by labor market discrimination. Productivity growth could be improved through *more* spending and intervention in these areas, not less.

There is some evidence that the quantity and quality of the nation's basic infrastructure, namely, transportation systems, sewer and water systems, and so forth, also have an impact upon a nation's productivity. There is also evidence that the slowing of public investment in infrastructure correlates with America's productivity slowdown. Deteriorating highways and difficulties with air traffic control systems may not figure prominently in explaining the slowdown, but the public sector must be vigilant in maintaining and improving transportation infrastructure to prevent drags on productivity growth.

While Conservatives argue vehemently on behalf of free trade, they seem to ignore that many of America's trading partners use industrial policies to obtain the best advantages from international commerce. This crosses over from the earlier point that government can use tax incentives or subsidies to target technological progress in promising industries to help bolster productivity growth. In other areas, America can make judicious use of selective trade barriers to give ailing industries time to reindustrialize.

In the face of sustained economic and employment growth in the 1990s, the American economy did not display above average gains in living standards until the last half of the decade. Conservatives initially said that productivity measures were not detecting the gains. When the same measures began recording a big acceleration, they proceeded to celebrate victory for a fairly predictable collection of Conservative favorites. Free markets, globalization, technological supremacy of American business enterprises, and reductions in affirmative action programs were credited. However, there was little Conservatives could say about their main obsession: onerous taxes wreaking havoc on incentives, productivity, and living standards. Clearly, supply-side tax policies have minimal influence on economic growth and stability, and Conservatives are having a hard time accepting it.

## Summary

Conservatives do not make a believable case against discretionary stabilization policy. No more convincing are their pronouncements of a shift in national sentiment toward the Conservative position and their claims that Conservative policies have led to rising productivity growth and living standards. Most thoughtful Americans would expect their living standards to be visibly improving if the United States were undergoing the productivity growth that Conservatives celebrate. However, it is mainly the elite few who have seen tangible gains in their own real income and wealth. Productivity growth is the engine for the development of future wealth. Sustaining it requires government to wage a strong and concerted effort to promote innovation, investment in human capital, and public investment, and adopt sensible industrial policies.

## THE RADICAL ARGUMENT

The debate between Liberal demand managers and Conservative supply-siders has produced considerable confusion among thoughtful Americans. The arguments have usually been framed in either/or terms: Either you intervene to manage the aggregate economy or you do not. Either an unregulated economy works better than a managed one or it does not. Given the record of the past seventy years of American economic history, there is little evidence to make either side's claims very convincing. Thus it is not surprising that modern macroeconomic policy debates produce more heat than light. In both actual policy making and the classroom teaching of economics, the result has been "a little of this and a little of that." From a Radical perspective, however, there is no confusion about the issues: both Liberals and Conservatives, albeit for different reasons, are *wrong*.

### Why Neither Demand-Side nor Supply-Side Efforts Work

The fundamental flaw of both Liberal and Conservative approaches begins from the same error: Neither truly understands what powers a capitalist economy. Although both agree that investment is the driving force, each sees investment as depending on different determinants.

Conservatives understand investment as being determined by the level of savings in the society. As savings grow, interest rates (the cost of borrowing) decline, and investors step forward in greater numbers to obtain funds. In turn, their investment actions propel the economy, providing growth and jobs. Accordingly, Conservative policy focuses on actions that will enhance savings. The Reagan tax cut of 1981 was called a supply-side tax cut (although it differed little from earlier demand-side cuts) because it was aimed at giving very large tax reductions to the very rich, who were expected to save their windfall, and to corporations, who were expected to translate after-tax profits directly into investment.

Similarly, Conservatives oppose government deficits that are financed in capital markets in competition with private seekers of funds. Government borrowing is supposed to *crowd out* private investment by raising interest rates (see the Conservative argument in Issue 7). In monetary policy matters, although low interest rates are attractive to investors, too-low rates are opposed because they might discourage saving and encourage consumer borrowing. Therefore, an expansionary money policy is discounted as having no useful effects on investment. In focusing on savings and the interest rate, along with their views on the excessive power of labor unions to raise wage rates, it is apparent that Conservatives take a cost-based approach to explaining how investment occurs and capitalism supposedly flourishes.

Liberals, meanwhile, see the chief determinant of investment as the actual level of aggregate demand. Abundant savings and low interest rates, they argue, will not induce a firm to invest if, as a result of an economic slump, it has a great deal of unused plants and equipment. As demand rises, utilization rates grow, and new investment becomes attractive as the firm actually seeks to expand output. Faced with an underemployed economy, Liberals are accordingly biased toward tax cuts that raise consumption, toward increases in government spending, and, under some circumstances, toward very low interest rates (which in their view encourage borrowing). Their built-in bias focuses on demand conditions. Increase demand to stimulate the economy; decrease it to slow down economic activity.

To be sure, Liberals and Conservatives view the "natural state" of the economy in two different ways. Conservatives assume that, left to itself and without government tinkering, an economy naturally runs at full employment and capacity utilization. Liberals view the natural state as being less than full employment but believe that full employment may be reached by means of adroit policy actions. In many other respects, Conservatives and Liberals are quite alike. Both zero in on business investment as the key that unlocks the economy; they differ, however, on their *cost* versus *demand* explanations of why investment takes place. *The difference is a very crucial one.*

To see this issue more clearly and to understand why Liberals and Conservatives are both wrong, we must first see that each is a little bit right in understanding how capitalism works. *Profit, not savings or aggregate demand, is the real determinant of investment.* Although few Liberals or Conservatives would disagree with the assertion that profit drives capitalism, they fail to recognize that profit has both a cost side and a demand side. Remember: Profit equals sales minus expenditures. Thus lower costs increase profits and increased sales raise profits, *ceteris paribus.* The trouble, of course, is with *ceteris paribus.*

The very actions aimed at lowering costs (the supply-side menu of cutting the taxes of only the rich, keeping government spending in check, balancing the budget, and so on) lowers demand and thus business sales.

Meanwhile, actions intended to increase demand (increased government spending, tax cuts to stimulate consumption, budget imbalance, and the like) raise costs as resource prices are bid upward in an expanding economy. This was precisely the dilemma of the 1970s, as we saw in the last issue.

Ironically, both demand-based and supply-based stabilization policy scenarios are doomed to fail in the long run. The problem lies deep in a production-for-profit system. The normal search for profits produces overproduction and underconsumption crises and falling profits. Marx identified both outcomes as inherent features of growth under capitalism. Why? Because capitalist competition compels businesses to squeeze every penny of profit from their payroll while simultaneously seeking new ways to automate and mechanize as many jobs as possible. In this way, technological change—rather than being some passive or neutral factor in the production process—has a very specific role and objective: to reduce the labor content in the production of any good or service. Thus, the capitalist system is always under threat because of its inherent labor-displacing tendency and continual need to exploit workers to increase profitability. Efforts to remedy overproduction and underconsumption through macroeconomic stabilization policies lead to rising costs and falling profits. In either case, profits, the driving force of the system, are perpetually threatened.

Over the past half century, stabilization policy has been simply a matter of trying first one and then the other of these bankrupt approaches. Although many economists have tried to reconcile the Liberal and Conservative extremes and build an eclectic system, that is bound to fail too. Invariably, cost-based and demand-based approaches come into conflict. The result is that they either negate each other or one comes to dominate the other.

### The Class Bias and Irrationality of Conventional Stabilization Policy Efforts

Regardless of its failure, stabilization policy efforts in our time have had one permanent effect: They have erected government as a central feature of the modern capitalist economy. In turn, the modern capitalist state has become a vehicle for class domination and increasing productive irrationality.

Liberals and Conservatives both hold that government policy is capable of being neutral; that is, tax cuts or money policy actions, regardless of the particular kind of action, are viewed as having only economic effects. The social and political biases of any of these policies are never put up front for examination. This misses an important aspect of public policy making, namely, its role as a class instrument, a tool for perpetuating ruling-class domination. Ordinary Americans better appreciate the social inequalities of stabilization policy than most economists admit, but they might usefully be laid out in detail.

There is an upper-income bias in taxation policy. A brief survey of important tax-cutting efforts to stimulate expansion—either the cuts of 1964 or those of 1981 or the most recent tax cuts of the Bush administration throughout 2001–3, for example—indicates that upper-middle-class and upper-income taxpayers received the largest percentage reduction and the bulk of the total cut. These same groups, of course, benefit the most from the legal loopholes of the tax system, such as the ability to deduct interest payments on home mortgages and home equity loans and business expenses from their tax bills. The poor and the lower middle class, without the benefits of tax loopholes (or even much opportunity to cheat), have lost economic ground in the tax-cutting measures of demand-side Keynesians and supply-side Conservatives. In the case of tax increases, the poor again are hit hardest. The recent increase in Social Security withholding taxes is a good example. Over the past few years, both the taxable base and the rate of the taxes have risen at the lower end of the income scale. (In 2005 the rate paid by employees was 6.2 percent on earnings up to $90,000.) Such taxes are regressive, since they fall most heavily on lower incomes. Moreover, nearly three out of four workers pay more in Social Security taxes than they do in federal income taxes. Obviously, the solution is to reduce significantly the payroll tax rate at the lower end of the income scale while imposing a progressive rate structure on *all* income.

Low-income Americans have also lost out on the spending side. While Conservatives and Liberals (for different reasons) point to the magnitude of federal transfers to the poor and indigent, this is a massive deception. The federal government's spending in this area amounts to about the same percentage of the GDP today as it did in the pre-Keynesian 1930s.* At the same time, transfers to large farmers, businesses, and professional work-

---

*This fact may seem startling to Americans, who are constantly bombarded with propaganda about the alleged extravagance of social spending on the poor. In reality,

ers have grown. Government spending for goods, meanwhile, directly benefits the ruling class and higher-income workers. A good illustration of the capitalized bias of such expenditures is military and space spending. The recipient firms are among the largest in the nation and also the most capital- and skill-intensive. Spending funneled into these firms strengthens capital's power and has little or no impact on creating jobs for less skilled and lower-paid workers (see Issue 11).

Looked at in this way, government spending, even for stabilization purposes, is not neutral at all. It actually heightens class divisions in the society. Spending on low-income housing, medical care, and other social goods that would improve the poor's quality of life has always ranked very low among fiscal priorities. This is because the poor, regardless of their numbers, are not yet a powerful constituency and also because spending for certain social goods would actually create competition with the private sector. Subsidized public housing would destroy the lucrative low-income housing market in the private sector, free clinics would bankrupt private hospitals, and so on. Moreover, when the stabilization experts call for a contraction in government spending (to balance the budget or reduce aggregate demand), services and transfers to the poor are the first items sacrificed.

Although Liberals in the heyday of Keynesian policy were less inclined to cut so deeply or so obviously, the Conservative budget cutters of the Reagan years brutalized the poor. In the name of "trickle-down" economics, poor children were told that catsup now qualified as a vegetable in the school lunch program, and the unskilled were told that there were plenty of jobs in most newspapers' classified sections. And all social service budgets were chopped.

Monetary policy is equally selective and unfair in its class effects. For instance, the 1982 pursuit of high interest rates (a tight money policy) as an anti-inflation tool especially burdened the working class. For consumers, high interest rates mean that greater portions of their income must go toward such necessities as home mortgages and for the "luxuries" provided by credit buying. Upper-income groups, of course, face the same interest rates, but their burdens are a much smaller proportion of their income and more easily borne without sacrifice of their living

---

we currently spend only a little over 2 percent of our output on programs directed specifically to low-income groups. In 1938, for example, the $1.5 billion spent on various poor relief programs by federal, state, and local governments amounted to a little less than 2 percent of the output.  ·

standards. Meanwhile, for workers, tight money translates into reduced business output and fewer jobs or lower pay.

Thus stabilization policy perpetuates and accentuates the normal class inequalities of capitalism. Expansionary policy never benefits the poor as much as the rich. And contraction always demands that the least affluent American citizens tighten their belts the most. The normal exploitative tendencies of traditional capitalism are merely reinforced under both Liberal and Conservative approaches.

Apart from the upper-class biases of stabilization policies, there is also the problem of the irrational production and consumption that it encourages. Foremost among these irrational activities are the huge amounts of government spending on the military. Presently, we are spending about $450 billion on national defense for goods and services that only waste the social surplus and have been a significant source of inflation during the postwar period. This is because once warplanes, tanks, guns, ordnance, and the like are produced, they can only be stockpiled and not recirculated throughout the economy. Although wages have been paid, there is no concomitant increase in socially useful output.

Second, while defense expenditures give the appearance of increasing GDP, in actuality they add little to the material well-being of the vast majority of workers. Furthermore, military expenditure programs are also extremely costly and untenable in an era of austerity and shrinking federal budgets. Thus, it should be obvious that rather than being a source of macroeconomic stability, defense expenditures are a persistent net drain on society's resources and need to be drastically curtailed. Significantly cutting the defense budget would have other salutary effects, such as lowering the national debt and deficit, freeing up money for needed social programs, and discouraging politicians from getting involved in unnecessary military adventures (such as the invasion of Iraq).

Rather than reconstructing a stable economy, uncritical and unplanned government spending policy has reinforced the irrational production and consumption patterns of a capitalist system.

With government nondefense spending now poised to be restrained by yet another round of supply-side tax and expenditure cutting, it would be erroneous to conclude that government has ceased contributing to productive irrationality. By cutting corporate taxes and reducing other burdens on the private sector, encouragement of irrational production and investment decisions has shifted from the spending side of the government budget to the revenue side. The technique differs, but the outcome is the same: more socially useless goods and a more meaningless life for consumers and workers.

## The Emerging Contradiction

Overall, the past forty years of public policy have heightened internal capitalist contradictions. The unequal distribution of benefits and losses has produced growing conflicts—big business versus little business, capital versus labor, worker versus worker, worker versus nonworker, and, always, rich versus poor. Overarching everything is the mounting evidence that Liberal economics cannot deliver on any of its promises of full employment, growth, and price stability. After peaking during the 1960s, the growth rate of real per capita income has been steadily falling (see Table 9.3). In fact, neither the Reagan nor Clinton administrations were able to reverse this long-term trend even as labor productivity accelerated right through the 2001 recession. In essence, American capitalism becomes more and more productive at the expense of worker's livelihoods and jobs.

The temporary rise of worn-out laissez-faire economics, however, may have one positive effect: revealing the class-biased nature of capitalism much more quickly. Consequently Americans may finally be willing to go beyond the narrow and oppressive economics of their past. When the Conservative ideology fails, as it must, and the Keynesian alternative remains discredited, we will be forced to consider an economic and social agenda we have evaded thus far. Under these circumstances, we will go beyond merely stabilizing the economy to reorganizing it and planning it so that oppression and irrationality no longer exist.

# Balancing the Federal Budget

## Should We Be Worried About the Rising Federal Deficit?

When national debts have once been accumulated to a certain degree, there is scarce, I believe, a single instance of their having been fairly and completely paid. The liberation of the public revenue, if it has ever been brought about at all, has always been brought about by a bankruptcy; sometimes by an avowed one, but always by a real one, though frequently by a pretended payment.

— *Adam Smith*, The Wealth of Nations, *1776*

A decline in income due to a decline in the level of employment, if it goes far, may even cause consumption to exceed income not only by individuals and institutions using up the financial reserves which they have accumulated in better times, but also by Government, which will be liable, willingly or unwillingly, to run a budgetary deficit.

— *John Maynard Keynes*, The General Theory of Employment, Interest, and Money, *1935*

We recognize loud and clear the surplus is not the government's money. The surplus is the people's money and we ought to trust them with their own money.

— *President George W. Bush, 2001*

A balanced budget amendment is a rigid, simple-minded approach to a very complex problem. Sometimes you need a deficit to kick-start a stalled economy. But that doesn't mean I think it's ok to run deficits year after year. Borrowing money from rich people is a cowardly substitute for taxing them.

— *Doug Henwood*, Left Business Observer, *2004*

## The Problem

Over the past seven decades, majority economic and political thinking on the question of government deficits has undergone a 360-degree swing. The prevailing view in the early 1930s, which had been held as long as economists had been speaking out on the subject, was that government budgets should be balanced annually. Experience had shown that when governments financed spending by printing new money or by borrowing, general economic misfortunes such as inflation, currency devaluation, and general financial instability tended to follow. Ironically, Franklin D. Roosevelt campaigned hard against Herbert Hoover in 1932, lambasting his "spendthrift" opponent for running deficits in the previous two years of depression.

The growing popularity of John Maynard Keynes's ideas in the 1930s and 1940s, along with the actual experience of watching budget deficits grow precisely as the economic gloom of depression receded, caused a shift in opinion. Few economists by the 1960s seriously advocated an annually balanced federal budget. A number talked about cyclically balanced budgets, in which expenditures and revenues should reach parity over a complete business cycle. The focus on the budget in such an approach was to use deficits to finance needed economic expansion while surpluses naturally accumulated during periods of prosperity. Clearly related to this view was "functional finance," which showed no real concern in any accounting sense for balance or imbalance at all but focused exclusively on using deficits or surpluses as policy tools. To the functional finance theorists, there was no fundamental limitation on government's capacity to create and finance deficits, regardless of the size of the debt.

It is important to recognize that the federal government deficit is different from the federal debt. The federal government experiences a *budget deficit* when its revenues are less than its expenditures during a given time period, typically a fiscal year or a calendar year. If deficits are not paid off and become a recurring phenomenon, then the government accumulates *debt*. Economists distinguish between a budget deficit and debt when speaking of government finance by referring to the revenue shortfall of a given year as a budget deficit and the year-to-year accumulation of budget deficits as the federal debt.

By the 1980s, the sudden explosion of the federal debt forced a change in majority economic thinking again. As Table 10.1 shows, both debt as a share of gross domestic product (GDP) and interest payments as a percent of GDP moved sharply upward. With debt and interest outlays on

Table 10.1

**Measures of the Federal Debt**

| Year | Public debt (billions of current dollars) | Real debt (billions of 2000 dollars) | Debt as percentage of GDP | Interest as percentage of GDP |
|------|------|------|------|------|
| 1929 | 16.9 | 98.8 | 16.0 | 0.7 |
| 1940 | 50.7 | 582.7 | 52.4 | 1.3 |
| 1945 | 260.1 | 2498.8 | 117.5 | 1.5 |
| 1950 | 256.9 | 1995.7 | 94.0 | 1.6 |
| 1955 | 274.4 | 1885.7 | 69.3 | 1.3 |
| 1960 | 290.5 | 1660.1 | 56.0 | 2.0 |
| 1965 | 322.3 | 1671.8 | 46.9 | 1.9 |
| 1970 | 380.9 | 1612.0 | 37.6 | 2.2 |
| 1975 | 541.9 | 1601.4 | 34.7 | 2.4 |
| 1980 | 909.0 | 1807.6 | 33.4 | 3.2 |
| 1985 | 1817.4 | 2680.2 | 43.8 | 4.9 |
| 1990 | 3206.3 | 4067.9 | 55.9 | 5.1 |
| 1995 | 4920.6 | 5395.4 | 67.2 | 4.8 |
| 2000 | 5628.7 | 5628.7 | 58.0 | 3.7 |
| 2003 | 6760.0 | 6396.0 | 62.4 | 1.4 |

*Source: Economic Report of the President* (Washington, DC: Government Printing Office, 2001) and data from Bureau of Economic Analysis.

Note: Entries for 1929 relied on gross national product figures. GDP = gross domestic product.

the debt growing faster than national output and also seeming to accompany an inflationary period of high unemployment and slow growth, many economists (mostly Conservatives at first but soon many Liberals as well) began to believe that deficits did have an adverse effect on the general economy. Needless to say, Conservatives have been increasingly vulnerable to Liberal criticism on the debt and deficit issues. The administrations of Ronald Reagan and George H. Bush, irrespective of their official condemnation of deficits and their posturing on behalf of spending restraint on budget balance, ran up in the 1980s the greatest deficits in American history to that point—nearly tripling the national debt (see Figure 10.1). Their defenders will correctly point out that Congress collaborated with the debt explosion too, but the irony of supposedly Conservative administrations being the most profligate is not lost on many observers.

Annual deficits mounted in the mid-1980s creating pressure for legal restraints on government's capacity to create debt. Proposals for a constitutional amendment that would require annually balanced federal budgets represented the strongest opposition to deficit spending. Whether or not

Figure 10.1    **Federal Budget Surplus or Deficit, 1969–2003**

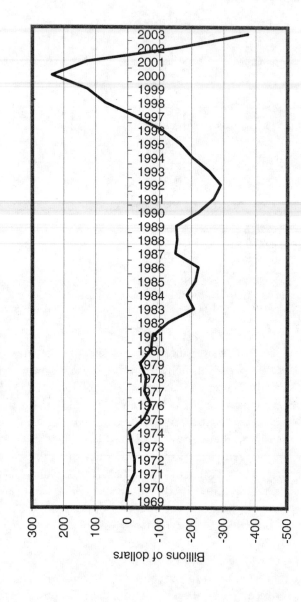

*Source: Economic Report of the President* (Washington, DC: Government Printing Office, 2004).

such an amendment will ever be passed remains to be seen. However, alarmed by their inability to slow the flow of red ink, Congress and President Reagan produced rather mechanical budget-balancing legislation in the form of the Gramm-Rudman-Hollings Act (GRH) in 1985. A schedule was laid out for obtaining annual budget balance by 1991, but this was later revised to 1993. Absolute deficit limits were imposed. If budgets came in at higher-than-allowed deficits, the act called for across-the-board cuts by the percentage of the excess deficit to all spending categories except Social Security and some defense outlays.

Few economists expressed much satisfaction with GRH's automatic, across-the-board budget-cutting machine as a substitute for human judgment and decision making about spending. Conservatives worried about defense spending cuts and insufficient cuts in social spending. Conservatives were also concerned about the distinct possibility that tax increases and not spending cuts would ultimately be used to meet deficit targets. Liberals and Radicals, on the other hand, saw the imposed cuts in social spending as "balancing the budget on the backs of the poor."

GRH's historical significance is that it *briefly* cooled debate about debt and deficits. The Black Monday meltdown of the stock market on October 19, 1987, reopened the debate. Postmortems of the securities market crash held that loss of investors' faith was traceable to America's "double deficits": the persistent federal deficit and the equally persistent deficit in international trade balances. Then the deficit reduction targets set by GRH were missed in 1988 and 1989 by more than the $10 billion margin for error allowed by the statute. The 1990 deficit was off target by more than $120 billion. In 1990, the Congress and the president eliminated the GRH mechanism and resorted to increasing taxes.

Agreeing to raise taxes in 1990 to reduce the deficit was the undoing of George H. Bush's presidency. Ironically, successor William Clinton promised and delivered higher tax rates at the upper end of the income scale. Top rates rose from 31 percent to 39.6 percent. Both the Clinton administration and the Congressional Budget Office had predicted rather modest deficit reduction using what turned out to be quite conservative forecasts of economic growth.

The expansion of the 1990s upstaged all tools of discretionary policy by outperforming even the most optimistic expectations of economic growth and deficit reduction. A deficit of $290 billion in 1992 shrank dramatically to a mere $22 billion in 1997. The year 2000 saw a $236 billion surplus in the federal budget. The best of all possible worlds had occurred: Economic growth had painlessly eliminated federal budget deficits. Federal debt as a percentage of GDP leveled off. Paying down the debt became a real option.

President George W. Bush's tax cutting policies, combined with the 2001 recession and initiation of war first against Afghanistan and then with Iraq, combined to move the federal budget from a position of record surplus to record deficit in just three years. In fact, with the exception of the Korean War, every major American armed conflict has been financed with debt. Historically, the financial capacity for the American economy to assume and manage very significant increases in wartime debt is rather remarkable. For example, during World War II the total stock of federal debt increased fivefold from 1940 to 1945 (see Table 10.1). The call for balanced budgets will likely become more vocal as the issue and its immediate effects will not disappear. As of this writing, financial markets remain nervous about prospective financing needs, and this has caused a notable increase in the yields on long-term federal government bonds. In sum, while there is fair agreement among all ideological shades that deficits do matter, it should also be clear that mainstream ideological differences could become quite blurry—especially during periods of national crises such as wars. Although the heyday of functional finance is over, there is wide disagreement on the precise consequences of deficits, on their real significance, and on how they might be eliminated.

### Synopsis

Conservatives oppose government budget imbalance because it is inherently destabilizing, producing inflation, rising interest rates, and reduced private investment. Furthermore, the discretionary nature of demand-management fiscal policy, which they see as the source of the rising debt, is singled out as particularly unwise. Liberals, although concerned with recent trends in debt growth (which they see as the result of Conservative management), generally view debt as a tool of fiscal management. Radicals see the debt issue as a reflection of the economy's general inability to realize surplus value. They point not only to the growth of public debt to support this view but also to the even faster growth of private debt.

---

### Anticipating the Arguments

- What is the logic of the Conservative argument that links budgetary deficits with inflationary pressures?

- Explain the Liberal argument that it is not the size of the deficit that is important but the way in which the deficit is acquired.
- Why do Radicals maintain that permanent elimination of the deficit is impossible?

## THE CONSERVATIVE ARGUMENT

If there is a particular gauge of the failure of demand-management policies, it must be the federal debt. The growth of the debt and a general indifference to this growth were, until comparatively recently, aspects of Liberal doctrine that were scarcely ever criticized. Introductory economics textbooks devoted a few pages to discussion of federal debt but quickly moved on to other topics, leaving the distinct impression that "debt doesn't matter." In fact, the debt does matter. Not only is it the undesirable outcome of wrong policy choices, but annual operating deficits by the federal government and mounting aggregate debt also throttle an economy, encouraging inflation and general economic stagnation.

Although Liberals have little understanding of the real problems posed by growing deficits, they are quick to point out that much of the current federal debt was acquired during a Conservative presidency. The implication is that what Conservatives say on the debt question is really just hot air. The charge is inaccurate and begs the evidence. Although the federal debt more than doubled during Reagan's years in office, this debt explosion was actually the result of pre-Reagan fiscal excesses and the reluctance of a Liberal Congress to cut federal spending. As much as ever, budget balance remains the central objective of Conservative fiscal thinking, and the debt expansion during the Reagan presidency—whatever its sources—does not change this.

### Deficits as a Source for Inflation and Unemployment

One of the more objectionable features of government's running high and persistent annual deficits is its inherent inflationary effect. When government spends more for goods and transfers than it collects in taxes, it increases the total demand for all goods produced in the economy. If an increase in the supply of goods equal to the increase in government-generated demand were instantaneously forthcoming, there would be no problem: more demand, more goods, prices unchanged. However, this is not how an economy works. Even in an underemployed economy capable of producing a greater output by simply adding productive resources, there is bound to be some *demand-pull* inflation as the existing output is bid upward in price. When the economy is operating near full employment levels, as it was through most of the 1960s and the early 1970s, and when government is at the same time piling up large annual deficits, the demand-pull pressure on prices is very much greater. Approaching the outer limits of the society's actual productive ability, demand increases by themselves cannot raise production.

Apart from their demand effect, deficits also have an inflationary effect through the money supply. Deficits must, after all, be financed. Two options are open: Bonds may be sold to financial institutions and the general public (which creates its own special problems, as we shall presently see), or the Federal Reserve System (the Fed) may purchase the new securities and in turn increase the Treasury's account, providing the government with funds to pay its mounting bills. When the latter takes place, as it will when the Fed attempts to complement an expansionary fiscal policy with an accommodative (and expansionary) monetary policy, new money is created.

To comprehend the effect of monetizing the debt, we need simply to understand the traditional explanation of inflation: too many dollars chasing too few goods.

The long-term growth of output and employment in any economy depends on the society's utilization of resources. Prices are nothing more than the measure by which money is exchanged for commodities. Accordingly, the general tendency of prices in any society will be determined by changes in the stock of money available for transactions. The stock of money, of course, must increase or decrease as the general level of economic output expands or contracts. A relative decrease in money stock compared to output must produce general price reductions. A money expansion rate above the rate of increase in output will lead to price expansion. Quite simply, more money does not, and by itself cannot, create more goods. Instead, it will be spent on the available goods at higher prices.

This analysis of the fundamental cause of inflation is amply supported by evidence. Every significant inflationary episode in U.S. history has followed excessive growth in the supply of money. However, neither logic nor the evidence has succeeded in deflecting modern state policy from pursuing an inflationary course. As we indicated in our discussions of stabilization policy and unemployment, public policy has been committed too long to the Keynesian belief that high levels of output can be created and maintained by manipulating aggregate demand. Through the 1960s and 1970s, deficits were the intended outcome of fiscal policy. Their excess demand effects were enlarged as the Fed, often pursuing an easy money policy, monetized the deficits.

Eventually, the economy was seized by an inflationary episode it could not control. The sequence of events producing the stagflation of the mid- and late 1970s should be carefully understood. The Conservative analysis of how underlying economic forces are affected runs as follows: The immediate impact of expansionary monetary and fiscal policy will probably be to induce new business investment and additional consumer spending. Thus an increase in output and employment may occur. However, the expansion is only temporary at best. Tricked by a sudden increase in earnings, businesses and consumers have overspent and overborrowed. While money income has risen, their real situation has not improved; indeed, it has probably worsened if they have overspent. Over time, however, people learn. Anticipated discretionary actions by monetary and fiscal authorities merely induce businesses and consumers—who, after all, are not stupid—to take any action they see fit to protect themselves. Their *rational expectations* negate the impact of the authorities' policies. Expansion of the money supply over time no longer stimulates economic expansion (even temporarily); it merely fuels demand inflation without any employment benefits. In fact, unemployment gets worse. The situation is a bit like a kitten chasing its tail. Excess demand inflation (aided by other Liberal tinkering with the market) lowers real income and demand for goods, which in turn lowers employment. Further economic intervention is therefore required to offset these employment losses. This in turn generates more inflationary pressures, which consequently lead to more unemployment. The more the kitten tries to catch its tail, the faster it must run.

### Crowding Out: The Impact of Deficits on Investment and Business

As noted earlier, the monetary authorities do have an option other than monetizing the debt. They can sell new government bonds, financing government's deficit spending out of private savings. While this is certainly less inflationary, it has equally undesirable effects. When government goes into financial markets as a borrower, it competes with private borrowers. With increased competition among all borrowers—government as well as private seekers of investment funds—interest rates (the price of borrowing) are pushed upward. For business borrowers, the cost of obtaining funds rises. The result is to *crowd out* some private business investment that would otherwise have taken place at a lower interest rate.

The magnitude of the crowding-out effect is a matter of some debate. A few economists hold that a dollar of government borrowing squeezes out a dollar of private investment. But even if the outcome is much smaller, government borrowing adversely affects the productive base of the economy, which is, after all, the real determinant of output and employment.

### Deficits and Trade Balances

By the early 1980s, it was apparent that the high and rising federal deficits had yet another undesirable consequence: They were adversely affecting our international trade position. This is examined in detail in Issue 14, so a brief outline here will suffice.

Through the 1970s and early 1980s, accompanying both the deficits and the deficit-generated inflationary pressures, there was a steady upward push in interest rates. From the perspective of lenders around the world, the comparatively high American interest rates made investment in all kinds of U.S. securities highly desirable. Large portions of the new government bond issues, floated to finance the swelling debt, were purchased abroad. To buy American securities, it was essential to obtain American dollars. The resulting demand for dollars pushed the price of dollars upward relative to other world currencies. With a strong and strengthening dollar (some would call it an overvalued dollar), American goods sold at relatively higher prices in foreign markets, while foreign goods sold relatively inexpensively in our own domestic markets. With imports rising and exports falling, the balance of trade turned decidedly against the United States.

While it is not accurate to lay all U.S. trade problems at the door of the deficit, it is obvious that insofar as deficit spending and deficit financing place upward pressure on interest rates, they helped create an artificially strong dollar, which translated directly into a worsening international trade position.

### Deficits Do Matter

The foregoing arguments make it clear that deficits have an extraordinary impact on the contemporary economy. Paradoxically, they bring about the opposite of their intended effects. Rather than leading to a demand-powered expansion of output and employment, as Liberals have long claimed, deficits lead in the other direction, toward inflation, rising interest rates, dwindling investment, and ultimately lower levels of output and employment.

The legislative process of budgeting is influenced by far too many powerful voting interests with personal stakes in keeping spending high and thus keeping deficits high. Too many candidates for high political office have learned that the briefly stimulating effects of a political fiscal policy that pumps up demand just before election time can ensure victory at the polls. A balanced budget amendment would solve this problem, but the political balance in the House and Senate has obstructed its enactment. The Cato Institute has proposed the alternative of a "balanced budget veto" amendment that would allow the president to exercise line-item veto power to reduce government spending only in years following a deficit. Congress would have the incentive to restrain spending to avoid losing control of the budgeting process. Thus, a check and balance would be restored in that the president's veto authority would be checked by the ability of Congress to balance its spending prerogatives against available revenues.

Conservatives maintain that mandatory budget balancing is the longterm solution to the problem of deficits and debt. The need for fiscal discipline is grounded in recognizing that the role of the central government must be curtailed. More aggressive efforts to privatize and contract out governmental operations to the private sector support that end. The savings and efficiencies from pursuit of these policies provide society with the rewards of a reduced tax burden and less government intrusion into economic affairs.

## THE LIBERAL ARGUMENT

During the Reagan presidency, when Conservative policy influence was at its greatest, the nation saw a near tripling of the federal debt. History seems to be repeating itself. The administration of George W. Bush has been relatively quiet about the exploding federal deficits it has induced on the heels of the comfortable surplus that it inherited. Yet, Conservatives still hold to the view that deficits are a profoundly evil economic undertaking and claim to remain committed to the ideal of a consistently balanced federal budget. Reconciling this inconsistency in Conservative philosophy versus policy presents a challenge to true Conservatives.

Conservatives are right in stressing that deficits do matter. What they do not seem to understand, however, is that they matter in how and why they come into being in the first place. *Some deficits matter much more than others.*

### Putting the Size of the Debt in Perspective

The recent focus on the deficit has been stimulated by public concern for both the absolute size and the rate of growth of the public debt. However, it is important to understand what the numbers really say. As Table 10.1 indicated, the *real* (or constant dollar) growth of the debt before its explosion during the Reagan years was substantially less than its *nominal* (or current dollar) growth. In constant dollars, the debt was less in 1980 than it had been at the end of World War II. As a percent of GDP, total debt was vastly smaller in 1980 than in 1945. Thus the argument that the growth of the debt was altering the American economic landscape is not very convincing, since the so-called spendthrift 1960s and 1970s did not have any impact on the real (as opposed to the nominal) level of federal debt.

The other misplaced emphasis of the Conservative argument, with regard to pre-Reagan debt accumulations, is to view the debt as a cause rather than the result of general economic conditions. *The simple fact is that a troubled economy produces deficits, not vice versa.*

### Understanding the Cause of the Debt

Conservative analyses of deficits make little effort to distinguish among different sources or causes of a given deficit. Actually, two major but quite different causes for the federal government's running a deficit are identifiable. First, there are deficits that are directly the result of a general economic slump. When recession strikes, government revenues decrease as taxable income falls, but expenditures rise automatically as more people qualify for unemployment benefits and various other transfer payments (including subsidies to business). Even if additional expenditures were not made, a gap between revenues and expenditures would develop since government outlays were planned before the slump and were based on anticipated revenues. This is called a *cyclical budget deficit*. It is estimated that every time the unemployment rate rises by one percentage point in a recession, the loss of revenues and the automatic rise in outlays create a $40 billion to $50 billion revenue-expenditure gap.

A second, and quite different, source of debt growth may come from a *structural budget deficit*. Structural deficits arise from some discretionary redirection of fiscal policy—the passage of a tax cut (decreasing revenue collections) or the introduction of a huge public works or military spending program (increasing outlays), for instance. Structural deficits may develop as the result of either wise or unwise policy making. They may also result from external conditions over which policy makers have no control (or very little), as in the case of World War II, Vietnam War spending, or the emergency relief associated with the World Trade Center and Pentagon disasters and the costs of waging the subsequent war.

With a little reflection, it should be obvious that it is essential to know whether a given deficit is the result of cyclical or structural events. Clearly, an attempt to balance a budget in a period of cyclical downturn—either by raising taxes or by reducing governmental outlays to the needy—is both economic and political foolishness that could make downturns worse and destabilize political institutions. In failing to distinguish between types of deficits and persistently calling for a constitutional amendment requiring a balanced budget, Conservatives are proposing the most destructive possible approach to government budgeting.

While Conservatives oppose all deficits, it is obvious that most of their attack is directed against structural deficits because they feel any manipulation of government revenues and expenditures for the purpose of demand management is wrong. Their conclusion is easily stated: Deficits, purely and simply, cause inflation and discourage investment. That judgment, however, is not unequivocally supported by theory or empirical evidence.

Consider an economy that has entered a recession. A structural deficit acquired when an economy is undergoing a cyclical downturn or when substantial underemployment of available resources exists need not create demand-pull inflation. The expansion of total demand resulting from a consciously developed structural deficit under these conditions can put the unemployed back to work and reemploy unused productive capacity without excessively bidding up wage and resource prices. This was the case in the early and mid-

1960s. The moderate deficits of the Kennedy and Johnson years (before Vietnam War spending generated demand-pull inflation pressures) lowered unemployment and stimulated the economy without pumping up prices. Moreover, most of the inflationary pressure that built up in the late 1970s came from supply-side shocks and cost-push inflationary effects, not from the demand side and government deficits. The Conservative view that all inflation results from excess demand and that government deficits are the primary source for excess demand is just not supported if the events of the 1970s are honestly reported and evaluated.

Structural deficits do not necessarily and under all conditions discourage or crowd out private investment demand that might otherwise be forthcoming. If crowding out exists at all, it can take place only when an economy is near full employment and is utilizing most of a fixed stock of investable funds. At any point below this level, "crowding in" is a much greater likelihood, with private investment rising as expansionary fiscal policy puts unemployed resources back to work. As output rises, new investment opportunities develop; they do not disappear.

Conservative logic is empirically contradicted by recent events when Conservatives were having their own way with budget making. Following Conservative reasoning, the enormous deficits following their so-called "supply-side" tax cuts in 1981 that were not matched by spending reductions should have generated enormous inflationary pressures. With the largest structural deficits in American history, we might also have expected the greatest price inflation. In actuality, prices did not rise very much. As any good Keynesian would have predicted, the economy expanded, and the cyclical deficit actually shrank.

Given an understanding of the foregoing points, Liberals are not about to cave in to Conservative and popular pressures and dispatch deficit spending to the junkyard of ill-conceived economic policies. Quite to the contrary of Conservative allegations, Liberals have always believed that deficits matter. When well planned and executed, they provide an important tool of economic management. However, Liberals also believe that deficits matter when they are piled up as the result of badly executed policies. The defense of deficit spending under certain conditions can in no way be extended to defend the deficits of the Reagan years. Likewise, the deficit-inducing policies of the present Bush administration defy convincing justification.

## The Reagan Debt Failure and the Balanced Budget Argument Examined

The loose fiscal policy of the Reagan years did not reflect a very rational approach to macroeconomic management. The near tripling of the federal debt over eight years did power the economy out of the 1981–82 recession, but unevenly and with lingering, troublesome side effects. Reagan's fiscal policies lacked a clear focus and were uncoordinated with monetary policy. As the federal budget was hemorrhaging from supply-side tax cuts, the administration encouraged a tight monetary policy to keep down the expected inflationary pressures. The effect was a bit like driving a car by depressing the accelerator and the brake at the same time. The car might move with some degree of control, but the equipment is being worn out. Suddenly it became apparent that as the recession lifted and prices held steady, a new problem had arisen. The higher interest rates resulting from the tight money policy had created a very strong dollar (that is, the high return on U.S. dollars put the dollar in great demand relative to other world currencies). As other currency values fell relative to the dollar, dollars bought more foreign goods, and domestically produced goods, denominated in dollars, cost more when sold overseas and paid for in cheaper foreign currencies. (We shall examine this problem in more detail in Issue 14.)

Conservatives maintain that the high-interest-rate policy was the direct result of deficits and deficit-inspired inflation. That is true only insofar as high interest rates were the ill-chosen Conservative reaction to the nonexistent problem of deficit-induced inflation. Conservatives had themselves to blame for a strong dollar and the resulting damage it caused to the economy. Ironically, under Conservative mismanagement, the nation succeeded in acquiring two very large deficits—the exploding federal debt and an international trade deficit. Paradoxically, the latter deficit served to negate many of the potentially positive effects of the former. The gains of an expansionary fiscal policy (even if it was a fiscal policy Conservatives did not want or understand) were offset by demand leakages resulting from a flood of foreign goods into American markets.

Whether the Conservative deficits were well planned or not is, of course, not the critical question. Nor is it really the first question we should ask. The question that reveals the truly important differences between Liberal and Conservative approaches to deficits is: Why would

Conservatives, who advocate budget balance, ever become associated with the greatest debt explosion in American history?

To unravel the question we need only remember the sources of the expanding deficit, the sequence of events that produced it, and the ultimate objectives of Conservative macroeconomic policy. The source of the Reagan deficit is no mystery. It resulted from two developments that were a critical part of the Conservative program and, when put in place, were bound to create a highly irrational fiscal strategy. As noted earlier, structural deficits could result from well-conceived programs or from wrong-headedness. In the case of the Reagan program, the wrong-headedness is abundantly clear.

The first part of the Reagan fiscal policy produced the personal and business tax cuts of 1981–83 and a gaping hemorrhage on the revenue side of the budget. The second part of the strategy was the incredible expansion of federal outlays resulting from a 50 percent or greater annual increase in military spending. Although social spending and entitlement programs (for example, Social Security) are usually singled out as the cause of growing debts, the charge obscures the fact that these programs, under the heaviest budget-cutting pressures, had shrunk as a share of the federal budget.

But was the deficit-expanding effect of cutting taxes and rising spending not understood? The answer is yes. It appears that the deficits were acquired by design. Only by making deficits and the size of the debt obnoxious would it be possible eventually to cap deficit spending with a balanced budget amendment. The sequence of events leading to $3 trillion of red ink should be understood. First, the tax cuts were obtained. Second, in the name of defense, military spending was increased. Third, growing deficits were accomplished. By giving people something good first—a tax cut and an improved defense posture—it became obvious that the only way the good things could be kept and not have the bad effects of deficits was to cut deeply into government social programs.

Some will say this is ascribing too much perversity and manipulation to Conservative politicians and economists. But it is the only explanation that makes sense if ultimate policy goals are to both shrink the size of government and neutralize fiscal policy by requiring a balanced budget. In other words, the Reagan red ink was not accidental or inherited but purposely created to frighten the nation into accepting a smaller, neutralized role for government in the economy.

The administration of President George W. Bush repeated this strategy in 2001. The comfortable position of budget surpluses made it relatively easy to gather popular and political support for a titanic $1.5 trillion tax reduction under the guise of letting people keep more of their own money, tax relief for marriage and children, and elimination of the estate tax. The passage of additional tax legislation in 2002–3 cut the tax rate on capital gains and dividends as well as granting businesses a significant increase in depreciation expense for equipment purchases.

The record deficit of 2003 vindicated the Liberal concern that President Bush's tax cuts have caused a return to mounting deficits. The events of September 11, 2001, only heightened such concerns: Necessary increases in government spending to cope with the aftermath of the terrorist attacks have only accelerated the transition toward deficits. Despite this fact, opinion polls in the past have indicated strong public support for a balanced-budget amendment. Immersion back into the sea of red ink, no matter how well justified, might prompt serious consideration of the amendment's adoption as the only way to tame the fiscal excesses of government. Yet, the expectation of a lengthy and protracted "War on Terrorism" as well as the massive cost of occupying and reconstructing Iraq suggests that the Bush administration must continue to use deficit financing to pay for tax cuts and foreign policies.

Fiscal mismanagement has once again set the stage for the neutralization of fiscal policy and renewed calls for a balanced-budget mandate. A constitutional law to balance the budget would require government to pursue policies that would worsen the business cycle. Taxes would rise and government spending would fall precisely when demand increases would be needed to offset a slump; and it is possible that an economic expansion could become an inflationary episode as increased tax collections are used to finance greater-than-needed public expenditures. For most Liberals, a legally required balanced budget is a leap back in time to an earlier era of failed economic thinking.

## THE RADICAL ARGUMENT

As we discussed in the previous two issues, the current stage of capitalist crisis may be distinguished from previous crises by the central role government has come to play in the economy. The other side of the past six decades' efforts to use government both as an agent to make up chronic deficiencies in the demand for goods and to lower business production costs has been the steady increase of government deficits. The current deficit crisis and the problems it imposes serve as a measure of the failure of the belief that the normal stagnation tendencies of capitalism can be corrected by government actions.

## Reaching the Outer Limits of Policy Management

Keynesians, as we have seen, perceived that the capitalist system could continue to obtain profits only as long as the demand for goods was sustained at high levels. Doubters simply disappeared as the levels of demand were pumped up first by World War II deficit spending and later by the deficits of the 1960s. Rather than competing with the private sector, as classical and neoclassical theory held, government spending (by all levels of government) reduced the pressures of chronic unemployment and excess capacity. It absorbed output and made the private realization of surplus value possible. As Table 10.2 shows, both the absolute magnitude of this spending and government outlays as a share of GDP have continued to grow. Amounting to a mere 7.4 percent of national output in 1903, government spending is now nearly one-third of the GDP. As we saw in the previous two issues, the expansion of government spending did slow the system's deterioration into crisis for a while, and although it seemed to work, no one talked much about government deficits. But by the late 1970s, deficits were seen as a source of trouble.

Of course, the trouble is that government spending in general and deficits in particular increase demand but at the same time raise costs to businesses, squeezing their profits. As we saw in the last two issues, the expansionary fiscal policy of the 1960s triggered upward pressures on the prices of resources and on wages. The present Conservative effort (and the efforts of some Liberals) to focus on these bad effects of activist fiscal policy and its resulting deficits merely reflects a redirection of American policy thinking away from the "demand solution" toward searches for a "cost solution" for sustaining profits. It does not represent a theoretical breakthrough for capitalism.

During the past two decades, neither demand-oriented policies of the Keynesian era nor supply-side solutions have benefited the vast majority of working Americans. If anything, the supply-side approach is simply a bold and naked effort to pick up the pieces of the demand-side failure. Indeed, the bulk of government spending largely benefits the upper classes in the form of lucrative contracts and subsidies. Meanwhile, the share of federal income taxes paid by corporations is at an all-

Table 10.2

**Government in the Economy**

| Year | GDP* (billions of dollars) | All government spending (billions of dollars) | Government spending as a percentage of GDP |
|---|---|---|---|
| 1903 | 23.0 | 1.7 | 7.4 |
| 1913 | 40.0 | 3.1 | 7.8 |
| 1929 | 103.4 | 8.0 | 7.7 |
| 1940 | 101.4 | 15.0 | 14.8 |
| 1950 | 293.8 | 59.3 | 20.2 |
| 1960 | 526.4 | 122.9 | 23.3 |
| 1970 | 1,038.5 | 294.8 | 28.4 |
| 1980 | 2,789.5 | 842.8 | 30.2 |
| 1990 | 5,803.1 | 1,872.6 | 32.3 |
| 2000 | 9,817.0 | 2,886.5 | 29.4 |
| 2002 | 10,480.8 | 3,224.0 | 30.8 |

*Source:* Bureau of Economic Analysis.
Note: GDP = gross domestic product.
*Figures prior to 1939 are gross national product (GNP).

time low. Accordingly, it is the American working class whose tax burden continually rises in order to pay off the wealthy owners of government bonds. Stagnant family incomes have necessitated an increase in personal debt just to maintain living standards. Since fiscal expansionism is no longer a meaningful political option for realizing surplus value, the accumulation of private debt by the working class has become critical for the continued viability of the system.

The supply-side actions to cut social spending and to end heavy taxation of the rich and the giant corporations are nothing more than efforts to maintain corporate profits by reducing the well-being of practically everyone but the very wealthy. The supply-sider wants not only to reduce taxes and social spending but also to roll back wages, permit monopoly power, and end consumer, job, and environmental protection. All such programs, it is argued, interfere with businesses' ability to invest, expand, and make profits. Of course, the supply-siders are right: Business does need greater freedom (read: ability to exploit) if it is to survive the growing profit squeeze. But if business survives this way, many people will not.

Yet there remains an irony in the supply-side emphasis on the cost effects of maintaining high levels of aggregate demand. Like a junkie hooked on drugs, giving up government deficits for good is difficult, probably impossible, regardless of the degree of human discomfort we are willing to impose on the general population. The fact is that enormous amounts of government spending are not demand-based at all but are directed toward the cost side. Spending has grown in a number of ways that are clearly aimed at lowering business operating costs and expanding profits. Since 2000, defense spending increased from about one-fifth to about one-quarter of all federal outlays. As the cost-overrun scandals by Haliburton and Brown and Root clearly show, defense expenditures are nothing less than a huge subsidy to very large American corporations. With America now deeply immersed in a protracted war on terrorism, the defense budget will continue to take an ever greater share of national income. Indeed, the stock prices of the large military contractors soared during one of the worst weeks for the stock market following the September 11 attacks. Meanwhile, building highways, subsidizing education, and even taking up most of the costs of maintaining adequate retirement and health programs for the elderly, which firms might have to pay for if Social Security did not, all have the effect of lowering business costs. Thus even Conservatives committed to balanced budgets have little real-world success in lowering government expenditures and balancing budgets. To make the irony a bit clearer: Like a junkie, the economy needs fiscal fixes to get high, but it also needs them just to stay even.

### The Misplaced Focus on Federal Deficits

The attention directed by both Liberals and Conservatives to the size and growth of the federal debt, predictable as it may be, obscures the real problems of the system, of which the debt, like the growth of government in general, is only a symptom.

By looking only at the federal deficit, we are deflected from looking at other types of borrowing. The result is a misleading impression because the federal debt amounts to only a small part of total borrowing in the United States, which includes consumer debt, mortgage debt, corporate debt, and state and local government debt. In fact, by 2000, federal debt, even with its explosion in the 1980s, amounted to only about 19 percent of all outstanding domestic debt. Since borrowing by consumers, businesses, and other government units has precisely the same result as federal borrowing in powering demand, the emphasis on the federal share of debt is especially myopic. More to the point, between 1960 and 1980, the period most frequently cited by Conservatives as that in which federal debt expansion first created and then fueled a destructive inflationary spiral, the federal debt grew more slowly than any other component of the nation's total debt. While Conservatives are essentially correct in arguing that borrowing means too many dollars chasing too few goods and thus, sooner or later, creates inflationary pressures, they focus on only one small slice of the debt pie. Even with the federal budget in balance, the debt-driven growth of demand has not been halted.

The Conservative view that federal deficits must be brought under control (a position also supported by many Liberals—though usually for quite different reasons) focuses only on the "too many dollars" aspect of the problem. These theorists do not understand that doing the reverse of what seems to cause inflation or raise interest rates will not necessarily result in relatively falling prices and interest rates. The fact is that tightening up on debts (federal as well as other kinds) will reduce the number of dollars chasing goods. However, as we saw in the late 1970s and early 1980s, it does not necessarily reduce price pressures. True, rising demand may bid up prices initially, but prices may stay up as a result of businesses continuing old and inefficient (high cost per unit of production) operations. After all, reducing demand by lowering federal deficits will not necessarily signal to business an impending improvement in general economic conditions. It will not induce them to modernize their production operations and lower their costs by taking on additional investments. There would be little point in adding plant and equipment that might not be used precisely because demand was being restricted. Only by bringing the economy virtually to its knees, through a deep recession that created enormous excess capacity, was the strong upward pressure on prices halted in the early 1980s. When few dollars are chasing whatever goods are available, it is elemental that prices must and do come down.

Government, with its persistent expansion of debt, must be seen for what it really is—simply one aspect of the fundamental contradiction that challenges a capitalist, production-for-profit economy. The recurring crisis of production outstripping consumption has not ceased in our time. This tendency has merely taken new forms, with the contradiction manifesting itself in the battle over government budgets and fiscal and monetary policy. Indeed, the modern capitalist state is a proxy for capi-

Table 10.3

**Outstanding Domestic American Debt, 1980–2000** (in billions of dollars)

| Year | Consumer debt | Mortgage debt | Corporate debt | State and local government debt | Federal debt | Total debt | GDP |
|------|------|------|------|------|------|------|------|
| 1980 | 358.0 | 932.0 | 909.1 | 344.4 | 735.0 | 3,957.9 | 2,789.5 |
| 1985 | 610.6 | 1,449.3 | 1,615.5 | 677.9 | 1,589.9 | 7,132.3 | 4,220.3 |
| 1990 | 824.4 | 2,504.1 | 2,533.1 | 992.3 | 2,498.1 | 10,849.6 | 5,803.1 |
| 1995 | 1,168.0 | 3,344.3 | 2,909.6 | 1,045.0 | 3,636.7 | 13,673.8 | 7,397.7 |
| 2000 | 1,719.0 | 4,837.4 | 4,538.8 | 1,192.3 | 3,385.1 | 18,098.8 | 9,817.0 |
| Change (in percent) | | | | | | | |
| 1980–1990 | 130 | 169 | 179 | 188 | 240 | 174 | 108 |
| 1980–2000 | 380 | 419 | 399 | 246 | 361 | 357 | 252 |

*Source:* Federal Reserve Board, "Flow of Funds," Table D.3, May 2004; *Economic Report of the President* (Washington, DC: Government Printing Office, 2004).
*Note:* GDP = gross domestic product.

talism itself. The state budget is the battleground among contending groups in the capitalist economy.

Yet it is a battleground on which victory is unobtainable. We have learned over the past seven decades that when overproduction appears (or demand lags), as it periodically does, we may offset it by increasing demand (through government and private borrowing). Indeed, a measure of our reliance upon debt to "float" the economy is illustrated in Table 10.3: Nearly every category of debt, public and private, has grown faster than national output (GDP) since 1980. We have also learned that increasing demand raises costs to firms by stimulating wage and resource price increases. The so-called cure for the resulting inflation is a full-blown economic slump that will force wages and costs down, and this slump would very likely be deeper and more protracted than the downturn that would have occurred if demand had not been stimulated in the first place.

In conclusion, then, Radicals are not confused about what federal deficits are or what they can and cannot do. First of all, deficits are not the problem. Second, and herein resides an important irony, neither deficits nor budget balancing offers any long-run solution to the chronic problems of a production-for-profit economic system.

# Unemployment

## Is Joblessness an Overrated Problem?

Once I built a railroad, made it run
Made it race against time
Once I built a railroad, now it's done
Brother, can you spare a dime?
> —*Popular song by Jay Gorney, 1932*

Capitalism forms an industrial reserve army that belongs to capital quite as absolute as if the latter had bred it at its own cost. Independently of the limits of the actual increase of population, it . . . creates a mass of human material always ready for exploitation.
> —*Karl Marx, 1867*

Outsourcing is just a new way of doing international trade. More things are tradable than were tradable in the past and that's a good thing.
> —*N. Gregory Mankiw, Chair, President's Council of Economic Advisors, 2004*

They've delivered a double blow to America's workers, 3 million jobs destroyed on their watch, and now they want to export more of our jobs overseas. What in the world are they thinking?
> —*Senator John Kerry, Presidential Candidate, 2004*

### The Problem

In the United States, episodes of high unemployment are not unlike a serious flu epidemic. When the flu is raging out of control, whether one is actually suffering from the disease or merely watching others suffer, the debilitating symptoms are a frightening thing to ponder. But when the epidemic recedes, so too does most popular recollection of the anxiety and genuine pain it earlier caused. Most citizens' reaction to an epidemic of joblessness is very much the same. When it is happening, the worst economic scenarios all seem possible to a fearful and worried public; when it has fallen to merely "normal" or "below normal" levels, it is hard for those not still suffering from the malady to recall the earlier uncertainties. By mid-2004, with unemployment rates holding stubbornly in the range of 5.5 percent or more, the U.S. economy had shown few convincing signs that low unemployment rates would be visited upon the U.S. labor force in the near future.

In point of fact, though, American attitudes toward unemployment have undergone a long process of evolution. Before the Great Depression of the 1930s, joblessness was generally understood as a personal problem and not a matter of public policy concern. Given the cyclical nature of general economic conditions, employment prospects were understood to be governed by the ordinary ebb and flow of the economy. Losing one's job from time to time, while certainly a matter of bad luck and often an event individuals could rightfully get angry about, was part of the normal course of economic life for great numbers of Americans.

Between the 1930s and the late 1960s, this outlook changed considerably. In the emerging "New Economics" of John Maynard Keynes, it was no longer necessary to accept the capriciousness of the business cycle with passivity. Public policy could be constructed to roll back hard times and regenerate employment. Accordingly, the notion that, through a variety of fiscal policy actions, government could maintain full employment became a matter of widely accepted economic belief. From the passage of the Employment Act of 1946 down to the passage of the Humphrey-Hawkins Full Employment and Balanced Growth Act of 1978, full employment, officially at least, was the goal of macroeconomic policy making.

However, even before the Humphrey-Hawkins Act was passed, it was apparent that the nature of American unemployment was changing. It was no longer only a cyclical event stemming from slowdowns in the general level of economic activity. Even during good times, by the 1970s unemployment rates stayed above the generally accepted 4 percent level then associated with "full employment." As Figure 11.1 indicates, between 1974 and 1991, unemployment fell below 6 percent only four times and never below 5.2 percent. What was becoming evident was that joblessness for great numbers of Americans was not a function of cyclical economic conditions at all.

Increasingly, it was evident that structural shifts in the American economy—how, where, and what goods were actually being produced and distributed—were permanently eliminating many jobs, while regional economic shifts, new skill and educational requirements, and perhaps even certain patterns of social outlook (racism, for instance) were making many would-be workers unemployable.

Public policy efforts to reduce unemployment were reoriented to improve the education, mobility, and flexibility of older workers as well as new workforce entrants and seemed to take on a special urgency. However, the new initiatives had their detractors. Some felt that the government efforts were too little too late. Others saw them as an enormous and unnecessary bureaucratic boondoggle and that a better cure in the end was simply to be patient as labor markets and individuals came to respond to the new employment realities. Some, especially those looking at the 4 percent unemployment rate attained in December 2000, argued that "full employment" actually had been obtained and worried aloud that, given the demographics of the American economy (with great numbers of baby boomers facing imminent retirement), labor shortages, not unemployment, were the real problem.

In fact, the U.S. economy tilted into recession in March of 2001 and suffered additional setbacks from the terrorist attacks of September 11, 2001. Though the recession was brief with the bottom of the downturn reached by November 2001, resumption of economic growth was reminiscent of the aftermath of the last recession of 1990–91: *a jobless recovery.* Structural changes in labor markets, largely associated with the long-running transformation of the manufacturing sector, appeared as accelerating outsourcing of jobs to foreign nations. To many Americans, diminished job opportunities and unemployment became a matter to be taken much more seriously than just a few years before.

## Synopsis

Conservatives see the present unemployment problem as largely the result of government efforts to manage labor markets. They therefore advocate

Figure 11.1   **Employment and Joblessness in the United States, 1950–2003**

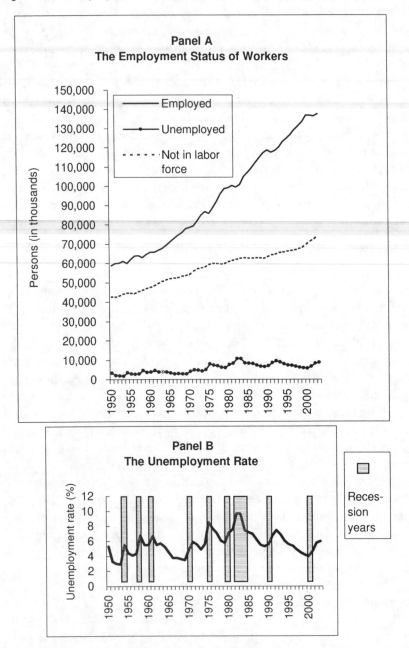

*Source:* Data from the Bureau of Labor Statistics.

minimum government involvement as the only long-run solution to job-lessness. Liberal arguments hold that much of our current unemployment is beyond the reach of usual stabilization policy tools. Thus new and en-larged job programs as well as curtailing the transfer of jobs to other coun-tries is necessary to compensate for the structural limitations of the economy that have created chronic unemployment. For Radicals, unemployment is characteristic of capitalism, a natural outgrowth of the system's tendency to produce surplus labor.

## Anticipating the Arguments

- How, according to Conservatives, have government actions increased unemployment?
- What do Liberals mean by structural unemployment, and how would they cure it?
- Why do Radicals believe that high levels of unemployment are char-acteristic of a capitalist system?

## THE CONSERVATIVE ARGUMENT

From the Conservative point of view, unemployment is logically unnec-essary. In an economy left to its own devices, involuntary unemploy-ment can result only from short-run market readjustments. Over the long term, as prices, wages, and output adjust, there is work for all at wages commensurate with their productive contributions. Individuals who value their labor higher than the market does or higher than its actual contri-bution to output, or who simply prefer leisure to work, may be jobless; however, their unemployment is voluntary and not a fundamental prob-lem demanding policy makers' attention. At least, this would be the situ-ation if labor markets were free of the interventions or stickiness and inefficiencies that abound in a world of Liberal social engineering, pow-erful labor unions, big government, and popular expectations that indi-viduals have the right to a certain level of wages irrespective of these individuals' actual contributions to production.

### A Rising Natural Rate of Unemployment

At all times, a natural rate of unemployment exists in a free market economy. By definition, this natural rate approximates the sum of frictional unemployment (voluntary joblessness as workers move from job to job) and structural unemployment (joblessness resulting from changes of skill-level demand and the willingness of workers to accept wage offers) in the economy at any particular time. It is the minimum unemployment level consistent with price stability. Any effort to lower the natural rate of joblessness would trigger inflationary wage and price pressures (because efforts to raise demand for workers will not create jobs for the frictionally or structurally unemployed but *will* bid up the wages of those presently employed). This concept of a natural rate of unemployment is associated with what economists call the *nonaccelerating inflation rate of unemployment* (NAIRU). NAIRU is defined as a rate of unemployment that is sustainable without generating acceleration in inflation.

Looked at from a slightly different perspective, the natural rate of unemployment—what some economists consider "full-employment unemployment"—is principally determined by structural conditions within the economy that affect the matching up of labor demand and labor supply. Of course, in an idealized economic world, in which wages and prices are perfectly flexible and workers are perfectly free to go wherever they desire in search of work, the natural rate would always tend to be near zero.

The natural rate of unemployment has been falling over the past ten years. The decline reflects the best operation of our economic system, while the periods when the natural rate rose were the product of a variety of measures originally intended to improve on the market economy's performance. The natural rate of unemployment rose because prices and wages were not flexible and because labor was not very mobile.

The lack of wage flexibility and labor mobility is the result of past Liberal efforts to intervene in the economy. However, presently concerned about rising "chronic" unemployment, they propose elaborate solutions that will guarantee greater unemployment and greater resource misallocation. To see the point, we need only examine a few of their past efforts.

### The Record of a Failed Employment Policy

To understand how labor markets have been made less mobile and less flexible and therefore characterized by a rising natural rate of unemployment, consider four areas of Liberal tinkering: support of unions, social legislation, antidiscrimination efforts, and actions to offset technological displacements.

Liberal support for labor unions in this century, while benefiting some workers, has cost many their jobs. Unions, by instinct and design, seek to restrict the number of jobs in order to force wages up for their members. The older craft unions specifically used this tactic to raise their members' wages. By having long periods of apprenticeship and limiting the number of apprentices, unions in the building trades, for instance, purposely reduced the supply of available labor. This maintained wages for carpenters, masons, and hod carriers, but it also kept large numbers of would-be workers out of the labor force. Large industrial unions also reduce employment. By imposing on management an industry wage that is higher than would otherwise prevail in a free labor market, the industry's total demand for labor is reduced. The union succeeds in keeping the wages of its members high, but unemployment—among both union and nonunion workers—is increased.

Legally mandated social legislation also depresses employment. Ironically, many of those programs aimed specifically at the poorest and least secure workers have worsened rather than improved their lot. For instance, Liberals invariably cite the passage of minimum-wage laws as one of their greatest triumphs; yet such laws have probably had the largest negative impact on employment of all of their social engineering endeavors. Setting minimum-wage rates above a market-determined wage has two immediate effects. First, more individuals enter the labor market, now willing to work at the higher wage, whereas before they opted for leisure. Second, the number of jobs available is reduced because employers cut back their hiring. Liberals have defended minimum-wage legislation as a boon to less-skilled workers; it has actually had the opposite effect. The least-skilled jobs, those with the lowest marginal contribution to a firm's earnings, must be the first eliminated in response to raising the minimum-wage floor. Thus part-time employment for teenagers and unskilled factory work for women and minorities has declined as the minimum wage advanced.

Two other popular pieces of social legislation—unemployment insurance and Social Security—illustrate various ways that well-intended efforts to benefit workers raise the natural rate of unemployment. With more generous unemployment benefits, the pain of joblessness is cushioned. However, the benefits also serve to subsidize, and therefore extend, the period of search for a new job. They also invite entry of some workers into the labor force purely to obtain the benefits. Social Security, meanwhile, works in a slightly different way to increase joblessness. With employers required to pay half of the contributions, Social Security amounts, from an employer's point of view, to a job tax and a hiring disincentive.

Discrimination may exist in the larger society, but competitive markets are the ultimate destroyers of such a practice. The reason is simple: Employers who discriminate, thereby excluding certain elements of the work force (minorities or women, for instance) from certain jobs, reduce their level of employment and, therefore, output compared to nondiscriminatory employers. This diminishes their profitability. The market takes no prisoners when irrational choices lead to noneconomic outcomes.

The fourth area to consider is Liberal tinkering to cushion job losses from technological progress. Periodic and quite natural shifts in the economy's structure produce short-run unemployment from time to time. Buggy makers do not become autoworkers overnight, and autoworkers cannot immediately be transformed into computer specialists. However, it is possible to make a temporarily bad employment situation permanently worse. Recent declining employment in the old, moribund basic industries—steel, automobiles, and farm machinery, for instance—has encouraged Liberals to call for special aid programs for the hard-hit industrial centers of the Northeast and Midwest and for direct aid to the old, failing industries. Such assistance may in fact lower unemployment for a time, just as aid to buggy makers would have softened the unemployment effects of Henry Ford's Model T production. But it also has the socially undesirable effect of halting economic change. By subsidizing antiquated, inefficient industries, we must tax the vital sectors in the economy. Detroit and Gary, Indiana, are kept afloat, but jobs are reduced in the high-tech centers of Texas, California, and Massachusetts.

Recently, Liberals have become fixated on losses in manufacturing employment caused by outsourcing. Some of these job losses are attributable to transferring production tasks to foreign locations and employing lower cost foreign workers. Other losses attributed to outsourcing are not losses at all; they merely reflect increased efficiencies obtained through business practices that rely more on contracted temporary workers. It is important not to confuse "doom and gloom" predictions about widespread job losses with the truth about manufacturing and service sector employment. Gains in output per worker in manufacturing have outpaced the economy as whole. This, combined with changing consumption patterns and businesses routinely seeking lower cost locations and production techniques, has indeed caused employment in textiles, apparel, primary metals industry, leather goods, and petroleum and coal products to contract. Yet, employment gains in retail and wholesale trade, business services, health services, and finance, insurance, and real estate have more than offset the losses—and generally at better levels of compensation than those offered in declining manufacturing industries.

Liberal proposals for special job programs, protection from foreign imports, and restrictions on outsourcing to deal with structural unemployment traceable to technological progress and other structural changes in the economy are both unnecessary and counterproductive. Despite more than four decades of federal expenditures for the education of young people, the retraining of older workers, and elaborate public service programs, as well as affirmative action programs to increase the employment of minorities and women, there is virtually no evidence that significant numbers of would-be workers have been helped. In fact, the tax bill for funding and operating these programs has probably had a negative impact on jobs because private-sector funds were diverted to these ineffective programs.

If Americans find the present natural rate of unemployment to be higher than they would like, we possess the means to lower it. Freeing up labor markets, reducing union power, eliminating costly and counterproductive social engineering programs, and letting the chips of technological change fall where they may would go a long way toward ending the present mismatch between labor demand and labor supply.

### The Unemployment Problem Is Overstated

The level of joblessness is overstated rather than understated. The overreaction to unemployment statistics has also directed attention away from recent positive employment developments. Even during periods of high unemployment in the recent past, the number of employed workers grew steadily. Since World War II, the market economy has exhibited less volatility and longer periods of expansion, thereby diminishing the severity of cyclical unemployment (Issue 8). In fact, since 1982, the American economy has experienced the longest, and second longest peacetime expansions on record. Likewise, unemployment resulting from structural changes has tended to be temporary, while the employment gains induced by such shifts in technology and patterns of production have surpassed the losses.

Finally, demographics have contributed to a lower natural unemployment rate. The Baby Boomers—who in sheer numbers contributed to a higher natural unemployment rate—are reaching retirement. The number of new entrants to replace these workers is comparatively small, and there are no signs that this trend will soon change. Already serious labor shortages are apparent in many regions of the country. These labor shortages will continue as the years pass. Indeed, a fair number of economists are arguing that policy makers and the public have the entire employment problem backward. The nation's long-term employment difficulties will be a matter of insufficient numbers of potential workers, not insufficient jobs. Lest this state of affairs be taken as a cause for rejoicing, we should remember that a smaller labor force, *ceteris paribus,* would also mean a smaller national output. Rather than worrying about how we can absorb the presently unemployed, we might be better served by figuring out how in the near future we intend to produce more with less labor.

## THE LIBERAL ARGUMENT

Liberals also know that a natural rate of unemployment exists. To be precise, there is some level of unemployment that corresponds with a nonaccelerating inflation rate of unemployment (NAIRU). If the economy pushes beyond this level of unemployment, the demand for labor produces wage-rate increases in excess of productivity gains, and the general price level begins to rise. While the concept of NAIRU makes considerable sense, we are left with much uncertainty about what might be the precise level of unemployment that conforms to price stability. For example, in 2000, NAIRU was (by then at least) much lower than the near 7 percent many economists agreed upon in the early 1990s. Prices rose at an annual rate of 3.4 percent in 2000 (in other words, this was an acceptable, nonaccelerating price increase), but the unemployment rate had fallen to 4 percent, a thirty-one-year low. By the 2000s, revised estimates of NAIRU were in the upper 5 percent range. Unemployment in 2003 spiked at 6 percent while consumer prices had ebbed to a mere 2.3 percent annual rate, worrying policy makers that unemployment was too high and prices were not rising fast enough. Clearly, gravitating to some "natural state" for unemployment and inflation rates is less elusive in theory than it is in practice. Natural rate theory has been a lousy source of guidance to policy makers for more than a decade.

On the issue of unemployment, Conservatives continue to advance the argument that "everything works well so long as it works well and when it doesn't, don't do anything about it." Having argued earlier (in Issue 8) that cyclical (lack-of-demand) unemployment is self-correcting and unworthy of economists' attention, Conservatives continue to repudiate the available empirical evidence by contending that structural unemployment is also self-correcting. Such slavish commitment to the principles and processes of laissez-faire markets was perhaps possible a century ago. Yet, optimistic theorizing about ridding the economy of the adverse effects of policies to deal with unemployment caused by cyclical downturns, structural dislocations, labor market discrimination, and outsourcing is difficult to reconcile with the real distress imposed by the experience of unemployment.

## The High Cost of Joblessness

In human terms, chronic unemployment erodes morale and self-esteem. Studies indicate that periods of prolonged unemployment destroy incentives and interest in work, even when the worker is later reemployed. Without employment, personal behavior patterns become erratic, leading to increased marital and family problems and greater child abuse. Unemployment also increases morbidity, mental illness, and crime. According to one study, a 1 percent increase in the unemployment rate will be associated with 37,000 deaths (including 20,000 heart attacks); 920 suicides; 650 homicides; 4,000 state mental hospital admissions; and 3,300 state prison admissions.* While it may be difficult (but not impossible) to put precise price tags on these human costs, we can measure the external or social costs of unemployment that result from (1) reduced tax collection, (2) rising unemployment insurance outlays, and (3) forgone production and sales. When all of these costs of permitting chronic unemployment are considered, the costs of special job programs to eliminate or reduce unemployment become insignificant.

## A Historical Overview of Structural Unemployment

To understand the importance of structural unemployment, we need to put it in historical perspective. Beginning in March 1991, the American

---

*Barry Bluestone, Bennett Harrison, and Lawrence Baker, *Corporate Flight: The Causes and Consequences of Economic Dislocation* (Washington, DC: Progressive Alliance, 1981), 20.

economy underwent an unprecedented 120-month expansion. Unfortunately, unemployment rates rose after the recession ended and remained high through 1995. A similar "jobless recovery" pattern has characterized the most recent recovery, which began in November 2001. Nevertheless, in both cases, unemployment was not the result of insufficient demand; rather, it was the result of subtle institutional changes in the American economy. The problems of unemployment require a new approach. Not only do we need policies to cure joblessness inflicted by recessions, but we must recognize that some unemployment is a chronic problem induced by a host of structural changes in the economy.

Since World War II, the American economy has enjoyed, with a few brief interruptions, phenomenal economic growth; however, the expansion has produced important technological changes and regional economic shifts that have contributed to unemployment. Rising globalization of industrial production aided by rapid growth in inexpensive information systems has given rise to the phenomenon of outsourcing jobs. The demand for older jobs and skills has declined as new goods and production techniques have revolutionized labor. At the same time, the geographic distribution of manufacturing has been altered. Meanwhile, the old employment bulwarks—steel, autos, and construction, for example—are undergoing a deep structural decline, both as employers and as contributors to the nation's output, with no prospects for reversal. The result has been to change the structure of labor markets.

Following are some examples of these structural shifts:

1. The continued decline in agricultural employment as farm production was increasingly mechanized.
2. The greater use of increasingly sophisticated technology in industrial production, thus reducing the relative demand for industrial labor in general and unskilled labor in particular.
3. The migration of many businesses and factories from the inner cities to suburban locations, and out of the country.
4. The greater concentration of economic activity in large metropolitan areas and the decline of employment in smaller cities.
5. The shift in the geographic location of industry to the West and South as new industries grew up in these areas and old plants left the industrial Northeast.
6. The sectoral shift in employment patterns as service industries and the government increased employment and the old

employers—in manufacturing, mining, and construction—declined. (In 1959, manufacturing, mining, and construction employed 36 percent of the workforce; by 2003, these industries employed less than 17 percent. Over the same period, service and government employment grew from 64 percent to over 83 percent of all employment.)

Across the nation, chronic structural unemployment was rooted in insufficient skills. Economic expansion or pumping up aggregate demand would not have much effect on an unemployed railroad worker in Altoona, Pennsylvania, an out-of-work miner in West Virginia, or an ex-steelworker in Gary, Indiana.

Changes in the composition of the labor force have added to the structural problems. Beginning in the 1960s, larger numbers of women began to look for work. Most of these new entrants possessed minimal skills and took, when they could get them, low-paying jobs in the service sector with little employment security. Many of the female job seekers were extremely immobile. Many were wives and mothers who had to seek work near their homes, which added a further restriction to their general lack of skills in obtaining work. Meanwhile, the entrance into the job market of the large number of people born in the post–World War II baby boom increased unemployment. As with women, many of the youthful job seekers did not meet the new employment demands. For urban, primarily black, youths, there were virtually no jobs at all. They had no desired skills and did not live near or have access to the few unskilled jobs available. As Figure 11.2 shows, the gap between blacks' and whites' employment opportunities has remained wide.

### Automation, Outsourcing, and the Demand for Labor

The adverse impacts of inexperience, immobility, race, and sex upon labor markets diminished by the 1990s. Nevertheless, since then, the twin structural forces of automation and outsourcing have significantly changed the demand for workers in both manufacturing and the broader service sectors. In manufacturing, the basic "problem" is that very strong productivity growth has allowed American firms to produce more and more goods with fewer and fewer workers. Since the fourth quarter of 2001, manufacturing productivity has averaged almost 6 percent per

274

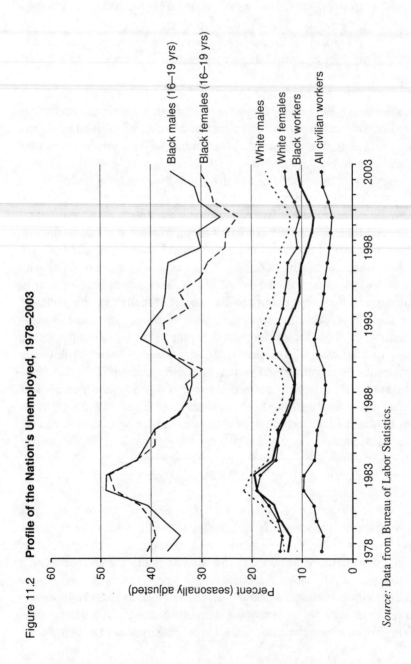

Figure 11.2    **Profile of the Nation's Unemployed, 1978–2003**

*Source:* Data from Bureau of Labor Statistics.

quarter (nearly twice the 1973–2000 average of 2.9 percent) while the high-wage jobs in manufacturing have steadily declined since 1998. The service sector has undergone similar transformations because of computerization, automation, and general technological change.

Since the end of the 2001 recession, much has been made of the growing threat to workers from "outsourcing," that is, the threat of job displacement emerging not from technology, but from the movement of jobs overseas. Global enterprises had long sought low-cost manufacturing havens in foreign nations. Job losses in the garment industry, television and electronic manufacturing, automobile assembly, motorcycles, household appliances, steel production, and much of the goods-producing sector of the economy set in gradually over decades. The pace of change in information technology blindsided many workers who had recently acquired what appeared to be highly valued skills in computing and management information systems during the technology boom from about 1993–2000.

Many back-office database management tasks and telemarketing projects among other things proved ripe for not just automation, but outsourcing to cheaper temporary workers, domestically and in other countries where the supply of workers possessing information systems skills is high and wages are low. Easy transmission of digitally encoded material has also made possible the outsourcing of medical diagnostics to freelance physicians around the world to read x-rays, examine slides of tissue samples, and offer consultative opinions. Even highly skilled, specialized service jobs can now be outsourced. The actual amount of employment that has migrated overseas is thus far a small fraction of the nation's 130 million jobs. But this ominous trend demands government policies that can provide for stable employment and income in the face of structural adjustments that continue to undermine good employment opportunities and confer joblessness on American workers.

## A Liberal Program

As we have noted, structural unemployment and joblessness resulting from changes in the composition of the work force are not responsive to efforts to pump up aggregate demand. Instead, specific job-creating programs and protection for American workers are necessary to provide full employment. However, unlike the make-work measures of the past (such as the Works Progress Administration in the 1930s), these programs should not be mere Band-Aids. Since lack of skills is the primary cause of chronic unemployment, federal programs should be constructed to improve the employability of would-be workers.

Getting the jobless back to work through retraining and job-incentive programs produces real social savings. Initial program costs are quickly offset by the taxes the newly employed pay and by the reduction of social outlays directly related to their unemployed condition (that is, welfare and unemployment compensation). As demographic evidence indicates, the workers are needed to offset a serious shortage of labor in the not-too-distant future. Accordingly, it becomes all the more important to provide the training and discipline required for the chronically unemployed to become employable.

The Workforce Investment Act of 1998 represents the most recent variation of training and job-incentive programs. It is focused upon assistance to disadvantaged individuals, dislocated workers, and youth. The act ties grants for work investment programs to the establishment of "one-stop delivery systems" in local areas. These one-stop career centers consolidate information and core services of numerous governmental programs to provide counseling, job search assistance, training, performance appraisals of training programs, and other resources. Unfortunately, funding and operations are highly dependent upon state and local governments, a pattern reminiscent of the 1996 welfare reform (see Issue 6). Consequently, the federal government is devolving a big part of its responsibility for implementation of employment policy onto the state and local levels. Liberals are concerned that this is yet another wrinkle in the Conservative strategy to shrink central government while gradually abdicating its obligation to full employment. Renewal of the Workforce Investment Act in the form of the Workforce Reinvestment and Adult Education Act of 2003 languished in a Senate committee into mid-2004. The 2003 bill also contained the Adult Basic Education Skills Act to continue state-sponsored adult education programs, and a reauthorization of the Rehabilitation Act of 1973 to help improve the employment prospects for disabled individuals.

Several job programs offer real opportunities for the so-called unemployables to join the labor force: youth programs, public service jobs, and wage subsidies.

### Youth Programs

With unemployment among teenagers the highest of all groups (17.1 percent among white teenage males and 36 percent among African American or black teenage males,* compared to an overall 6 percent rate in 2003), youth unemployment demands special attention. The problem has grown worse since 2000. Teenagers account for about 14 percent of all the unemployed. Most teenage unemployment, especially among African Americans, is found in urban areas. Also, among the teenage unemployed there is a high educational dropout rate. Thus, employment programs for this group should be urban in focus and organized to encourage completion of public education. While learning useful skills, many youths will learn the workplace discipline that is necessary for retaining employment. A long-run improvement of youth unemployment problems is fairly certain as the past decade's declining birth rate makes itself felt in labor markets. The Department of Labor's Employment and Training Administration is charged with operating rather modest job programs to combat youth unemployment. Much of the effort is oriented at managing grants distributed to states to deal with improving employment prospects for youth. How well this has worked is unclear in the performance appraisals issued by the government. Combined with quite limited funding, one can conclude that commitment to addressing this problem is low.

### Public Service Jobs

Beginning in 1973, the Comprehensive Employment and Training Act (CETA) instituted federal funding for local government hiring of public workers for limited employment periods. Rather than creating an overloaded federal bureaucracy, this approach allowed local communities to set and meet their own public service needs. Workers, meanwhile, obtained important on-the-job experience before their CETA employment ended in 1982.

By contrast, the Workforce Investment Act reoriented public policy in the direction of making the prospective trainee an informed "consumer" of training services with the hope of maximizing a successful transition to a good job. While laudable, this would be more effective if combined with on-the-job experience that could be supplied through greater availability of public service jobs. Unfortunately, the concept of publicly provided employment opportunities has fallen into disfavor. Customer service to the unemployed seems to have become the main

---

*Data represent changes in classification from "black and other" to "black or African American," reflecting changes in the Bureau of Labor Statistics data series beginning 2003.

priority of government agencies whose mission weighs more heavily on supplying information, cutting costs, and constructing performance indicators. A pleasant experience with the agency seems to have greater importance than actually reducing the unemployment rate.

### Wage Subsidies

A third approach to chronic unemployment is to subsidize private sector employment of the unskilled. The bonus paid to private corporations is intended to offset the expected lower productivity of workers in this program. Somewhat paradoxically, Columbia University economist Edmund Phelps, credited with the development of natural rate theory, endorsed wage subsidies in his 1997 book *Rewarding Work.** The argument is that economical social engineering is obtained by "mainstreaming" the unemployed into the world of work through wage subsidies. In turn, the social costs of crime, drug abuse, welfare, medical care, and other burdens associated with unemployment are reduced by more than the expense of the subsidies.

## THE RADICAL ARGUMENT

Both Conservatives and Liberals misunderstand the role of unemployment in a capitalist society. To the Conservative advocating a free market economy, there would be virtually no unemployment if the market were to work freely, that is, unimpeded by government action, labor unions, and so on. To the Liberal, unemployment is at least a periodic, and perhaps chronic, condition of capitalist economies, but it can be controlled by "enlightened" public policy. Neither position sees unemployment as central to capitalist organization, as necessary to the actual functioning of the system. The simple fact is that capitalism, regulated or unregulated, cannot help but create unemployment.

### Unemployment: Capitalism as Usual

As capitalists accumulate and successfully translate past labor into what they see as profit-producing capital and investment, the need for an ab-

---

Edmund S. Phelps, *Rewarding Work: How to Restore Participation and Self-Support to Free Enterprise* (Cambridge, MA: Harvard University Press, 1997).

solute or growing volume of labor diminishes. This must be true by simple definition. The object of capital development is to increase production without increased (or with decreased) costs. Labor-saving machinery is cost-saving machinery only because labor is paid less per unit of output. More output can be obtained by employing more capital and less labor. Thus increased capitalization and technological growth, all things being equal, must produce growing surplus labor. This is the historical tendency of capitalism that is even confirmed in the official productivity and unemployment statistics over the past couple of years.

The growth of unemployment tends to be in recessionary clusters rather than in a steady, unbroken upward movement; however, the official unemployment rate has been trending upward over a long period (only recently and mildly reversed during the Clinton-era boom). Since the mid-1950s we have seen the official unemployment rate (itself a statistical understatement of the problem) move relentlessly higher even in comparatively good years. In other words, the percentage of the labor force in what Marx called "the reserve army of the unemployed" is constantly expanding. No doubt this unemployment would have been even higher in the past had government not pursued the expansionary policies. In fact, the situation has been getting progressively worse despite elaborate governmental efforts to hold down unemployment. Neither the free market nor Keynesian tinkering halts this tendency.

The failure of expansionary fiscal policy to deal with the problem of chronic unemployment is particularly evident if we go back to the tax cut of 1964. This was perhaps the first self-consciously Keynesian effort to use fiscal policy to reduce unemployment (then at 5 or 6 percent). The $11 billion Kennedy-Johnson tax reduction did spur business investment and increase national output. Between 1964 and 1966, investment increased by more than 22 percent—more than twice the rate of the previous two years. The gross domestic product (GDP) grew by 13 percent during the same period, compared to a growth rate of less than 10 percent in the earlier period. However, reported unemployment fell by only 900,000 between 1964 and 1966, despite the fact that government alone increased its payroll by 1.7 million persons. Thus any real reduction in unemployment came not from tax cutting à la Keynes but from good old government hiring.

An additional case against the supposed effectiveness of "full-employment" fiscal policy is the hyperexpansion of government spending that took place during the Vietnam War. Although government policy during the war may now be represented by Liberals as unintended and undesired (in other words, determined on political rather than economic grounds), it did not result in the employment growth that modern Keynesians associate with expansionary fiscal policy. Between 1966 and 1969, during the height of war appropriations, unemployment fell by less than 100,000. Meanwhile, direct government employment added an additional 1.6 million workers to public payrolls. Direct government hiring, not private sector job growth, brought unemployment rates down during the middle and late 1960s.

The point of these examples should not be misunderstood. Fiscal expansionism does create demand for workers. After the 1964 tax cut, during the Vietnam War boom, and after the 1981 Reagan tax cut, unemployment rates did fall a bit. But in each case, normal unemployment (what Conservatives euphemistically call the natural rate of unemployment) leveled off at a higher level: 3.5 percent in the mid-1960s, 5 percent in the early 1970s, and 7 percent or more in the mid-1980s. What was happening was that "full employment" was being achieved at successively higher levels of normal unemployment, with the pressures of an expanding economy having no useful effect on many workers who were falling out of the employable labor force altogether. Meanwhile, as we shall see below, the "improving" unemployment rates of the 1990s are a massive deception.

### Capitalism Benefits from Unemployment

Political rhetoric to the contrary, the fact is that capitalism benefits from surplus labor—at least to a certain degree. Surplus labor usually forces wages downward or at least slows upward pressures. Workers compete with one another, and employers have a pleasant buyer's market. Even the prospects of important union wage gains are diminished by the competitive threat of the swelling ranks of unemployed. Recently, corporations have shamelessly used the specter of growing unemployment to force the labor union elite of the working class to sign new contracts with "givebacks." Wage gains and fringe benefits struggled for in the past were wiped out as rising unemployment weakened the unions' bargaining position. The old-line management bargaining tactic of "take it or leave it" was once again successful.

The declining rates of reported unemployment in the 1990s, at first glance, seem to suggest that the long upward trend in unemployment has been arrested. This is not so. First of all, the rising levels of employment mask the fact that a very large number of relatively high-paying jobs were lost in the 1970s and 1980s. Automation, downsizing, and the overseas flight of firms and jobs cut deeply into premium employment opportunities. The fact that average real wages in the United States are still below their 1974 levels illustrates the effect of such employment losses. Indeed, if a greater number of Americans are actually working (and we will address this data manipulation question shortly), a very large proportion of them are working at lower wages, and not uncommonly at more than one job. Ironically, on the same day in early 1998 that the Bureau of Labor Statistics reported a low 4.6 percent unemployment rate, the nation's largest charitable hunger relief agency released a study showing it had distributed food to 21 million needy individuals in 1997 and that 39 percent of these recipients were employed—about half of them working at full-time jobs.

Celebration of a lowering unemployment rate is a silly undertaking if reductions in joblessness have been accomplished through "spreading the work around" by dint of driving wages down and using part-time employment. Having a job one cannot survive on is cold comfort indeed.

### Understating the Problem

Radicals are always amused by conventional economists' use of data in support of their ideological outlook. Perhaps no important set of statistics is more misleading than the official data that are released on American employment and unemployment. After figuring out how the employed and the unemployed are counted, one can see that official statistics always understate the size of the unemployment problem, whatever the general conditions of the economy.

Bad as it appears to be, our unemployment problem is really much worse than we realize because we understate the number of unemployed in at least three ways. First, the average annual rate does not show the number of people affected by some type of annual unemployment. For instance, in 2001 at least 16 million Americans experienced some involuntary unemployment during the year. Looked at this way, unemployment touched at least one in every ten American workers during the year. Even if an unemployed worker suffered only a week or two of lost labor, the effect on savings, retirement plans, and the educational hopes of the worker's children could be devastating. Second, our statistics tend to overestimate the actual number employed. In 2003, the "employed" included 24 million Americans who worked only part time. Such calculations expand the total employed category but do not show how slight their employment is. Third, official statistics do not indicate those who are socially underemployed from the standpoint of earnings. At least 6 million full-time workers earn wages below the official poverty income level. Fourth, the "unemployed" category does not include people who want a job, but have given up looking or made few attempts to find a job. No precise measures are available, but it is estimated that if this group were added to our known unemployment, actual unemployment in 2003 probably stood at about 7 percent rather than the reported 6 percent.

Deeper structural problems continue to plague the economy. Since the end of the last recession in November 2001, the official unemployment rate has fallen from about 6.3 percent to 5.5 percent. Unfortunately, the labor market remains in a severe slump as a result of an unprecedented two and half years of job losses despite positive GDP growth. Additionally, the lack of job growth combined with an expanding working-age population has created an employment deficit of about 7 million jobs.

It is important to understand not only the real size but also the composition of unemployment in the United States. Clearly, job possibilities are poorer if one is black, female, or young. This discrimination in employment is not surprising. It reflects the general contraction of labor markets and the resulting exclusion of newcomers. On one hand, such discrimination has served the system well, because many of the unemployed are not visible but hidden away in the ghetto or home. On the other hand, obvious discrimination of this kind creates considerable political development among the affected groups, who quite consciously and correctly see themselves as an exploited class. Liberals, aware of this tendency, have proposed make-work and on-the-job training programs aimed at quashing the discontent of the hard-core unemployed. But such programs have no long-run effect on improving employment. Undaunted by failure, still weirder twists in employment policy such as requiring the Employment Training Administration to devise ways to spend a portion of its budget to improve employment opportunities within the context of "faith-based initiatives" have emerged.

There is obviously a limit to how large the surplus labor army can grow—not just an economic limit but also a political one. Unemployment breeds contempt for the existing order and sows the seeds of revolution. Therefore, capitalism faces the constant problem of devising expensive legitimization schemes. Ironically, given our "soak the poor" tax structure, employed workers are increasingly burdened by taxes to support unemployed workers. This situation has so far only set workers against nonworkers, rather than uniting all against the system that oppresses them.

In any case, modern public policy can do little or nothing about the significant increase in the duration of unemployment, especially among older and higher educated workers. In 2003, about 22 percent of all unemployed workers had been out of work more than six months—a worse situation than in the previous four expansions. The blight of long-term unemployment took an unusual toll on two groups that should be prime workers in the labor force: college graduates and workers over forty-five years of age. Instead, they have been the most vulnerable with college graduates constituting 20 percent and workers forty-five years of age and older accounting for 35 percent of long-term unemployment. Thus, membership in the reserve army of the unemployed is not evaded because of skills, education, or even a proven track record in the job market.

Short-run manipulation and trade-offs with inflation (see the following issue) are possible, but the structural foundations of capitalist unemployment remain. Nor do special job-creating programs for the chronically unemployed offer a long-run solution. At best, they only buy a little time through deceptive but unfulfilled promises of future jobs. Small wonder that officials have no wish to tabulate all the unemployed. But their statistical manipulation does not change the historical tendency of capitalism.

# Inflation

## Can Price Pressures Be Kept Under Control?

The recognition that substantial inflation is always and everywhere a monetary phenomenon is only the beginnings of an understanding of the cause and cure of inflation.

*—Milton Friedman, 1979*

Future price levels and, hence rates of inflation should be reasonably predictable, a pattern that in practice requires the average rate of inflation to be low.

*—Robert Barro, 1996*

Thus inflation is unjust and deflation is inexpedient. Of the two perhaps deflation is, if we rule out exaggerated inflations such as that of Germany, the worse; because it is worse in an impoverished world to provoke unemployment than to disappoint the rentier.

*—John Maynard Keynes, 1923*

Prices are thus high or low not because more or less money is in circulation, but there is more money in circulation because prices are high or low. This is one of the principal economic laws, and the detailed substantiation of it based on the history of prices is perhaps the only achievement of the post–Ricardian English economists.

*—Karl Marx, 1859*

Lenin was certainly right. There is no subtler, no surer means of overturning the existing basis of society than to debauch the currency. The process engages all hidden forces of economic law on the side of destruction, and does it in a manner which not one man in a million is able to diagnose.

*—John Maynard Keynes, 1919*

## The Problem

Inflation is understood by economists as a sustained rise in the general (or average) level of prices. For the uninitiated, such a phenomenon may not seem to be a particularly threatening event, especially if such a rise in prices is at least offset by an equivalent or greater rate of increase in personal incomes. In that kind of situation, *real income* (a person's price-adjusted purchasing power) is unaffected or even possibly rises, with the net result that no decline takes place in most citizens' standard of living.

Yet in the deeper recesses of accumulated human intellect, there abides a profound fear about inflation and its possible consequences. Possibly our receptivity to such recurrent anxiety goes all the way back to a more primitive time in human development. No worry could have been greater among our cave-dwelling ancestors than the possibility of some unpropitious event—bad weather, depredations by wild animals, invasions by hostile fellow humans, or similar occurrences—that denied cave dwellers access to their regular source of food supplies and also destroyed the family larder. In more modern times, humans have learned that price inflation under certain circumstances can produce precisely the same kind of personal predicament. When inflationary rates continue to rise rapidly, displaying runaway or hyperinflationary characteristics, they can quickly surpass any wage gains and wipe out family savings (the larder), producing destitution as great as any unfortunate cave dweller ever experienced.

Happily, the occurrence of such extreme inflationary episodes is not common, but these events are not easily forgotten either. For instance, the hyperinflationary episode that gripped Germany immediately after World War I (1918–23) still haunts European economic consciousness.

The German hyperinflation was brought on by the impact of the war and war-induced price increases, defeat and the imposition of war reparations, and finally a bankrupt central government that—unable to pay its own bills—resorted to turning on the printing presses and daily issuing (by the tons!) ever larger denominations of increasingly worthless, paper currency. The proportions of the hyperinflation that resulted were staggering and are difficult to grasp: Between peacetime 1913 and the armistice in 1918, the value of the German mark fell by 3,400 percent. Thus, it took 34 marks in late 1918 to purchase a commodity that sold for just 1 mark five years earlier.

By mid-1922, as inflation began to accelerate, the same 1913 product would have required an outlay of 24,000 marks. By the middle of 1923, six months before the collapse and reorganization of the German currency and financial system, it would have commanded a price of 1.4 billion marks. The astronomical rate of increase was, of course, somewhat cushioned by the fact that wages also increased at extraordinary rates, but not nearly as swiftly as prices advanced. German workers, paid no longer in pay- envelopes but in cartons filled with bricks of paper currency, saw their real (inflation-adjusted) wages fall to about one-third of their prewar level by 1923. Near the end of the hyperinflationary experience, banks were paying 18 to 20 percent interest *per day* on savings accounts, but that was scarcely half the average daily inflationary rate.

The episode came to an end in late 1923 with the reformation of the German banking and monetary system, but not until most Germans had lost their savings and were forced to accept a drastically reduced standard of living. A few benefited from it all: Large landowners paid off their mortgages and industrialists their debts in inflation-devalued paper money and reconsolidated their power over the German economy. And, of course, the residual legatee of greatest gain during those awful years was Adolf Hitler and his Nazi Party, first gaining support from many Germans with their promise of building a "new order" in Germany and finally foisting on the world the pain and cost of Germany's hyperinflation in the form of humankind's bloodiest of wars (World War II). Small wonder that Europeans have a special fear of inflation.

While the American economy has never experienced anything like the European hyperinflation of the 1920s, persistent increases in prices remain a central concern of economic policy makers. Fifty years from now, when economic historians look back on the American economy of the late twentieth and early twenty-first centuries, they will surely remark on the great effort expended to both understand and control inflation. Taking a longer-term view of the problem, the thoughtful reader should recognize that persistent inflation has *not* been the norm in the long sweep of American economic development. In fact, *deflation,* or a fall in the overall level of prices, occurred during most of the nineteenth century and during the Great Depression of the 1930s. Nevertheless, the consequences of a systematic rise in overall prices are easy to grasp: Inflation reduces the purchasing power of money and the value of any financial asset that yields a fixed return. Moreover, inflation generally causes interest rates ( the "price" of money) to increase as lenders try to hedge their losses by reducing their supply of loanable funds. With a reduction in the supply of bank loans, businesses find it more expensive to finance new plants and equipment; consequently they cut back on employment and output. In this way, inflation can have a very deleterious effect on the economy because it discourages investment and savings and introduces great uncertainty into the decisions of both firms and households. Thus, the problem of maintaining a stable price level has been a long-standing concern of both private and public policy makers. However, as with other economic phenomena, widespread observation does not imply a consensus as to its ultimate cause and cure. Before we explore the different explanations for inflation, it is important to grasp some of the patterns regarding long-term price fluctuations.

Looking back over the past two hundred years of American economic history, it is possible to identify specific periods when the rate of change in the aggregate price level fell (deflation), rose (inflation), or slowed (disinflation). Figure 12.1 shows how the aggregate level of retail prices—as measured by the consumer price index (CPI)—has performed.

Generally, stable or falling prices prevailed into the early part of the twentieth century. There was a notable acceleration in prices from 1911 to 1920, mostly associated with the inflation caused by World War I and the demand for military goods. Yet this was followed in the Roaring Twenties with a reversal in price movements.

The decade of the 1930s is mostly remembered for the protracted decline in national income, output, and employment, but it also was a time of falling prices. While a stable price level became a primary concern of the governments in most advanced industrial nations, one of the leading economists of the time, John Maynard Keynes, cautioned against the effects of persistent deflation. Prior to Keynes, conventional economic doctrine assumed that flexible prices would automatically cure any imbalance between supply and demand in particular markets or for the economy as a whole. Keynes opposed the logic of this argument by claiming that deteriorating economic conditions in the advanced industrial economies of the 1930s were not going to reverse themselves. If the capitalist system was going to survive the Great Depression, government actions that superseded the market—such as deficit spending to raise national income—were absolutely essential.

Government efforts to increase aggregate income through deficit financing have been widely credited with rescuing the stagnant capitalist economies of the 1930s. However, since the 1930s, price stability has been an elusive achievement for macroeconomic policy makers.

The great ungluing of the American economy after 1966 was due to a confluence of both domestic and international political economic forces.

Figure 12.1    **Consumer Price Index, 1800–2003**

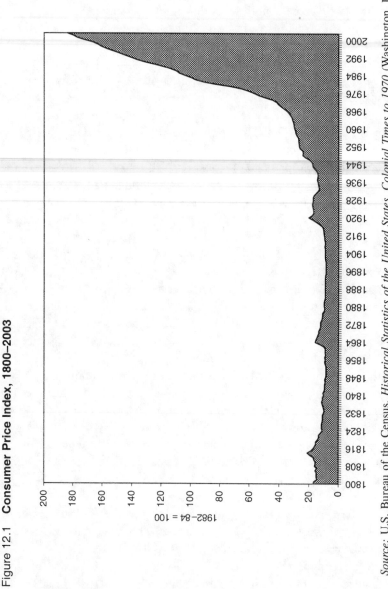

*Source:* U.S. Bureau of the Census, *Historical Statistics of the United States, Colonial Times to 1970* (Washington, DC: Government Printing Office, 2003) and data from the Bureau of Labor Statistics.

The persistent and accelerating rise in overall prices posed profound questions for conventional explanations of inflation. While it was generally believed by Keynesians that government tax and expenditure policies could always ensure a stable balance between inflation, employment, and output growth, by the mid-1970s the tried-and-true tools of macroeconomic policy had broken down. The unprecedented inflation of the late 1970s and early 1980s generated a backlash against Keynesian demand-side macroeconomic policies. America seemed demoralized by the lack of resolve on the part of policy makers to bring down inflation. Paul Volcker, chairman of the Federal Reserve, had spearheaded the attack on inflation by raising short-term interest rates to an unprecedented 19 percent, which induced one of the worst downturns in economic activity since the Great Depression of the 1930s. Volcker's strategy was to accept an economic slowdown as the price for bringing inflation under control.

Since the mid-1980s, inflation has been on a steady downward trajectory. Over the past decade, inflation has averaged about 2.5 percent, a trend that had not been experienced by Americans since the mid-1960s. History will judge whether this portends a return to the long-term tendency of only gradual increases in the overall price level, interrupted by short intervals of significant inflation. Currently, while measured inflation is low, there are several potential risks on the horizon, including the significant increase in oil and raw material prices that are by-products of both the Iraq war and China's demand for raw materials. The current challenge is to understand how recent experiences with inflation have shaped the logic of the different paradigms.

## Synopsis

Inflation, from the Conservative perspective, is caused by a combination of government interference in the market and misguided attempts by the monetary authorities to manipulate the money supply over the business cycle. According to Conservatives, inflation can best be contained by eliminating excessive regulations, which raise the costs of doing business, and by keeping money supply growth at a pace commensurate with the long-run trend in output.

Liberals interpret the inflation record of the past quite differently, pointing out that random shocks over which economists had little or no control were largely responsible for the high inflation of the 1970s. The record low inflation rates of the past several years support the Liberal contention that responsible regulatory and fiscal policies, combined with a reasonably flexible monetary policy, will provide the economy with a solid foundation to ensure steady growth in output and employment.

For Radicals, inflation partly reflects the chaotic and uncontrolled nature of capitalist production itself, and the inherent conflict and struggle between capital and labor over the social surplus. Radicals recognize that while inflation can quickly destroy the livelihoods and savings of workers, current macroeconomic policies to control inflation are having the same effect. As long as the banking and financial system is controlled and run by the capitalist and rentier classes, workers will be forced to accept lower wages and living standards in the interest of achieving price stability.

---

## Anticipating the Arguments

- Conservatives maintain that inflation is primarily caused by discretionary actions by the monetary authorities. Why do they claim that such policies are inherently inflationary?
- Why do Liberals believe that it is more important to maintain low interest rates than to worry about actual or expected inflation?
- Why do Radicals claim that financial institutions and finance capital will always try to keep inflation low at the expense of the working and lower classes?

## THE CONSERVATIVE ARGUMENT

Americans learned a very costly lesson from the failed Keynesian fiscal and monetary policies of the 1960s and 1970s: Long-run prosperity cannot be ensured by government interference in the economy. Moreover, attempts by the Federal Reserve to manage the supply of money to accommodate a particular rate of gross domestic product (GDP) growth are destined to fail. What the 1980s amply demonstrated was that a sound monetary policy and reduced government regulations could yield strong growth, with low inflation and a rising standard of living for all.

Producers and consumers understand that government expenditures can result only in a higher level of prices because those are largely unproductive expenditures that do not contribute to the accumulation of profits. In addition, borrowing by the state to finance such spending *crowds out* private consumption and investment from the market. As we first learned from Adam Smith, profits are the source of new capital investment, which in turn determines an economy's rate of growth and standard of living.

While it is true that government spending programs can provide the economy with a temporary stimulus (e.g., hiring unemployed workers to clean streets), over the long run these activities do not add to national wealth. Finally, even public works programs to build bridges and schools must ultimately be funded by taxing businesses and workers.

A second lesson to be learned from the economic history of the past twenty-odd years is that government deregulation policies have had a salutary effect on price levels. Lower prices for airplane tickets and phone calls and higher rates of return on consumer bank accounts are just some of the benefits derived from deregulation efforts. Free and unfettered global competition has also been directly responsible for lowering resource prices, which has translated into lower prices for consumer goods. This has been a great benefit to consumers, equivalent to a significant tax reduction. However, low or zero inflation will become a permanent feature of the American economy only when *all* prices are allowed to be determined in free and open markets. Government can ensure a steady price level if it continues to encourage price competition and permits the market mechanism to be the final arbiter of the allocation, distribution, and production of goods and services.

On the other hand, government interference in a dynamic market economy will result in the inefficient allocation of scarce resources, which is the basic cause of inflation. For example, when the public sector either purchases goods or services and/or hires workers, it bids up the cost of land, labor, and capital. Similarly, any attempt by government to obtain loans to finance its deficit can only result in bidding up interest rates. Furthermore, when government engages in expensive and unnecessary construction and social welfare programs, it also drives up the price for scarce commodities and services. In this way the government sector "crowds out" private investment and spending and causes a general rise in the price level. Inflation and the expectation of further price increases (due to more public spending and debt issuance) become embedded in product, labor, and financial markets so that prices rise in anticipation of actual changes. This sets the stage for an upward spiral in prices that threatens to undermine the market system.

At this point it should be quite evident that price stability is also contingent upon limited government involvement in the economy. Just as important, most Conservatives believe, is a policy that only permits the money supply to grow at a constant rate. This principle, known as *monetarism,* presumes that there is a stable and predictable relationship between the amount of goods and services in the economy and the amount of money and credit required to produce, circulate, and consume them. Since a capitalist economy has a natural tendency to grow, persistent inflation must result when the money supply expands faster than real economic activity. Obviously, short-term disturbances in the production process, such as floods, droughts, and other weather-related factors, can cause a temporary rise in prices. Nevertheless, free markets have a profound capacity to adjust to such sudden shocks by eventually bringing supply and demand back into balance. Crucial to the maintenance of this balance is the one factor that should be controlled by government— the supply of money and credit.

### Lessons from the 1980s

Inflation is one of the most regressive and punitive taxes because it reduces the purchasing power of those who are least able to resist or bear its effects: wage earners and retirees on fixed incomes. More than his program of tax cuts, Ronald Reagan probably will be most remembered for breaking the back of the high inflation that had gripped the American economy prior to his election in 1980. How did Reagan do it? By adhering to the basic tenets that undergird any successful free market economy: a sound monetary policy and reduced government interference in markets. Voters responded to the clarity and success of Reagan's inflation-fighting program by electing him to two successive terms. In the broadest sense, Ronald Reagan understood that attempts by governments to interfere in the economic decisions of private individuals would serve to distort the price system and bring on inflation.

Figure 12.2 shows that the policies of the Ronald Reagan and George H. Bush administrations were quite successful in fighting inflation. From 1982 to 1992 price increases averaged 4.0 percent, compared to 8.1 percent over the prior ten years. Thus, supply-side economic policies to deregulate the economy were quite successful in reducing persistent inflation and high interest rates. Conservative policies also provided a stimulus to the economy that far exceeded what could have been expected from a Keynesian tax-and-spend program. With many years of low inflation behind us, businesses are now more secure about future costs and revenues. Companies are able to operate at higher rates of capacity utilization and lower rates of unemployment relative to the 1970s because they are confident that inflation will remain sub-

Figure 12.2 **Measures of Inflation**

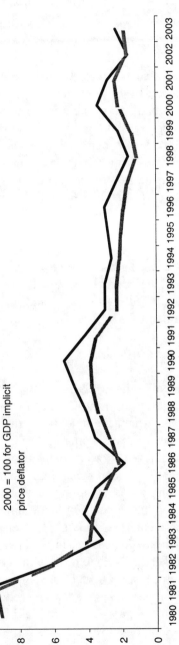
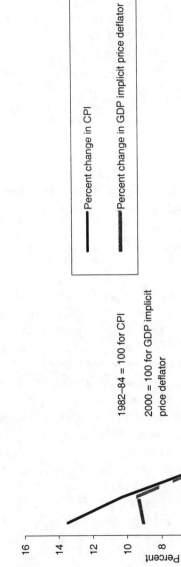

1982–84 = 100 for CPI

2000 = 100 for GDP implicit price deflator

Percent change in CPI

Percent change in GDP implicit price deflator

Percent

1980 1981 1982 1983 1984 1985 1986 1987 1988 1989 1990 1991 1992 1993 1994 1995 1996 1997 1998 1999 2000 2001 2002 2003

*Source:* Data from the Bureau of Labor Statistics and the Bureau of Economic Analysis.

dued. Moreover, lower interest rates were brought about by restrictive monetary policies to permanently wring inflation out of the economy. The resurgence in American manufacturing productivity has largely been due to cheaper long-term financing for new plants, property, and equipment.

Consumers and workers also have benefited greatly from the low-inflation policies of the previous decade. Housing is much more affordable because banks are once again comfortable with underwriting long-term mortgages at fixed rates of interest. There is also much less fear in the broader financial markets that inflation will eat away at the fixed stream of earnings from bond or mortgage portfolios. A low inflation environment has brought strong earnings growth to many corporations, and the surge in the rate of return from holding U.S. stocks is also largely due to the persistence of stable prices since the mid-1980s. In addition, the decline in interest rates on consumer loans to finance purchases of automobiles and consumer durables has been a key factor in maintaining overall growth. Once again, a stable price environment has allowed both lenders and borrowers to engage in profitable transactions that have facilitated consumption and increased the pool of private investment capital.

### Keep the Lid on Inflation

Since the end of both the 1990–91 and 2001 recessions, there have been calls for a relaxation in the Federal Reserve's vigilance against inflation. While it is true that employment growth lagged behind other postwar recoveries, this was primarily because of fundamental changes in the structure of production and demand, which could not be easily influenced by changes in economic policy. For example, the globalization of production, foreign competition, and technological change have permanently changed the demand for labor in the U.S. economy. On balance, however, these changes are likely to keep the overall level of domestic price inflation low. This is because increased foreign competition from overseas workers is likely to restrain the growth in U.S. wages and salaries. Employment costs—which are generally a firm's largest expense—will also be tempered by rising labor productivity in the service sectors. For example, consumers are paying less for many services because the transaction costs of those activities have dramatically fallen over the past decade. Banking, insurance, retail, convenience food, and many other labor-intensive services have experienced notable improvements in the quality of delivery and production because of the widespread adoption of computers and new information technologies. Since the service sector now employs the vast majority of workers, the fight against wage-driven inflation will become increasingly dependent upon additional productivity-enhancing automation.

Finally, there is much evidence that historical price inflation—as measured by the government's Bureau of Labor Statistics (BLS)—has been greatly overstated. A couple of problems associated with the construction of the index are worth noting. First, the CPI was subject to a *substitution bias*—that is, it was not adjusted to reflect the fact that consumers could switch to lower-priced, substitute goods if the price of a particular product rose. In fact, the BLS used to *exclude* cheaper generic drugs from the calculation of the CPI although most health insurance programs required their customers to buy generics. Thus, price increases for pharmaceuticals propelled the entire CPI upward despite the fact that consumers might be able to dodge the higher prices by switching from brand-name medications to generic substitutes. Indeed, it is not possible to build a perfect CPI that will account for people switching to cookies if the price of doughnuts rises or resorting to video rentals if movie theater ticket prices increase.

Second, the CPI tracks the prices of a market basket of goods in a base year period. The quality of this market basket of goods can change considerably. Additionally, the actual market basket of goods varies as new products are introduced. For example, analog stereos progressed to superior multichannel digital systems, personal computers (once not even imagined as occupying the consumer's basket of goods) became faster, medical care improved, automobiles sport global positioning systems, and so forth. In short, it is difficult to tell if increases in consumer prices that are captured by the CPI reflect improved product quality or pure inflation. Given general improvements in product quality and changes in the composition of consumption purchases because of new and improved products, one can safely conclude that the CPI has tended to exaggerate inflation.

Relying on the CPI, the government overstated inflation in the past and at considerable cost to the economy. Wages, other resource prices and contracts often are tied or indexed to the CPI. In addition, taxpayers are burdened with unjustified cost-of-living increases for Social Security and other public sector expenditures that are also linked to overall change in the CPI.

Recognition of the defects in computing the CPI has prompted the development of adjustments to the CPI to correct for some of the substitution bias and account for the effect that improved quality has upon product prices. Conservatives agree with advocates who favor alternative indices, such as the GDP implicit price deflator shown in Figure 12.2, as better measures of the general level of prices and the pace of change in prices in the economy.

In sum, the Conservative program to fight inflation—deregulation of the economy and a responsible monetary policy—has proven to be quite successful. Critics would be well advised to reflect on the changes sweeping the world that favor free markets and reject government-dominated economies. Underlying the discontent with centrally planned socialist economies was recognition of their inability to maintain a reasonable standard of living for the common person. Out-of-control inflation during the early years of Russia's transition to capitalism is the most dramatic example of the fundamental failure of an economy previously organized along collectivist ideas. On the other hand, countries that rapidly embraced capitalist economic principles, such as the Czech Republic, Poland, and Hungary, experienced a dramatic decline in inflation and a simultaneous rise in per capita income. The emerging economic leaders of tomorrow realize that stable prices are essential for prosperity, and have readily adopted Conservative policies to ensure political and social success in the future.

## THE LIBERAL ARGUMENT

It has become quite fashionable in recent times to lay the blame for most economic problems at the doorstep of Keynesian economics. With respect to inflation, most Conservatives argue that demand-side economic policies have an inflationary bias because they ignore microeconomic and monetary factors. It is further claimed that policies developed in the 1930s to fight economy-wide deflation, falling income, and output are no longer relevant or useful for a modern, globally oriented capitalist economy. According to the Conservative paradigm, inflation is mostly a monetary phenomenon that is best controlled by steady growth in the money supply.

While it is true that Keynes's economic policies were unquestionably influenced by the conditions of the Great Depression, Keynes never denigrated the importance of a stable price level to ensure growth and prosperity. Having observed the German hyperinflation of the 1920s, Keynes was well aware of the relationship between monetary factors and prices. It should also be remembered that Keynes had experience as both an academic and government economist, as well as serving as the president of a life insurance company. Thus he clearly understood the adverse impact that inflation has on financial assets with fixed returns. Indeed, Keynes was so concerned about understanding the interrelationships between production, finance, and money that he titled his most famous book *The General Theory of Employment, Interest, and Money.*

Since that book's publication in 1936, the advanced industrialized nations have had to grapple with numerous changes in the performance and structure of their respective economies. As we have seen, persistent gains in the overall price level did not become a widespread problem until the late 1960s. Prior to that time, the inflation record of demand-side policies compared rather favorably with the experience of the so-called supply-side era. For example, the average change in the CPI between 1961 and 1969 was 2.4 percent compared to the supply-side era's 4.0 percent. While Conservatives blame the expansionary fiscal policies of the Democratic Johnson and Kennedy administrations for stimulating inflation, it was during the Republican Nixon and Ford regimes that price controls were imposed in an unsuccessful attempt to suppress inflation.

### Random Shocks and Structural Changes

The eruption of inflation during the 1970s and early 1980s was not, in fact, due to the failure of Keynesian stabilization policies. Rather, it was the result of a series of random events and structural changes that built an inflationary bias into the economy. For example, between 1971 and 1973, the Nixon administration attempted to devalue the dollar to ease worsening U.S. balance-of-payments problems (which were caused mostly by our Vietnam War spending). While American goods were more attractive in foreign markets because of devaluation, foreign goods became expensive to U.S. consumers. The result was that domestic prices of imported goods went up. In October 1973, the United States exported 19 million tons of wheat to the Soviet Union, substantially reducing American supplies of grain, resulting in higher food prices, especially for bread. Beginning in the 1970s, the oil-producing nations banded together in a cartel that effectively raised crude oil prices from less than

$2 per barrel in the early 1970s to nearly $40 by 1981, forcing all prices upward. Inflationary pressures were also being generated by the slow-down in labor productivity as a result of lagging investment and the influx of a growing cohort of younger and more inexperienced workers into labor markets.

These inflationary shocks and pressures created a general inflation-ary psychology: Since people *expected* prices to rise, they quickly bought up currently available goods in the market. This had the effect of *realizing* those expectations. Each event seemed to support the view that prices would continue to go up. These expectations of future in-flation induced both labor unions and businesses to act to protect them-selves from future inflationary shocks. Wages and prices began to go up even faster than the rise caused by the random inflationary events. The effect of this general inflationary increase, which caused the CPI to more than double between 1970 and 1980, was to lower consumers' real purchasing power. The "inflation tax" reduced the spendable in-come of ordinary consumers and businesses, and aggregate demand fell. With falling demand and slowing economic growth, there was an accompanying rise in unemployment.

To many Liberals, the situation called for capping inflationary in-creases by some use of price controls while maintaining employment and growth through appropriate fiscal policy. This was not to be the case. Democratic president Jimmy Carter's efforts at voluntary wage-price guidelines, in 1978 and 1979, were a complete failure. At the same time, expansionary efforts to reduce unemployment were blocked by Conservatives who had decided that inflation was the biggest problem and who wrongly concluded that inflation was the result of past fiscal policy excesses.

### The Monetarist Program of the 1980s

The central disagreement that Liberals have with Conservatives regard-ing the attainment of a stable price level involves two distinct issues: the role of monetary policy and how to cope with the changing structure of the economy. First, the Conservative fixation on steady and predictable growth in the money supply to guarantee a stable price level will be shown to be without merit. Second, the traditional relationship between inflation and unemployment has also been undermined by recent eco-nomic history, as steady declines in real average hourly earnings have not brought the economy to full employment. Indeed, technological change, global competition, and greater income inequality have exerted powerful downward pressures on prices, wages, and income. With fiscal policy paralyzed by political gridlock and an unreasoned fear of federal deficits, the responsibility for macroeconomic coordination lies squarely in the hands of the chairman of the Federal Reserve Board (the Fed). Nevertheless, the preoccupation of the monetary authorities with fighting *past* bouts of inflation has led to its imposition of unnecessarily high interest rates. This policy of *tight money* continues to act as a powerful restraining force on aggregate growth.

The Conservative program for maintaining a stable price level assumes that economic growth is primarily determined by the growth in the money supply. That is, the central bank should fix money supply growth at a rate that is consistent with the economy's long-run potential for growth. Milton Friedman, who has been the foremost proponent of monetarism, has argued that we should eliminate the Fed and replace it with a computer that allows the money supply to grow at a fixed rate. By 1980, with inflation raging, monetarism was given a perfect opportunity to rescue a stagnant and listless economy. Ironically, during the 1980s, when inflation was being subdued, money supply growth was accelerating into the double-digit range. While monetarism has not been totally discredited, no less an authority than the Federal Reserve Bank of New York acknowledged the breakdown in the relationship between the growth in the money supply and the rate of inflation.

While one might have thought that the 1980s would have settled the question of the best monetary theory and policy, unfortunately political and economic realities interfered. The basic political problem confronting Reagan's administration was how to pay for promised tax cuts, increase military spending, and balance the federal budget. In order to carry out his program, Reagan needed the Fed's cooperation. At that time, the Fed had been pursuing an extremely tight monetary policy, which caused interest rates to rise while output and employment declined. The recession of 1982 quickly quelled inflation, but the unemployment rate reached nearly 11 percent, a level not seen since the Great Depression of the 1930s.

With the nation in deep recession in late 1982, Reagan sought to jump-start the economy by increasing defense expenditures and reducing taxes. The tax cuts, combined with very strong money supply growth (courtesy of the Fed), stimulated economic activity and set the conditions for a recovery. Monetarist theory notwithstanding, interest rates continued to move downward through the mid-1980s, precisely as both the money supply and the federal deficit were exploding. While monetarist theory would have predicted severe inflation, perhaps even hyperinflation, disinflation (a slowing in the growth rate of overall prices) actually persisted while employment and output proceeded to expand until mid-1990. As the economy moved into the mid-1980s and beyond, it became evident that there was little relationship between money supply growth and retail inflation (as measured by changes in the consumer price index). Moreover, by the late-1990s inflation exhibited an *inverse* relationship to money supply growth.

For all of his Conservative beliefs and contrary to the picture that Conservatives portray, Ronald Reagan followed a textbook Keynesian policy of *easy money* and tax cuts to move the economy out of a recession. Had the Fed's monetary policy not been as "accommodating" (letting the money supply expand to absorb the demand generated from a rising budget deficit), it is doubtful that Reagan's fiscal policies would have provided enough stimulus to prevent a recession. Moreover, the Reagan administration's approach of very rapidly growing the federal deficit was a crucial, yet unheralded, component of its political success. Thus, it is clear that monetary and fiscal coordination between the government and the Fed often plays a vital role in determining the macroeconomic performance of the U.S. economy.

### Managing Inflation in the Here and Now

Monetary policy has drifted away from targeting the money supply. In recent years, the Federal Reserve seems to have aligned with, but does not formally acknowledge the use of, the "Taylor Rule." Conceived by Stanford University economist John Taylor, short-term interest rates are the principal focus. They are manipulated to achieve a desired balance, or acceptable trade-off, between full employment and long-run inflation rates. This view operates from the perspective that *some* level of inflation is both a normal and necessary characteristic of an expanding economy. Policy makers are spurred to raising short-term interest rates when existing rates entice borrowing that threatens to allow inflation to exceed an estimated target that is consistent with full employment. On the other hand, if actual GDP were falling short of the potential GDP (full employment), monetary policy makers would pursue a lower interest rate strategy as long as it is consistent with the long-run inflation target.

The fact that some variant of Taylor's Rule seems to guide policy making is not really a revelation to anyone's thinking about how short-term interest rates might be altered to fight inflation or to counter an economic slump. The key is that the Conservative-favored monetary rule does not dominate the scene when it comes to managing inflation in the real world. Analysis of modern policy making acknowledges that policy makers form preferences about how much deviation in inflation and output will be tolerated before they *act* to counter an ominous turn in economic conditions. Thus, the "rule" of contemporary monetary policy is really a matter of when to exercise discretionary intervention, not a matter of avoiding intervention.

While the American economy faces potential inflationary pressures, it is unlikely to accelerate to an unacceptable pace. The globalization of production, increased energy efficiencies in both homes and businesses, and productivity gains from the widespread use of computers have helped and will continue to help, keep inflation in check. On the other hand, the record of the Fed has not been good in promoting balanced economic growth over the past several years. The Fed increased the short-term interest rate on lending between banking institutions (the federal funds rate) to 6.5 percent throughout 1999–2000 based upon what proved to be an unfounded fear of potential inflation. However, with unprecedented speed the Fed resorted to a striking reversal of policy when confronted with the very real prospect of recession, the destabilizing impact of the terrorist attacks of September 11, and a growing fear of *deflation.* Thirteen successive interest rate cuts dropped rates to 1 percent by June 2003. The federal funds rate remained at a 45-year low, which helped to lower mortgage costs and fuel the rapid rise in home ownership. By June 2004, the Fed raised short-term rates by 1/4 percent, thus beginning another round of successive rate increases to stave off inflation. Much to the chagrin of Conservatives, activist policy is alive and well.

## THE RADICAL ARGUMENT

Central to Marx's economic critique of capitalism is his perception of the inherent tendency in capitalism toward ever greater instability. Marx expected violent fluctuations in output, employment, and prices to be the necessary outcome of increased competition and struggle between firms. Driven to realize ever-greater amounts of profit on an ever growing scale of production, businesses must employ any means necessary, including price cutting, price gouging, sabotage, and fraud, to destroy their competitors. Persistent intra- and interindustry warfare results in greater macroeconomic instability. For Radicals, the historical record of price movements in the United States reflects both the incredible development of the forces of production and their growing incompatibility with the needs and social relations of working people. As we have seen, Conservatives and Liberals view the recent success at fighting inflation to be the result of decisive Federal Reserve actions, deregulation, increased foreign competition, and technological change. In contrast, Radicals would argue that the persistence of high *real* interest rates and a declining *real* wage lie at the core of capitalists' macroeconomic policy efforts designed to achieve price stability on the backs of the working people in America.

### Inflation versus Unemployment: The False Trade-off

Rather than being simply a macroeconomic goal, Radicals argue that the traditional means employed by both Conservatives and Liberals to fight inflation have ended up destroying the livelihoods and living standards of the vast majority of workers. Bankers and financiers understand price stability to mean *no* increase in the overall price level (literally, 0 percent inflation). To ensure this goal, a nonelected body of elite managers of the monetary system—the Federal Reserve System—is granted nearly total control over the economy. This group is not concerned if their policies require interest rates to rise and stay at levels that result in high unemployment and falling wages. Their sole objective is to make sure that prices do not rise so that they might preserve the value of bond and mortgage portfolios held by financial institutions. To do this, the Federal Reserve had to maintain high inflation-adjusted interest rates throughout the 1980s and 1990s.

The destruction of America's industrial heartland and, with it, thousands of high-paying manufacturing jobs was largely the result of Conservative policies to reduce inflation through tight monetary policies and an avowed antiunion stance. The data convincingly demonstrate the "success" of the supply-side programs of the 1980s, which brought about unprecedented high real interest and thus destroyed the manufacturing sector and its workforce. This period also began with Reagan's busting of the air traffic controllers' union (PATCO), which not only set the tone for future labor relations but also was hailed as the first victory by Conservatives over inflation.

Of course, the broader objective was to reduce overall labor costs by breaking the power of unions to impose wage demands or to organize and bargain in a collective fashion. This is particularly important to capitalists as they invest in new service-based sectors where labor expenses make up a relatively larger share of total production costs. Although services are also generally much more labor-intensive than manufacturing industries, they have proved to be rather susceptible to productivity gains from automation and mechanization. Given these structural changes in the economy, it is no wonder that Conservatives believe that price stability can be achieved only by repressing labor costs and pursuing virulent antiunion policies. In fact, the recent official government data on falling unit labor costs confirm the success of these policies. Furthermore, it is essential that advanced capitalist economies maintain what Marx termed a "reserve army" of unemployed workers who are always willing to work at wages below prevailing norms. While Liberals may say they wish to return to the full-employment/high-wage era of the mid-1960s, Radicals realize that this is impossible under the present rules governing our economic system. What's more, even though the U.S. economy experienced unprecedented low unemployment during the late 1990s, real average hourly wages have continued to decline. Unlike the prediction of supply-and-demand theory, an increase in the demand for labor has not been accompanied by a concomitant rise in the real wage. Finally, while the Fed is obsessed with peremptorily restraining wage growth, it will do nothing to stop a real inflationary threat: the 20 percent gain in corporate profits over the past two years. This only further confirms the inherent class bias in monetary policy in the service of corporate and banking interests.

Even if workers are able to exert political pressure to restore some of their lost earnings (e.g., by increasing the minimum wage), their efforts are likely to be overwhelmed by the efforts of government and corporate leaders to maintain a stable price level by exposing American workers to greater global competition. Radicals clearly recognize that free trade agreements such as the North American Free Trade Agreement (NAFTA) and the globalization agenda of the World Trade Organization (WTO) seek to encourage capital mobility across borders. While supporters of increased foreign competition claim that it will make American industry more competitive and efficient, the effect on workers will only be lower wages and fewer jobs. Importing cheap foreign goods may serve to check inflation, but the continued globalization of domestic production will lead to a reduction in the standard of living for most wage and salary earners.

## Inflation, the Fed, and Class Interests

Capitalism's past and recent experiences with inflation have not been good for the vast majority of working people. As has been noted, high rates of inflation create a sense that the economy is out of control. This undermines confidence in politicians and political institutions. During such periods of turmoil, people often become willing to accept reactionary or authoritarian regimes that promise to get inflation under control. Imposing harsh reductions in government services, employment, and social spending, combined with "sound" (i.e., tight) monetary policies that create high interest rates and result in high unemployment, is the typical means used by repressive governments to bring inflation under control. Chile, Argentina, Brazil, and Poland have all employed such tactics with the active support of the World Bank and the International Monetary Fund. While these actions hurt the working poor and middle class the most, political elites, foreign creditors, and upper classes generally applaud these oppressive measures.

Inflation was not a threat in the 1990s, but the Fed aligned monetary policy with the interests of banks and the financial services industry by keeping real interest rates high to maintain the incomes of creditors and speculators. The high costs of borrowing increasingly burdened working people to the point where bankruptcies and nonperforming loans produced a worrisome state of affairs. Not until the stock market began to exhibit clear signs of downturn in 2000, jolting the intoxicated casino mentality of the financial elite, did the Fed act to lower interest rates. Financial institutions, brokerage firms, mutual funds, and globalization advocates applauded the aggressive interest rate cutting undertaken by the Fed through the spring and summer of 2001.

Then came the terrorist attacks on New York and Washington on September 11, 2001. On the heels of a slowing economy, Wall Street reacted as if the events were nothing less than catastrophic and the plunge in the stock market spurred the Fed to action with more interest rate reductions. Ironically, the economic calamity facing working people for the preceding decade had received no attention from the Fed. Interest rates were held at unnecessarily high levels to fend off inflation. Only when the financial sector began to have trouble did the Fed forsake anti-inflationary regimen.

Long-term price stability should be an important part of the Radical economic policy agenda. Liberals are soft on fighting inflation because they instinctively associate its cure with the repressive policies of Conservatives. They miss the point that a more humane program must be offered. The core of such a program would seek to change the balance of financial power in the American economy away from large creditors such as banks and insurance companies and toward workers and small businesses. Put simply, since bankers and bondholders prefer slow growth and tight monetary conditions to fend off any hint of inflation, they will always endorse central bank policies that result in unnecessarily high real interest rates and unemployment. What's more, bank presidents also sit on the board of directors of most of the twelve regional Federal Reserve banks and their views strongly influence Fed policy. Thus, the goal of a Radical program for stable prices should seek to create a single worker-controlled and state-owned bank, the nationalization of financial markets, and the mandatory distribution of equity rights in all corporations to workers.

### Equity and Price Stability

Ensuring a stable price environment cannot be left to the unelected monetary authority of the Fed, the financial markets, or politicians. As the industrial and financial structure of the American economy becomes increasingly concentrated and centralized, the threat of increased inflation because of monopoly pricing power intensifies. Currently, there is no governmental or public institution exerting a meaningful challenge to the growing economic and political power of large financial corporations. As their power and influence grow, the monetary and political authorities will continue to bend to the dictates of financial capital. Furthermore, the current structure of the Fed provides negligible oversight from Congress: Its budget is immune from congressional appropriations and its primary decision-making body—the Federal Open Market Committee (FOMC)—is vested with too much power over the lives of Americans.

While reforming the Fed would be an important first step, a more important change would be to abolish the distinction between commercial and central banking so that a worker-controlled state-owned bank could be responsible for all banking transactions. Such an institution would be first and foremost concerned with the social consequences of fighting inflation, and represent the interests of average Americans and not bankers and their wealthy constituents. A central bank operated and controlled by working people would allocate investments where they are most needed—low-income housing, day care, and child health care facilities—and away from unproductive activities such as speculation in commercial real estate and the stock market. Moreover, various groups devoted to community purposes could be organized around local branches of publicly owned banks. These local and regional banks would take in all deposits and make low-interest loans to enterprises in their respective communities.

Finally, in order to guard against excessive asset inflation, financial markets would have to be nationalized and heavily regulated. In addition, there would have to be a mandatory distribution of equity rights to all employees. This would have the effect of redistributing ownership and power to workers and making sure that their interests were considered before the narrow interests of corporate managers. With a democratized financial structure, the investment environment would be much more conducive for long-term investments in productive ventures that provide the goods and services needed by the vast majority of people while simultaneously employing large numbers of workers.

In sum, inflation must be understood as the natural outcome of the irrationality of an economy organized along the principles of capitalist competition. Inflation, whether generated by price gouging, financial speculation, or the production of socially useless goods, is part of a broader economic logic that subordinates the needs of people to profit and greed. The continuing decline in real wages demonstrates that inflation is *not* the result of overpaid workers, although workers are sure to suffer if inflation flares up again. To that end, price stability can be assured only if the operations of the financial system are directed by public institutions that are accountable to the working people of America. Furthermore, there must be a radical reorientation of both private and government resources into investments that will raise the living standards of average wage earners.

# The New Population Problem
## Can We Save Our Social Security System?

Among our objectives I place the security of men, women
and children of the nation first. . . . Hence I am looking for
a sound means which I can recommend to provide security
against several of the great disturbing factors in life—
especially those which relate to unemployment and old age.
—*President Franklin D. Roosevelt, June 8, 1934*

All in all, Social Security is an excellent example of
Director's law in operation, namely, "Public expenditures
are made for the primary benefit of the middle class, and
financed with taxes which are borne in considerable part by
the poor and the rich."

—*Milton Friedman, 1980*

Cutting back on benefits will undermine people's faith in the
integrity of the whole system—they will feel double-crossed.
—*Wilbur J. Cohen, former Health, Education,
and Welfare official, 1981*

The retirement of the Baby Boom generation will double
the number of retirees. . . . The timing of their retirement
will affect the composition and the productivity of the
workforce. The increased number of retirees will have an
impact on the costs of entitlements, including increased
retirement benefits, and a labor shortage with fewer
workers to fill existing positions.
—*Patricia P. Pine, Ph.D., New York State
Office for the Aging, 2004*

## The Problem

Among the first macroeconomic concerns pondered by economists was the possible connection between the size of a nation's population and the general well-being of its people. Looking at the world at the end of the eighteenth century, the great British economist, Thomas Malthus (1766–1834), concluded that population growth would sooner or later impose important restrictions on human progress. Based on available evidence, Malthus and his disciples concluded that starvation would be a permanent and ultimate check on population growth and the fortunes of most of the human species.

This was so because populations had the capacity to expand geometrically (1, 2, 4, 8, 16 . . . ) while agricultural output (food) could only expand arithmetically (1, 2, 3, 4, 5 . . .). In point of fact, the dark Malthusian world never materialized. To be sure, starvation indeed would raise its ugly head across the globe from time to time but according to evolving economic wisdom, such events were local concerns and nothing that a rapid increase in agriculture productivity could not cure.

In a mostly unexpected way, however, the contemporary American economy finds itself confronted with a new population problem. The dilemma does not arise out of the sheer numbers of its population, but rather from the numbers of that portion of its population that have entered, or are about to enter, their postemployment years. Put simply as a question, the problem is: How and what resources can be provided for sustaining the increasing proportion of the society that, by virtue of age or disability, no longer contributes to national income?

Long an institution and a federal budgetary outlay that has enjoyed immense popularity, America's Social Security system is on the verge of becoming an enormously divisive issue that pits the younger working population against a growing population of elderly citizens. To understand the roots of the generational crisis that promises to threaten the American program of Old-Age, Survivors, and Disability Insurance (OASDI), it is perhaps informative to tear a page from natural history before turning to concrete political and economic realities.

The North American beaver is a prolific and industrious mammal that lives in highly social communities. "Busy as a beaver" is a well-known euphemism, the roots of which acknowledge the fact that this single-minded and disagreeable little animal stands second only to human beings among warm-blooded creatures in its physical alteration of the natural landscape.

Like human beings, beavers are also subject to aging and infirmity and the probable accompaniment of diminishing capacity for work. Accordingly, a situation develops in which the old beaver's output—measured in cutting and collecting sapling boughs and carrying on maintenance of the dam and the lodge—is less than the inputs needed to sustain the oldster. The growing gap between the old beaver's contribution to the colony and the colony's cost in sustaining the old fellow becomes immediately apparent when the food supply (for whatever reason) dwindles to the point where the young beavers and the community itself are in danger of starvation. The oldster is driven out, and the old beaver swims downstream. If lucky enough to reach a river or a lake, he will take refuge in an abandoned burrow and spend his remaining time gnawing on the very tough trunks of large trees and on freshly fallen branches until extinguished by starvation or a predator.

The *beaver solution* represents one social and economic approach to the process of aging. Brutal as such a solution may seem to contemporary human beings of civilized pretensions, the beaver solution remains the only sure-fire cure for societies suddenly overwhelmed by age-based dependency problems. *And* it is a model to which human cultures have turned from time to time if the community itself was to survive.

The urgent demographic problem of the United States (and a great many other countries) and the urgency for coming to terms with the costs that an aging population imposes on the larger society simply cannot be ignored. Failure to tackle this problem in humane and rational ways means that some variation of "the beaver solution" will (must) inevitably evolve.

Until the twentieth century, the existence of a large elderly and postemployment population was rarely viewed as an economic problem. The principal reason was not a matter of voluntary charity but rather reflected mortality statistics. As late as 1920, the average life expectancy at birth in the United States stood at 53.6 years for men and 54.6 years for women. It is no overstatement to say most of the population "worked until they died" and the handful of others who survived a few years between work and death passed their time in a relative's home or in sordid public facilities. From the perspective of public policy, America had no program for the elderly other than individual adaptations of the beaver solution.

In the 1930s, however, the problem of the dependent elderly could no longer be ignored. People were living longer and well past the years where they could find, given their accumulating disabilities, employment. A few industries, such as the railroads, had been forced by labor unions to provide retirement benefits, but most American retirement programs were developed long after the creation of the Social Security system.

In any event, when the bottom fell out of the American economy after 1929, unemployed old folks with few or no sources of income (since their kids were out of work too) were finally recognized as a social and economic problem that was not going to go away even after the Great Depression. In 1935, at the urging of President Franklin D. Roosevelt, Congress passed the Social Security Act.

In truth, the original act was not a particularly grand commitment. It compared poorly with old age and disability plans in place in most western European nations, some of which had been operating for forty years or more. Under the 1935 act, eligible workers would contribute to a fund one-half of 1 percent (matched by an equal employer contribution) of the first $3,000 of annual earnings. It was estimated the first wave of recipients would receive from $10 to $85 per month from the Social Security Administration upon reaching age sixty-five (which was three years beyond the then existing life-expectancy of males). From the beginning, the OASDI program was not an insurance program at all. It was, and never really changed from, a "pay-as-you-go" financing arrangement. When OASDI went into effect in 1938, only about 42 percent of American workers qualified for participation—modest beginnings, indeed, for the most popular social welfare program ever introduced in the United States.

Over the years OASDI grew. In 1940, the 78,000 retired workers eligible to receive Social Security checks got an average $22 per month; 30,000 retired workers "with aged wife" averaged $36 per month and widows with children under age fourteen got checks averaging $35 per month. By 1950, the average monthly benefit check climbed to $59, reached $125 in 1970, and shot up to $382 by 1980. In 2003 the average monthly Social Security check was $922. If adjusted for inflation, the increase in benefits-paid tarnishes a bit, but not enough to dim the fact that great numbers of older Americans enjoy a standard of living scarcely dreamed of a half century or even a quarter century ago. With the addition of Medicare, to cover a substantial share of seniors' medical costs in the mid-1960s, it was evident America had abandoned the beaver solution.

However, an increasingly important question remained to be answered: Could the nation pay for its beneficence to its elderly? There was, after all, the enormous generation of Baby Boomers (over 70 million of them) who would start drawing on their Social Security benefits somewhere around

2010. By the 1980s, a lot of economists and politicians began to argue that the Social Security system had serious long-term funding problems, and, in 1984, some modest but important changes in the administration of system accounts deferred (but did not eliminate) doomsday scenarios.

By 2003, a number of Bush administration studies "proved" (at least to the administration's satisfaction) that short of *immediately* raising the federal income tax rate by 69 percent, raising payroll taxes (OASDI contributions) by 95 percent, cutting Social Security benefits by 45 percent, *or* some combination of the preceding, *and* holding the line on these changes through 2075, OASDI insolvency was a long-term certainty. Interestingly though, fully 80 percent of the $45 trillion "fiscal gap" (the difference between projected outlays and projected Social Security receipts) that would pile up by 2075 if no action were taken, would come directly from projected Medicare outlays. For the record, $45 trillion is "serious money"—about equal to the private net worth (assets minus liabilities) of all Americans, about seven times the size of the present federal debt, or four times as large as 2004 gross domestic product (GDP).

The fact that so much of the fiscal gap derives from Medicare reveals a problem not much considered until recently: More people are getting older . . . and older. Average life expectancy at birth today is seventy-six (it was sixty-two in 1935 and sixty-eight in 1945, about the time the Baby Boomers started arriving). But once you reach considerable age, modern medicine—at considerable cost—continues to increase life expectancy. Between 1985 and 1995, the death rates of those aged eighty to eighty-four fell by 8 percent.

In any event, America is a swiftly aging society in which maintenance of the elderly will lay an increasing claim upon national output. Presently, Social Security and Medicare outlays amount to 7 percent of GDP. Even after placing a freeze on benefits, a recent Congressional study estimates, this share will rise to 15 percent by 2037 and to 22 percent by 2075.

The problem is not one without solutions, but no solution is painless:

1. increase the eligibility age for benefits
2. increase the Social Security tax burden on those paying into the system
3. increase general (income) tax collections to fund pay-as-you-go outlays
4. lower the outlays paid to Social Security recipients
5. drop the system as it exists altogether and fashion something new.

The nation faces some tough choices.

## Synopsis

Conservatives maintain that the defenders of the Social Security system have fraudulently promised elderly Americans a retirement income that simply cannot be afforded by the nation. Meanwhile, the very concept of an "involuntary" Social Security program erodes individuals' rights and operates as a drag on the entire economy in its discouraging of private savings. Liberals respond that Social Security is both a solemn promise and the only protection that many have from abject poverty in their declining years. Liberals also maintain that the fear of the Social Security system going bankrupt is a pure scare tactic used by its opponents. Radicals see the eventual sacrificing of Social Security as an illustration of the fiscal crisis confronting government—an inability to provide both outlays that benefit capital and expenditures for people's needs. Thus, Social Security and other social outlays must be constantly reduced.

## Anticipating the Arguments

- On the basis of what evidence do Conservatives maintain we cannot "afford" the Social Security program?
- How do Conservatives and Liberals disagree on the question of an individual's responsibility and choice in the matter of providing for retirement?
- Why do Radicals believe that the growing attack on the Social Security system really masks a fundamental problem in state financing? What do they see as the cause of this problem?

## THE CONSERVATIVE ARGUMENT

As with most social programs, Social Security is an excellent example of how Americans have been deluded and manipulated since the incipient drift toward welfare statism began under Franklin Roosevelt. Ironically, most Americans simply do not understand that Social Security and other "giveaway" programs are pushing the national economy to the brink of disaster. It is not simply a "type" of program that Conservatives oppose for philosophical reasons. The opposition is based on simple economic sense: There is no such thing as a free lunch. And the cost of the Social Security banquet, despite its immense popularity, is prohibitive.

## Myth versus Reality

The managers and political supporters of the Social Security system have created a number of self-serving myths about their programs that persist in spite of common sense and overwhelming evidence to the contrary. Perhaps the most enduring myth is that Social Security is merely a pension program, in which government holds tax payments in a pool and then pays them out on an actualized basis, just as a private pension insurance company would. Even a catchy and inventive TV commercial on behalf of the Social Security system a few years ago perpetuated this belief when it announced: "It's your money!" Nothing could be further from the truth. The insurance-fund approach to the Social Security system was abandoned long ago. What remains of the old funds (Old-Age Survivors Insurance Trust Fund, Disability Insurance Trust Fund, and Medicare Trust Fund) will be exhausted in the near future. The fact is that Social Security is operated on a pay-as-you-go basis; consequently, next to nothing is accumulated. Any surplus funds must be used to purchase U.S. government securities, which, because the securities are issued to finance the federal deficits, amounts to a backdoor means of taxation. No investments are made in the usual capital markets patronized by private pensions that result in accumulation of dividends and interest—things that, after all, make it possible for private pension insurers to operate not only with solvency but with profitability.

A pay-as-you-go system means it is not "your money" when you retire, but someone else's. Your money, meanwhile, is—or will be—going to support someone else. On the surface that may seem fair enough, as long as someone else's money is available to finance retirees' needs. Most recipient's retirement benefits (skipping the various nonretirement programs of Social Security) are paid out of current taxes *and* exceed the actual contribution of the retiree (because benefits tend to grow much faster than contributions). Retirees are receiving more than they paid into the system. In other words, they are receiving transfer payments from those who are productively at work. The simple fact is that a Social Security pensioner is just as certainly on welfare as is a mother supported by Temporary Assistance to Needy Families or a food stamp recipient.

This leads to a second myth: Retirement monies, whether provided by insurance or a welfare system, will be ensured upon retirement. It seems fair that if you pay for someone else, someone should pay for

you. However, this is possible only by a relentless increase in the contribution rate. The current demographic profile of the population makes
it a certainty that the number of recipients will grow faster than the
number of contributors. The situation is a bit like the old pyramid game
or a chain letter: Those near the bottom of the list have to muster a far
larger money contribution or required number of letters over those
higher on the list. But like the pyramid or chain letter, the burden for
those on the bottom sooner or later becomes too great compared to the
estimated rewards, and the link is broken. It is a simple political fact
that the relative level of benefits for Social Security retirees will not
be continued when contributors are faced with an excessive burden
and little hope that they will ever get back anything close to their contributions. There is no economic "proof" that workers in the year 2050
will not pay 30 to 50 percent of their salaries in order to sustain retirees at present standards, but it seems likely that such demands on workers will be unacceptable.

Meanwhile, the immense popularity of the Social Security system, as
well as its economic difficulties, stem largely from another myth: Social
Security was intended to provide all with a comfortable standard of living upon retirement. Even by Franklin Roosevelt's liberal standards,
Social Security was only supposed to provide "safeguards from misfortune." Framers of the act did not have in mind sending New York retirees to Florida condos to bask in the sun. Social Security was intended to
protect the very poor and elderly from total destitution. It was, for the
more fortunate, to be a small bonus to their personal retirement savings.
Except for the very poor, benefits were to equal what the individual had
paid in, which in the 1930s and 1940s was not very much. All that has
changed today. Many Americans see their Social Security benefits—
which far exceed their contributions—as *their entire retirement program.*
They believe that Social Security is both a substitute for savings and a
reason not to save.

### Undesired Effects

Because of the persuasiveness of the mythology, there is practically
universal acceptance by Americans of the Social Security system.
People who might grumble about "welfare queens" driving Cadillacs
and who would never accept food stamps, accept Social Security payments without a second thought. Moreover, senior citizens see Social

Security as a right and are quite willing to vote against any honest politician who has the audacity to question either the philosophy or the economics of the system.

Older citizens act as a powerful political lobby through organizations such as the American Association of Retired Persons (AARP). They make ending the system impossible and reducing the system's actual benefits practically impossible. As a result, this political lobby of kindly but uninformed older citizens keeps pushing Social Security and ultimately the entire economy down the road to disaster. Only a serious reeducation effort can halt this trend.

One of the first steps is to see that the Social Security system is a badly designed tax system. Both Social Security and Medicare are financed through the imposition of a constant tax rate imposed on employees and employers. Currently (2005), the Social Security tax is 12.4 percent, split between employee and employer at 6.2 percent on the first $90,000 of income. Medicare is also equally split at 1.45 percent apiece but on *all* earned income. The effect of this rate structure is to burden low-income earners more than high-income individuals. The irony is that low-wage earners, who most desperately depend on Social Security in retirement, have all their labor income subjected to the Social Security tax, while higher incomes, particularly those above the $90,000 base, experience less of an impact.

Another disadvantage of this method of taxation is that it discourages job creation. Because employers are required to match the employee's contribution rate, employers find it advantageous to hire fewer workers. This may occur in one of two ways. First, each worker represents a hidden tax payment because employers are required to match employee contributions. By keeping numbers of workers down, taxes and costs are lowered. Second, where employers are already paying the maximum tax because workers are at their maximum wage for paying Social Security contributions, it is desirable to require more work from present workers (and pay more in wages) than to hire new workers and pay the additional employment tax. The outcome of such a tax system is to reduce employment, but Liberals rarely come forth to criticize these arrangements.

The distortions caused by the Social Security tax are accompanied by an inequitable scheme of benefits payments. Payments are determined neither by the amount paid in nor by the individual's needs. While some limits to benefits are set according to lifetime contributions to the system, the benefit schedule is connected only loosely to actual contribution rates. To a considerable extent, conditions totally unconnected to either need or contributions determine payments to the Social Security recipient. Married persons receive greater benefits than the unmarried because a spouse who never worked qualifies for an amount equal to half the benefit received by the retired working spouse upon reaching full retirement age. Dependent children also make families eligible for additional benefit payments. A widow or widower who never worked is able to get the late spouse's pension.

Perhaps the greatest inequity is imposed upon low-income workers who never exceed Social Security's taxable income base and out of economic necessity must continue to work beyond the full retirement age. Consequently, all of their income is subjected to the Social Security tax while those whose incomes exceed the taxable income base experience a lower effective tax rate. High-income individuals are more likely to have private pensions and other assets that allow them to retire early or at least stop working when they reach Social Security's demarcation of full retirement age. The size of the monthly benefit check is determined by the years of highest earnings so the regressivity of the tax is reinforced by the regressive distribution of benefits. To make matters worse, low-income earners have shorter life expectancies than high-income earners. In short, low-income workers are taxed hardest, receive the least, and find they are literally working to death for the Social Security system.

Part insurance in philosophy and part welfare, the benefit program is both unfair to the needy and inequitable to the contributor. Welfare to the truly indigent is perfectly acceptable to a Conservative. Even a system by which a contributor received benefits equal to his or her contribution can be defended logically (so long as the contributions are voluntary). However, we have neither.

An undesirable macroeconomic outcome of the Social Security program has been its impact on savings. As we noted before, the initial object of Social Security was to provide a bare cushion for those who lost their savings in the Depression years. However, as the coverage and benefits of the program—not just old age benefits but everything from educational to health benefits—has grown, Social Security has increasingly been treated as a substitute for personal savings. According to respected estimates, Social Security depresses personal savings by 30 to 50 percent. The Social Security "contributions" collected by the government are not saved but rather spent on a pay-as-you-go basis. Thus government-forced saving (in withheld contributions) does not replace lost personal savings. The macroeconomic effect of dwindling savings rates is not difficult to estimate. In particular, it denies the nation the fund of savings that would otherwise be available for expanded investment. More consumption and less savings mean less capital. Accordingly, with investment lowered, employment is lowered and unemployment increased. The negative macroeconomic effects of Social Security cannot be overlooked in their impact. Martin Feldstein (chair of the President's Council of Economic Advisors in the Regan administration) and others have estimated the drag on the GDP to be very great. National output may be reduced by as much as 15 to 20 percent as a result of Social Security's discouragement of savings.

## An Intermediate Solution

Conservatives understand that reforming Social Security cannot take place overnight. Americans need to be weaned slowly from Social Security dependency. The goal for OASDI reform, of course, must be to transform the existing bureaucratic system through successive increments of privatization.

As a simple matter of fairness, those now collecting Social Security benefits should be able to continue to do so. And, those near retirement age and who have already made their retirement plans should have access to existing options. Yet, even these groups must understand that future increments of government largess will be small and infrequent. In other words, effective caps on present giveaways must be put in place, and put in place in such a way that they are not subject to political change of heart. After all, Hell knoweth no fury like that of a senior citizen politically scorned.

For those who are some distance from retirement, a privatized alternative to the present system should be established. Workers would be able to direct all or a portion of their Social Security contributions into a private—essentially personal—account, which they or their agents will invest so as to maximize accumulations when retirement age is reached. It should go without saying, that—over time—no investment alternative outperforms equity markets. Ideally, no restrictions should be placed on the account holder's range of choices. However, as a practical matter, it would be unwieldy to allow frequent transactions among a wide array of investments for so many personal account holders with initially small balances. Additionally, a substantial share of the participants—if not the vast majority—will not have enough expertise to assess risky investment opportunities. A limited list of funds and some restrictions on the number of exchanges among funds would be necessary to hold down transaction costs and curtail foolish speculation that would reduce accumulations for retirement. Yet, transition to a private system will cause people to realize that this time it really is *their money.*

The contributions to, and earned accumulations of the account, will be exempt from taxes in the accumulation years. Upon reaching retirement age, they shall be taxed as ordinary income once the recipient starts drawing down the account. Moreover, and in a decided improvement over the unfairness of the present system, early death will not cut off the recipient's heirs or designees from access to the accumulated funds, regardless of whether the recipient has actually reached retirement age.

With respect to funds already paid into the system (before the privatization strategy is enacted into law), a change in benefit calculation should be introduced. With respect to existing Social Security accumulations, rather than basing future payout benefits according to the recipient's wages (as exists presently), future benefits would be indexed to price changes. In other words, benefit payments obtained up to the time privatization is introduced would be fixed in their real dollar value and would never grow because of increases in earnings. If it is clear that accumulated benefits will not increase (legally speaking, *cannot* increase), the "bounce effect" of political tinkering will be eliminated. And, it is the only fair thing to do.

Obviously, prudent workers will move as quickly as possible to privatize their future Social Security contributions—perhaps even rolling over past fund accumulations into their personal account (but only on the basis of a "real dollar" adjustment to determine the real value of current fund accumulations). Over time, workers will recognize that the market, not government bureaucrats and politicians, will provide the better long-run return from payroll deductions. With a little more time, and the introduction of an investment option, most will recognize they would be better served by not being compelled to pay "payroll taxes," and can opt out of the intermediate Social Security system altogether. When we reach that point, "Amen" can be said to the biggest political boondoggle America has ever contrived.

## THE LIBERAL ARGUMENT

Conservatives are correct when they assert that the Social Security system is the showpiece and the keystone of American social legislation. They are dead wrong, however, when they claim it "proves" the foolishness of government efforts to maintain minimum social welfare conditions. The Conservative allegation with regard to the "bankruptcy" of Social Security financing and their charge that we simply cannot afford the excessive benefits of Social Security are misrepresentations of the facts.

The differing perspectives of Liberals and Conservatives should be evident by this point. However, it needs to be pointed out that no issue so clearly sets out the differences in our respective ideologies than the matter of how the nation's elderly citizens should be treated. Central to the Conservative faith and its approach to the Social Security question is the notion that people do not count; only markets do. Liberals, on the other hand, approach every economic policy matter with a basic standard in mind: *What is the fair outcome?* The dismantling of Social Security or its eventual privatization is decidedly *unfair.*

### *The Importance of Social Security*

Steeped as it is in the philosophy of voluntarism and individualistic social behavior, the Conservative argument preaches that it is each person's responsibility to provide for his or her old age or illness. Their arguments, however, fail to point out that this was precisely the kind of social philosophy that prevailed before the New Deal era and before Social Security. Such an individualistic approach to national social welfare was found wanting at that time and nothing has happened to change the situation. Even in the best of times, the average industrial worker had only the most limited opportunity to set aside a "nest egg" for his or her retirement years. Indeed, most workers in the pre–New Deal era worked until they were physically unable to go on any longer or, more likely, until bosses interested in hiring younger, more productive workers fired them. The "declining years" of an elderly worker were often spent in the back bedroom of a son's or daughter's home. This extended family condition has received praise from Conservative social theorists who emphasize the values of family and togetherness. Reality was usually different. Having an old person live with you meant, sooner or later, increased medical bills for the family and almost always long hours of tending the elderly when they became bedridden. Not many who had to go through this sort of thing—neither the old parent nor the children—found life quite so idyllic as mod-ern exponents of the extended family make it seem.

For other poor workers, without savings *and* without family, there was the grim prospect of wasting away in a public institution. "Going to the poorhouse" was not just gallows humor among workers; it was a very real possibility. Usually located on the outskirts of a city, "county homes" and "state homes" had an exquisite institutional ugliness. Workers usually lived dormitory-style; thus husband and wife were separated save for an occasional walk on the premises. The food was of equal quality and quantity to the fare offered at the county jail. There were few social programs for residents to enjoy, just utter boredom until the end.

While Conservatives anguish over the adverse effects of Social Security on private savings habits, their concerns overlook the fact that few American workers were able to save anyway. After the introduction of the Social Security system, saving was not only possible but also required, as workers and their employers put income aside in trust funds.

For those workers who did succeed in putting away some savings for their later years, the Great Depression of the 1930s demonstrated that there was little virtue in voluntary frugality. As the stock market crashed and banking and financial institutions went under, the elderly of the era watched their savings vanish. Practically overnight, the diligent citizen who had planned ahead for retirement was no better off than the poorest worker or the most profligate. This was the situation when the Social Security Act was passed in 1935. Far from being a destructive "give-away," it was a very modest attempt to pull millions of elderly Americans out of the terrible insecurity of economic dependency. Conservatives represent Social Security as a step into the collectivist state; the irony is that it returned many elderly people to a condition of economic self-sufficiency and individualism.

As the years passed after 1935, the Social Security system was broadened. First, many additional workers and their dependents came to be covered under the law. Second, Social Security was extended to provide health and disability benefits. Third, the payments under Social Security provisions were enlarged. As a result, Americans came to rely on Social Security to handle the economic problems of their retirement years. It became part of a new social contract between government and its citizens, and it is almost universally popular.

It would be wrong to conclude, as Conservatives suggest, that we no longer need Social Security, that the modern-day affluence of Americans would allow a private and voluntary accumulation of savings that would be a "better deal" for workers than the Social Security system. Comparisons with private pension programs are downright misleading. No private insurance company can offer—regardless of the price—a retirement package that includes a pension, health insurance, disability, and life insurance where the benefits are protected from inflation and are largely tax free. Not only is no better plan available, but also many workers simply cannot be certain of meeting their payments for a private program. Thus they would run the risk, if jobs and income decline, of forfeiting their retirement plan. Very quickly, Americans could return to the cruel economic conditions that beset the elderly before 1935.

### The "Dependency Ratio" Myth and the Need to "Grow" the Economy

Among the favored Conservative devices to discredit the existing Social Security system is to maintain that the increasing ratio of retired workers to employed workers will soon reach a level at which those working simply cannot—without impoverishing themselves—sustain the existing number of Social Security recipients. The argument frequently takes on tangible form as illustrated in Figure 13.1. The dependency ratio projections rest on existing demographic projections with respect to life expectancy and on the assumption that currently available benefits to Social Security recipients will remain (in real terms) constant.

Figure 13.1 charts the present and projected ratio of Social Security beneficiaries per one hundred workers from 2003 through 2080. The dependency ratio rises from about thirty in 2003 to about forty in 2020 and on to fifty-five in 2080. The gray line depicts the Conservatives' projection of how the rising dependency ratio drags up the benefit outlays that must be paid by working Americans. Social Security payouts amount to about 11 percent of workers' earnings in 2003, rise to about 13 percent by 2020, and shoot up to nearly 20 percent by 2080.

The data as presented are alleged to illustrate that a rising dependency ratio necessarily edges the nation toward a point where the existing numbers of workers will be unable—by virtue of insufficient numbers—to sustain, out of pocket, the transfers that are mandated to be paid to a grow-

322

Figure 13.1    **Projected Beneficiaries per 100 Workers and Cost of Social Security**

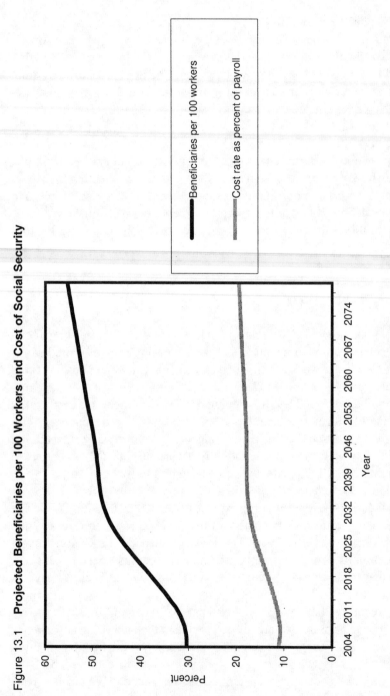

*Source:* Data from the *2004 Annual Report of the Board of Trustees of the Federal Old-Age and Survivors Insurance and Disability Insurance.*

ing number of oldsters. Curiously, the argument takes on a vague Marxist preconception: that a nation's output value is simply equal to the labor value of those working—hence nonworkers are simply appropriating the fruits of workers' labor. The obvious fact that GDP (and hence GDP per capita) is not simply a function of numbers of people employed is completely missed. The entire concept of improving labor productivity and its effects receives no direct consideration in graphics dwelling on a "dependency ratio" that report the ratio of retirees to workers.

This assertion is easily proved by looking back to the late 1950s and using a slightly different dependency ratio that compares paid workers with nonworkers (retirees, the extraordinary numbers of young Baby Boomers and their nonworking Moms, as well as others not in the labor force). As a simple matter of "dependency," there were fewer workers in comparison to nonworkers (of all kinds) in 1960 than there will be (given existing demographic projections) in 2020 or 2050 or 2080.

However, the really important point to remember is that the high dependency ratio at the end of the 1950s in no way signaled impending stagnation. In fact, between 1960 and 1973, real GDP increased by 70 percent, which facilitated a 50 percent increase in employment, and a 44 percent increase in real median income (as well as a 43 percent increase in real outlays paid by the Social Security system). Not only is the whining about "dependency ratios" misleading, it evades the real problem: the currently slow rate of growth in GDP per capita—a matter addressed in Issue 9.

### We Can Afford It

Before reform of the Social Security system in the mid-1980s, a convincing argument could be made for the fact that OASDI and Medicare were quickly going broke. However, the reforms have had a beneficial effect on all four of the system's trust funds. Between 1980 and 2003, the balance in the Old-Age and Survivors Insurance Trust ballooned from $22.8 billion to $1,355.3 billion, the Disability Insurance Trust balance grew from $3.6 billion to $175.4 billion, and the Hospital Insurance Trust went from $14.5 billion to $251.1 billion. Only the Supplemental Medical Insurance Trust remains grossly underfunded, scarcely holding its own in real terms with a current balance of less than $24.8 billion. Doomsday projections for Social Security funding are based upon rather low estimates of labor productivity, which, taken together with a rising dependency ratio, results in forecasts of depleted fund balances and high costs.

Indeed, the problems of the Medical trust fund are illustrative of the truly serious problem the system faces: exploding Medicare outlays. Even examination of the George W. Bush administration's generous overstating of the fiscal gap the Social Security system faces reveals that the real problem is rising medical costs. Of the $40 to $50 trillion gap they allege exists between estimated income and estimated outlays between now and 2075, more than 80 percent is the result of projected medical cost increases.

Quite simply, the fiscal gap disappears (or at least becomes small enough so as to be susceptible to disappearance with a little fine-tuning of income and outlays and a little more economic growth) *if we bring medical and hospital costs under control.*

In fact the medical cost problem is not just a Medicare problem. In league with the pharmaceutical companies and the HMOs, the Bush administration has shamelessly stood aside, as everyone's medical costs have increased at four or five times the rate of the consumer price index increases. With 44 million Americans of all ages not having any medical insurance coverage, rising medical costs are not just the problem of the elderly.

The simple fact is that the nation needs a freestanding national health insurance program that holds down medical costs and guarantees universal coverage, whatever one's income or age. With that in place, we could return Social Security to its original purpose: to make it possible for every citizen to be assured in their old age of a reasonably comfortable and independent lifestyle.

Alas, Conservatives do not want an affordable Social Security system. For that matter, they do not want a successful, freestanding national health insurance program either. In a highly calculated fashion, the Bush administration has done about everything in its power to eliminate the creation or enlargement of any government social program. The device for doing this: eliminate the availability of funds by driving up annual federal deficits. It was not by accident (or even a war) that a projected $5 trillion federal surplus between 2001 and 2015 was transformed into the currently projected accumulation of $5 trillion of deficits—mostly by way of excessive tax cuts that bestowed great rewards on the wealthiest of Americans.

This intentional creation of federal deficits has been—among the general population—a mostly unnoticed and quiet strategy aimed at convincing Americans we cannot afford *any* social outlay that requires increasing government outlays. However, paraphrasing President Lincoln, while it's possible to fool some of the people all the time and all the people some of the time, *it's not possible to fool all the people all the time.*

## THE RADICAL ARGUMENT

The current crisis in the American Social Security system cannot be understood apart from the general fiscal crisis that grips the government budgets of all modern capitalist economies. From the Radical perspective, we must go beyond the narrow and partisan claims of Liberal and Conservative adversaries and look deeper into the fundamental relations of the state and capitalist enterprise. These real economic relationships, not merely political prejudices, set the actual limits to the growth and development of social spending.

### *The State Budget within Capitalist Economies*

Within a capitalist economic system, the object is always to employ capital and to produce goods in such a way that profits (or surplus over the costs of production) continue to rise. It should be remembered that this is not an arbitrary and doctrinaire definition. Conservatives as well as Liberals know full well that "profit is the name of the game." Conservatives, of course, maintain that government appropriation of some share of production (government taxes and their budgetary allocations) comes *at the expense* of the private sector. In other words, what government takes and redistributes is a subtraction from what businesses would otherwise receive. Liberals, on the other hand, also see the government taxing and budgetary process as redistributive but defend it on the grounds that either such redistribution is socially desirable or that government spending in fact generates output that would not otherwise take place (see the Liberal argument in Issue 9). Both views, however, miss the important role played by government taxing and budgeting within the modern capitalist state because they fail to grasp the central place of the state in the process of accumulating capital *and* maintaining social and economic order. In consequence, neither understands the central issues involved in the political and economic struggle over social spending in general or the Social Security system in particular.

If we examine the taxing and budgeting activities of modern capitalist states, it becomes apparent that they pursue two basically different objectives: "accumulation" and "legitimation."* On one hand, the state undertakes actions that are aimed directly at stimulating economic growth and encouraging business profits (providing for capital accumulation). On the other hand, the state attempts to create and maintain general conditions of social harmony, thus legitimating the operation of a capitalist society.

If in fact the state could provide the desired levels of accumulation and legitimation at the same time, there would be no crisis. Nor, of course, would there be much reason to study economics because, in such an Alice in Wonderland world, scarcity would not exist. In the real world, however, these two objectives are competing uses for the state budget. Moreover, as we shall see, outlays for one purpose may be in direct contradiction to the goals of the other objective. The contradiction has become particularly sharp in our era of lagging capitalist growth. Presently, it is obvious that there are very real limits to the budgetary outlays that government can make in these two general areas without (1) raising to unacceptable levels the taxes on the society or on certain groups within the society or (2) generating excessive inflationary pressures (see Issues 9 and 10).

To see how the "accumulation" and "legitimation" functions of the capitalist state budget work, we need only dissect the budget according to these functions. First, there is a broad category of social capital outlays that either *directly* increase capitalist output (social investment) or *indirectly* lower the cost of capitalist production (social consumption). Social investment and social consumption spending add to the accumulation of capital in a variety of ways. Social investment includes outlays for roads, airports, and industrial parks, that is, outlays that increase private-sector output by having government pay for part of the investment cost. Social consumption expenditures such as education and unemployment insurance are useful to business *indirectly,* since the enterprise does not have to pay for training its workers or for sustaining them when economic conditions deteriorate. While social investment and social consumption spending primarily serve the accumulating function, it is obvious that they also work to legitimate the capitalist system. Meanwhile, certain other outlays, which we shall call social expenses,

---

*The following analysis adopts the terminology and concepts of the now classic work of James O'Connor: *Fiscal Crisis of the State* (New York: St. Martin's Press, 1973).

have not the slightest impact on accumulation and work only to achieve legitimation. This is the service performed by those budgetary outlays that commonly are called "welfare"—payments to the surplus or unemployed portion of the population for the purpose of bribing them into complacency and political acceptance of the economic order.

The categories may seem confusing, and in truth the confusion is heightened by the fact that some government outlays serve both accumulation and legitimation ends. Social Security, for instance, lowers the production cost of employers (by having government provide pension funds) and legitimates by sustaining otherwise "useless" workers. Nevertheless, with a little reflection it is possible to categorize government outlays according to how they serve one or both of these basic functions. Such an approach is important because it demystifies the otherwise obscure organization of the government budget. We can begin to see just what certain spending categories are intended to do.

### The Growing Fiscal Crisis

Viewing the budget according to the categories of accumulation and legitimation ties together nicely the Radical critique offered in the earlier issues dealing with stabilization policy, unemployment, deficits, and even international economic policy. By looking at how the government budget is constructed according to the conflicting demands of accumulation and legitimation, we can gain insight into the problems of modern macroeconomic policy making. The issue of Social Security becomes understood in the context of a much larger political and economic crisis.

The general fiscal crisis of the modern capitalist state (within which the Social Security crisis is but one small element) can be put simply enough: There are rising demands for government outlays and a dwindling capacity or willingness to pay for such outlays through taxes. Thus the crisis takes a number of forms. First, there is the problem of rising accumulation and legitimation demands. In a period of economic stagnation, business (in particular the big business or monopoly sector) requires greater outlays (or what amounts to the same thing, tax cuts) to lower production costs and facilitate capital accumulation. Thus, farm subsidies and business "investment credit" programs have continued to expand. Some direct aids to business—such as the "enterprise zone" concept—have been presented inaccurately, as if they were really aid to the unemployed worker. Meanwhile, there has been a rise in legitimation claims, more so in an economy deeply committed to rising levels of mass consumption.

Second, with claims rising, there has been a steady pressure for tax increases. In the 1980s, this stimulated a considerable number of tax-payer revolts such as California's Proposition 13 and dozens of similar efforts to force down taxes. The victory of Ronald Reagan in 1980, perhaps more than anything else, signaled a popular reaction among taxpayers to hold down spending and even to cut it back. Yet when we look back at the fiscal restraint actually produced by the tax revolts and by Reagan's victory in 1980, we find that few ordinary people have benefited.

The budgetary cuts forced by the fiscal crisis have come primarily from the "legitimation" activities of government. In other words, using Marxist terminology, the budget has become increasingly an instrument of class oppression and domination. Thus budgetary actions that primarily benefit big business and the upper-income groups' abilities to accumulate profits and capital have been protected or have actually expanded, while budget items aimed at maintaining a minimum level of personal well-being have been sacrificed. Quite simply, it is a matter of profits for General Motors and Microsoft *first*. Conservatives, with their supply-side and trickle-down theories, have been surprisingly honest in putting forth this objective. Even more surprisingly, people who have nothing to gain from such an approach have accepted this nonsense, but only up to a point. Social Security is a good example of how the fiscal crisis can explode into a serious political crisis.

### Social Security and the Fiscal Crisis

The recent shrinkage of purely "legitimation" outlays within the budget, while painful to welfare recipients, never held out much possibility for solving the fiscal crisis. Quite simply, our outlays for the poor always have been too small to provide a significant amount of savings that can be transferred to needed accumulation activities. Moreover, even the wildest-eyed Conservative knows at heart that literally starving the poor to death would bring more political chaos than the system could handle. After all, some minimum outlay must be made for legitimation. To state the matter bluntly, "the beaver solution" is not a policy option in a capitalist order that seeks to sustain its political viability.

Social Security, with its $471 billion in outlays each year, is certainly an attractive area from which to obtain some accumulation gains. Since "everybody" pays into Social Security and receives its benefits, the class nature of raiding Social Security is not so immediately obvious. If we look beneath the surface, however, we find that the Social Security crisis is an illustrative case showing the basic class nature of government spending and taxing.

On the revenue side, Social Security taxes are collected only on earned income. No taxes are paid from income received from rents, interest, and dividends. Thus the owners of wealth and property are exempted from any payments. Second, the payroll tax itself is regressive, with a constant percentage levied from the first dollar up to a maximum earned-income level. The result is that low-income groups must pay a higher portion of their income in Social Security taxes. Currently these people are told that Social Security can be saved only by making the tax more regressive, that is, by raising the percentage contribution (and modestly expanding the taxable income level) or by taxing the benefits actually received. This regressive tax structure is encouraged by the fiction that Social Security is self-funding, or that you get according to what you pay in. By keeping the self-funding myth alive, workers are told simply that they can get only what they pay for. If the funds go bankrupt, contributions must increase or benefits must go down. This successfully evades the whole question of guaranteeing minimum retirement benefits irrespective of contributions and allows us to avoid the question of establishing minimum welfare standards for the elderly and the ill. It maintains the capitalist faith that we are responsible only for ourselves and not for others.

Class bias also appears on the benefits side of the Social Security system. Proposals to lengthen the period for retirement eligibility work against the low-income production worker whose ability to work productively is diminished by the physical demands of his or her job. Being forced into early retirement because of health means accepting greatly reduced benefits for the rest of one's life. Meanwhile, well-to-do professionals, who do not suffer from health-damaging employment, are permitted to collect benefits *and* earned income after retirement age has been reached.

The assault on the Social Security system reveals much about capitalism in general and specifically about the current (but well-disguised) crisis of the capitalist order. First, by attacking Social Security as well as such traditional "legitimation" functions as welfare spending, the defenders of capitalism reveal just how far and how deep the fiscal crisis has developed. The trade-off between accumulation and legitimation activities by the state has become quite severe, a much greater problem certainly than well-meaning Liberal defenders of Social Security understand. Second, both the attack on Social Security and the proposed efforts to save it amount to a new "disciplining" of the working population. Even with its many flaws, Social Security has been an important social welfare program and has been immensely popular with most Americans. Its promise far exceeded its delivery, but it did create a widely held belief that society would indeed protect individuals. Reneging on Social Security sends the signal that this commitment will no longer be honored. Whether Americans are willing to accept a new discipline of reduced social welfare remains to be seen, but the old Liberal program for a system that delivered both accumulation and legitimation is being undone, even if this fact is not reported by the media nor understood by ordinary citizens.

Meanwhile, the reader should put in the context of capitalist needs and habits the likelihood of the geriatric-care industry receiving a serious "spanking" such as Liberals propose. Similarly, the plausibility of the long-term Conservative plan to get rid of Social Security must be weighed against the political disorder that would surely arise thereafter. From a Radical perspective, Conservatives and Liberals, as usual, are offering cures upon which they simply cannot deliver because capitalists will not allow it. Recognition of this reality goes a long way to clear the head of self-mystification about what American macroeconomic policy making *is* and *is not* about.

# International Economics

## Where Does America Fit into the New World Order?

Under a system of a perfectly free commerce, each country naturally devotes its capital and labor to such employments as are most beneficial to each. This pursuit of individual advantage is admirably connected with the universal good of the whole.

—*David Ricardo, 1817*

If nations can learn to provide themselves with full employment by their domestic policy . . . international trade would cease to be what it is, namely, a desperate expedient to maintain employment at home by forcing sales on foreign markets and restricting purchases which if successful will merely shift the problem of unemployment to the neighbor.

—*John Maynard Keynes, 1936*

On the whole, capitalism is growing far more rapidly than before; but this growth is not only becoming more and more uneven in general, its unevenness also manifests itself, in particular, in the decay of countries richest in capital.

—*V.I. Lenin, 1916*

We live in a global economy that is characterized by free trade in goods and services and even more by the free movement of capital. As a result, interest rates, exchange rates, and stock prices in various countries are intimately interrelated, and global financial markets exert tremendous influence on economic conditions everywhere. Financial capital enjoys a privileged position. Capital is more mobile than other factors of production, and financial capital is even more mobile than other forms of capital.

*—George Soros, 2000*

The cranes on the docks of Shanghai, Hong Kong, and Tianjin are not simply loading containers for export to the United States. They are also unloading huge amounts of American machinery, American farm products, American aircraft, and American electronics.

*—Robert Zoellick, U.S. trade representative, 2004*

## The Problem

Until comparatively recently, Americans have not paid much attention to international economic affairs. From the end of World War II to the 1970s, the preeminent position of America in both international trade and finance was pretty much taken for granted by Americans (and by most of the rest of the world too), very much as we took for granted our international political preeminence. Unlike many nations whose very existence depended on foreign trade and commerce, American imports and exports of goods had never been very large, not amounting to much more than 6 percent of our gross domestic product (Figure 14.1). As one economist observed of the American tendency to worry little about matters of foreign trade and finance, to do otherwise "would be to let the tail wag the dog."*

To understand how we have moved away from our earlier insular, unconcerned attitude about the rest of the world and toward pondering the impact of international events on the domestic American economy, we need only look at the following chain of representative events over the past three decades:

- In early 1987, the United States becomes the largest debtor nation in the world, largely attributable to an uninterrupted string of annual trade deficits since 1976.
- In 1989, the United States and Canada (America's most significant trading partner) sign a free trade agreement.
- In 1991, the European Community leaps beyond free trade with the Treaty of Maastricht, establishing a plan for political and economic unification.
- In 1991, the United States leads a coalition of many nations to reverse Iraq's occupation of Kuwait, which ends in a smashing military success. The cold war era ends in the same year with the dissolution of the Soviet Union into fifteen independent states.
- By 1993, Mexico (America's third-largest trading partner), Canada, and the United States enact the North American Free Trade Agreement (NAFTA). Thereafter, efforts begin in earnest among many North, Central and South American, and Caribbean nations to create

*Campbell R. McConnell, *Economics: Principles, Problems, and Policies*, 7th ed. (New York: McGraw-Hill, 1977), 918.

Figure 14.1 **Exports and Imports as a Percentage of Gross Domestic Product, 1929–2003**

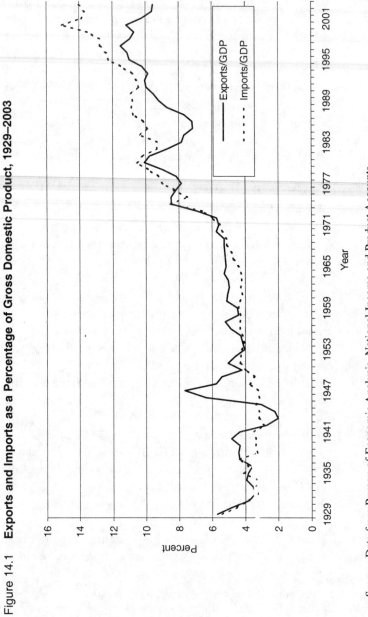

*Source:* Data from Bureau of Economic Analysis, National Income and Product Accounts.

a hemispheric free trade zone under the Free Trade Agreement of the Americas (FTAA).

- In 2001, the nation reels from the collapse of a long economic boom and the bursting of a stock market bubble, and finds itself involved in a "war on terror" after September 11.
- In 2003, the United States and the United Kingdom along with a relatively small group of cooperating allies initiate a second Gulf War against Iraq and quickly dislodge the government of Saddam Hussein. More than a year later, the battle drags on in the streets of Iraqi cities. International support wears thin, oil prices skyrocket, and the U.S. trade deficit continues to grow.
- By early 2004, a component of a hemispheric trade initiative emerges in the form of the Central American Free Trade Agreement (CAFTA). Separately, the United States and Australia sign a free trade agreement in May of 2004. The U.S. zeal for free trade is shadowed by its dependency on capital inflows from abroad.
- By 2004, the dollar's weakness against the euro and other major currencies seems like a permanent condition. Meanwhile, China's rising importance in international trade as well as the "outsourcing" of U.S. jobs impact the domestic political agenda.

These and other events show that (1) the long-held American economic and political preeminence in the world is in retreat; (2) America now depends more on the world for trade and capital, and also chronically buys more than it sells; and (3) the conditions of domestic well-being are intricately connected to the nation's international trade and financial condition. Alas, the tail *was* wagging the dog.

Understanding international interdependence and appreciating the influence of the country's international position requires comprehension of how international trade takes place. Although discussions of international economic issues invariably become quite complicated, mastery of the fundamental reasoning involved is easier than many noneconomists realize. The conditions affecting trade among nations are not very different from the conditions affecting trade among individuals in a simple market. Just as an individual's ability to sell his or her goods is basically determined by (1) the price of the goods and (2) the ability and willingness of buyers to pay that price, so it is with exports and imports. Whatever America or any other exporting nation is able to sell to the rest of the world is determined by the prices that must be charged for their exported goods and by foreign purchasers' willingness and ability to pay such prices. Similarly, the amount of goods we buy from abroad (import) depends on the prices we are charged and our willingness or ability to pay these prices.

Accordingly, it becomes obvious that the various factors that affect the prices of a nation's goods and the ability of world buyers to purchase the goods at the prices offered are the basic variables in determining any particular nation's export or import position. Some examples serve to make the point clearer. All things being equal, anything that might raise the price of American goods relative to the prices being charged by other (non-American) sellers of the same goods would obviously discourage foreign purchases of American products. Higher production costs, resulting from rising factor prices, various production inefficiencies, or domestic inflation would raise the prices of exports. And, so too could a situation where fluctuations in international exchange rates result in the exporting nation's currency becoming strong (high-priced) relative to importing nations' currencies.* These forces push export prices upward, which would likely lead to a decline of American exports. And what makes exports unattractive to foreigners usually makes imports attractive at home. When foreign goods are cheaper than American goods, American consumers would choose to buy foreign products. In other words, U.S. exports would be lower and imports higher. The opposite would be true if our prices were relatively lower than prices charged by the rest of the world (that is, our exports higher and our imports lower as a result of this type of price disparity).

However, even if U.S. prices were competitive with world prices (or were even lower), exporting goods and services would be difficult if the rest of the world was gripped by a serious recession that greatly reduced other nations' ability to buy imported products and services. On the other hand, the United States would expect to be able to sell more in the world— as long as its prices were attractive—if the world was enjoying prosperity.

---

*A strong (relative to other nations) currency will not necessarily work against a nation's exports and balance of payments. Other factors are important, such as the relative prices of goods in the first place. However, in the mid-1980s, high interest rates in the United States led to foreigners' seeking American dollars to purchase high-return American investments. The result was "an exceptionally strong dollar" even though the United States was already in a serious trade deficit situation. The higher-priced dollar meant that when U.S. goods were sold overseas, after the conversion of dollar prices to the local currency, they were priced quite high. The result was to depress American exports even further. Meanwhile, imported goods enjoyed, after price conversion into dollars, low prices that encouraged U.S. imports to soar.

This comparatively simple model of world trade, however, becomes more complicated when more than prices are at work. For instance, consider what will happen if American prices are relatively high compared to the rest of the world and the American economy is experiencing a modest expansion while most of the world is in an economic slump. U.S. exports will be relatively low because of higher prices *and* because of diminished worldwide ability to buy U.S. goods. Meanwhile, the United States imports more because its capacity to purchase is fairly high and foreign goods are cheaper than American-made products. Indeed, this was precisely the real-world situation in the mid-1980s as the United States began to run up very large trade deficits. A significant reversal in the early 1990s gave way to ballooning, followed by record-breaking, trade deficits.

The main influences upon exports and imports are rather easily explained, but greater complexity lurks beyond the basics. Explanations about the relative international trade and financial position of the United States are scarcely matters of universal agreement among economists. However, near unanimity exists on one point: *The U.S. economy is more interconnected with the rest of the world than ever before.* As a result, domestic economic policies—both in their immediate objectives and in their longer-term effects—must always be seen within the context of an international economy, not just the domestic economy. Other nations can surely be expected to respond to U.S. policy initiatives. Their actions in turn rebound on the United States, perhaps negating or distorting the outcomes we sought with our original domestic policy. For American economic policy makers, economic interdependence is a two-way street and the world has become a much smaller, more complicated place in the past few decades.

## Synopsis

Conservatives argue that U.S. trade and currency problems are traceable to protectionism, pegged exchange rates, and ill-conceived domestic economic policy. Liberals oppose the Conservative remedy of free trade and floating exchange rates, maintaining that the cost in terms of jobs and industrial decline in the United States would surpass any benefits. They hold that only stimulation of the domestic economy will ensure international vitality. Radicals assert that the present international trade and finance problems are a gauge of the nation's decline from power and a further measure of the chronic capitalist crisis of production and distribution.

## Anticipating the Arguments

- According to Conservatives, what particular economic problems are caused by protectionism?
- Why do Liberals believe that even worse problems would be caused by free trade and floating exchange rates?
- What do Radicals identify as the cause for recent U.S. balance-of-payments problems?

## THE CONSERVATIVE ARGUMENT

Perhaps the severest test of personal commitment to a free and open capitalist economy arises with respect to international trade and finance. Economists, politicians, and especially business leaders who perceive the advantages of competition and the market and who ardently oppose any type of controls or intervention in domestic activities are tempted to abandon their philosophy at the nation's borders. Perhaps it is a narrow nationalism or a basic parochialism in economic thought, but the logic of free markets is too easily abandoned when international issues are raised. For the consistent Conservative, however, there should be no exceptions. Free economic arrangements are as crucial internationally as they are domestically.

### The Necessity of Free Trade

The first requirement for free trade is the elimination of all tariffs, quotas, and bilateral or multilateral trade agreements that inhibit the free operation of international markets. Each nation must be free to sell its goods to any other, and each nation must be open to any other's goods. Regrettably, however, the desire for protectionism runs very deep among nations. This remnant of outmoded mercantilist philosophy persistently reappears when one nation gains a production or price advantage over another in a particular product or line of products. In the United States, it appears when firms or industries act as special-interest groups lobbying Congress to raise duties on hated imports or to set quotas on these imports. Supposedly, by limiting the ability of foreign firms to compete through price or other means, American industry's position is enhanced.

Conservatives acknowledge that part of society's difficulty in adhering to free trade is one of perception. The costs of trade appear in highly visible ways: displaced workers, bankrupted steel manufacturers, and prominent properties wistfully lost to foreign ownership. However, the benefits of trade in the form of lower prices to consumers, the redirection of resources to higher value purposes such as the manufacture of silicon chips instead of fueling blast furnaces, and the enjoyment of infusions of capital from abroad are easily lost on the ordinary person. Rarely does free trade receive credit for a birthday or Christmas being celebrated more fervently because the absence of trade barriers made it possible to buy twice as many goods. Nor do many people immediately acknowledge the technological and economic necessity of employment shifting from steel production to computer memory production. At the same time, shifting labor to chauffeuring luxury limousines from stagecoach driving is readily accepted as an improvement and no one would venture to assert that low-wage rickshaw drivers in Asia threaten the employment prospects of U.S. workers.

Ironically, labor unions in affected industries very often ally themselves with the corporation in their lobbying effort. For example, in 2002, the United Steelworkers joined with the majority of the steel industry to urge import tariffs on steel. President George W. Bush acceded to imposing the tariffs of 8 to 30 percent on various steel products for a period of three years. From the union's point of view, the object is always to protect jobs. The real outcome is quite different, however, for several reasons.

First, protectionism is costly. It raises the prices of imported goods for all consumers or artificially holds up the price of competing domestic goods. This may mean jobs and income for steelworkers and steel companies in Gary, Indiana, but it means reduced buying power and lost jobs elsewhere. Tariffs and quotas have not protected American earnings, but have merely redistributed income and jobs and raised prices for everybody.

Second, protectionism encourages inefficiency. Without the incentive provided by competition, neither business nor labor is induced to increase productivity or to modernize production techniques. In turn, consumers must pay for an industry's protected inefficiency, which can be quite costly over time because it tends to grow cumulatively. The limits on foreign competition are very often increased as production gaps grow between a vibrant overseas producer and a lethargic domestic industry.

Third, protectionism invites retaliation. Other nations will be induced to follow the same protectionist path if their goods are effectively priced out of our domestic markets. Thus we may find the threat of foreign steel eliminated at the cost of being unable to sell U.S. tractors in foreign markets. The result may be the end of trade altogether. Recognition of this fact arose shortly after the Bush administration imposed tariffs on imported steel in 2002. Outrage from foreign producers coalesced in a dispute mediated by the World Trade Organization (WTO). The steel tariffs were deemed unfair trade by the WTO and the United States faced $2.2 billion in retaliatory tariffs from the European Union. Rescinding the tariffs in December of 2003 averted a retaliatory response that could have impacted a whole range of American firms, not just steel companies.

Fourth, protectionism invites other undesirable tinkering with trade, exchange rates, and capital flows to effect political solutions to economic problems. For instance, Liberals would attempt to artificially improve our international balance of payments through a variety of interventions. Practically disregarding the favorable effect of inflows of foreign earnings by U.S. businesses on our balance of payments, many Liberals have incorrectly singled out the export of U.S. capital as a primary cause for balance-of-payments deficits. Their shortsighted cure is to restrict U.S. overseas investment. As with all protectionist actions, the effect has been counterproductive for the economy. American businesses are placed at a competitive disadvantage in world markets at precisely the time when they should be developing strength.

Free trade and free overseas movement of U.S. capital may indeed mean the end of some American industries and may throw some workers out of jobs. However, other production possibilities are opened. Let the Koreans concentrate on toy or textile production and the United States exploit its computer technology. Indeed, let each nation develop its comparative advantages so that trade between them is possible.

Milton Friedman has emphasized the significance of a commitment to free trade this way:

> There are few measures we could take that would do more to promote the cause of freedom at home and abroad. Instead of making grants to foreign governments in the name of economic aid—and thereby promoting socialism—while at the same time imposing restrictions on the products they succeed in producing—and thereby hindering free enterprise—we

could assume a consistent and principled stance. We could say to the rest of the world: We believe in freedom and intend to practice it. No one can force you to be free. That is your business. But we can offer you full co-operation on equal terms to all. Our market is open to you. Sell here what you can and wish to. Use the proceeds to buy what you wish. In this way co-operation among individuals can be worldwide yet free.*

## The Necessity of Floating Exchange Rates

Despite the central importance of free trade policies in developing an efficient and mutually beneficial system of international commerce, free trade alone will not bring freedom to international markets. The other side of the free trade coin is the maintenance of freely floating exchange rates. Indeed, the two must proceed together.

To understand the advantages of flexible exchange rates, we need to see how they work and how pegged rates cause trading difficulties. Take two countries, the United States and Great Britain, for instance. Consider also a particular bundle of representative goods. In Britain, this bundle of goods can presently be purchased for £50, and in the United States an identical bundle costs $100. Accordingly, we can say that £50 buys $100 worth of goods, and vice versa. Thus we can conclude that in terms of a free or floating exchange, £50 = $100, or £1 = $2, or $1 = £0.5. Now consider that inflationary pressures develop in the United States, causing the dollar price of our bundle of goods to rise to $200. If the exchange rates are still floating freely, the new exchange rate will be £1 = $4. Inflation has reduced, both at home and overseas, the buying power of the dollar, which is exactly the effect we would expect of inflation. However, if the United States tried to maintain the old $2 = £1 rate, the official exchange value of dollars to pounds would be overvalued. The price of American goods in Britain would be artificially high. Rather than getting an equivalent bundle of goods for £50, Britons would get only half a bundle for their money if they bought American goods. Meanwhile, in the United States, British goods would be relatively cheaper than American goods. It would take only $2 to buy goods denominated at £1 rather than the $4 that would be required if we had a freely floating exchange rate reflecting the

---

*Milton Friedman, *Capitalism and Freedom* (Chicago: University of Chicago Press, 1962), 74.

actual 4 : 1 dollars-to-pounds ratio. It becomes immediately obvious that pegged rates that are either above or below the real purchasing power parity (based on our identical bundles of goods) make it impossible for stability to exist in international markets. Nations with currencies that are overvalued relative to those of other nations will actually encourage a worsening balance of trade as import prices are held down and export prices are held up. And so it was for the United States during the mid- and late 1980s as certain domestic economic policies tended to produce a strong and expensive dollar. Meanwhile—and this is a strategy not lost on most nations—undervaluation of a nation's currency tends to encourage exports and discourage imports.

From the end of World War II until the 1970s, the world used a fixed exchange-rate system. Under what was known as the Bretton Woods arrangements, the U.S. dollar replaced gold, the traditional international unit of account, as the instrument for measuring and making international payments.*

To oversee these international transactions, the International Monetary Fund (IMF) was created. The pound, the French franc, the German mark, the yen, and all other currencies were valued by the IMF against the dollar. (The franc and mark have since been replaced by the euro, the common currency of most member countries in the European Union.) Thus when a nation experienced domestic inflation that raised the price of its goods relative to those of other nations, it was obliged, for international money exchange purposes, to devalue its currency in relation to the dollar. If, for instance, the British experienced an inflation that doubled the price (in pounds) of British goods, the only way to bring the inflated British currency into proper balance with unchanged dollars (and other currencies) would be to devalue the pound by one-half. Each dollar would now buy twice as many pounds and twice as much British goods as was possible before the revaluing. If the British did not devalue their currency, trading nations would shun either their products or their currency, and the domestic crisis would be worsened. To forestall short-term shortages of funds for international payments and to avoid the anarchy of devaluation wars as

---

*Meeting at Bretton Woods, New Hampshire, toward the end of World War II, the Allied powers agreed to an "adjustable-peg" system. While exchange rates for individual currencies were pegged to the dollar, their value in dollar terms could be changed to reflect overvaluation or undervaluation.

each nation sought to gain a brief currency advantage over others, the trading nations maintained reserve balances with the IMF or could borrow from the fund. Meanwhile, the fund pegged currencies to the dollar, adjusting values from time to time as economic conditions within nations changed. So long as the dollar was sound, the problems of inflation or unemployment could be limited to the affected country. The system's weakness, however, was what everyone had thought to be its strength—the dollar.

During the 1950s and 1960s, the previously weakened European and Japanese economies strengthened precisely as the American economy slowed. For the United States, the pegged exchange rate meant maintaining an overvalued dollar. The result was a growing balance-of-payments deficit during the 1970s as overpriced American goods sold poorly in foreign markets while cheaper foreign goods flooded the United States. Under a pegged system, the only options to eliminate the balance-of-payment deficits were to (1) pay out gold to creditors (so long as we were on an international gold standard); (2) engineer a domestic recession to lower import demand and reduce the prices of exported goods (thus increasing export volume); (3) establish import controls; or (4) resort to an official devaluation of the nation's currency. For a variety of reasons, each of these options has such serious political or economic effects that the balance-of-payments deficit could not be eliminated. As a result, the worsening U.S. payments situation through the early 1970s was directly traceable to the Bretton Woods–IMF system of fixed exchange rates.

Furthermore, the flow of dollars into European markets and the effects of U.S. government efforts to impose exchange controls created extensive internal currency problems for all nations. The initial flood of U.S. dollars and the attempt to maintain the value of these dollars forced an unwanted inflation on many European nations as their central banks purchased all dollars presented to them. With foreigners now holding more dollars than they wanted—dollars that were believed overvalued by the old Bretton Woods pegging system—the United States was forced to take action. On August 15, 1971, President Nixon suspended the dollar's convertibility to gold. At the time, foreign dollar holdings were four times greater than the value of the U.S. gold stock, the price of which was then officially stated as $35 per ounce. Gold henceforth became a speculative commodity having no official role in international payments. It climbed to over $900 per ounce in 1980 before tumbling back to between $300 and $400 by the mid-1980s.

After the United States ceased gold conversion, there were periodic efforts to revalue the dollar under the old pegging system. However, even after several devaluations of the dollar, it became obvious that the era of fixed exchange rates was over. Each nation now let its currency "float" to whatever value the market established, and neither gold nor U.S. dollars served as the international currency. Instead, the IMF kept national payment accounts in order through a kind of "paper gold" (SDRs, special drawing rights) that were made available to members on a quote system. The value of the SDRs was based on an average of five leading nations' currencies.*

The drift toward floating exchange rates was a desirable development. If practiced honestly and without the slightest tinkering by governments, floating rates allow nations to trade goods based on their real values as opposed to the manipulated values under pegged rates.

Over the long run, flexible exchange rates eliminate balance-of-payments deficits and associated problems. The market forces of supply and demand for a nation's currency create an equilibrium. Assume that two nations are trading. An excess of imports over exports in nation A will bid up the price of the currency of the exporting nation B (or lower the value of the importer's currency relative to that of the exporter). The currency of importing nation A is now devalued. However, this means that its goods are now priced lower than before, and its exports to B will rise while its imports from B will fall until equilibrium between the two trading nations is reached.

From the point of view of most Conservatives, the abandonment of pegged exchange rates and the international gold standard has freed international trade from some of the tyrannies of the past. In theory at least, floating exchange rates can reflect increasingly the real value of a nation's currency against that of other nations. However, this latter situation has not yet been attained. The present managed float system still allows member nations great latitude in determining their own exchange rates and in taking individual actions to bolster their currency. Until exchange rates are freely flexible and until free trade prin-

---

*SDR valuation is now based on the euro, Japanese yen, pound sterling, and the U.S. dollar.

ciples are generally accepted, international trade and currency crises will continue.*

## International Crisis as Failure of Domestic Policies

The creation of free trade and freely floating rates, desirable as they are, will not protect a nation that is hell-bent to cut its own throat. The recent exchange rate and trading difficulties of the United States are the direct result of foolish domestic policies. In particular, the expansionary fiscal and monetary policies of the 1970s triggered an inflationary situation that, to our benefit, did drive the price of the dollar downward, but also caused soaring product prices (relative to the rest of the world) that overwhelmed any exchange rate gains. The net result was a decrease in U.S. exports and a rise in U.S. imports. Moreover, in an effort to protect themselves from "importing" the American inflation, a number of our trading partners undertook contractionary economic policies at home. Correspondingly, as the German, Japanese, and other economies cooled down, the ability of the United States to sell in these nations was further reduced.

To prove the point once again that domestic policies are interconnected with international economic conditions, consider what the costs were in the 1980s as America came to grips with the chronic inflation that had gnawed deep into the economy through the 1970s. To halt the inflationary pressures, the Federal Reserve had been required to use a tight-money, high-interest-rate policy. However, the high American interest rates (and the relative stability of the United States as a place for investment) were attractive to foreign investors, who now sought dollars to buy high-yield U.S. securities. Their actions bid up the price of the dollar, and with its rise, the price of American goods rose relative to foreign goods. Soon an unfavorable trade balance changed sharply for the worse. It also produced a growing pressure to return to the bad old days of protective tariffs and pegged exchange rates. The old lie—that

---

*The argument on behalf of floating exchange rates presented here is the "traditional" Conservative view. It should be noted, however, that some Conservatives, led recently by Robert Mundell, favor a return to the gold standard. This view argues that tying the domestic and international monetary arrangements to a fixed gold standard will create greater stability, making it impossible for nations to export their domestic inflationary policies and to "manipulate" exchange rates to their own advantage.

trade balances and currency values can be manipulated as desired through public policy efforts—surfaced again.

Yet America's recent trade problems were not, at bottom, the result of flexible exchange rates and free trade, which were singled out as the culprits by some Liberals. The problems began with domestic inflation, and the problems would only ease by ending inflation—even though the means for fighting inflation might have to be even worse short-term trade deficits. At any rate, the lesson to be learned here is that we cannot separate the domestic economy, either in its general conditions or in the policies undertaken to correct these conditions, from the international economy. To avoid the spillover of domestic policy effects into world markets and back again into the domestic economy, the only certain strategy is to let domestic trends work themselves out naturally and to undertake a minimum domestic policy strategy because supposed public policy "cures" for macroeconomic problems only make the situation worse.

### The Trend Toward Freer Trade

Fortunately, historical experience and a better understanding of the merits of free trade have moved trade liberalization to the front of both domestic and international agendas. The development of a North American free trade zone among the countries of Canada, Mexico, and the United States via NAFTA; the FTAA's progress in creating a free trade area throughout much of the Western Hemisphere; expansion of the European Union; the U.S.-Australia Free Trade Agreement; increased participation in the free trade agreements of the Association of Southeast Asia Nations (ASEAN); and the expanded role of the World Trade Organization in managing trade disputes, advancing freer trade, and promoting economic integration is refreshing. It is difficult to determine if this evolution truly represents a change in philosophy among policy makers who in the past have been beholden to Liberal or even Radical views about trade or if they have been overwhelmed by the inevitable failure of public policies designed to obstruct trade.

The Conservative position is absolutely clear with respect to efforts to set up trade barriers to protect American markets and to manipulate currency values to expand exports: All such interference with the market mechanism, despite the short-term painful effects of an unfavorable balance of trade, must be opposed if we are ever to obtain the benefits of free international trade. The negative numbers for the three major gauges of trade balances shown in Figure 14.2 are bound to be cited by Liberals and Radicals as cause for alarm and used as justification for a return to increased meddling with international trade and finance. In fact, recent trade deficits reflect the enviable strength of the U.S. economy. The flexibility of an open, market-based economy has allowed the country to assert its advantages in the production and export of capital goods, technology, and services. America should eschew protectionism and interventionism in favor of focusing on an agenda that can result in improved trade balances such as increasing the domestic saving rate (Issue 7) and abiding by more disciplined monetary and fiscal policies (Issue 9).

## THE LIBERAL ARGUMENT

Typically, Conservatives remain detached from reality and hopelessly utopian in their advocacy of free trade: the perfect solution for an imperfect world. Although there are, theoretically, greater long-run benefits to be obtained under free trade than under protectionism, Conservatives are calling for America to act as a free trader in a very unfree international economic environment. Playing by the rules while most of the rest of the world cheats has already cost us dearly.

### A Background to the Trade Crisis of the 1980s

According to the Conservative scenario, free trade and floating exchange rates go hand in hand to produce harmony and equilibrium in international trade and finance. Quite naturally, they oppose any efforts at protection or manipulation of exchange rates. However, they do not seem to make any connection between their own domestic economic policies and the nation's recent trade deficits, preferring to blame it all on past Liberal economic policy.

In point of fact, the incredible decline of American exports and the even more incredible flood of imports after 1980 were the direct result of Conservative domestic policies that had adverse international effects for the United States *precisely because* we had followed a free trade, floating-exchange-rate path. The scenario went like this: The incorrect Conservative view that the inflationary pressures of the late 1970s were demand-based (too much spending by government, business, and consumers) led to the adoption of a tight money policy by the Federal Re-

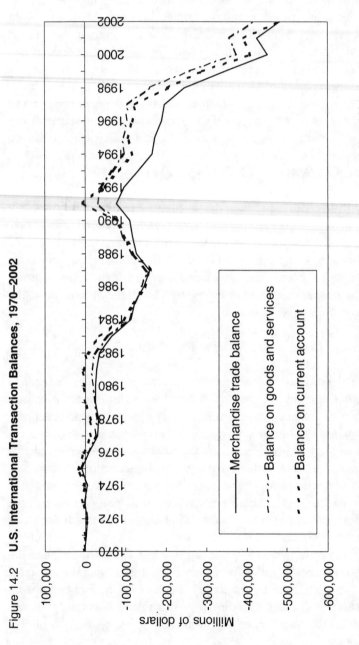

Figure 14.2  **U.S. International Transaction Balances, 1970–2002**

Merchandise trade balance

Balance on goods and services

Balance on current account

*Source:* Data from *Economic Report of the President* (Washington, DC: Government Printing Office, 2004).

serve System. Consistent with our macroeconomic understandings, this led to rising real interest rates and eventually to a domestic recession. On the surface, the recession might have been expected to have a stimulating effect on exports as prices of domestic goods steadied or even fell a bit. However, this did not happen. Instead, in an economic world where exchange rates had become more flexible (after the collapse of the old pegging system), high interest rates in the United States suddenly became attractive to foreign investors. The demand for dollars (to invest in the United States) grew, and as demand grew, the price of the dollar rose. With the dollar now strengthening relative to other currencies, dollar-denominated goods became more expensive in foreign markets while goods denominated in yen, marks, francs, and other currencies became cheaper in the United States. The effect was to depress U.S. exports and invite an explosive increase in imports. The recession in the domestic economy, stemming as it did from the original tight money policy, was in fact worsened as many key industries were closed out of foreign markets precisely as they were being battered at home by imports.

It suddenly became apparent that domestic economic policies could have unintended international effects in a world of floating exchange rates and free trade. Of course, free traders will argue at this point that sooner or later the overvalued dollar will fall in value as exchange rates adjust. All this supposes, naturally, that exchange rates are in actual fact freely floating, and it presumes that an overvalued dollar will not continue to be propped up by a high-interest-rate money policy that is in place to fight domestic inflation.

While it is easy for economic theorists of any political preference to dismiss protectionism as "beggar thy neighbor" economic policy, the recent protectionist sentiment, from a Liberal point of view, is perfectly explainable and not entirely without justification. The lesson from the trade problems of the 1980s is that pursuit of free trade in a world where some nations practice free trade and maintenance of floating exchange rates while others manage their rates can lead to unacceptable economic costs. These costs materialize in the destruction of certain domestic industries and greatly increased American unemployment. Trade liberalization has encouraged U.S. firms to outsource operations and jobs to less-developed countries with fewer regulatory restraints and lower wages. In short, for all its theoretical attractiveness, free trade and floating exchange rates can, under certain conditions, deliver the opposite of what they promise.

## *The Case for Modified Protectionism*

As Figure 14.3 shows, U.S. tariffs have fallen steadily since World War II and stand at historical lows. Duties collected amount to less than 5 percent of the value of imports. In the 1930s, duties stood at about 60 percent. Moreover, since the Kennedy years the U.S. government has conducted serious trade negotiations to reduce restrictive tariffs and import quotas throughout the trading world.

But reduction of trade restraints must be a two-way street. Reductions of restrictions on U.S. goods should be expected from nations desiring or obtaining benefits from the United States. Otherwise, the United States throws its doors open to foreign goods while its goods are effectively excluded from foreign ports. Nor are tariffs and quotas the only devices nations use for creating trade advantages. The Japanese, for instance, have provided extensive governmental subsidies for their manufacturers, thus creating artificially low prices. Legitimate health and safety concerns to prevent fire blight from being spread to Japan on American apples degenerated into overly stringent regulations that effectively bar most apple imports from the United States despite the fact that the apples are blight-free. Their notorious dumping of such under priced commodities as TVs, cameras, specialty steel items, and the like has provoked the United States to take restrictive trade actions.

The reality of contemporary trade arrangements is one in which the United States must frequently exert muscle through trade restrictions to respond to unfair tactics by other nations. As of February 2004, the U.S. International Trade Commission reported 358 antidumping and countervailing duty orders against 51 countries in retaliation for unfair trade practices. Some of these sanctions were imposed more than two decades ago and have been continued because the offending countries refuse to reform their trade practices.

When these real-world obstacles to trade are considered, it is apparent that the road to free trade is much bumpier than Conservatives admit. Apart from the difficulty of inducing all trading nations to accept the principles of free trade (which would be a minimum requirement even under Conservative logic), the serious domestic problems that might follow the hurried or reckless adoption of free trade must be considered.

First, the failure to employ protective tariffs might deal a deathblow to many American industries. Among these would be firms that are critical to the country's ability to defend itself militarily or to its continued eco-

Figure 14.3 **Major U.S. Tariff Laws, Trade Agreements, and Level of Effective Tariffs**

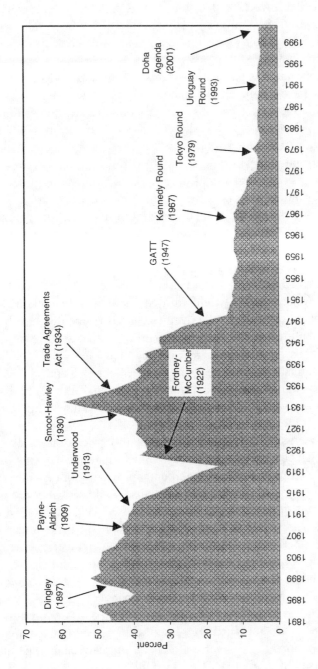

*Source:* Data from U.S. International Trade Commission.

nomic well-being if world trade is interrupted in the future. In brief, the military and political significance of self-sufficiency in certain goods and raw materials would outweigh the argument of greater efficiency resulting from free trade.

Second, concentrating production efforts only in industrial areas where a nation may have a comparative trade advantage would tend to create an undiversified and possibly unstable economy. As the domestic production mix became more specialized and concentrated, it would become more vulnerable (not stronger, as Conservatives argue) when there was any interruption in world markets. The serious impact that overseas shortages of critical goods might have domestically has been demonstrated amply by the crises caused by the OPEC energy cartel. Similarly, the United States might experience interruptions in the purchase of its specialized goods when buyers disappear. The result would be massive layoffs and recession at home.

Third, and closely associated with the first two points, free trade might have the effect of closing off the development of new (infant) industries. Established overseas firms would enjoy marketing and capital advantages that could not be overcome. Limited, industry-focused tariff protection would allow new industries to emerge and mature. The strategy of industry-focused protection can also be applied to provide "breathing room" for established industries that have been buffeted and smothered by fierce, and often unfair, competition from abroad. The steel tariffs of 2002 were conceived with the intent of providing breathing room for the steel industry to restructure and revitalize itself.

Fourth, American firms might be completely priced out of certain markets by cheaper foreign labor or by foreign dumping, causing massive domestic economic upheaval and unemployment. In the short run, free trade, without any quotas or restrictions, would probably produce massive unemployment in basic industries such as steel and autos, which would make our current unemployment problems in these industries look inconsequential. Even if, in the long run, new industries emerged to fill the employment gap, billions would be spent on unemployment insurance, welfare, and job retraining. Whole areas of the nation would be disrupted as our nation's production mix changed. Such costs would more than offset the efficiency advantages proposed by Conservatives.

Fifth, Liberals are not strictly obsessed with protecting the domestic economy from potentially adverse effects of international competition. The Generalized System of Preferences (GSP) allows developing countries duty-free sales to America for certain goods. This is less expensive than gifts of foreign aid as a way to help poor countries and certainly preferable to a noninterventionist stance of survival of the fittest, which would not allow such assistance.

## The Need for Rules and Enforcement

Managing international exchange is nothing new and is practically unavoidable. Increasing *globalization* or *internationalization* of world markets has not been automatically accompanied by implicit rules of free exchange that all trading nations abide by and understand. Trade policy has been increasingly engineered by governments, especially since the inception of the General Agreement on Tariffs and Trade (GATT) in 1947 and its subsequent passage into the World Trade Organization. GATT began with 23 signatory nations and expanded to 147 countries under WTO, accounting for more than 90 percent of world trade. WTO supplies a mechanism by which countries can resolve trade disputes. America has its own antidumping statutes and trade laws that can be invoked in response to specific unfair tactics. The phasing in of free trade to allow time to discern the effect upon particular industries and allow time for adjustments among the signatory nations indicates that NAFTA, FTAA, the U.S.-Australia Free Trade Agreement, and other "free trade agreements" are inclined more toward managed trade than free trade.

Conservatives are correct in asserting that pegging international exchange rates by tying them to gold or the U.S. dollar is misguided. However, the period following the demise of the Bretton Woods system is not characterized by freely floating exchange rates. Central banks of the world and national government, principally of the G-10 countries,* are actively engaged in *managed float*. That is, they have adopted a policy of intervention in foreign exchange markets to maintain orderly market conditions. This vague wording is generally understood to mean offsetting disruptive, short-term variations in exchange rates.

---

*G-10 or "Group of Ten" countries included at the time the United States, United Kingdom, France, Germany, Japan, Belgium, Canada, Italy, Netherlands, Sweden, and Switzerland. The G-10 actually numbered eleven with the addition of Switzerland in 1984. A new forum called the G-20, was composed of big trading nations' finance ministers and central bank governors, and was formed in 1999.

In the 1970s, the United States worked in concert with foreign central banks to reverse the dollar's depreciation, which had been caused by oil crises, inflation, and trade deficits. Subsequently, recession and high interest rates sent the dollar soaring on foreign exchange markets. The Reagan administration was predictably noninterventionist in its first term. However, by the second term of the Reagan presidency the sustained and rapid rise in the dollar was constricting exports and enlarging the trade deficit. Collective action on the part of the major industrialized countries ensued in 1985 in a conscious effort to drive down the value of the dollar and marked the resumption of intervention.

The bottom line is that free trade and freely floating exchange rates are not really the exclusive coordinating mechanism in the world of international trade. For example, a country may attempt to drive down the value of its currency in an effort to offset a trade deficit, which may have been caused by the lowering of trade barriers. Unless the economic nationalism of states can be brought under control through international agreements that are vigorously enforced, the benefits of free trade will always elude those nations that maintain floating exchange rates and open markets.

## Putting the International Economy in Perspective

Regardless of what happens in the development and enforcement of international "rules of the game," the United States cannot withdraw from the world economy. Probably the most significant problem posed by free trade and floating exchange rates is that the domestic economy is subordinated in international economic affairs. Policies aimed at correcting balance-of-payments and exchange rate problems may actually worsen domestic problems. For instance, unemployment in the United States would have to grow and an extended domestic recession would be required as the price of ending our international payments deficit.

Free traders may resolve this conflict between needed expansionary policies at home and the required contractionary actions to put international payments in balance by glibly saying, "We must bite the bullet." Matters are not that simple. Indeed, the contraction might be so unbearable as to trigger extensive political reactions in the United States that would destroy not only our political institutions but also the market economy so beloved by Conservatives.

The necessity for strong and enforced trading and exchange rules has never been greater. The American economy is no longer dominant, nor is it insulated from the rest of the world. With the continuing integration of the European economies, the United States will no longer be the largest of the world economies. Requiring that the rest of the world play by the rules of the trading game (and penalizing those who do not) is, after all, only fair. However, given the degree of cheating in the past, as well as our diminished stature in the world economy, the United States may have to act unilaterally to protect itself.

The real measure of a nation's strength in international affairs is the strength of its domestic economy. Accordingly, the United States may have to undertake limited protectionism and exchange rate intervention to shield itself. Such actions, of course, must be complemented by domestic microeconomic and macroeconomic policies to stimulate investment and productivity growth; otherwise, the Conservative scenario of a nation decaying behind its own protectionist walls is a distinct possibility.

## THE RADICAL ARGUMENT

Although the Conservative and Liberal scenarios of international trade and exchange problems seem to be quite different, a closer examination indicates that they are similar. Both arguments accept as a matter of fact or "right" the continued dominance of the United States in world trade. The remedies that they suggest for current problems, whether the free trade approach of the Conservatives or the administrative emphasis of the Liberals, are intended primarily to restore and strengthen the American position. Moreover, their underestimation of the significance of international trade and finance and of the degree of crisis now existing in these areas is a dangerous error of judgment.

Capitalist nations do not trade and expand their international influence merely to improve efficiency or to benefit mutually from each nation's exploitation of its comparative advantage. Profit making, pure and simple, is the engine that drives overseas trade and investment. Indeed, the overseas search for markets, cheap resources, and profitable investment is absolutely essential for any capitalist system's continued expansion. Rather than trade and international economic affairs being mere aspects of capitalism, as Conservatives and Liberals suggest, they are the central features of modern production-for-profit economies. The international trade and exchange crisis is thus the result of the insatiable drive of individual capitalist nations to exploit the rest of the world for their own gain.

## The Rise of the American Empire

Americans tend to think of themselves as reluctant internationalists drawn into world affairs only to save the rest of the world from itself. However, the facts support quite a different explanation. By the turn of the twentieth century, American capitalism had exhausted its domestic markets. The long decade of depression in the 1890s suggested to many the need for overseas expansion either to obtain markets for surplus goods or to gain access to cheap raw materials and foreign labor. The United States steadily enlarged its world trade between the 1890s and the 1960s, exporting ever-larger amounts of expensive manufactured goods and importing greater quantities of cheap raw materials. At the same time, to secure markets and assume control over raw materials, Americans exported vast amounts of capital (see Table 14.1).

The old trading powers of Europe exhausted themselves in two world wars—wars that had been fundamentally economic wars for trade supremacy—while the United States continued to expand its overseas sales, purchases, and investment. By the 1960s, the United States, in terms of comparative development, had reached the peak of its international economic power. The rise to this height and the later fall are important and instructive enough to examine in some detail.

In 1950, U.S. gross domestic output was about equal to that of the rest of the world combined. Great Britain's output was only 13 percent of America's, while those of France, West Germany, and Japan were 10, 8, and 4 percent, respectively. During World War II, the United States, as principal supplier of arms, had accumulated almost the entire world's gold stock, as well as many other overseas assets. Our exports accounted for about one-third of all the world's exports and more than one quarter of all manufactured exports.

Meanwhile, as a result of Marshall Plan aid and other dollar grants to noncommunist European economies, other capitalist nations fell into a client relationship with the United States. Dependent economically on aid and trade programs and militarily (in the cold war years) on America's armed forces and mutual defense treaties (such as NATO) that were dominated by the United States, the older capitalist nations became part of the American economic sphere. At the same time, the United States expanded

Table 14.1

**Value of U.S. Foreign Investment, Selected Years, 1880–2001** (in billions of dollars)

| Year | Direct investment abroad |
|------|--------------------------|
| 1880 | 1.6 |
| 1890 | 2.9 |
| 1900 | 2.5 |
| 1914 | 3.5 |
| 1920 | 7.0 |
| 1930 | 17.2 |
| 1940 | 12.2 |
| 1950 | 19.0 |
| 1960 | 40.2 |
| 1970 | 75.5 |
| 1980 | 215.4 |
| 1990 | 620.0 |
| 2001 | 1,598.1 |

*Source:* U.S. Bureau of the Census, *Historical Statistics of the United States* (Washington, DC: Government Printing Office), *Economic Report of the President* (Washington, DC: Government Printing Office, 2001), and *Economic Report of the President* (Washington, DC: Government Printing Office, 2004).

its penetration into the Third World, establishing a new, informal colonial system. Within this imperial system, the resource-rich remnants of the former European colonial empire in Africa and Asia joined Latin America as part of the U.S. sphere of influence. Through development aid and especially through supporting friendly but repressive regimes with military assistance, the United States established a neocolonial system without resorting to the old tactic of territorial seizure.

By the late 1950s, the United States enjoyed virtually unchallenged economic hegemony over the noncommunist world, comprising the Western European and Japanese economies and much of the Third World. Supposedly international agencies such as the International Monetary Fund, the World Bank, and the United Nations became arms of American foreign economic and political policy. Under such conditions, it is small wonder that the American dollar became the international medium of exchange and that the international financial situation of the United States appeared so secure. We could virtually dictate exchange rates, and we could hide any balance-of-payments problem by compelling foreign governments to accept and hold dollars rather than demand gold. The ultimate fall from this pinnacle of international power was to be a terrifying experience for Americans.

## The Collapse of the Empire

The fall from power was speeded by events overseas and at home. First, the ·Soviet challenge failed to disappear. The Soviet economy rose swiftly from the ruins of World War II. Despite the Korean War and dozens of other cold war confrontations, the power of cold war ideology in holding the American–Western European alliance together waned as Europeans reevaluated their position within the American empire. This, as much as anything, directed Europe to a more middle-ground approach.

Second, the European economies made their own rapid recoveries in the 1960s. By 1972, the combined gross domestic output of Western Europe and Japan exceeded that of the United States. Accordingly, the U.S. share of world markets declined drastically. Between 1950 and 1972, our share of passenger vehicle production fell from 82 to 29 percent; similarly, the share of steel production fell from 55 to 20 percent and that of energy production from 50 to 33 percent. At the same time, other industrial nations began to claim larger shares of the American market. Finished manufactured imports increased almost 300 percent between 1965 and 1970, while U.S. exports of manufactured goods grew by only 80 percent in the same period.

Third, U.S. domination of the Third World declined. Wars of national liberation and the emergence of new regimes committed to an independent political course eroded American influence. The failure of our effort in Vietnam to stem the tide of Third World nationalism only accelerated the decline of the empire. By 1973, the United States was helpless in dealing with the OPEC oil embargo. In 1979, it could only stand aside quietly as Iran, perhaps one of the most crucial parts of our earlier neocolonial system, threw out its pro-American government.

Fourth, the emergence of American multinational corporations further weakened the United States. The flight of U.S. capital overseas to the expanding economies in Europe and the Third World accelerated the decline of the U.S. balance-of-payments position. The multinationals' flight left investment and employment gaps at home, with which the nation was ill prepared to deal. By 1971, the United States registered the first trade imbalance in the century, as imports exceeded exports.

## *Global Competition and the Race to the Bottom*

The 1990s ushered in a new era of heightened capitalist competition, where the needs and demands of giant multinational corporations are displacing the sovereignty of individual nations. Unelected bureaucrats at such supranational capitalist institutions as the World Bank, the International Monetary Fund, and the World Trade Organization are dictating the rules of world trade while preventing governments from blocking or restricting capital mobility. Corporations and their propagandists have mounted a ferocious campaign against those who challenge or suggest any alternative other than a model of so-called "export-led" growth. By creating an unassailable myth of the benefits of free trade, the neoliberal mantra of "no alternative to the market" has repressed any debate over the winners and losers in the new capitalist world order.

While global capitalism may be presented as the best of all possible worlds, in reality it is a ruthless, anarchic system that destroys everything in its relentless search for profits. In addition, it is inherently self-limiting both because of its wasteful and irrational use of natural, productive, and human resources and because world trade cannot continue to grow much faster than world income. The recent collapse of several Asian economies, combined with the sluggishness in the economies of Europe and Japan, underscores just how vulnerable the entire system is to its own internally generated limits. An obvious question that is never asked by Conservative and Liberal economists is: If all nations are to become rich by exporting to their competitors, who is importing and what is the source of their income? The fact is they have no answer because capitalism is incapable of sustaining balanced and sustainable growth for the benefit of the vast majority of people living under its domination.

Conservative and Liberal economists focus on the trade balance of particular countries, not on international firms, and therefore continue to fail to grasp the growing power of transnational corporations over individual nations. The World Bank estimates that about one-third of total world trade consists of transfers *within* the 350 largest multinational corporations. Intracompany trade, say between Ford plants in America and Mexico, often consists of sending parts or raw materials to one country and finished products back to the other. Such trade is also largely immune from import taxes and jobs are effectively outsourced to other countries. Nevertheless, free trade agreements such as NAFTA and the FTAA are designed to allow greater freedom for transnational capital to move across borders and thus take advantage of lower labor costs.

What about the supposed improvements in U.S. living standards due to the lowering of domestic trade barriers? While it is true that an infusion of foreign capital often entails the acquisition of state-of-the-art production facilities, rarely do the benefits trickle down to the average worker who will use the new machines and equipment. In fact, manufacturing plants in Mexico that employ the most advanced technologies have achieved quality and productivity standards that meet or exceed those in the United States. At this point, traditional economic theory would predict that real manufacturing wages would *have* to increase to U.S. levels following such a notable increase in Mexican labor productivity. Yet workers in Mexico earn much, much less on an hourly basis compared to American workers. Even allowing for generous assumptions about labor market reforms—including minimum wage, health, and safety standards—wages and working conditions remain much lower in Mexico than in the United States. In fact, while Mexico's manufacturing productivity rose by about 40 percent from 1980 to 1992, wages and benefits for manufacturing workers were only about two-thirds of their 1980 levels.

Neither increased job training nor a more efficient structure of production will guarantee a higher standard of living for American workers. This is because the rapid diffusion of technology and heightened competition in both labor and financial markets are swiftly destroying economic advantages that traditionally accrued to industrialized economies for relatively long periods of time. For example, computer programming and design were once thought to be the strict purview of highly trained "knowledge workers" living in the United States. Moreover, a range of high-tech support activities—especially data entry, coding, and computer support services—were also thought to be impervious to competition from workers in low-wage countries. But the widespread use of telecommunications satellites has enabled domestic corporations to employ Third World technical and professional workers at a fraction of the cost of their American counterparts. Today, a U.S. insurance company can hire a computer programmer in India and data entry clerks in Ireland—at one-half to one-third of American wages—to perform all data-processing tasks. Similarly, several high-technology companies such as Texas Instruments are employing mathematicians and other scientists in Russia to write computer software. Clearly, the relatively low value of the ruble and the rupee against the dollar make such arrangements highly profitable.

From a Radical perspective, the problem has been predictable. The internationalization of capital is only a further step in capitalism's irrational development. The strength of the American overseas economic operations of the 1950s and 1960s was the result of its power to exploit the so-called free world. This country's gains were others' losses. What Americans saw as a normal situation was an exceptional one. As the United States' capacity to exploit was successfully challenged by developing socialist countries and by increasing Third World independence and then by other capitalist economies, its premier position in world trade and finance has declined. As overseas growth ends, domestic contraction sets in. The specter of another worldwide capitalist depression looms larger. The crisis is, of course, a production crisis—too many goods and too few buyers. The newly industrialized nations of Southeast Asia have recently experienced such a crisis and have watched gains in living standards fizzle out. Even Japan, the once vaunted industrial powerhouse, faced a collapse of its financial system, despite an overabundance of savings and investment capital and nearly negligible interest rates. Economic growth in Japan has ranged from negligible to nonexistent for more than a decade.

### What Is to Be Done?

The globalization of capitalism poses a vexing problem for mainstream economic theory. On one hand, the "triumph" of free markets over centrally planned socialist economies suggests that the private accumulation of capital is a fundamental precondition of political freedom. Nonetheless, it is also clear that placeless transnational corporations are undermining the economic sovereignty of capitalist democracies. Just as the classical English economist David Ricardo feared in 1817, global competition no longer allows "men of property to be satisfied with a low rate of profits in their own country." Even many Conservatives who extol the virtues of the capitalist work ethic (over sloth-promoting social welfare programs) harshly denounce free trade advocates and managed trade technocrats for their unpatriotic policies. Increasingly insecure about their futures, voters are courted by demagogic economic nationalists who want to close the borders to foreign capital and labor.

Is closing the borders to international trade the only viable solution? Not likely. Given the mobility of multinational corporations to move productive resources around the globe, actions by individual governments to control the movement of private capital are not expected to have much effect. Moreover, the growing role of international money managers and currency traders to rapidly mobilize and deploy huge amounts of financial capital is also undermining the power of central banks to control currency and monetary flows. Using sophisticated computer and communications technologies, these managers can instantaneously enter and exit stock and bond markets virtually anywhere in the world. The 1998 hedge fund crises are but one small example of the downside of bringing together technology and capital mobility for private gain.

The fundamental incompatibility between capital mobility and national sovereignty poses a profound, if not intractable, problem for world capitalism. The breakdown of international economic agreements, such as the Bretton Woods accords to control exchange rates, clearly suggests that the self-regulation of fundamentally irrational currency markets is not possible. Free-floating exchange rates can only result in short-term gains for currency traders and economic dislocation and crisis for the vast majority of people throughout the world. Thus it is incumbent on working people throughout the world not only to organize domestically, but also to reach out to their fellow workers outside their borders. Unions need to mobilize their political and economic resources with their counterparts all over the world to break the growing power of multinational financial capital. Unless international corporations are forced to equalize working conditions and wage-and-benefit standards for *all* workers, the relentless search for profits will compel them to drive down labor costs to levels existing in the poorest countries. Furthermore, international governmental organizations cannot be relied upon, or trusted, to act in the interests of workers; time and again organizations such as the WTO and IMF have shown themselves to be completely beholden to capitalists' interests, especially regarding the exercise of labor rights and environmental regulations. Without direct transnational solidarity between working people, standing together to challenge and overthrow the capitalist grip on the world economy, there is little hope. The new international economic order can only result in continued deterioration in the standard of living and overall quality of life for the vast majority of people living on the planet.

# Part IV

# Conclusion

# The Market Versus Planning and Controls
## Which Strategy Works Better?

Whenever the legislature attempts to regulate the differences between the masters and their workmen, its counsellors are always the masters.

*—Adam Smith, 1776*

The world is not so governed from above that private and social interests coincide. It is not so managed here below that in practice they coincide. It is not a correct deduction from the Principles of Economics that enlightened self-interest always operates in the public interest.

*—John Maynard Keynes, 1926*

It used to seem to me that the drift of all Western countries was toward something like socialism. But now, when I reflect on what is happening . . . it is not so clear. There is a sense of return to the market, because the task of planning in a modern economy is so complex.

*—Robert Heilbroner, 1986*

Off-the-shelf utopias may be useful thought experiments, but they're of limited political use, except maybe as long-term inspiration. A future society has to emerge out of this one, on the basis of experimentation and struggle.

*—Doug Henwood, 1997*

## The Problem

Throughout our examination of contemporary economic issues, there has been a consistent tension among the Conservative defense of a free and unregulated economy, the limited regulation objectives of the Liberals, and the general assault on free markets by Radicals. At issue has been the question of exactly how free or how planned the economy should be. In our closing debate, it is appropriate to deal with this question directly: Which strategy—the free market or some degree of planning and controls—is more likely to provide desirable outcomes?

Based on recent public opinion surveys, trends in American political rhetoric and practice, and events beyond the borders of the United States, an ordinary observer might quickly conclude that planning is in full retreat. Public support for the Keynesian social-engineering efforts of the 1960s and early 1970s withered by the late 1970s. Between 1980 and 1992, first with Ronald Reagan and then with George Bush, Americans elected presidents who, at least in terms of their public posture, were emphatically promarket. Democrat Bill Clinton entered office in 1992 sporting a sort of moderate Liberal posture, briefly turned leftward, and then, after his party lost both houses of Congress in 1994, moved toward a safer middle-ground position. He was reelected in 1996 after announcing that the era of big government was over. Meanwhile, within the domestic economy, "privatization" became an important new buzzword as extended discussions began to take place about spinning off certain longtime bastions of government power to the private sector. Schools, prison systems, and certain public welfare operations were in fact privatized in some areas of the country, and by 1997 there was serious talk of privatizing the Social Security system. With George W. Bush's election in 2000, the nation's political leadership took an obvious and clearly defined Conservative posture.

Beyond the nation's borders, however, the drift toward privatization and the introduction of market economic policies were much more striking, mostly because these shifts were taking place in economies long in the camp of the central planners. The collapse of the Soviet Union first opened Eastern Europe in 1989 to extensive experimentation with and implementation of a wide variety of market-directed economic policies. By 1990–91, in its reconstitution as Russia, the principal remnant of the former Soviet Union had hired a team of American free market advocates to advise the Russian authorities on the transition from a centrally planned communist state to a more democratically open and market-driven political economy.

However, the perilous decline in Russian living standards and life expectancy has undermined popular support for further privatization schemes. Meanwhile, China introduced *enterprise zones* and some limited experimentation with market economics in some of its southeastern provinces. However, the Chinese effort, promising as it is to free market advocates, remains suspect, still laboring under the cloud of that government's brutal reaction to the Beijing student uprising in the spring of 1989 and the considerable repression that persists throughout most of the nation.

Understandably, promarket advocates are quick to draw final conclusions on the basis of these trends. Yet what can we really conclude with certainty? Seven decades ago, in a world caught up in abject economic depression, the market system stood discredited in the eyes of many. However, market-based economics has obviously enjoyed a rebirth in recent years. The failure of the communist-bloc economies may say more about the effects of poor planning and the shortcomings of imposing ideology through the planning apparatus than about planning in general. After all, economic planning in various degrees remains alive and well in many nations, not the least of which are the highly successful cases of Sweden, France, and Germany. Nor can we ignore the fact that economic planning efforts have deep roots in the American past.

Someone unfamiliar with American history might conclude that current economic trends are a ringing and final referendum against any effort to construct even a modestly planned economy. Such a judgment would likely be premature. Popular political belief in the possibilities of national economic planning has frequently surfaced in the past and has been translated into policy. From Alexander Hamilton's *Report on Manufactures* to Henry Clay's American Plan to Woodrow Wilson's progressive New Freedom to Franklin Roosevelt's New Deal, the United States has undergone a number of periods in which varieties of faith in central planning were applied to the nation's economy. Nor were these experiments with planning mere artifacts of a distant political past.

As recently as the 1980–82 recession, even with a staunch defender of free market economics in the White House, another vision of central planning attracted considerable attention, this time with startlingly strong support in the business community. "Industrial policy," as it was known, promised to revitalize American industry through, among other things, the creation of a federal investment bank that would act as a lender of last resort to businesses, especially those rustbelt industries that were particularly hard pressed. Some industrial policy advocates urged that the United States develop its own version of Japan's then highly successful MITI (Ministry of International Trade and Industry). MITI had operated since shortly after World War II, directing Japanese industrial development and targeting winners and losers in Japan's export and domestic markets through its control over research and development funds, investment sources, and imports. However, industrial policy did have its critics in the United States, and it never developed to the point of proposing specific legislation. At any rate, its attractiveness diminished as the recession of the early 1980s lifted.

While the 1980s and 1990s will doubtless be remembered for the resurgence of market economic philosophy in the United States, some observers can be excused if they wondered aloud just how deep this redirection in American economic thinking really went. After all, the scare provided by the stock market crash of Black Monday, October 19, 1987, produced all manner of pleas from members of the business and financial communities for greater controls over securities trading. Similarly, the savings and loan crisis of 1988–89 triggered calls for greater regulation of American banking. And despite the expansive arguments on behalf of deregulation in general, surveys of public attitudes indicate no diminishing of the general population's support for environmental and consumer protection activities by government. In the fall of 2001, as smoke was still rising from the World Trade Center, the public clamored for "sky marshals" and federalized airport security while the airlines and segments of the tourist industry waited for federal assistance. Meanwhile, the 2001 bursting of the stock market bubble and increasing incidents of corporate fraud among such corporate giants as Enron and WorldCom pushed mindless devotion to market capitalism off center stage.

Given the cyclical nature of economic planning's popularity and its tendency to arise precisely as the general economy's performance sags, it is entirely possible that a national debate about industrial policy, full-employment planning, or perhaps even more radical and far-reaching planning efforts simply await the next significant slump in the economy.

## Synopsis

For Conservatives, the adoption of national economic planning would mean the ending of capitalism as a social system and the imposition of an inefficient dictatorship in its place. Liberals, however, see planning as compatible with our mixed capitalist economy, since the essential elements of the system (private property and economic and political freedom) would actually be enhanced by the increased stability that planning would provide. To be sure, Liberals advocate only a limited system of planning. Radicals, meanwhile, see present planning proposals only as efforts to maintain the present inequalities and exploitativeness of the capitalist system. To them, planning is essential, but it must be done at the level of human needs, not those of the corporation.

## Anticipating the Arguments

- What is the Conservatives' fundamental philosophical disagreement with centralized planning efforts?
- How do Liberals argue that planning and a basically capitalistic economic system are compatible?
- What do Radicals mean when they call for planning "for and by people"?

## THE CONSERVATIVE ARGUMENT

At this stage in our discussion of contemporary economic problems, the Conservative response to the idea of national economic planning should be obvious—or perhaps it would be better to say *familiar.* National economic planning, in the sense that it means nonmarket, administrative decisions on output, pricing, employment, capital, and so on, is to be opposed as vigorously as possible. Planning is the final collectivist victory over freedom and individualism. When economic and political authorities, whether they be fascists or communists or even well-meaning Liberals, have the power to determine all important matters in the economy, there is little else left in life that is beyond their ability to control. The frightening scenarios in such books as *Brave New World* and *1984* are no longer merely science fiction.

The economic criticism of central planning is quickly summarized. First of all, it is profoundly inefficient in terms of theoretical economic principles. Second, empirical evidence on efforts at national economic planning (which is abundant) proves that such planning is ineffective.

### National Planning: Theoretically Inefficient

As we know, under a market system prices are the signals for economic activity. The decision to produce a particular good can be calculated both in terms of the actual production costs of labor, capital, or resources and in terms of what that particular good costs compared to other goods. As long as the market designates the prices of the factors of production (labor, capital, and resources) and the prices of final goods, we have a rational basis for allocating resources to their best possible uses. As consumers or producers, we can make choices based on a steady and reliable measure of costs and benefits. This is not to say that prices will not fluctuate. Of course they will. They are supposed to fluctuate to reflect changes in demand and supply and thus changes in the cost structure or in consumer satisfaction.

Far from being anarchy, the market *is* a planning mechanism. The market works like a system and, as Adam Smith observed in an essay on astronomy written long before his *Wealth of Nations,* "a system is like a little machine." Like a machine, a market-planned economy has regulators that keep it in balance.

Administrative planning, on the other hand, has no natural internal or external checks on its effectiveness. In an administered economy, levels of output, employment, and the mix of goods are purely matters of political determination. It is not really important whether these goals are set by commissars, Harvard economists, or the duly elected representatives of the people; they are the result of human judgments. They reflect particular individual or collective biases. Not even a computer can tell what output and employment goals are correct unless it is programmed (by humans) to respond to certain criteria (selected by humans).

Defenders of planning may point out that high levels of growth and employment have been attained in certain planned economies. There is some truth to this, but the argument misses the point. Administrative planning in the Soviet Union during World War II and immediately afterward, and in developing nations more recently, was bound to have some success because of these nations' very primitive level of economic development. When you have nothing and plan something, you can hardly lose, especially if you have authoritarian control over the labor force. It is quite another matter, however, to maintain efficient administrative planning in an advanced, complex economy. This, of course, is exactly what the Russians, the East Europeans, and, to some extent, the Chinese discovered in the 1980s, as decades of inefficient planning brought economic growth to a standstill and discredited communism as an economic and political system.

Like market economies, most administered economies use prices to direct economic activity toward predetermined goals. But it should be remembered that these prices, like the goals themselves, are administratively determined. Prices, therefore, do not reflect costs as we speak of them but are merely a rationing technique used to direct labor, capital, output, and, ultimately, social behavior toward certain imposed objectives.

Space prohibits a more detailed theoretical attack on the output and pricing behavior of planned economies, but a brief survey of some of the problems encountered by such economies may demonstrate the essence of the Conservative critique.

### National Planning: Ineffective in Practice

The Soviet Union was a striking example of what can happen when economic mechanisms are subordinated to clearly political objectives. Not unlike legislation American Liberals have sought to pass since the "glory days" of Roosevelt's New Deal, Soviet goals also included full employment, enforced price stability, and specific production targets for certain goods.

In the Soviet case, full employment meant a job for everyone. In an authoritarian collectivist society, this was not a great problem, but there is a big difference between putting people in jobs and having them perform productively. For instance, Soviet plant managers, given output goals by state planners (which were to be met *or else*), often feared a shortage of labor in the future and commonly hoarded workers. On other occasions, they had to hire labor as directed by state authorities, whether or not they needed it. In either case, the workers in question were underemployed. In terms of economic analysis, the result is obvious: inefficiency. Workers were hired without any view to their productivity. Wages were set by state planners, who had little or no knowledge of costs of production at a plant. Thus managers might reach their output targets, with workers *fully employed,* but the actual cost of goods (as reckoned by alternative uses of labor and capital) often were much higher than the planners could cover in setting a price. In real terms this meant that the whole society had to pay the actual costs by forgoing other goods. An inefficiently made tractor often "cost" many thousands of nonproduced consumer items.

The tendency to think only in output (quantitative) terms has qualitative effects too. Production rushed to meet a planner's goal may encourage defective and shoddy manufacture. Quick and flexible adaptation of production to meet changes in goals is very difficult. Planners lack the signals of prices based on supply and demand to tell them when and how to change the production mix. Plans become rigid, at both the plant and planning levels.

In the Soviet Union many of the worst features of central planning were eliminated over time. The introduction of linear programming, input-output analysis, and, finally, the computer did improve the accumulation and flow of information. The incredible lapses of mind that earlier had led to the production of motor vehicle engines and chassis but not the needed ball bearings for their wheels had generally disappeared by the 1980s. In fact, Soviet industry had achieved a measure of technological success in some cases (for example, space-related industries). However, as Gorbachev took over, the overall microeconomic decision-making process remained bogged down by the political administration of prices and wages and by mind-boggling distributional inadequacies. Even after years of sacrifice to build the industrial base of the society, ordinary Russians remained as they had always been—the balancing item in the central plan ledger. The errors of planners, even those with computers, were still to be paid for in relinquished consumer goods and in a scarcely improving standard of living. In the end, Gorbachev's timid efforts were his and the Soviet Union's undoing. Racked by strikes, internal economic crises and political disarray, and the secession of key states in the union, the USSR passed into history. Gorbachev was removed from power in December 1991, and in the fall of 1992, the Constitutional Court of Russia ruled that while communists could still enjoy local political rights and protections, the Communist Party, as a national political party, was illegal. Meanwhile, the party's financial assets and real property were placed under the control of the Russian Federation. The foremost model of the centrally planned, authoritarian state came to an end after a mere seventy-five years of existence.

### Putting Planning Within an American Context

Critics will argue that the Soviet case is irrelevant to any planning situation affecting the United States. They will maintain, of course, that American *mixed capitalism*—a combination of a dependence on the market and relevant interventions to correct the market—is much different from a fully planned, authoritarian economic system. To Conservatives, though, the threat of planning is quite real. Talk of national economic planning goes back a long way in American history, and, as is evident in day-to-day government reaction to the issues discussed in this book, the tendency toward collectivist solutions to all economic problems, although diminishing a bit lately, remains strong. History shows that, once commenced, the march toward collectivism is hard to reverse. Today we may be talking merely of obtaining additional data for national planning or making full employment a law. Tomorrow the managed-economy objectives may be more personal to all of us— determining where we live, where we work, what we buy, and so on.

Conservatives are not anarchists. Indeed, they believe in planning, and today we have a high order of acceptable planning in the economy. This planning, however, is a function of *individual choices collectively expressed in the market.* As Milton Friedman has observed:

> Fundamentally, there are only two ways of coordinating the economic activities of millions. One is central direction involving the use of coercion—the technique of the army and of the modern totalitarian state. The other is voluntary cooperation of individuals—the technique of the market place. . . . Exchange can bring about coordination without coercion.*

The present in-between, never-never land of mixed American capitalism cannot continue long. *We must go either one way or the other in the future.*

### The Dynamism of the Market

Critics of the market economy have always stressed that the fundamental weakness of a truly capitalist economic system is its recurring propensity toward varieties of instability. Such an idea is both overworked and misleading. As our earlier discussion should have pointed out, the failure of planned economic systems—such as the old Soviet Union— to meet individual needs can be vastly greater than the uncertainties a market order might create.

Yet, the critics do have a point. Market capitalism can be a disruptive system. Indeed, it should be. The driving force of a production-for-profit

---

*Milton Friedman, *Capitalism and Freedom* (Chicago: University of Chicago Press, 1962), 13.

market system is *change*—change in the goods that are produced, change in the way goods are produced and sold, and change from time to time in the distribution of the goods and the distribution of claims to goods produced. The great Austrian economist who for many years taught at Harvard University, Joseph Alois Schumpeter, called this process of capitalist uncertainty and change "creative destruction."

In the very processes of invention, innovation, and the resulting rise of new investment and production opportunities—always events encouraged in a market economic order—the society, said Schumpeter, would be swept by "gales of creative destruction." Perfectly serviceable factories and machines could be rendered obsolete instantly. Old capital investments could rapidly depreciate to scrap. Once-valued skilled labor could become redundant. Great redistributions of income and economic power could take place as new entrepreneurs with new ideas, driven by the desire to profit from their inventions and innovations, turned the old economic order upside down. But, Schumpeter maintained, the resulting destruction was worth the cost to everyone. Better goods, more efficiently produced, provided society with net positive gains even after the costs of destruction were subtracted.

Yet, as Schumpeter knew, there was always a variety of social groups who entrenched themselves against creative destruction. Labor unions, monopolistic business enterprises, bureaucracies of any kind, and their principal agent, government, all stand ready to protect the status quo by controlling, really strangling, change.

Those Liberal and Radical opponents of the market are not just advocates of a different view of economic progress and the benefits that thereby might be accorded. They are, in their hearts and minds, the enemies of progress itself.

## THE LIBERAL ARGUMENT

By this point the Liberal propensity to approach contemporary economic problems in pragmatic and nondogmatic ways should be self-evident. Equally, it should be evident that both Conservatives and Radicals, despite their vastly different ideological agendas, share a peculiar tendency: to present economic behavior and economics itself as largely deterministic and mechanistic processes. That is, economic thinking and economic undertakings are viewed not as matters of human choice or as matters of cultural habit but as the unfolding of abstract and eternal verities that, quite simply, exist independently of human beings and of human history. The Radical argument has for the time being been shoved off into history's dustbin as a result of the failure of the Soviet Union. However, and regrettably for the discipline of economics, the Conservative vision has recently come to exercise considerable influence in mainstream American economic thought. It has also been gaining greater influence outside of the United States. Liberals cannot let this development go unchallenged and the debate over the comparative virtues of *the market* versus *employing planning and controls* is a good place to reveal the analytical and practical weakness of the Conservative argument.

### The Narrow and Unrealistic Assumptions of Market-Logic Advocates

To see where Conservatives think they are going, it is necessary to understand the logic from which their argument proceeds. The argument, of course, was first set out by Adam Smith a bit over two hundred years ago and augmented and enriched a hundred years later by neoclassical economics. Together Smith and the neoclassical traditions are the foundations of modern Conservative emphasis upon market logic.

Market logic, first of all, presumes the existence of cultural and political stability as a given. Only amid this general external stability is it possible for a market to work according to a fairly consistent and predictable set of expectations. Second, market logic assumes the presence of *rational maximizing* behavior on the part of all individuals as a central element in the popular will of that society. Without social stability and without popular support for individual self-interest, the seeds of market logic cannot take root and give rise to appropriate practices of production-for-profit behavior. A third requirement specifies a *minimum government* condition to be present; in other words, a popular willingness never to tinker collectively with market outcomes. And, although the caveat hardly needs to be added, Conservatives believe the market, left essentially to its own dynamic, will be a competitive market. It should be remembered that all of these conditions are not viewed as mere accidental matters but as normal conditions that will naturally arise over time.

Right away, it becomes evident that a goodly portion of the world's population lives outside the conditions where a truly market-driven economic system could flourish. For instance, consider the problem of rational maximizing. The assertion that human beings are first and foremost acquisitive and self-interested individualists is impossible to prove and is easily disputed by real-world events. It goes without saying that much of the world is ruled by very different outlooks. The dominance of nationalistic, religious, and tribal orthodoxies that militate against individualistic and materialistic values poses an important practical problem in many nations for the development of a personal and social behavior that market-logic theorists describe as "human behavior" and as "natural." Much more troubling to market-logic adherents, however, is the fact that, even in social systems that have been receptive to individualist and materialist values and to the broad outlines of market logic, the tendency to tinker with and try to improve upon free market outcomes has been irresistible. While market-logic advocates rail against big government and its interference in the workings of the market, they offer no convincing explanation for the rise of this clearly *unnatural* tendency in the first place. After all the Conservative arguments against state interference in economic affairs have been reviewed, it still seems fairly obvious that big government with its planning and controls was not invented for the purpose of creating economic inefficiency and dependency.

Certainly in the United States, big government emerged initially as a corrective "political response" to problems viewed as inherent to free markets. It was from practical political experience, not an ignorance of economic logic, that Americans came to understand that a high order of personal freedom entailed much more than just having the right to be a rational maximizer and that individual economic freedom in no way ensured all individuals would enjoy fair and just outcomes in the marketplace.

The principal problem, then, that Conservatives have with regard to the accuracy of their market model and the relevance of its rational maximizer prescription is that none of the world's nations spells out citizens' rights and responsibilities in purely economic terms. The various freedoms and nonfreedoms that individuals have in virtually any society are derived from the prevailing political and social conventions deemed essential by that society to perpetuate and protect itself. Any particular society's taste for economic individualism and for free markets is necessarily constrained by these realities. In any case, the *political* requirements of a social order are set first and the acceptable range of economic behavior follows—a very different reality from the market-logic vision of things.

## Putting the Role of the State in the Correct Perspective

Quite apart from the logical problems of Conservatives, there is the practical matter that history offers no convincing example of a successful free market economy. To be sure, there may have been some near misses. Perhaps England of the 1830s, the United States of the 1850s, possibly even Singapore a couple of decades ago demonstrated certain free market characteristics that were reminiscent of market-logic inspiration, but, on closer look, they were pretty pale copies, clearly not meeting the required standards.

With the possible exception of theological belief associated with religious faith, probably no set of formal arguments has endured so long in the absence of any convincing real-world evidence of their practicality and validity as those laid out by the classical advocates of market logic. Even formal scientific postulates in biology, astronomy, and physics have proven to be more adaptive to real-world constraints and the force of empirical evidence. Accordingly, for a very long time now, Conservative economic thinkers have had to spend much of their time explaining why their free market vision has not come to pass. Indeed, these explanations generally occupy more space in Conservative writings than the real body of Conservative analytical doctrine.

Variously over the years, labor unions, monopolistic business enterprise, socialists, communists, intellectuals, and many other groups have been singled out as part of the general "conspiracy" against free markets. And always the device these conspirators have employed to destroy or subvert true economic freedom has been the most malignant of human institutions: government. In any case, it is a heavy burden for Conservatives to bear, constantly having to explain why the "natural" conditions of a free economic order are forever undermined by "unnatural" conspiracies and events.

The Conservative assault on government, apart from its logical irrelevance, as we have earlier noted, rests on a revealing irony. It is true, of course, that Adam Smith intended his articulation of a market economy to free economic thinking (at least English economic thinking) from the hold long imposed by the mercantilist state. But Smith was no anarchist. He continued to assign to government, in his own version of state power, fairly considerable economic responsibilities. These powers Smith's followers ever sought to diminish. Yet, irony of ironies, the English classical economic tradition, the precursor of all market-logic efforts, only gained practical influence through its own, quite unnatural manipulation of government.

In England, as in other nations undergoing industrialization during the first half of the nineteenth century, it was the machinery of government—not the absence of such machinery—that was essential in rolling back the paternalism and protectionism of the feudal and mercantilist past. Repeal in 1846 of the Corn Laws protecting English agriculture, passage in 1832 of a new Poor Law that set aside the social protection of the unemployed in the name of a free labor market, and enactment of the Banking Act of 1844, which set Great Britain upon a gold standard, were efforts *by the state,* supported of course by the advocates of free markets, that paved the way for the temporary flourishing of laissez-faire economic conditions. As Karl Polanyi pointed out many years ago: "Laissez-faire itself was enforced by the state. . . . Laissez-faire was not a method to achieve a thing, it was the thing to be achieved."*

From the beginning, everywhere market capitalism surfaced in its varied forms, the state was the instrumentality through which it came into being. Capitalism was not obtained, as Conservative doctrine might lead one to believe, through evolutionary practice and the "natural" march of economic progress. Indeed, without the state's acting on behalf of a market capitalist agenda, there was no surety that capitalism—or at least capitalism as most Western nations have come to know it—would have emerged at all. And, when the experiments with a laissez-faire market system experienced difficulties from time to time, the state was to be used again and again in either its maintenance or its reform. By regulating away capitalism's more obnoxious social effects, and thereby at least maintaining the basic elements of production-for-profit, practical men of affairs, if hardly ever Conservative economic thinkers, recognized that saving half a loaf was better than no bread at all.

To be sure, many of the market-driven economic tools of Conservative economic theory have been and continue to be useful analytic devices. Liberal economic analysis, as it is known and taught in the United States, is built, after all, on the foundation of classical economics. But the larger vision of Conservatives is another matter. Their faith in the efficient and fair functioning of an economy free of all planning and controls is blind to the flaws of its own logic and overlooks the evidence of history. It is a hopelessly mechanical argument in which iron-clad

---

*Karl Polanyi, *The Great Transformation* (New York: Rinehart, 1944), 250.

economic "laws" can be used to justify great varieties of inequity and unnecessary pain. Capitalism as a system may be able to function and thrive, but only with periodic adjustment and repair.

## The Objectives of Liberal Interventionism

A quick review of the Liberal arguments in each of the preceding economic issues provides a range of the types of tinkering Liberals are content to support. The Liberal view is certainly not the collectivist vision Conservatives assign to it.

Contrary to the Conservative outlook, planning is not necessarily communism, nor is it authoritarianism of any special breed. Planning is essential to maintaining the American democratic capitalist tradition. To the Liberal, of course, "democratic" is much more important than "capitalist" in a generic sense. The economic experiences of the United States and all other basically capitalist countries indicate quite clearly that only planning can save the private-property, production-for-profit system from self-destruction.

Although he has not always been in the mainstream of Liberal opinion, John Kenneth Galbraith's observations of over three decades ago fairly represent the Liberal position of today. After weighing the growing problems of American industrial society, Galbraith concluded:

> It is through the state that the society must assert the superior claim of aesthetic over economic goals and particularly of environment over cost. It is to the state we must look for freedom of individual choice as to toil. ... If the state is to serve these ends, the scientific and educational estate and larger intellectual community must be aware of their power and their opportunity and they must use them. There is no one else.*

## THE RADICAL ARGUMENT

Despite the current Conservative celebration of a renaissance of free market thought and practice, capitalism has for a considerable period of time moved inexorably toward greater central control. Although there is much debate on how close we really are to a formally planned and con-

---

*John K. Galbraith, *The New Industrial State* (Boston: Houghton Mifflin, 1967), 335.

trolled economy, Radicals would generally agree that it is the next great leap in capitalist development. From laissez-faire to monopoly capitalism to state-corporate regulation to formal planning, capitalism runs its course in its effort to secure profit and protect itself. The obvious irony, of course, is that planned capitalism is a contradiction in terms. As the basic economics textbooks tell us, capitalism emerged as a philosophy espousing, in theory at least, total economic and personal freedom. Alas, in the practical world, it ends as a statement on behalf of authoritarianism.

From the Radical perspective, it is necessary to get beyond the thoughtless celebration of market economics that presently pervades popular opinion and political rhetoric in the United States. Quite simply, this resuscitation of capitalist ideology has served to obscure the capitalist reality we in fact live in and to mystify for many the actual workings of modern capitalism. Yet the symbiotic relationship between capitalist enterprise and the modern capitalist state persists just below the surface of everyday economic life if only we care to dig beneath the veneer of Conservative ideology.

## *Capitalism Needs Planning*

Ideologies, even after they have proved worthless, die hard, often convulsively. It remains to be seen how the outmoded rhetoric of laissez-faire or even the more sophisticated mixed-economy philosophies will pass into history. They are deeply rooted in the individual practice and thought of American citizens, and their public defenders are still loud and shrill. Nevertheless, as our discussions of other contemporary issues should indicate, the use of government controls and planning in the economy is apparent everywhere.

This process is not really very new. It originated in the late nineteenth-century response to the growing crises of American capitalism. Troubled by periodic panics or recessions (in 1873, 1884, 1893, and 1907), chronic excess capacity and overproduction, and anarchic market conditions, and threatened by increasingly radicalized labor strife, American capitalism depended more and more on state intervention. We have elaborated on these interventions in our discussions of stabilization policy, government deficits, unemployment, and international trade. As the state became a partner in supporting business, American corporations enlarged their monopoly powers through concentration and control.

This growth of state-corporate integration has been euphemistically termed the "mixed economy" in economics texts. Uninformed Conservatives have attacked this integration as the domination of business by the state, without even stopping to ask just whose interests the state has represented. They fail to see that, quite as Marx specified, "the State is the form in which the individuals of the ruling class assert their common interests."

Capitalist production has proved to be extraordinarily rational in a microeconomic sense. The organization of production, labor, and capital for any particular firm is governed by economic rules of behavior (we call it the price system) that, for an individual entrepreneur, give key signals on how best to attain profit objectives. Yet, in totality, the capitalist system is irrational. Though the actions of any given firm are rationally planned or calculated with profit in mind, the actions of all firms taken together produce macroeconomic and social disorder. There is a lack of coordination and integration, even among monopolistic capitalists, in dealing with different industries and different sectors of the economy. Rational control of the whole labor force, of total output, and of investment alternatives is lacking.

The boom-bust rhythm of the business cycle, although recently muted when compared to the past, is still evident—but with a difference. Today's highly integrated and automated production is extremely vulnerable to even the slightest variations in sales, profits, and output. In the past, when industry was predominantly labor-intensive, a business downturn amounted mainly to sending the workers home with empty pay envelopes and waiting until things got better. Today, with greater capital usage and production on an international scale, nonproduction presents a firm with greater losses. These, in turn, adversely affect financial markets and the international structure of business.

Moreover, modern capitalism has so penetrated the world that it is limited in its ability to acquire new markets, so essential to its survival. At the same time, as we have noted repeatedly before, capitalist production can be carried on at higher output levels using less labor power. As a result, the crowning irrationality of the system is that it can produce more and more, but labor becomes increasingly redundant and markets harder to find.

The chronic tendency toward unemployment and excess capacity, the steady threat of inflation, and the worsening balance-of-trade situation leave few options for American capitalism. As the Liberal John Kenneth

Galbraith has argued for years, the next step in capitalist development is to transcend the market and modern Keynesian efforts to correct it and to move straight toward direct economic planning and controls. Only through such efforts can capitalist irrationality be controlled. Planning presents possibilities for reorganizing the capitalist processes of production and accumulation and at the same time can legitimize or bring order to labor markets.

## Planning for Profits, Not People

One of the great self-deceptions of Conservative economic thought is the doctrinaire view that planning is inimical to market-based economic behavior. It is wrongheaded as a logical matter and a positively silly notion as a matter of real-world practice. Capitalists, whether we are talking of giant corporations or small mom-and-pop operations, do not earn their profits accidentally. In any case, it would be absurd to suggest that Microsoft, General Motors, and Citicorp do not have a plan for their business operations, that at the end of the year of producing and selling goods and services willy-nilly they are randomly surprised or dismayed when they tally their sales and expenses.

No one in their right mind would seriously argue that planning is not an essential element of every business enterprise's operations. Planning within the modern enterprise is, of course, much more important than it was at the dawn of the capitalist era when Adam Smith and his colleagues were working out the "rules" of a market economy. This does not reflect so much a philosophical change in capitalists' approach to the everyday matter of obtaining profit as it does the vastly increased complexity of the goods they make and the techniques necessary to manufacture and sell these goods.

However, if planning is important as an everyday operational function within a business, why are planning efforts between and among businesses and planning utilizing government not seen as natural progressions for capitalism as a system? Obviously, the Conservative assault upon planning is a spurious argument not taken seriously by real-world practitioners of production for profit.

In fact, business enterprisers—especially large business enterprisers—see real gains and opportunities to be obtained from planning. During the late 1970s and into the 1980s, as the American economy sagged through a particularly unimpressive period of slow growth, high unemployment, and lowered profits, many in the business community flirted publicly with the idea of enlarging the federal government's role as a central planner. Many spoke warmly on behalf of an *industrial policy* that embraced a joint government-business coordination of investment, labor, and trade policies to deal with the then preoccupying concern about the *deindustrialization* of America. To be sure, this enthusiasm for planning has flagged a bit over the past two decades as the American economy's performance and prospects brightened. But when the boom turns to bust, as it surely will and as it always has, it is reasonable to expect that capitalists will rediscover industrial policy.

Regardless of the simplistic Conservative notion that all centralized efforts at economic planning and control are threats to a production-for-profit system, Radicals understand the real issues in any discussion of planning to be very different matters. The crucial question that any inquiry into economic planning should raise is: planning by whom and for what objective? Planning of an industrial policy variety still operates within the capitalist firmament. It amounts to planning by capitalists, or their agents, for the purpose of maintaining profits for business enter-prises and profit-making as a social objective. The name of the game in capitalism is still profits, and, contrary to Liberal apologists, the name does not change when essentially capitalist systems adopt centralist plan-ning techniques.

As long as business profitability is the guiding force of planning ef-forts, Americans will never be able to transcend the limitations of the social order under which they live. Quite literally, all human experience will remain subservient to and positively limited by the eternal quest for *the bottom line*. Radicals have a different prescription for the economic order: Planning should first and foremost be about meeting the needs of real living and breathing people.

### The Radical Alternative: Planning for and by People

Although Radicals may be divided on the means by which social plan-ning is to be achieved, there is greater agreement on *how* such planning should proceed once it is established. Most American Radicals would reject out of hand the varieties of social planning demonstrated by such socialist nations as the Soviet Union or China. These efforts at state planning simply lost sight of the major objective of any rational and humane planning: *people*. In these cases, plans were developed and imposed from above by central planning or political authorities whose decisions had no more to do with workers' and consumers' needs than decisions currently being made by Exxon or IBM officials.

The first and unifying rule for Radicals with regard to planning is that the planning process must begin with popular participation and must be conceived to deal with people's problems.

The complexity of modern economies and the immensity of providing people with the opportunities to plan such economies, of course, seem so formidable as to make most citizens believe that popular planning is simply impossible. Radicals reject such a view out of hand. To do anything else would be to submit to the tyranny that is the capitalist mode of production. There are, of course, many levels of planning, from decisions pertaining to a particular plant or factory to broad national output targets. Obviously, the more distant the level of planning, the more difficult individual participation becomes. Nevertheless, society now has the appropriate means of production, such as computer and information processing technologies, to make widespread planned coordination between producers and consumers a reality. Innovations such as bar code technologies and integrated communication and computer networks can facilitate a speed and depth of coordination and allocation that is far superior to anarchic capitalist markets. Recognizing that the Soviet and Chinese communist cases are examples of what can happen when planning lacks the requisite information processing and coordination capabilities and becomes too abstracted from popular input, the object is always to keep as much of the decision making at the lower levels as possible and, when that is no longer a reasonable alternative, to devise the broader elements of the plan through as democratic a means as possible.

Workers or their directly elected representatives must be the basis for local output, pricing, and workplace decisions. Such decisions, of course, must be made with an eye to the general welfare. No worker or group of workers has the right to earnings obtained by sacrificing consumers or some other group of workers. That would merely be capitalism reappearing in the disguise of socialism, and it would lead to the same kind of exploitative conditions we now live under. Thus it is obvious that workers must be joined by consumers in the local or lower-level planning activities. Organizing broad popular participation in the planning process will not be easy, nor is there absolute certainty that a democratically devised plan will not be guilty of error and even failure. It is com-

paratively easy for Conservatives and Liberals to paint a picture of chaotic planning meetings as various representatives of workers, managers,
and consumers determine key economic objectives. However, they miss
two very important points. First, the failures of such planning efforts
can be little worse than the current private planning "successes." Second, even at its worst, planning based on workers' and consumers' participation *is* democratic planning and *is* consistent with the professed
ideals of a democratic society.

Regardless of the precise methods ultimately devised to facilitate
participatory planning—and trial and error will certainly play a role in
selecting planning goals—the Radical holds to a basic belief that the
people must be the architects of their own society. The basic economic
decisions of *what* is produced, *how,* and *for whom* must not be entrusted
to an elite, whether they be capitalists, political commissars, or
excommissars turned capitalist.

The late Radical economic and social historian William Appleman
Williams put it this way:

> Hence the issue is not whether to decentralize the economy and politics
> of the country, but rather how to do so. . . . This literal reconstructing and
> rebuilding of American society offers the only physical and intellectual
> challenge capable of absorbing and giving focus to the physical and in-
> tellectual resources of the country during the next generation. . . .
>
> Throughout such a process, moreover, the participants will be educat-
> ing themselves . . . for their membership in the truly human community
> they will be creating. In the end they will have built a physical America
> which will be beautiful instead of ugly, and which will facilitate human
> relationships instead of dividing men into separate functional elements.
> They will have evolved a political system which is democratic in form
> and social in content. And they will be prepared . . . to function as men
> and women who can define their own identity, and their relationships
> with each other, outside the confining limits of property and the bruising
> and destructive dynamics of the competitive marketplace. They will be
> ready to explore the frontier of their own humanity.*

---

*William A. Williams, *The Great Evasion* (Chicago: Quadrangle Books, 1964),
175–76.

# Final Thoughts and Suggested Readings

Having reached the end of this volume of debates on contemporary economic issues, it is probable that the reader expects (perhaps even hopes for) the authors to make their pitches—to say straight out which of the representative paradigms is correct and which is not, perhaps each one to unveil his own grand program. Indeed, the opportunity is tempting. For an economist, it is practically a reflex to try to get in the last word, especially one's own last word. However, after much thought, we decided that such conclusions would spoil the entire effort. This book was undertaken to present the differing ideological alternatives as objectively as space and writing talents allowed so that the reader would be free to make personal choices on matters of economic policy.

We can hear some readers complaining: "Cop-out! You're avoiding presenting your own preferences and your own conclusions. You've taken the easy way out of the swamp." Not so. Delivering our own final polemics would in truth be ever so easy. But the book has been about questions and choices. The reader, then, shall be left in the uncomfortable position of making a choice among the paradigms and policy questions surveyed here. And that is the way it should be.

This perspective, however, must not be misunderstood. The authors have not intended to produce a relativistic conclusion in which any choice will do and one choice is as good as any other. The point is for the reader to make a *good* choice, and some policy choices *are* better than others. However, only a reasoned analysis of the facts and a critical study of the truths of this world will permit any of us to make wise choices.

The British economist Joan Robinson has said it best:

> Social life will always present mankind with a choice of evils. No metaphysical solution that can ever be formulated will seem satisfactory for long. The solutions offered by economists were no less delusory than those of the theologians that they displaced.
>
> All the same we must not abandon the hope that economics can make an advance towards science, or the faith that enlightenment is not useless. It is necessary to clear the decaying remnants of obsolete metaphysics out of the way before we can go forward.
>
> The first essential for economists, arguing amongst themselves, is to "very seriously," as Professor Popper says that natural scientists do, "try to avoid talking at cross purposes."*

Before we can "avoid talking at cross purposes" on economic matters, we must understand our fundamental differences in opinion and interpretation. We hope this book has identified some of these important differences for the reader.

In undertaking this task, the authors were sorely tested. While trying to submerge our personal biases, we also had to master the biases of others. Perhaps we have not entirely succeeded on either count. Only the reader can judge. Nevertheless, such an endeavor has been extremely educational.

For readers who desire to dig deeper into economic ideologies and their application to contemporary issues, the following bibliography offers some landmark readings in the respective Conservative, Liberal, and Radical schools of economic thought.

## Conservative

Banfield, Edward C. *The Unheavenly City.* Boston: Little, Brown, 1970.
Buckley, William. *Up from Liberalism.* New York: Honor Books, 1959.
Friedman, Milton. *Capitalism and Freedom.* Chicago: University of Chicago Press, 1962.
———. *Free to Choose.* New York: Harcourt Brace Jovanovich, 1980.
Gilder, George. *Wealth and Power.* New York: Basic Books, 1981.
Hazlitt, Henry. *The Failure of the "New Economics": An Analysis of the Keynesian Fallacies.* New York: Van Nostrand, 1959.
Kirk, Russell. *The Conservative Mind.* Chicago: Regnery, 1954.

---

*Joan Robinson, *Economic Philosophy* (Garden City, NY: Anchor Books, 1964), 147–48.

Klamer, Arjo. *Conversations with Economists.* Totowa, NJ: Rowman and Allanhold, 1983.

Knight, Frank. *Freedom and Reform.* New York: Harper and Row, 1947.

Malabre, Alfred E., Jr. *Living Beyond Our Means.* New York: Vintage Books, 1987.

Marshall, Alfred. *Principles of Economics.* New York: Macmillan, 1890.

Rand, Ayn. *Capitalism: The Unknown Ideal.* New York: New American Library Signet Books, 1967.

Schumpeter, Joseph. *Capitalism, Socialism, and Democracy.* New York: Harper Brothers, 1942.

Simon, William E. *A Time for Action.* New York: Berkley, 1980.

Simons, Henry C. *A Positive Program for Laissez-Faire.* Chicago: University of Chicago Press, 1934.

Smith, Adam. *An Inquiry into the Nature and Causes of the Wealth of Nations,* 1776.

Stein, Herbert. *Presidential Economics: The Making of Economic Policy from Roosevelt to Reagan and Beyond.* New York: Simon and Schuster, 1985.

Von Hayek, Friedrich. *The Road to Serfdom.* Chicago: University of Chicago Press, 1944.

Von Mises, Ludwig. *Socialism: An Economic and Sociological Analysis.* New Haven: Yale University Press, 1959.

## Liberal

Berle, Adolf A. *The Twentieth-Century Capitalist Revolution.* New York: Harcourt Brace Jovanovich, 1954.

Clark, John M. *Alternative to Serfdom.* New York: Random House/Vintage Books, 1960.

———. *Social Control of Business.* New York: McGraw-Hill, 1939.

Friedman, Benjamin. *Day of Reckoning.* New York: Random House, 1988.

Galbraith, John Kenneth. *The New Industrial State.* Boston: Houghton Mifflin, 1967.

———. *The Affluent Society.* Boston: Houghton Mifflin, 1971.

———. *Economics and the Public Purpose.* Boston: Houghton Mifflin, 1973.

———. *Economics in Perspective.* Boston: Houghton Mifflin, 1987.

Hansen, Alvin. *The American Economy.* New York: McGraw-Hill, 1957.

Heilbroner, Robert. "The Future of Capitalism" in *The Limits of American Capitalism.* New York: Harper and Row, 1966.

———. *The Nature and Logic of Capitalism.* New York: Norton, 1985.

Heller, Walter W. *The Economy: Old Myths and New Realities.* New York: Norton, 1976.

Keynes, John M. *The General Theory of Employment, Interest, and Money.* New York: Harcourt Brace Jovanovich, 1936.

Lekachman, Robert. *The Age of Keynes.* New York: Random House, 1966.

Okun, Arthur M. *The Political Economy of Prosperity.* New York: Norton, 1970.

Reagan, Michael D. *The Managed Economy.* New York: Oxford University Press, 1963.

Reich, Robert B. *Tales of a New America.* New York: Times Books, 1987.

Shonfield, Andres. *Modern Capitalism: The Changing Balance of Public and Private Power.* New York: Oxford University Press, 1965.

Thurow, Lester C. *Dangerous Currents.* New York: Basic Books, 1980.

———. *The Zero-Sum Solution.* New York: Simon and Schuster, 1985.

## Radical

Baran, Paul. *The Political Economy of Growth.* New York: Monthly Review Press, 1957.

Baran, Paul, and Paul M. Sweezy. *Monopoly Capital.* New York: Monthly Review Press, 1966.

Botwinick, Howard. *Persistent Inequalities.* Princeton, NJ: Princeton University Press, 1993.

Bowles, Samuel, and Herbert Gintis. *Property, Community, and the Contradictions of Modern Social Thought.* New York: Basic Books, 1986.

Bowles, Samuel, and Richard Edwards. *Understanding Capitalism.* New York: Harper and Row, 1985.

Brouwer, Steve. *Sharing the Pie: A Citizen's Guide to Wealth and Power in America.* New York: Henry Holt and Company, 1998.

Domhoff, William. *Who Rules America?* Englewood Cliffs, NJ: Prentice-Hall, 1967.

Dowd, Douglas. *The Twisted Dream.* Cambridge, MA: Winthrop, 1974.

Duboff, Richard. *Accumulation and Capital.* Armonk, NY: M.E. Sharpe, 1990.

Franklin, Raymond S. *American Captialism: Two Visions.* New York: Random House, 1977.

Gordon, David M. *Fat and Mean.* New York: The Free Press, 1996.

Henwood, Doug. *Wall Street.* London: Verso, 1997.

Kolko, Gabriel. *Wealth and Power in America.* New York: Praeger, 1962.

Magdoff, Harry. *The Age of Imperialism.* New York: Monthly Review Press, 1967.

Mandel, Ernest. *Marxist Economic Theory.* New York: Monthly Review Press, 1967.

Marx, Karl. *Capital.* 1867.

O'Connor, James. *The Fiscal Crisis of the State.* New York: St. Martin's Press, 1973.

Robinson, Joan. *An Essay on Marxian Economics.* London: Macmillan, 1942.

Shaikh, Anwar M., and E. Ahmet Tonak. *Measuring the Wealth of Nations.* Cambridge: Cambridge University Press, 1994.

Sherman, Howard. *Radical Political Economy.* New York: Basic Books, 1972.

———. *Stagflation: A Radical Theory of Unemployment and Inflation.* New York: Harper and Row, 1976.

Strachey, John. *The Nature of Capitalist Crisis.* New York: Covici, Friede, 1933.

———. *The Theory and Practice of Socialism.* New York: Random House, 1936.

Sweezy, Paul. *The Theory of Capitalist Development.* New York: Monthly Review Press, 1942.

Williams, William A. *The Great Evasion.* Chicago: Quadrangle Books, 1964.

# Index

# About the Authors

**Robert B. Carson** is professor emeritus with the Division of Economics and Business at the State University of New York College at Oneonta. He pioneered the unique approach of teaching economics by addressing economic issues from the Conservative, Liberal, and Radical positions with the first edition of *Economic Issues Today* in 1978. He has authored twelve books on economics, including *What Economists Know* (1990), which has been reprinted abroad in Spanish, Portuguese, Russian, and Arabic editions. Dr. Carson is an expert on the public regulation of American railroads.

**Wade L. Thomas** is professor of economics and assistant dean of the Division of Economics and Business at the State University of New York College at Oneonta. Dr. Thomas served two terms as president of the New York State Economics Association, and serves as the organization's Web coordinator, and received the association's Distinguished Fellow Award in 2004. In addition to publishing journal articles on the economics of franchising, health care, and antitrust, he coauthored *The American Economy: Contemporary Problems and Analysis* (1993) with Robert B. Carson.

**Jason Hecht** is associate professor of finance in the School of Administration and Business at Ramapo College of New Jersey. He has published in both academic and business publications including the *Journal of Economics and Business* and the *Cambridge Journal of Economics*. Dr. Hecht previously worked as an economist in the property-liability insurance industry for many years and continues to consult for this industry.